SOURCES OF CONFLICT
IN THE POST COLONIAL AFRICAN STATE

SOURCES OF CONFLICT IN THE POST COLONIAL AFRICAN STATE

Ademola Araoye

AFRICA WORLD PRESS
TRENTON | LONDON | CAPE TOWN | NAIROBI | ADDIS ABABA | ASMARA | IBADAN | NEW DELHI

AFRICA WORLD PRESS
541 West Ingham Avenue | Suite B
Trenton, New Jersey 08638

Book and cover design: Saverance Publishing Services

Library of Congress Cataloging-in-Publication Data

Araoye, Lasisi Ademola, author.
Sources of conflict in the postcolonial African state / Ademola Araoye.
    pages cm
Includes bibliographical references and index.
ISBN 978-1-59221-974-2 (hardback) -- ISBN 978-1-59221-975-9 (pbk.) 1. Africa--Politics and government--1960- 2. Social conflict--Political aspects--Africa. 3. Postcolonialism--Africa. I. Masilela, Ntongela, writer of preface. II. Title.
  DT30.5.A73 2014
  320.96--dc23
                        2013041921

A bouquet
To the vessels of hope
For the next generation:

Oyindamola Sinmisola Adebimpe

Table of Contents

List of Acronyms

ACS	**American Colonization Society**
AFDLC	Alliance of Democratic Forces for the Liberation of Congo
AFL	Armed Forces of Liberia
ALCOP	All Liberians Coalition Party
APC	All Peoples Congress
APD	Alliance for Peace and Democracy
COTOL	**Coalition for the Transformation of Liberia**
CPA	Comprehensive Peace Accord
CPLP	Community of Portuguese Speaking Peoples
DF	**Democratic Front**
DSF	Social Democratic Front
DRC	Democratic Republic of Congo
ECOMOG	**Economic Community of West African States Monitoring Group**
ECOWAS	Economic Community of West African States
EDD	Europe of Democrats and Diversities
ELDR	European Liberal Democrats and Reformist Party
EPP-ED	European People's Party (Christian Democrats) and European Democrats
EUL/NGL	European United Left/Nordic Green Left
EU	European Union

FAR	**Forces Armees Rwandaise/Rwandese Armed Forces**
FCG-SD	Guinean Civic Forum/Social Democracy
FLING	Front for the Liberation of Guinea (Bissau)
GOSS	**Government of Southern Sudan**
Greens/EPAD	Green European Free Alliance
ICGL	**International contact Group on Liberia**
ICJ	International Court of Justice
IFES	International Foundation for Electoral System
IGNU	Interim Government of National Unity
INPFL	Independent National Patriotic Front of Liberia
IWG	International Working Group
LAP	**Liberia Action Party**
LICPA	Liberian Institute of Certified Public Accountants
LIPE	Guinea League for Ecological Protection
LRA	Lord Resistance Army
LURD	Liberians United for Reconciliation and Democracy
MCDDI	**Congolese Movement for Democracy and Integral Development**
MFDC	Movement of Democratic Forces of Casamance
MJP	Movement for Justice and Peace
MNC	Congolese National Movement
MODEL	Movement for Democracy in Liberia
MOJA	Movement for Justice in Africa
MPCI	Patriotic Movement of Cote d'Ivoire
MPIGO	Ivorian Popular Movement of the Great West
MPLA	Movimento Popular de Libertação de Angola / Popular Movement for the Liberation of Angola
MPR	Popular Movement of the Revolution

NDPL	**National Democratic Party of Liberia**
NEC	National Elections Commission
NDP	National Development Party
NPC	Northern Peoples Congress
NPFL	National Patriotic Front of Liberia
NPN	National Party of Nigeria
NPP	National Patriotic Party
NRP	National Reformation Party
NTGL	National Transitional Government of Liberia
NTLA	National Transitional Legislative Assembly
OAU	**Organization of African Unity**
OCAM	Organisation Commune Africaine et malgache
PAIGC	**Pan African Party for the Independence of Guinea Bissau and Cape Verde**
PAL	Progressive Alliance of Liberians
PCD	Party for Democratic Convergence
PES	Party of European Socialists
PRC	People's Redemption Council
PRP	Party for Renewal and Progress
PRP	Peoples Redemption Party
PRS	Party for Social Renewal
PSD	Social Democratic Party
PTC	Parti Congolais des Travailleurs/ Congolese Workers party
PUDS	United party for Social Democracy
RDL	**Rally for Democracy and Liberty**
RGB/BM	Guinea Bissau Resistance Bafata Movement
RUF	Revolutionary United Front
SCAPO	**Southern Cameroon's Peoples Organization**
SLPP	Sierra Leone People's Party

SPLA/M	Sudanese People's Liberation Army/Movement
UAM	**Union Africaine et Malgache**
UEMOA	Economic and Monetary Union of West African States
UEN	Union for Europe of the nations
ULIMO	United Liberation Movement of Liberia for Democracy
ULIMO/J	United Liberation Movement of Liberia for Democracy/ Johnson
ULIMO/K	United Liberation Movement of Liberia for Democracy/ Kromah
UM	Uniao para Mudanca/ Union for Change
UN	United Nations
UNDP	National Union for Democracy and Progress
UNITA	Uniao Para a Independencia Total de Angola
UP	Unity Party
UPDS	Union for Progress and Social Democracy

Acknowledgements

My tour of duty in Congo Brazzaville as a Political Counselor at the Embassy of the Federal Republic of Nigeria from August, 1990, to August, 1993, decidedly left imprints on my intellectual journey. The daily litter of deaths and systematic nightly executions orchestrated by rivals in the struggle for political power on the open streets, as well as in the nooks, crevices and corners of Brazzaville shattered my naivete. The troubling experience in Brazzaville was again starkly reinforced by the heart wrenching replication of the same scenario, and on a much larger scale, across the Congo River in Kinshasa. In neighboring Zaire (now Democratic Republic of Congo), the struggles of the national sovereign conference, the longest on the continent, led by the Sacred Union to achieve a peaceful transition to a new republic, was confronted with violent suppression from the Mobutiste dinosaur state. Cadavers in their twisted contortions often floated on the abused Congo River from Kinshasa to the port of Brazzaville. The Democratic Republic of Congo, as I refine the original piece done in Rialto, CA, in Monrovia, Liberia, in March 2010, has known no respite from its sanguinary trajectory since the 1990s. I wish to acknowledge the agony of these known, even if uncodified, victims of this madness as the drivers of my search.

Meanwhile, my return to the Foreign Office in Abuja in 1994, after a year at the Claremont Graduate School, Claremont, California, found me saddled with the unpopular Liberia desk under the supportive Ambassador Thadeus. D. Hart, then Head of West Africa, later Ambassador to the Hague, Head of the Foreign Service and finally Senior Special Advisor to the President of the Federal Republic of Nigeria. I enjoyed the personal encouragement of Ambassador Oluremi Esan, Director-General of the Africa Directorate, in the very difficult years of hounds and hyenas in the Ministry of Foreign Affairs - a reflection of the sickening conjuncture of Nigeria's own history at that point in time. The late Ambassador Joshua Iroha, Special Representative of the ECOWAS Secretary General to Liberia, was generous with his insights whenever he stormed into the department in Abuja or when huddled together in Accra, Ghana, to unravel some of the perennial mysteries that the Liberian conflict always threw up. I wish to acknowledge the debts of respect and encouragement received from these very senior and inspiring professional officers. I also pay tribute to my late boss, Ambassador George Adetuberu, former Ambassador to the Republic of Congo, who sustained his personal interest in my development until his passing away.

The second incarnation- of my career saw me in Guinea Bissau- a call to witness to a human tragedy of unimaginable proportions , in a Cote d'Ivoire locked in a titanic struggle to define its future and finally in a Liberia just emerging from the trauma of mindless violence that had spanned a whole generation. In effect, the dynamic of inexplicable bloodletting set out in these volumes are also personal testimonies of the human cost exacted by the myth and the peculiar construction of the postcolonial African state. In bearing these testimonies, I express my gratitude to Felix Downes Thomas-Executive Director and "Oga mi"- for his unshakable faith and for anchoring the haven of kindred spirits at great personal costs. Ambassador Raph Uwechue, senior statesman and Special Representative of the Economic Commission of West African States (ECOWAS) to Cote d'Ivoire, was kind in his open invitation to the residence and office. He was generous with his experience as he illuminated the difficult dynamics of the Ivorian crisis and of Africa as a whole. This period was enriched by the sustained friendship and sterling collegiality of Comfort Ero, now Vice President (Africa) of the International Crisis Group, Akinyemi Adegbola and Deborah Schein. The immense camaraderie was so often characterized by rancorous discourses over the *problematique Africaine.* Abdourahmane Diallo and Gonleh Jenkins Bakar's personal commitments to the project were expressed in their boundless energy as volunteer research assistants. Michi Ebata and Adeola Bodunrin read the first draft and made useful suggestions. Lukas Rust pored over the chapter on Liberia and assisted with very constructive comments. I also wish to record my appreciation of the inspiring enthusiasm of "Egbon" Segun Omolayo in editing this volume. Carol Crichlow was generous with her helping hands.

Prof Ntongela Masilela at Pitzer College, Claremont, CA, instigated these volumes. Without his nagging persistence and encouragement through a decade, this book would never have been. The final outcome bears the imprint of his formidable intellect that he so often brought to bear in midwifing these volumes. This is also a payment of sorts for the free weekly breakfasts at his home through the mid and late nineties; a great incentive for an indigent African student in California. The outlandish theses that emerged from our dissection of the anatomy of the African malaise have found their way into these volumes.

I acknowledge my eternal indebtedness to Professors Dean McHenry, Jr. and Thomas Rochon, at the Claremont Graduate University, Prof Ed Haley at Claremont/McKenna College and Prof Nathaniel Davis, former United States

Assistant Secretary of State for African Affairs, at Harvey Mudd College, Claremont, California, for instilling integrity as the soul of all intellectual, indeed all, endeavors. I am still wary of simple answers to complex social challenges as they taught me. I am very privileged to be a student of theirs. By their exemplary trails, they set me on this course. To conclude,"K", Dr Karolee Rosen, would remain special for her kindness and magnanimity.

Notwithstanding these beneficial influences, I bear sole responsibility for the contents of this book.

ADEMOLA ARAOYE.
Rialto, CA, USA/Monrovia, Liberia.
March, 2010.

This book has been produced in the author's personal capacity. The views expressed in this work are those of the author only and do not represent the views or opinions of the Department of Peacekeeping Operations or the United Nations.

Foreword

MAPPING THE GENESIS AND STRUCTURE OF THE CRISIS OF THE POST-COLONIAL AFRICAN STATE

BY NTONGELA MASILELA

A demola Araoye has given us in these two interrelated books, *Sources of Conflict in the Post-Colonial African State* and *Cote d'Ivoire: The Conundrum of a Still Wretched of the Earth*, which are in fact a singular book, one of the most acute analysis of the political crisis that began besetting Africa within a few years of the heydays of African Independence Movement in the early 1960s. The crisis has emerged in the political form of the legitimacy of the African political state in the postcolonial era. The crisis itself was coterminous with the decolonization process. Retrospectively, the beginnings of the crisis can be traced to the Congo Crisis of the 1960s, which resulted in the tragic death of the great Patrice Lumumba, when European and American imperialism(s) under the aegis of the ideology of white supremacy enforced and imposed on African history a political and economic mechanism whereby the decolonization process became simultaneously the actualization of neocolonialism. This was the conundrum that traumatized the then emergent political leadership from Modibo Keita in Mali to Jomo Kenyatta in Kenya, from Sekou Toure in Guinea to Julius Nyerere in Tanganyika (Tanzania).

The Congo Crisis was one of the seminal events of the revolutionary decade of the 1960s. Perhaps the most important in that its tremors and consequences have not disappeared from world history, whereas those of French May 1968, the Cuban Missile Crisis of 1962, the assassination of Ernesto Che Guevara in Bolivia in 1967 by American imperialism as he was initiating the Latin American Revolution, the Prague Spring 1968, the Vietnamese Tet Offensive also of 1968, have all seamlessly interwoven themselves into the movement of history. Several instances can be mentioned to indicate the world historical nature of the Congo Crisis.

First, the most important and dramatic reaction was of Fidel Castro and Ernesto Che Guevara in deciding to link the Cuban Revolution with the then emergent Africa Revolution, the latter having been initiated by the Algerian Revolution of 1954-1962. Guevara spent nearly the whole year of 1965 secretly fighting in the Congo; a fact made public to the world thirty years later with the publication of his posthumous book, The African Dream: The Diaries of the Revolutionary War in the Congo (1999 [2000]). In subsequent years the Cuban Revolution was to support the Ethiopian Revolution of 1974, the Angolan Revolution of 1975, and eventually the liberation struggle in South Africa that led to the historic democratic elections of 1994. Given all this, it is not accidental that of all the approximately a hundred Heads of State and Monarchies assembled in South Africa in May 1994 to witness the swearing in of Nelson Rolihlahla Mandela to the presidency of a new democratic nation, Fidel Castro was the most acclaimed by the populace.

Second, Amilcar Cabral, the preeminent African Marxist of the twentieth century, decided to link the Guinea-Bissau Revolution to the Cuban Revolution by giving a most extraordinary presentation in Havana in 1966 entitled The Weapon of Theory (now in Amilcar Cabral: Unity and Struggle, 1980) at the Plenary Session of the First Solidarity Conference of the Peoples of Africa, Asia and Latin America. It needs no adding here that this is one of the most astute philosophic documents to come from Africa in the past century.

Third, Kwame Nkrumah, the President of Ghana and the most prominent Pan-Africanist among African leaders, reacted not only by writing The Challenge of the Congo: A Case Study of Foreign Pressures in an Independent State (1967) denouncing imperialism in Africa, but also by gravitating away from Pan-Africanism into wholeheartedly embracing Marxism-Leninism.

Fourth, Jean-Paul Sartre, the last classical European philosopher before the emergence of postmodernism in the 1960s, who had shifted from Existentialism to Marxism partly as consequence of the Algerian Revolution, in penning a memorial essay on Patrice Lumumba that originally appeared in Presence Africaine and later as an Introduction to Lumumba's writings: Lumumba, Fanon: these two great dead men represent Africa. Not only their nations: the entire continent... Fanon often spoke to me of Lumumba; though he was immediately on the alert when an African political party proved to be vague about reforming structures or reluctant to do so ... Everything still remains to be said about Fanon. Lumumba was better known; nonetheless he has kept many a secret to himself (Lumumba Speaks: The Speeches and Writings, 1972). With this essay Sartre wrote one the most damning documents about European imperialism, even surpassing his celebrated Preface to Frantz Fanon's The Wretched of the Earth (1961 [1965]), began embracing the concept of the Third World articulated by his protege Fanon. Perhaps it is necessary to recall here that Sartre was the first major European intellectual to support the eventuation of the Cuban Revolution by writing a text of unsurpassed analytical rigor: Sartre on Cuba (1961).

Lastly, Fanon, mourning for Lumumba, dramatically swerved from being the ideologue of the Algerian Revolution to being the prophet of the African Revolution as it was made evident by the essay Lumumba's Death: Could We Do Otherwise?, now part of a collection of combative essays, reflections and presentations posthumously published in Toward the African Revolution (1964, [1968]). Like Sartre, or coincidentally, Fanon himself found it necessary to support the Cuban Revolution in The Wretched of the Earth as an event of world historical proportions. With this gesture, Fanon, in effect, was calling on the Cuban Revolution's support on the emerging African Revolution, of which he himself and Cabral were its supreme ideologues.

More about Fanon needs to be said here because what he prophetically warned Africa against in his political masterpiece or manifesto, The Wretched of the Earth, this brilliant Nigerian scholar, political scientist, diplomat has with tremendous sorrow surgically diagnosed the consequences that have shattered a large part of the continent. Although Ademola Araoye does not mention the Antillean revolutionary intellectual at all in this two-volume study, this work is imprinted by the understanding of the nature of the crisis of the African state that Fanon foresaw at the very moment of its historical emergence. Araoye also, as though guided by the historical imprint of this great thinker, diagnoses the abysmal nature of African political leadership in the postcolonial era. Since Fanon was not in a position to give immediate historical explanations to his acute and profound observations of the political and sociological crises about to ravage and devastate the continent, given the terminal illness then engulfing him as well as the contingent needs of the Algerian Revolution which he had to spontaneously analyze since he was its major ideologue, Araoye has had to appropriate the historical imagination of the African revolutionary thinker of the 1960s, Amilcar Cabral, in order to undertake a retrospective analysis of the past as the present and a sociological analysis of the present as the historical. Also regarding Cabral, he is hardly mentioned in this voluminous study. Cabral becomes an obvious imprint in those sections of the book that are directly concerned with the crises that engulfed Guinea-Bissau following the coup d'etat that overthrow the political leadership of Cabral's younger brother, Luis Cabral, in 1980.

This two-volume study makes clear that the reflections of Fanon and Cabral are inescapable or unavoidable in any serious search of the historical explanations for the African political crises.

Given that Lumumba was assassinated by imperialist and neo-colonialist forces led by United States on January 17, 1961, and Fanon himself was to succumb to leukemia on December 6 in the same year, the essay on Lumumba was not only written as Fanon was struggling to complete The Wretched of the Earth, but also both texts resonate thematically with each other in an uncanny manner. In fact, the essay could be viewed as a prolegomenon of the book. The essay is an encapsulated presentation of the one of the three great chapters of the book: The Pitfalls of National Consciousness. Fanon viewed Lumumba as epitomizing the most rigorous forms African patriotism and African nationalism which he found pitifully absent in most of African nationalist leaders at the dawn of a new era of decolonization in African history. One of the African leaders whom Fanon in the book is unsparing in bitterly criticizing as lacking in what Lumumba exemplified was the then leader of Ivory Coast Felix Houphouét-Boigny, who was to misrule the country from its independence in 1960 to his death in 1993, with tragic consequences that Ademola analytically reveals in Cote-d'Ivoire: The Conundrum of a Still Wretched of the Earth. It is perhaps necessary to quote Fanon in The Wretched of the Earth what he had to say prophetically about Ivory Coast in just the first year of Houphouet-Boigny's misrule: In the Ivory Coast, the anti-Dahoman and anti-Voltaic [Burkina Faso] troubles are in fact racial riots. The Dahoman and Voltaic peoples, who control the greater part of the petty trade, are, once independence is declared, the object of hostile manifestations on the part of the people of the Ivory Coast. From nationalism we have passed to ultra-nationalism, to chauvinism, and finally to racism. These foreigners are called on to leave; their shops are burned, their street stalls are wrecked, and in fact the government of the Ivory Coast commands them to go, thus giving their nationals satisfaction.

Of course, these problems were not only confined to Ivory Coast, but also in other African countries, and as recently as 2006 when they occurred in my country South Africa. Fanon was clear that whenever African political leadership lacked a proper national consciousness, informed of African patriotism and African nationalism, these problems would invariably emerge. Fanon believed Lumumba to an exception to this national chauvinism, even though he was aware that Lumumba governed for less than a year.

Lumumba's Death: Could We Do Otherwise? possesses an absolutely singular importance in Fanon's intellectual trajectory because in it he formulated one of his politico-philosophical credos that he was to amplify and intensify in The Wretched of the Earth, at the moment when he was uncertain whether he would be able to complete the book given his terminal illness. This paragraph summarizes the nature of the African political crisis that preoccupied Fanon as death was approaching: Africa's first great crisis, for she will have to decide whether to go forward or backward. She must understand that it is no longer possible to advance by regions, that, like a great body that refuses any mutilation, she must advance in totality, that there will not be one Africa that fights against colonialism and another that attempts to make arrangements with colonialism. Africa, that is to say the Africans, must understand that there is never any greatness in procrastination and that there is never any dishonor in saying what one is and what one wants and that in reality the cleverness of the colonized can in the last analysis only be his courage, the lucid consciousness of his objectives and of his alliances, the tenacity that he brings to his liberation.

Indeed, the Congo Crisis was the first political trauma of postcolonial African history. The other remarkable chapter too in *The Wretched of the Earth*, Spontaneity: Its Strength and Weakness, could also be viewed as presenting the historical and political correctives that Fanon thought would prevent Africa from sliding further and further into the snares of neo-colonialism. Both chapters in all probability were intended as primers for the emergent African political leadership to move in the direction of political unity, decisiveness, and the shaping of an awakened national consciousness, not to be confused with nationalism, that would correspond to a correct social consciousness. This is what Fanon understood as his historical mission in Africa, as he stated it in the essay This Africa To Come, one of the essays assembled in Toward the African Revolution: To put Africa in motion, to cooperate in its organization, in its regrouping, behind revolutionary principles. To participate in the ordered movement of a continent—this was really the work I had chosen . . . To the East, Lumumba was marking time. The Congo which constituted the second landing beach for revolutionary ideas was caught in an inextricable network of sterile contradictions. It is these contradictions that Ademola Araoye seeks to understand and map out in his two-volume study.

The historical correctives that Fanon desperately sought to impart to the African political leadership that seems to have situated itself in a political position that made them unfathomable. In Spontaneity: Its Strength and Weakness, he formulated the following propositions among many others: First, that the African intelligentsia who formed the central segment of the new African political leadership had failed to transform itself into a revolutionary leadership that would represent the fundamental interests of the whole nation, especially those revolutionary peasant class, rather than defend its sectional middle class interests. With this formulation Fanon was postulating his celebrated and controversial position that in the former colonized African countries, the peasantry was the only spontaneously revolutionary class, whereas the small and incipient African working class was a privileged segment of the population. To argue otherwise, he characterized this as a misapplication of European historical imperatives to African history. Fanon was well aware that a contra-logic regarding the positioning of the two classes was operative in Western European historical theatre. It was in this context Fanon stated that Marxism in Third World countries should be stretched to accommodate new realities. This position was subsequently challenged by Amilcar Cabral in the essay, National Liberation and Culture, assembled in Return to the Source: Selected Speeches of Amilcar Cabral, who argued that the peasantry is certainly a dominant class demographically in ex-colonial or postcolonial African countries, but it is not revolutionary regarding historical consciousness. But for our immediate purposes here, it is important to register that just as Fanon had argued for the uniqueness of the class structure in the postcolonial African state, Ademola Araoye, in *Sources of Conflict in the Post-Colonial African State*, argues for the singularity of the postcolonial African state, in fact barely its existence or its fundamental dysfunctionality given its location in perpetually shifting ethnic mosaics that are not governed by the logic national boundaries constructed by the imperatives of neo-colonialism and imperialism. Regarding this epistemic theme, the book takes on a remarkable conceptual force. Ademola Araoye reiterates a constant refrain: the historical logic that made the Westphalian state possible is inherently contradictory to the logic of African history.

Fanon was critical of African political parties in believing their functional methods to be similar to those of Western European countries, the ex-colonial powers but new neo-colonizing entities. First and foremost, he was enraged that these political parties confined their political practice to the urban areas, totally disregarding the rural areas where the majority of the African people resided. Whereas for Fanon it was clear that modernity had for intents and purposes practically abolished the historical divide between the rural and urban in highly industrialized countries, this was manifestly not the case in African countries that were just beginning in earnest to undertake the industrialization process. Since the population in the rural areas of the emergent postcolonial countries in the Third World far exceeded that in cities, in contradistinction to the situation in First World modern countries, a new type of political party was necessary that would emphasize the interests of the peasantry above that of the working. Fanon was well aware that this was the opposite of the situation prevailing in Western European countries in which he postulated that the working class was structurally and demographically stronger while the peasantry was largely reactionary. In Third World countries Fanon repeatedly argued that the peasantry was ever in a state of combativeness and characterized by spontaneity for revolutionary action. This problem of a political party that is not extensively integrated to the will of the nation is compounded by the failure of the national intelligentsia in developing or constructing a national ideology that expressively articulates the imperatives of a national history. Though Fanon was generally hostile to nationalism, he very much embraced national consciousness as necessary in forging a nation. He was very explicit in warning of the dire consequences that would follow in the failure of the national bourgeoisie in constructing or formulating an ideology. In another section of the seminal essay This Africa To Come was clear about this matter: Colonialism and its derivatives do not, as a matter of fact, constitute the present enemies of Africa. In short time this continent will be liberated. For my part, the deeper I enter into the cultures and the political circles the surer I am that the great danger that threatens Africa is the absence of ideology. Old Europe had toiled for centuries before completing the national unity of the States.

In case study after case study in the many African countries in the 1970s and 1980s in which the state disintegrated for years if not for decades, Ademola Araoye shows with acuity that the disintegration occurred in situations where the ideology was weak, consequently tribalism displaced or was substituted for ideology and national consciousness, and poor leadership replaced the party. For sure, in each country this tragedy occurred accordance with its own historical imperatives, whether it be Sierra Leone or Central African Republic or Guinea-Bissau or Uganda or Zimbabwe. What is impressive is the detailed grasp Ademola Araoye has of these matters: each country is analyzed in its distinctiveness and particularity.

The tribalism that emerged from the failure of political leadership and the nationalist parties to forge an ideology that would give rise a national consciousness, Fanon believed inevitably leads to regionalism and all forms of chauvinisms that challenged national unity and the historical legitimacy of the State. It is in regard to this point that Ademola Araoye has formulated his startling thesis: the postcolonial African state is hybrid entity that did not emerge organically in the evolution and development of African social formations. It is a foreign contraption that was imposed on Africa in the interest of Western imperial nations. Its perpetual lurching towards disintegration is an index of its absolute foreignness. In the Introduction: The Double Instrumentality of the Postcolonial African State to the book he delineates his thesis with these words: The terrible developmental and humanitarian cost of the pervasive dynamic of disintegration in the postcolonial African state and the profound instability of its inter state system provide ample causes to re-examine the axiomatic understandings of the Westphalian state system in postcolonial Africa. The moral resources engendered by the stagnant postcolonial state imposes a critical need to reappraise statehood as the only legitimate form of political community . . . It is here postulated that there exists a linkage between the structure of the postcolonial African state, the character of its inter-state system generated by the peculiarities of its structure and instability in the postcolonial African state. There is also a turbulent interactive dynamic emanating from the incongruous structure of the postcolonial African state and conflict within it and the systematic instability of the state system in the postcolonial African environment. (p. 5-6)

This rigorous lucidity in the formulation of the historical problem is a prelude to a remarkable conceptual untangling of its complexity, convolutions and contortions. There follows a critical analysis of unmatched amplitude that traverses practically the whole terrain of the African political state system in sub-Sahara Africa. In this analysis Ademola Araoye combines theoretical rigor and empirical evidence in an exemplary manner that is expected of serious scholarly undertakings. Let me add in passing that this Nigerian scholar witnessed many of the events and situations he describes in the books in many of the West African countries for over the past decade or so. He was truly a witness at the making and unmaking of contemporary African political history.

Arguing persuasively that the postcolonial African state is not a proper classic state but rather a hybrid state or proto state or an instrumentalist state, Ademola Araoye searches for reasons for this historical conundrum that has haunted Africa for many decades. Making the observation that Frantz Fanon had noted sixty years earlier in the early 1960s under different circumstances, he makes the following observation: Cross border problems between Liberia and Cote d'Ivoire, as in much of West Africa and indeed across much of black Africa, emanate from the flow of cultural affinities of ethnic groups and communities across international boundaries between the two countries. These historically entrenched social affiliations across border areas generate ethnic identity consciousness that combine with communally shared religious faiths to contest for preeminence over citizenship obligations and loyalty to the respective states. (p. 20)

It is the effect of these transnational sociological affiliations that are at the center of the perpetual instability of the postcolonial African state. Fanon in The Wretched of the Earth characterized the same phenomenon with these words: The working class in the towns, the masses of unemployed, the small artisans and craftsmen for heir part line up behind this nationalist attitude [chauvinistic sloganeering]; but in all justice let it be said, they only follow in the steps of their bourgeoisie. If the national bourgeoisie goes into competition with the Europeans, the artisans and craftsmen start a fight against non-national Africans. In the Ivory Coast [Cote dÆIvoire], the anti- Dahoman [Benin] and anti-Voltaic [Burkina Faso] troubles are in fact racial riots. The Dahoman and Voltaic peoples, who control the greater part of the petty trade, are, once independence is declared, the object of hostile manifestations on the part of the people of the Ivory Coast. From nationalism we have passed to ultra-nationalism, to chauvinism, and finally to racism. These foreigners are called on to leave; their shops are burned, their streets stalls are wrecked, and in fact the government of the Ivory Coast commands them to go, thus giving their nationals satisfaction.   [p. 156]

The same phenomenon repeated itself in my country South Africa in early 2008 when approximately nineteen Somalians were killed by my black compatriots. So, the profound historical crisis of the postcolonial African state continues into the twenty-first century enveloping the relatively recent liberated states such as Zimbabwe and South Africa.

In tracing the disintegration of the social consciousness of national unity or African unity due to the collapse of proper national consciousness, which inevitably leads to horrendous religious, ethnic, racial (Arab versus African) antagonisms and conflicts, Frantz Fanon criticized the tragic role of the national parties in both the liberation phase and in the postcolonial phase of modern African history. He blames this tragedy largely on the failure of the African national bourgeoisie to lead the nation and the mechanisms and machinations of European imperialism and neocolonialism, both of which are the center subject of the Foreword to the accompany book: *Cote d'Ivoire: The Conundrum of A Still Wretched of the Earth*. Among the problems Fanon noted was the tribalizing of the national party; accompanied by the political leader of the party, who is invariably the head of state, substituting himself in place of the political organization. The cult and dictatorship of leadership leads to the destruction of the party and the democratic process.

Also on this matter of political parties, the parallel between Fanon and Ademola Araoye is instructive and fascinating. Here is Ademola Araoye take: Several attributes of the construction of society in the postcolonial socio- political space must be understood if we are carefully going to plot the locus of the state in relation to civil society and understand the problematic nexus between the character of society and the travails of the state. Inter communal relations in postcolonial states may be defined as mutually antagonistic. This antagonism runs through the whole gamut of processes that constitute national life, including the political, economic and social . . . Political parties in the postcolonial African state are the acceptable mechanisms for conducting formal inter ethnic struggles, as long as they are dressed in the right cloak of a political party. This is a critical distinguishing element in differentiating the political process of postcolonial states from the political processes of other kinds of states; the pre-Westphalian, the modern and the postmodern state . . . A political party in a postcolonial African state conventionally brings together peoples of similar ethnic or tribal backgrounds and those who share common myths of antecedence to struggle for the domination of political space. It is a parochial mechanism. To facilitate the articulation of this sectional goal, universal political goals and ideas are espoused to cloak this generally acknowledged character of the ethnic grouping. [p. 45-46]

The book is studded with such acute observations and brilliant theoretical formulations.

Specifying the failure of the postcolonial African state in relation to the expected norms of a modern state, Ademola Araoye writes: The postcolonial African state then deviates significantly in four major attributes of the modern Westphalian state. Examined on the degree of its institutional differentiation, the unification of the state through a development of a monistic structure entailing one locus of power, the pacification of society leading to the ascendancy of a common identity that revolves around the state and the emancipation of the political realm from the social domain, the postcolonial African state emerges in terms of its internal development as only a few decades from the state of 1648. In terms of its political capacity, the postcolonial African state is very weak. He illustrates these formulates with a detailed study of two African countries: Liberia and Guineau-Bissau. He could easily have chosen other countries.

In the early pages of the companion volume to this one, *Cote d'Ivoire: The Conundrum of a Still Wretched of the Earth*, Ademola Araoye writes a long paragraph of extraordinary pithiness that articulates the central causative factors and reasons for the crisis of the postcolonial African state: It is further advanced that there is an interactive dynamic between the difficult internal structure of the postcolonial state and the problematic structure of the postcolonial state system. The problematic structure of the state system flows directly from the transnational affinities of the constituent groups that are both within and transcend the formal state territories. This structure drives conflicts both in the state and in its immediate state system. The conflicts and the dynamics of conflicts, we argue derive from systemic structural dislocations that run across the frontiers of the various states. The dislocations of major groups within the state and across transnational frontiers underpin conflicts in the respective states. Through transnational structural linkages conflicts in any of the interacting states have a tendency to destabilize the immediate inter state system. In West Africa, sociological affinities flow in a westerly-easterly direction, while the territories of postcolonial state and the borders are aligned from south to north. The opposing latitudinal and longitudinal flow of historical and ethnic affiliations on the one hand against the territorial alignment of the state locates the postcolonial state in an intermestic environment in which extraterritorial stakeholders perceive legitimate interests to be pursued in developments within those states. The postcolonial state is thus an instrument to be captured by competing constituent groups and extraterritorial allies across the formal boundaries of the state to advance their parochial agenda. The national interests in the intermestic situation equate the interests of the dominant constituent groups in the respective states. Resulting from this, both the postcolonial states and the inter state systems constituted by them have problems that are intrinsic to them as micro and macro units and which, through an interactive dynamic, immensely aid conflicts and instability within its intermestic environment and across the constituent states of the sub system. [p. 8, my italics]

With these extraordinary words Ademola Araoye announces himself as an intellectual descendant of Frantz Fanon.

Claremont [Los Angeles], California,
February 2010.

Introduction

THE DOUBLE INSTRUMENTALITY OF THE POST COLONIAL AFRICAN STATE

Alarmingly, most of Africa remains in conflict, lawlessness and societal col-lapse, and vulnerable to the ravages of disease and natural disasters. African states are the world's poorest, weakest and most artificial states launched into the international arena, raising questions as to how such states have managed to survive. The question has also been asked as to what extent the survival of those states is now threatened.[1] Yet long term solutions to Africa's crises remain as elusive as they are essential.[2] Whole sub-regions in Africa are in chaos. At the start of the new millennium, crises and wars were raging in Sierra Leone, Liberia, Cote d'Ivoire and Senegal in West Africa; the Democratic Republic of Congo, Congo (Brazzaville), and Central African Republic in Central Africa; Angola in the East; and Sudan, Ethiopia, Somalia and Eritrea in the north and the Horn of Africa. Tribal, religious, economic and political tensions threatened to precipitate new bloodshed in Burundi, Nigeria, Guinea Bissau, Cameroun, Guinea Conakry and Zimbabwe. The sovereignty of the post-colonial African state is often being challenged, even as attempts to forge nations out of them continue to flounder. In West Africa and Central Africa, Southern Camerou-nian groups are challenging in law courts in neighbouring Nigeria the legality of the claims to sovereignty over the territory and peoples of that region by the central government of the Republic du Cameroun. They also urged the court "to restrain the government of Nigeria whether by herself, her servants, agents and or representatives or otherwise howsoever, from treating or continuing to treat as regard the Southern Cameroun and the people of the territory as an integral part of La Republic du Cameroun".[3] With the states imploding with their numerous crises, Africa is the primary region of operational engagement of the United Nations. UN troops, numbering 57, 334 and constituting over a third of the UN's blue helmeted forces, are deployed there, and most of them are from countries outside Africa.[4] The 2004 appropriations for UN peacekeeping operations in seven African conflict situations cost US$2,377,660,000 .[5] In these circumstances, queries may be raised again, not the least, about whether the post-colonial African state is the most effective principle of political organization for the promotion of the peace and stability of African societies.

Long before the present predicament, confronted with a similar situation in the years between the two great wars of the twentieth century, it had been envisioned that some things had to change, including the basic unit of world politics, the nation state, which could no longer be regarded as the most effective means of promoting the welfare and security of European societies.[6] The terrible developmental and humanitarian cost of the pervasive dynamic of disintegration in the post colonial African state and the profound instability of its inter-state system provide ample causes to re-examine the axiomatic understandings of the Westphalian state system in post-colonial Africa. The moral resources engendered by the stagnant post-colonial state impose a critical need to reappraise statehood as the only legitimate form of political community. Preceding the emergence of the post-colonial state and the attendant crises, the problems of the Westphalian state had led to the imagining of new forms of political community as a major enterprise in the contemporary theory of modern and international relations.[7] The crisis of the post colonial African state and its humanitarian costs have added some immediacy to the suspended interrogation of the state as the sole form of social and political organization. Or is the challenge in the nature of the expression of the Westphalian state in the African environment? And if so, what unique attributes of this genre of state render it prone to perennial failure and implosion?

It is here postulated that there exists a linkage between the structure of the post-colonial African state and the character of its inter-state system generated by the peculiarities of its structure, on the one hand, and instability in the state, on the other hand. There is also a turbulent interactive dynamic emanating from the incongruous structure of the post-colonial African state and conflict within it and the systemic instability of the state system in the African environment. The crisis of the post colonial African state and its state system, however much it may appear to be a problem internal to the respective states, actually derives from the structure of the inter-state system. It is thus a systemic problem as well. The internal constructions of the various states constituting the state system are significant elements in defining the structure of the inter-state system of the post-colonial African state environment. The structures of both the state and the inter-state system give their environments their unique attributes. It is proposed that there is an interactive dynamic between the difficult structure of the post colonial state and the problematic structure of its state system which drives conflicts both in the state and in its immediate state system. The dynamic of conflicts and the conflicts in themselves, we argue, derive from systemic structural dislocations that are expressed in the incongruous internal construction of the post-colonial state and reflected in the difficult alignments of the frontiers of the various states. These dislocations underpin conflicts in the respective states as well as, through structural linkages, destabilize the immediate inter-state system.

In West Africa, sociological affinities flow in a westerly –easterly direction, while the territories of the post-colonial states and the borders are aligned from south to north. The opposing latitudinal flow of political, historical and ethnic affiliations, on the one hand, aligned against the longitudinal territorial alignment of the state on the other hand, locates the post-colonial African state in an intermestic environment. This environment is populated by extraterritorial stakeholders that abound just outside the boundaries of all the states who perceive legitimate interests to be pursued in developments within those states. In concert with their natural allies within a particular post-colonial state, they are perpetually engaged in the process of seizing control of the state to the benefit of their corporate group, who are both within and outside the formal boundaries of the state. The post-colonial African state is thus an instrument to be captured by competing constituent groups and their extraterritorial allies across the formal boundaries of the state to advance their parochial agenda. The official national interests in this intermestic situation equate the interests of the dominant constituent groups in the respective states. Notwithstanding the power of the center in the post-colonial African state, there are other centers of power competing for ascendancy at all times. This deviates from the monistic conception of power associated with the conventional state. Resulting from this, both the post-colonial states and the inter-state systems constituted by them have problems that are intrinsic to them as micro-and macro-units and which, through an interactive dynamic, immensely aid conflicts and instability within its intermestic environment and across the constituent states of the sub-system.

The complex linkages between the internal construction of the post colonial African state and the structure of the immediate environment in which it is located set it and its state system apart from the conventional modern and post modern Westphalian state and their respective state systems. Deriving from this complexity, it is the main thrust in this book that conflict in the post-colonial African state and instability in its state system result from the attempt to appropriate the state by major domestic constituent groups acting in collaboration with their respective allied extra-territorial stakeholders. These stakeholders are members of the larger corporate trans-national communities of which the constituent group in the post-colonial state and its national society are a part of. Such stakeholders are pre-existing trans-national nationalities and groups with historical affinities which may be largely tribes or religiously based communities. Common ethnic identification and religious affinities present a certain understanding of the cosmology, universe and a defined worldview that may not only compete with others, but may also be the basis to challenge the emergence of new and common values as well as principles to legitimize the nascent state.

These competing ideational sub-structures of the numerous societies are often expressed in a fragmented civil society that is unable to develop an integrated national social capital base. Social capital abounds, but it is non-integrative, atomized and limited within networks of clearly defined corporate identities. The strength and resilience of the social capital that is derivable from informal structural linkages of the disparate transnational communities in the post-colonial African state and its intermestic environment have a deleterious bearing on the process of generating new and unifying identities and consciousness for competing compatriots of the state. The disparate identities and groups compete to impose their respective partisan and narrow conflicting political agendas that can only be concretized through the total control of the social, economic and political space. The highly exclusive agenda of the contending forces can only be fulfilled through domination of the state and all its pivots of power. Power in that context is conceived in terms of the successful appropriation of the state for the imposition of a hegemonic agenda. At the cultural level, this includes the entrenchment of the symbols and images of the hegemonic group, its worldview, the norms and values as well as conceptions of the universe of the dominant group as synonymous with that of the appropriated state.

Flowing from the peculiar construction of the system of the post-colonial African states, conflicts hardly occur as isolated developments in any one state. These conflicts often implicate and engulf the whole sub-region. Indeed a pattern of systematic systemic conflict may be said to have emerged. The structural incongruity of the interstate system leads to the existence of interests and stakeholders of these interests outside the frontiers of the state. The extra-territorial stakeholders, who are allied with lead domestic interest groups, are directly implicated in the turbulent political bargaining process in the respective sovereign entities. The extra-territorial interests, acting in concert with extensions of their communities within the post-colonial African state across international frontiers, express themselves in mainly disruptive intrusions in the affairs of that post colonial state. The shared loyalties of the community are perceived as preeminent and superior to those conferred on formal polities and their structures and institutions that are largely considered as illegitimate in seeking to redefine pre-existing identities and interests through forced integration. The interest of the post-colonial African state is subordinate to the perceived interests of the respective trans-national communities that abound in its environment. These transnational communities are corporate units, internally cohesive groups and defined by strong affinities and loyalties that often predate the new states whose borders go through the territorial boundaries of the groups. Despite attempts by the post-colonial African states to claim their loyalties, transnational groups straddling international frontiers first identify themselves as part of the transnational identity groups rather than as citizens of the new state. As a result the post-colonial state environment is constituted by numerous transnational forces that contest against one another for domination in all the various post-colonial state entities in which their members are present. Shared borders facilitate the intrusion of these groups in the affairs of the various states. For one thing, the territorial legitimacy of many of the newly independent states rested more on the establishment of their frontiers by prior international agreement between the former colonial powers than on any sense of nationhood or common identity among peoples of the territories themselves.[8] These unique attributes give rise to an intermestic character of the immediate environment of the post colonial state in which structural linkages between communities lead to intrusions of trans-national stakeholders in the affairs of the state.

This intermestic environment, which is defined by unique collaborative or adversarial relationships among and between trans-national communities across international borders, impact not only on the internal processes of the post-colonial state but also affect stability in their immediate neighbourhood. Intermestic relations derive from informal relationships existing between communities and are distinct from the relations formally pursued by the state authorities. Depending on a host of factors, the perspectives of state authorities may not always coincide with the interests of communities that are formally within its territories. In other instances, intermestic factors have influenced formal policies adopted in relations between post-colonial states that are located in the same intermestic environment. The demographic structure of the specific intermestic environment in which the post-colonial state is located is critical in this regard. An exploration of this neglected layer of analytical landscape may import significant consequences for our understanding of the internal processes of the post colonial state and of the facility with which whole sub-regions in the post colonial state system have imploded in conflict.

The peculiar difficulties of the African state and its inter-state system raise issues with the very conception of Westphalian statehood and its inter-state system in Africa.[9] Conventional analytical frameworks have treated conflicts in African states in an atomistic fashion. In this tradition of scholarship, the state is taken as an ontological given, despite the numerous queries raised on the claims of many political entities to statehood.[10] Though a lot of narrative essays have been generated on the post-colonial African state, this genre of state, including the nature of its inter-state system, is significantly under-theorised. The missing element relates to the paucity of theorization on the very nature of the post colonial African state. The post colonial African state is treated just like any other state in the global inter-state system, even if most of its vital attributes and internal dynamics, including the logic governing its internal and external security and role in the international systems, deviate significantly from those of the original Westphalian state. Unlike most states in the true Westphalian universe, the political authority of the African state is more over geographical space and territory and less over peoples in this space. Its major security threat is internal since its society is fragmented and is not pacified. Parallel authorities over peoples transcend international frontiers in the interstate system of these states. There are informal parallel institutions to every attempt to construct a formal state institution. Indeed group and individual behavioral patterns tend to conform more to the set of principles, norms, and rules of informal institutions than those of the formal ones. Informal institutions have survived longer than the new and formal ones. They have also demonstrated more resilience, persistence, relevance and durability. In the face of the pretensions and challenges posed by the Westphalian state, domestic groups and societies tend to negotiate with the compass of the old institutions. Some have observed that the basic institutional structures of most of the new states were indigenously determined.[11]

The post-colonial African inter-state system is a product of an attempt at crisis management by the colonial powers at the Berlin Conference of 1884. These powerful elite actors are as engaged in Africa in the post-Cold War era as during the Cold War. While the practical expressions of this engagement have altered with the display of greater circumspection, it has not diminished in the manner in which some analysts have posited in the post-Cold War era. Basically, the African state was designed by its foreign creators as an instrument for the articulation of the interest of hegemonic forces. The broad outline of the African state system is a reflection of the perceived historical claims of contending colonial forces to various areas of influence on the continent by 1884. The growth or lack of institutions by the post colonial African state and the lack of evolution of state systems are also largely the consequences of the pattern of engagement imposed on the state by their original colonizers. The major institutions of the post-colonial African state were designed to protect the interests of their colonizers rather than to serve the new state. Also, the post colonial African state lacks an organic will for its very existence as its creation did not result from a manifest will of its people. On its own, this state is not grounded on any principles nor underpinned by any philosophical understandings commonly shared by the peoples. At the domestic level, which incorporates stake-holders in the outcome of internal political processes in a state, including those who live outside the territorial confines of that state, the emergence of the state signals the beginning of a struggle for appropriation by all significant contend-ing forces in the new political space.

The major fault-line in this struggle is demarcated by ideational affinities and value convergences among the contending constituent communities in the new states. The concrete vessels of these normative affinities may be tribes, clans or religious faiths. Political violence and conflicts reflect an inability to bridge over systemic ideational and value dissonance within the context of new political mechanisms that are premised on control over geographical spaces rather than over peoples. Such inability exacerbates conflicts as the struggle to define the essence and character of the state becomes critical. In whose image is the state crafted? What are its major symbolisms and which of the contend-ing worldviews would be dominant in the new political space opened up by the creation of a new state? The African state is thus an instrumental state at two levels; at the level of internal struggle for the articulation of an internal hegemony; and as a handmaiden in the larger clashes of global forces, which may be expressed in terms of the interests of metropolitan states or a global force in the form of a religion. The African state ultimately remains an instrument at two levels, internal and external. Conflicts in the post colonial African state and in its inter-state system derive from this double instrumental character of the post-colonial African state.

We posit in this book that it is the instrumentality of the post-colonial African state at these two levels that is at the heart of conflicts in the state and accounts for crisis in its inter-state system.

Notes

1. Christopher Clapham, *Africa and the International System: The Politics of State Survival*, Cambridge University, 1996.

2. "Africa Newsfile," August 29, 2000, *Time*: http://www.time.com.daily/newsfile/africa/central.html, p. 1-2.

3. Dr Kevin Ngang and 11 others vrs the Federal Government of Nigeria before Justice Roseline Ukeje of Federal High Court in Abuja, Federal Republic of Nigeria. February –March 2002.

4. Cyrus Sami, Peace Operations in Africa: Capacity, Operations, and Implications, Report from the 34th annual Vienna Peacemaking and Peacekeeping Seminar.

5. Cyrus Sami, ibid., p.

6. Andrew Linklater, "The Transformation of Political Community: E.H. Carr, Critical Theory and International Relations," *Review of International Studies* 23, 1997, p. 321-338.

7. Andrew Linklater, ibid., p. 321-338.

8. Christopher Clapham, *Africa and the International System: The Politics of State Survival*, Cambridge University Press, Cambridge, 1996, p. 19

9. Georg Sorensen, "An Analysis of Contemporary Statehood: Consequences for Conflict and Cooperation," *Review of International Studies* 23, 1997, p. 253-269. Georg Sorensen observes that beyond juridical sovereignty, states in Africa do not share much in common with the modern Westphalian European nation state.

10. Stephen Krasner, "Compromising Westphalia," *International Security* 20, no. 3 (Winter), 1995-96, p. 115. Krasner argues that the Westphalia model has never been an accurate description of many of the entities that have been called states. He submits that the Westphalia system of political authority based on territory and autonomy. Territoriality means that political authority is exercised over a geographic space rather than, for instance, over people, as would be the case in a tribal form of political order. Autonomy means that no external actor enjoys authority within the borders of the state.

11. Stephen D. Krasner, *Sovereignty: Organized Hypocrisy*, Princeton University Press, Princeton, 1999, p. 201.

Chapter I

THE CRISIS OF THE POST-COLONIAL AFRICAN STATE AND ITS STATE SYSTEM

The post-colonial African state and its inter-state system are in crisis. In 1996, civil war and strife raged in at least 17 African countries.[1] By 2002, many more countries had joined the dismal list of imploding and unstable polities. In 2006, 18 African states in West, East and Southern Africa, as well as in the Horn of Africa were either attempting to exit from conflict or still struggling to embark on the peacemaking process.[2] Many of the states involved share contiguous frontiers. Indeed, it is possible to talk of conglomerates of unstable states with contiguous borders in various sub regions in Africa. African states, in the post cold war era, do not just implode, whole sub-regions are simply falling apart. Some of the states were born and remained in chaos for a considerable period of their statehood. For example, Angola was embroiled in civil war for 27 years, that is,over the entire quarter century of its existence after independence. The Portuguese colonial architects that crafted the project of its statehood hurriedly abandoned their resistance to the struggles among a number of feuding indigenous forces who were contending for the control of the emerging state.

A few states, such as Somalia, Liberia, and Sierra Leone have collapsed. Attempts at reconstituting them into functional political entities continue. Somalia has disintegrated into four political entities that all claim to be sovereign states. From 1980 to 2005, Liberia, one of the oldest states in Africa, experienced a brutal war, interspersed with short spells of lulls. For about 8 years the country was bifurcated into two with one headquarters in Gbarnga with a virtually independent administration run by a rebel movement, the National

Patriotic Front of Liberia. By 1998, the capital Monrovia was held by four rebel movements and the residue of government forces loyal to the central administration of Charles Taylor. The Republic du Tchad has faced intermittent wars since France's departure from the country in 1960. The country has endured over three decades of civil war and resistance from rebel and insurgent groups as insurgents and rebels alternated in and out of power through wars and when overthrown, always regrouping to challenge their old adversaries in government.

In May and July 2006, Chadian rebels attacked from the eastern border with Sudan. Chad's president Idriss Derby Itno accused Sudan's President Omar Hassan al-Bashir of backing Chad's eastern based rebels. The Chadian rebels are also seen to be allied to Sudanese government-backed Janjaweed who have a reputation for brutal attacks on black Christian and animist population in the Sudan. In addition to the ongoing violence, 200,000 Sudanese refugees are living in Eastern Chad – straining the already limited agricultural resources of the country. Some other states have irreparably broken up in violence. Insurgencies abound against the Khartoum government in every corner of Sudan; north, south, east and west. In the south, it contends with the Southern Peoples Liberation Army and a host of splinter movements. In the western region, there is the rebellion in Darfur. There are armed rebels also in the east and the north.[3]

Tension between Chad and Sudan has escalated since late 2005 when Chad accused Sudan of arming and financing Chadian rebels in the east. In turn, Sudan has accused Chad of supporting rebel groups in Darfur province in the west of Sudan, many of whom are drawn from the same ethnic Zagawa group as Chad's President Idris Derby.[4] President Derby, at the same time, has been accused by Chadians of doing too little to help Sudanese in Darfur who share ethnic links with many Chadians[5]. The leader of opposing Rally for Democracy and Liberty (RDL), Mahmat Nour, who has led attacks against Derby, is from the eastern Chadian Tama tribe, a tribe which also spans the border into Darfur. It's a small African tribe but has powerful historical alliances with Chad's Arab tribe.[6] Meanwhile, the apparent alliance of Chadian rebels [7]with Sudanese Janjaweed also increases border tensions, with Chadian and Sudanese officials trading blames over rebel attacks despite a string of top-level government agreements to mend ties. The complicity of both the Sudanese and Tchadian governments in the instability in their immediate neighborhood aptly reflects their difficult internal constructions respectively.

The alliances that emerge are between the central governments of the two states with allied extra-territorial kinsmen who are minorities in the two states respectively. In the case of Sudan, it must conquer to the south and the west in Darfur in order for the dominant Arab community to fully occupy the political space and consolidate Islam as state religion.

Sudan provides a particularly clear example of the changes in external alliances which followed from changes in the domestic structure of power, and from conceptions of Sudanese nationhood espoused by Kharoum. Any Sudanese government faced a fundamental choice between strategies designed to conciliate the Christian communities of the south on the one hand, or to control or conquer them on the other; as part of the either strategy, it also needed to manage complex division both within the south of the country and within the Moslem and largely Arabic speaking north...

In short, foreign policy management was intricately linked to domestic political control.[8]

The complexity of the interconnectedness of conflict between Sudan and its neighbors is also replicated in the linkages that lock the conflicts in Somalia, Ethiopia and Eritrea into a sub-systemic instability. The problems confronting the splintered Somali state is compounded by the situation in the Ogaden region of Ethiopia, which is at the center of a long running armed contention between Ethiopia and Somali's Islamic rulers. Against the background of the pervasive brutalities unfolding in the region, the situation has been described as characterized by "drought, war and darkness".[9] The recent history of the region is clouded by conflict since the British ceded it to Ethiopia in 1954. This has generated a war of independence waged by Somalis who live in the province under the umbrella of the Ogaden National Liberation Front against the Ethiopian government. The Ogaden National Liberation Front is backed by Somalia, which has declared Ogaden part of Greater Somalia. For some Somalis, the land taken by Ethiopia cannot be forgotten because it is attached to Somali blood and nationalists who died during the war 1977/78. They claim that

Ethiopia mistreats the Somalis under their administration. The land was given to them by colonialists and we will seek justice to resolve the crisis that is dividing the two countries.[10]

There are strong cultural and social affinities between Ethiopian Somalis and their kin in Somalia and northern Kenya. The transnational Somali community thus feels like one cohesive cultural group that must cope with the intrusion of unwanted international frontiers. Ethiopian Somalis feel culturally and socially closer to their ethnic affiliates in Somalia and Kenya than they do to their compatriots Ethiopian highlanders. They trade more with Somalia than with the rest of Ethiopia and have adopted the Somali shilling as the main currency in the region occupied by them. The Ogaden problem has developed into complex entanglements between the two states as well as in developments within their respective countries. Against this background, and to protect its interests, Ethiopia has backed the formation of the transition government of Somalia, led by its ally Abdulahhi Yusuf as president and sent troops to protect Somalia's interim government in Badoa against Islamists in Somalia. Meanwhile, Eritrea, a recent breakaway state from Ethiopia has been arming the Islamist militia, a development that has led to fears of wider regional instability.[11]

A number of states, yet still, which Nigeria, the Democratic Republic of the Congo and Republic of Sudan aptly exemplify, have also simmered in unending internal conflicts since their very emergence as states.

UNSTABLE NEIGHBOURHOODS

Conflicts and disintegration within the post-colonial African state as well as the instability of its state system defy major colonially-inspired divisions throughout Africa. It has equally affected Anglophone, Arabic, Francophone and Lusophone states. The proneness to conflict and instability has also defied the size of state. Guinea Bissau and Cape Verde, which jointly fought a long brutal war of liberation, effectively abandoned the movement towards full political union in 1980. Guinea Bissau, with a population of 1.6 million, in turn has fought intermittent civil wars since 1997. A medium-level state like Senegal has experienced instability in an irredentist war in the Casamance province that has gone on for over two decades. Large states like Sudan and the Democratic Republic of Congo have not been immune to the pervasive affliction of conflict of the post-colonial state in Africa. The post-colonial Westphalian state and the state system constituted by them are thus unstable. From whatever theoretical perspective the phenomenon of conflict in the post-colonial African state is approached or whatever analytical lenses are adopted (*realist, liberal institutional or constructivist*), the state and its system have failed.

On 12 June, 2006 the Greentree Agreement was signed by President Olusegun Obasanjo of Nigeria to cede the strategic Bakasi Peninsula in dispute between Nigeria and Cameroun to the latter. The Nigerian indigenes of the peninsula were presented with a choice of retaining their Nigerian citizenship and being resettled in mainland Nigeria or acquiring the citizenship of Cameroun. Following the signing of the agreement, in July 2006, the Nigerian indigenes of Bakassi and the representatives of the peoples of Southern Cameroons, who were already engaged in disputing the sovereignty of Republic du Cameroun over Southern Cameroun, published an open letter to President Olusegun Obasanjo, the Secretary General of the United Nations, Mr. Kofi Annan, and the President of the Republic of Cameroon, Mr. Paul Biya, stating their resolve to launch a new republic immediately after the withdrawal of Nigerian troops from the Peninsula. They also rejected the Greentree Agreement reached on June 12 by Nigeria, the UN Secretary General, and the President of Cameroun, which gave effect to the October 2002 ruling of the International Court of Justice (ICJ).

In the open letter, the Southern Cameroons Peoples Organisation (SCAPO), the umbrella body of the peoples of Southern Cameroun, challenged the legality of the Greentreee agreement, which was done without their consent. SCAPO's leader, Dr. Kevin Gwang Gumne, who signed the open letter said that the Republic of Ambazania, which would rule over the Southern Cameroons and Bakassi Peninsula, would take off soon as Nigerian troops moved out of the troubled territory. The organization announced its intentions to create a new Republic of Ambazania that would have dominion over Bakassi Peninsula as it remains a country recognized under international laws. It further stated that the ruling of the International Court of Justice (ICJ) did not state which of the Cameroons had control over the disputed territory. It gave reasons that

> The people of Southern Cameroons believe that the ICJ ruling of October 2002 was correct only in the sense that it determined that the sovereignty over the Bakassi Peninsula does not belong to Nigeria. However in that ruling, the sovereignty belongs to Cameroon, the ICJ failed to specify which Cameroon it was referring to. To the extent that there has never been any formal union between the Southern Cameroons and La Republic du Cameroon, which attained independence on January 1 1961 with defined and internationally recognised borders, we believe that the sovereignty over the Peninsula belongs unquestionably to the Southern Cameroons and not the La Republic du Cameroun,[12]

The group stated that its claim is strengthened by the fact that no formal agreement exists between the Southern Cameroons and the La Republic du Cameroun.[13]

Chaos at Creation

As the case of Cameroun and other states to be discussed later depict, the crisis in post-colonial African states began almost immediately as these political units emerged by fiat in the global inter-state system as independent political actors claiming the attributes of statehood and its implied sovereignty. The claims to sovereignty by the new state were often challenged at two levels: internally by constituent units, usually pre existing nationalities, contesting the legitimacy of the institutions of the new state; and externally, by elite state actors in the international system, who seek to appropriate or consolidate their control over the emerging state as an element in a larger global strategic canvass during the cold war era. In the post Cold War, the process of the consolidation of the pre-Cold War agenda to build the world in the image of rival hegemonic forces has continued unabated. The pursuit of control over subordinate members of the global inter-state system by rival colonial and hegemonic forces that were suspended at the end of World War II as a result of new compelling security challenges and the uncertain process of realignment of the global configuration of power dictated by the Cold War, has resumed after the cold war era. The end of the struggle for ideological supremacy at the global level has established clearly defined principles that would underpin the way human affairs would be conducted henceforth.

The end of the Cold War introduced a number of factors to which the African continent and its host of post-colonial polities are still responding. While the strategic value of the continent diminished for the major powers[14], the triumph of liberal democratic principles has engendered a universal acceptance of the framework of the post-Cold War global order. Despite this, the envisaged stability as a result of the post Cold War configuration of power at the global level has become elusive. These principles have legitimated the new order, including its structure, within which context some form of competition, limited in scope, among major actors can resume. A legitimate order, however, does not make conflicts impossible, it simply limits its scope.[15] Many of the new conflicts in the global system, paradoxically, are consequences of the changed structure of the international system deriving from the end of the Cold War. In the post Cold War period, the competition for continued hegemonic control of post-colonial African states continue unabated within the constraints posed by the relative stability of the global inter-state system. Thus while the heightened considerations for global security associated with the Cold War have been deprioritized, designs for continued hegemonic control continue to unfold. Traditional rivalries of neo-colonial and metropolitan states have resumed between hitherto Cold War allies. The occasional rhetoric of jointly pursuing common agenda in the continent imposed by the evolved character of relations among these rival states in the post-Cold War has not dampened the enthusiasm to pursue traditional interests of the various states. Sometimes, the processes entailed in the recrudescent rivalries of neo-colonial powers may be explicit but most times nuanced.

Events in the Democratic Republic of the Congo in the 1960s was an early signal of the deadly dynamic of conflict that was going to revolve around the simultaneous struggles for the appropriation of the state at two levels: the contention for ascendancy in the new political space by diverse domestic forces and their extraterritorial allies and stakeholders at the first level; and the continuing search to consolidate control of the post-colonial African political entity through the appropriation of the new state by external actors at the other level. Congo Kinshasa thus presaged the future direction of statehood in Africa when it plunged into civil strife on the eve of independence. Internally, Katanga sought to break away from the new Republic in order to appropriate its resources. This agenda converged with Belgian notions of creating a micro state out of the rich enclave in the perceived interest of the departing colonial power. Externally still, the emerging post-colonial Democratic Republic of the Congo was being co-opted as an element in the larger global Cold War of elite states in the state system.

PROBLEMATIC STATEHOODS

The problematic statehoods of three biggest states, one of which is also the most populous, namely, Democratic Republic of Congo, Federal Republic of Nigeria and the Republic of Sudan, are symptomatic of the malaise of the very conception of the African state. These countries have since independence lurched from the brink of one major disaster to another. It is against this background that the African state has been described as a mere container of peoples.[16] The very notion of sovereignty has been questioned, and calls for the re-definition of the concept of security have been made by some leaders.[17]

The Democratic Republic of Congo (formerly Zaire) was born into chaos in June 1960. The process toward independence was short. The emergence of Congolese political parties is dated by Crawford Young from the first elections in colonial Congo in December 1957.[18] In the two and a half years before independence, the Belgian colonial authorities attempted to retain effective control of the independent Congo after what was to be merely a flag independence. At independence, among other strategies, the Belgians provoked fights among the indigenous population along ethnic lines to create confusion. The 'rubble of a decolonization process that went awry' were riots which led to an abrupt flight of the Belgians from the colony.[19] What was described by the United Nations as a constitutional issue and an internal conflict in the young multi-national state degenerated into armed hostilities. This was the result of a Belgian-inspired attempted secession of the province of Katanga from the new republic. The Katagan secession involved the collaboration of the Belgian military, ethnic Katangese and European settlers in Katanga.[20] That immediate post-independence internal crisis, in the context of the prevailing international climate of the time, naturally invited the attention of the super powers. The super powers stamped on the internal Congolese crisis a Cold War imprint that was to define the character, nature and internal dynamic of the Zairoise/Congolese state and the external politics of Mobutiste Zaire for three decades. This problematic scheme of the dinosaur state remained in place until May 1997.[21] The brutal civil war of 1960 - 1964 and the Katangese secession were only brought to an end by the force of arms of the United Nations. Since then, under the dictator-ship of Mobutu Sese Seko, two major invasions of Shaba province on March 8, 1977 (Shaba I), and on May 13, 1978 (Shaba II), by Zairoise dissidents and opponents of the regime and many other skirmishes have taken place. These invasions were repelled by France, in collaboration with the United States, by mobilizing their allies such as Morocco and Senegal, to intervene in these wars. At no time did any of the neighboring states of Zaire overtly intervene in its domestic crises.

By late 1993, a long-drawn democratization process in Zaire, which began in 1990 through the convening of a sovereign national conference, was becom-ing violent and futile. At the instigation of Mobutu, military detachments were sealing off the premises of the conference and harassing its members. The powers and decisions of the Conference were constantly being undermined and challenged by Mobutu. By October 1996, on the eve of the Kabila rebellion, the Zairoise 'dinosaur' state had all but collapsed. Provinces such as East Kasai had started asserting their autonomy from the disintegrating state. Before the Kabila rebellion overthrew the Mobutu regime, the province managed its own currency, promoted its own development project and had just opened its own university all outside the institutional framework of the Zairoise state.[22]

This provided a vital backdrop to the Kabila rebellion in October 1996. Kabila and his forces attracted the overt support of Uganda, Rwanda, Angola, the Sudanese Peoples Liberation Army/Movement, who supplied troops, mate-riel and logistical support for the Kabila led Alliance of Democratic Forces for the Liberation of the Congo/Zaire (ADFL).[23] Other states such as Eritrea, Ethiopia, Zambia and Zimbabwe offered critical diplomatic support for the Alliance against the government of Mobutu. The Mobutu government was supported by Sudan with military supplies and by the Uniao para a Indepen-dencia Total de Angola (UNITA) and members of the former Hutu dominated national army of Rwanda, the Forces Armee Rwandaise (FAR) with men in effective participation in the battles. France bankrolled Serbian mercenaries in support of Mobutu forces in combat and worked to find a negotiated settlement to the conflict.[24] The interplay of multiple internal and external forces produced an implosion that warranted one of the earliest massive foreign interventions, both overt and covert, in the internal affairs of a nascent state in Africa. The Democratic Republic of the Congo has yet to reconstitute itself into a function-ing state. The state has not only gone through the travails of a vicious dictator-ship in the dinosaur state of Mobutu, but it also continues to remain unstable as a result of continuing interventions from actors in its intermestic environment and elite actors in the global system. Georges Nzongola-Ntalaja observes that

The current war is a function of both external and internal factors. The external factor relates to the national security interests that Rwanda and Uganda have with respect to the north-eastern region of the Congo. These interests include issues of cross-border violence as well as economic and geopolitical stakes, which led the two countries to support the war of liberation against the Mobutu regime in 1996-97. Today, the two countries seem determined to impose a weak regime in Kinshasa, one that would not question their control over the eastern part of the country and its considerable natural wealth, now being openly exploited by their political authorities and businesspeople. As for Kabila's new allies, the defense of international law and OAU principles is a convenient pretext for their own economic and geopolitical calculations. The case of Zimbabwe is particularly revealing in this regard.[25]

The fate of the Democratic Republic of the Congo is as uncertain as the very concept of the Westphalian state in Africa. The viability of the various inter-state systems in the various sub-regions in Africa, West, East and Central Africa, including the Great Lakes region, the Horn, North and Southern Africa, hangs in the balance. The situation in Nigeria exemplifies this.

Instability in Nigeria, which gained independence in October 1960, led to the declaration of a state of emergency in Western Region of the state in 1962, only two years after independence. Before then the amalgamation of the constituent communities into colonial Nigeria had been declared a mistake.[26] The crisis enveloping the Nigerian state, arising from the struggles for internal hegemony by major domestic forces, culminated in the Biafran attempt at secession in 1967. This led to three years of bloob bath in a civil war. The major backers of secession in Nigeria were francophone countries in Africa, goaded by France. In the fourth decade of its existence, Nigeria was still perceived as a mere geographical expression.[27] For decades after the declaration of an end to its civil war in 1970, Nigeria remained under the yoke of brutal military dictatorships. It has been riddled by domestic violence that rivals any of the formal civil wars in its sub-region. Even though Nigeria is not formally at war, lives and properties lost exceed casualties in communities faced everyday with machine guns, armored cars and high-capacity bombs from guided missiles and warplanes.

Ethno-religious conflicts have become integral to national life in Nigeria. In 2002 to 2003, there was conflict in the Middle Belt (lower Benue valley) involving Tiv in Benue, Taraba and Nasarawa and the Jukun of Taraba states and other tribes in Nasarawa state. During the same period, there were conflicts between Moslems and non Moslems over the implementation of Sharia law in Jigawa, Kano and Kaduna States.[28] Conservative estimates put fatalities from politically motivated violence related to the introduction of Sharia in northern states of

Nigeria as far higher than that resulting from perennial conflict between Israel and the Palestinians.[29] Fatalities from communal or religious violence across the country in three years is put at least 10,000.[30] In July 2009, the Boko Haram, a fanatical Islamic group began a Jihad with the intent to Islamize the whole of Nigeria, in particular the "evil West and South" of the country. In clashes between members of the group and the military and Police, 800 were killed as government forces fought to contain the spread of the mayhem initiated by the group in five of Nigeria's northern states.

Conflict on ethno-religious lines in Nigeria however pales into insignificance against the the newly emered threat of fundamentalist salafist group, the Boko Haram, that is waging a war to islamize Nigeria. The war of this terrorist organization has heightened the threat to the longevity of the Nigeria state. Before the advent of Boko Haram, a long-standing, low-intensity conflict that has pitted a number of militias in the Niger Delta and the Nigerian military forces over the control of oil resources mined in that region. The Niger Delta area accounts for 90% of the country's oil and gas export earnings, but since independence it has remained severely underdeveloped and politically marginalized.[31] The greatest immediate challenge to Nigeria's stability emanates from the Niger Delta, where political grievance, criminal opportunism and militia violence, all fuelled by major oil theft operations and a massive influx of increasingly sophisticated weaponry, are creating an ever more dangerous dispensation.[32] The year 2005 witnessed an alarming escalation of the conflict with illegal arms flows into the Delta, with militia groups increasing their personnel and armament strength

> Among the militias, the Movement for the Emancipation of the Niger Delta (MEND) is currently the most recognized, having gained notoriety in early 2006 with a series of attacks on oil installations, kidnappings of foreign oil workers, and most recently, by detonating a car bomb- the first in Nigeria's history- in the city of Port Harcourt. Reports of training camps led by former military officials and of the arms caches located throughout the region led observers to suggest that conflict in the Delta may be transitioning towards insurgency.[33]

The future of the Nigerian state, like many other post-colonial states in Africa, remains at stake. Ason Bur observes the steady rise and increase in the number and operations of ethnic militias in Nigeria since 1999

> These organizations or ethnic militias come from South west, South South, South East and some Northern parts of Nigeria's six

geo-political zones. In the South West there is the emergence of the Odu'a Peoples Congress (OPC) led by Dr Frederick Fasheun and Otunba Gani Adams who are agitating for self governance of the Yoruba speaking areas.

In the South East, there is also a militant organization, the Movement for the Actualization of the Sovereign State of Biafra (MASSOB), headed by Chief Ralph Uwazuruike. This organization, as the name implies, seeks to actualize the sovereign state of Biafra. It is very influential among the Igbos in the South East geo political zone....It is alleged that they have a Radio Biafra in America and have Biafran currency circulating in Abia and Imo states...In the Niger Delta area of the South South geopolitical zoned inhabited largely by oil producing states, militia groups have emerged since 1999 demanding 100% resources control or political independence for the Niger Delta region. These are mainly Niger Delta People Volunteer Force (NDPVF) headed by Alhaji Asari Dokunbo.[34]

As the 2007 democratic elections drew near, the political process in Nigeria was heated up, as the North, the South and the South-South, all clamored to take over the Presidency from President Olusegun Obasanjo, a Yoruba from the South West. Victor E. Dike observed that

As the 2007 election gets nearer, the drumbeat of power-shift (or retention) politics gets louder, irritating, insulting, confusing and destabilizing. The politicians from North and South are throwing political punches at each other, as each is claiming ownership of the Presidency. The pitch of the political trumpet gets higher among ethnic politicians that are furiously and arrogantly thumbing their nose, swearing in the name of their political gods that the world would cave in if the presidency were not dropped on their doorstep. In their bid to achieve their selfish purpose, each region is stereo-typing and insulting one another. And the minority groups within the regions are equally claiming the presidency for varied reasons. While some of them are saying that the presidency should be given to them because they feed the nation, others are arguing that they have been politically marginalized and, therefore, should be allowed to occupy Aso Rock, in 2007. However, the irksome noise have (sic) caused political birds of unlike feathers to flock together to actualize their selfish zonal ambition without anyone taking cognizance of the damages their actions are doing to the democratization process and the unity of Nigeria.

The power shift (or retention) palaver is also creating ripple within the geo-political zones, as there abound stories of how the political gladiators in the zones are scheming to out maneuver (sic)

one another in the political crossfire that is reminiscent of the 2003 political era.[35]

Before the assumption of statehood by South Sudan on 9 July, 2011, having seceded from the Republic of Sudan through a referenum in January 2011, Sudan had become the forgotten war. In its case, attempts at forcible Islamisation and Arabization of the predominantly Christian south by the dominant Islamic and Arabized North has led to a permanent state of war in the country. The Sudan has the unfortunate distinction of harboring the longest conflict in Africa in which millions of people have died. Its civil war began in the early 1960s when a major guerrilla war developed in the South against the Khartoum government that was denounced as a regime of Arab domination.[36] Since independence from the UK in 1956, the governments of Sudan have been largely military regimes that have favored Islamization of the country through forcible conversion of Christian south non-Arab population. This policy has embroiled the country in two prolonged civil wars during most of the remainder of the 20th century. These conflicts were also rooted in northern economic, political, and social domination of largely non-Muslim, non-Arab Southern Sudanese and became more poignant and critical with the discovery of oil in the South. The first civil war ended in 1972, but broke out again in 1983. The second war and famine-related effects resulted in more than 4 million people displaced and, according to rebel estimates, more than 2 million deaths over a period of two decades. Peace talks gained momentum in 2002-04 with the signing of several accords; a final Naivasha peace treaty of January 2005 granted the southern rebels autonomy for six years, after which a referendum for independence would be held. A separate conflict that broke out in the western region of Darfur in 2003 has resulted in at least 200,000 deaths and nearly 2 million displaced; as of late 2005, peacekeeping troops were struggling to stabilize the situation.[37] Neighboring states, Uganda, Kenya and Chad have been implicated in the crisis of the Sudanese state.

The problem of extra territorial minorities acting in concert with their cousins across state frontiers to capture or destabilize the states led the government of Niger to declare a minority Arab population along its borders with Chad as non-Nigerien and to expel them from the country. In October 2006, Niger's government, alleging that the minority Arab community, known as Mahamid, was engaged in criminal activities ordered them to leave the country. The protestations of the community that they are citizens of Niger who have no other country to go to, went unheeded. At the expiration of a five day ultimatum given to the community to leave Niger, the government began rounding the Mahamid and transporting them up to the borders of Chad. The Mahamid have indicated their intentions to take their case to the United Nations Security Council. Many members of this Arab community came to Niger from neighboring Chad following the 1974 drought in Chad. Others who came to seek refuge from fighting in Chad arrived in the1980s. Since then they have lived in Niger. Many still have lived in the country for up to 50 years. Notwithstanding that the Mahamids have risen to senior positions in the military, local adminis-tration and in business, the governor of Diffa State, where most of the Mahamid live, affirmed that it was "high time" for them to pack and return to Chad. Niger's Interior Minister Mounkaila Modi reiterated that this represented the position of the government of Niger as he declared the Mahamid as foreigners who possessed illegal firearms and were a serious threat to the security of local communities. He added that the camels of the Mahamid were draining local oases. He reaffirmed the quit order on the Arab community, reiterating that:

> We have decided, starting today, to expel these nomadic Arab 'Mohamides' to their home countries,...These foreigners have shown no respect to the rights of the natives and they're putting pressure on pastures in this region. We can no longer accept seeing our ecosys-tem degraded by foreigners. [38]

INTERMESTICITY AND THE POST-COLD WAR ERA

The transnational communities perceive themselves as one people, despite international boundaries that pass through the territories that they have tradi-tionally claimed for their respective communities. They behave as cohesive units with common interests and stakes in their interaction with other transnational communities that they encounter in those spaces. These encounters may take place in the context of conflicting interests in the various states sharing contigu-ous borders in which their members are represented in varying strengths. Often, there are as many transnational communities as the number of communities that straddle the international borders of the post-colonial African state. They are recognized as competing units with legitimate stakes in the informal discourses and interactions in the intermestic environment in which the post- colonial African state is located. They are natural stakeholders in developments within each formal political entity in which its members are represented, whether as a majority group or a minority. In both instances, the ultimate well being of the community is paramount. This has become more evident in the post-Cold War era that has been marked by behavioral transformations of African states.[39]

Post-colonial African states and, more importantly, communities acting as corporate non state entities overtly intervene militarily in the affairs of one another. This is with a view to promoting partisan goals of their allies. In the case of extra-territorial communities intervening in the conflict across international frontiers, the goals sought may or may not be consistent with the agenda of the dominant group or even of its own government. Its intervention is supportive of the determined interests of the forces to which it is affiliated in the struggle it is wading into across international frontiers. The conflict in Angola reverberated in instability in the Democratic Republic of Congo and implicated communities in Congo Brazzaville and Zambia, Angola, Zaire/Democratic Republic of Congo. The unending chaos in the immediate sub-region reflects the dire circumstance of the state in Africa and the problematic character of its inter-state system. Angola-Democratic Republic of Congo-Republic of Congo Brazzaville-Rwanda-Burundi-Sudan-Uganda constitutes one discernible orbit of conflict. This conflict zone stretches from the Great Lakes region into Central Africa. The patchwork of the states of Sierra Leone –Liberia-Guinea Conakry-Senegal-Guinea Bissau, which stretch across the vast length of the West African coast, is a well known aggregation of failing states in Africa. Implicated in these conflicts are networks of transnational communities who have to be taken account of in formulating the peace process for the so-called domestic conflict. Some have estimated that these states and the sub-regions have produced over 25 million refugees and internally displaced persons every year since the early eighties.

The problem of interconnectedness and the intermesticity elicited by this are also expressed in the complex linkages between instability in Uganda and Sudan and the continued massing of the Ugandan Lord Resistance Army (LRA) in the North-East of the Republic of Congo (Kinshasa). The government in Khartoum has provided material support for the LRA, which has used southern Sudan as a rear base in their continuing offensives against the Ugandan Government. Sudan's President Omar Hassan Ahmed el Bashir's regime has sought good relations with Kinshasa to protect the LRA. As a result, Ugandan troops that have often entered southern Sudan to hunt LRA rebels now stay in Southern Sudan. In the post-January 2005 Comprehensive Peace Agreement with Khartoum that grants Southern Sudan autonomy leading to the formation of the Government of Southern Sudan (GOSS), neutralizing the Khartoum backed LRA in that province would boost the GOSS among the Southern Sudanese. Even more importantly, Southerners conjectured that Khartoum will use the LRA to destabilize the GOSS before independence referendum that was held in 2011. Meanwhile, outspoken northern Ugandan politicians have threatened secession by the north and the formation of a "Nilotic state", by joining with Southern Sudan. This brings warning signals in Juba about the historic aspirations of Sudan's southernmost region, Equatorial, to secede.[40]

CROSS–BORDER PROBLEMS BETWEEN LIBERIA AND COTE D'IVOIRE

Cross-border problems between Liberia and Cote d'Ivoire, as in much of West Africa and indeed across much of black Africa, emanate from the flow of cultural affinities of ethnic groups and communities across international boundaries between the two countries. These historically entrenched social affiliations across border areas generate ethnic identity consciousness that combine with communally shared religious faiths to contest for preeminence over citizenship obligations and loyalty to the respective states. Between Liberia and Cote d'Ivoire, communal identities flow horizontally across international frontiers, while citizenship of the states is vertically aligned within the states. The problematic sociological layout of border communities has been exploited by political forces to the detriment of political stability, economic development and social harmony in the border regions as well as the state system as a whole. Cross-border security problems between Liberia and Cote d'Ivoire are thus mainly attributable to antagonisms and divergent political interests that are manipulated along ethnic and cultural lines. These contrived political differences create cleavages that feed into the strategic permutations and policies of key political actors in the sub-region. The interplay of the two forces has invariably instigated a vicious process of mutual destabilization that has weakened the two contiguous states and victimized all the communities caught in the throes of the destructive dynamic. These factors underpin cross-border allegiances of communities that straddle the Liberia-Cote d'Ivoire borders and, as such, determine the alignments of ethnic armed elements that criss-cross not only the Liberian and Ivorian common frontiers, but impact as far north as in Burkina Faso and Mali. Manifestations of cross-border problems between Liberia and Cote d'Ivoire are abundantly expressed in linkages between the major protagonists and their supporters in the sub region.

The impact of transnational affiliations among the peoples in the sub-region, including ethnic groups in member countries of the Mano River Union and Cote d'Ivoire, are illustrated in close interaction between them at the social, political and economic levels. They are also expressed in a complex security and humanitarian nexus that underpins security developments in the four countries. This interconnectedness defines these states together as an autonomous sub-system in many respects. This fact notwithstanding, the interplay of transnational affinities among communities seriously impacts on security among states that share common borders. They are also critical in the management of humanitarian challenges that flow from conflicts in the sub-region. This has come to the fore in the nature of social and economic crisis as well as political uncertainties as they underline both state and communally-inspired strategic alliances that emerge.

In its humanitarian expression, these affinities partly determine the flow of refugees in the direction of their ethnic cousins across international frontiers. In the medium to long term, refugees along the borders become factors in the calculus of conflict in the border areas. They provide new recruiting grounds for the next generation of armed elements. Cross-border problems between

Liberia and Cote d'Ivoire exemplify this security conundrum. In the economic domain, persistent instability on the Liberian-Ivorian border areas has led to the development of a unique political economy that is associated with conflict and brings together conniving states, international business and the various rebel movements that operate across the borders. This peculiar economy of war, which funds conflict in the border areas across West Africa, thrives on illicit logging, mining, and proliferation of small arms, prostitution and the diversion of agricultural produce from official state marketing channels to the international market. This was pronounced during the war.

Cross border problems between Liberia and Cote d'Ivoire are, first, manifest in the prevailing difficult security dynamic that revolves around the deployment of ethnically organized bands of armed elements who are engaged in active combat on the two sides of the common borders. These ethnic mercenaries are often instruments of official state policy, or may be in the service of rebellious movements between the two countries. The activities of these organized renegades have contributed to the weakening of Liberia and Cote d'Ivoire and pose a serious challenge to the very conception of the state system in the sub-region. The activities of the roaming bands of ethnic mercenaries along the Liberian and Ivorian international borders may be dated to the Liberian conflict in 1989. It is believed that the Charles Taylor led NPFL was sponsored by Cote d'Ivoire and Burkina Faso against the Samuel Doe regime. The war not only contributed to the demise of the Doe government but ultimately to the implosion of the Liberian state. It also gave rise to the emergence of a rival proto Liberian state with its headquarters in Gbarnga for over seven years. On the Ivorian side, the partition of the state since September 2002 up to the conteoversial elections of 2010 had been sustained by the support of Liberian armed elements of different ethnic hues that are fighting on all sides in the Ivorian divide. These armed elements perceive themselves as helping their Ivorian ethnic cousins to achieve political goals.

This volatile security situation created along the Liberian-Ivorian borders has entailed humanitarian challenges of mammoth proportions. In Guiglo, over 5000 Liberian refugees lived in the peace-town refugee camp. They condition their return to Liberia on the neutralization of all pro-Taylor forces in the country. Paradoxically, residues of the Taylor elements are themselves embroiled in the conflict in Cote d'Ivoire.

ETHNIC ALLIANCES ACROSS THE BORDERS OF LIBERIA AND COTE D'IVOIRE AND THE SECURITY CONUNDRUM SINCE 1989

As far back as 1989, Cote d'Ivoire, under President Felix Houphouet Boigny, supported the incursion of Charles Taylor's National Patriotic Front of Liberia

(NPFL) into Liberia to begin the conflict that raged in that country for 14 years. Cote d'Ivoire supplied arms, logistical support and the diplomatic leverage that helped to strengthen the perceptions of the legitimacy about the NPFL within the international community. Ivorian territory served as a base and outlet of pro Taylor international businessmen whose activities in illicit commercial logging and in the mining sector funded his rebellion. About the same time, Diola / Madingo irredentism in the sub-region, which had instigated strategic alliances in the sub region in relation to the conflict in the Casamance basin of Senegal and lately in the tripartite Madingo/Balanta/ Metisse political contentions in Guinea Bissau, expressed itself in the Liberian conflict through the formation of Raleigh Seekie's United Liberation Movement (ULIMO) in Sierra Leone. The split into the Kromah ("K") and Johnson ("J") factions highlighted the devolution of ULIMO into instruments of ethnic political aggrandizement. ULIMO "K" sourced funds mainly from Madingo elements in Guinea and Sierra Leone. In more recent times, the Liberia United for Reconciliation and Development (LURD), founded in 1999 whose command structure had 90% ULIMO antecedents, and initially led by Sekou Damate Conneh, Jr. and Chayee Doe, the brother of late Samuel Doe, was a reincarnation of the first consolidated ULIMO. The fractious split of LURD merely repeated the break up of the first ULIMO under pressure from transnational ethnic pressures. In this connection, the emergence of MODEL from the LURD has been attributed to initiatives of the Ivorian government. The Liberia United for Reconstruction and Development (LURD) has strong affiliation to Guinea and Sierra Leone, while MODEL consolidated Krahn and Kru elements from Liberia and Cote d'Ivoire.

IMPLICATIONS FOR CONFLICT ANALYSIS

The post-colonial African state is a weak political institution. It largely depends on coercion to assure compliance. This, in turn, undermines its tenuous legitimacy. The formal state institutions thus have very limited impact, or, at best, are superficial indicators of behavioral expectations of the state and society in the state. Paradoxically, the post-colonial state survives at the expense of the international community. Whatever their limitations in terms of internal contentions about domestic sovereignty, the basic rule of international legal sovereignty is that recognition is extended to entities, states, with territory and formal juridical autonomy. This state is thus treated by other actors in the international state system in the same manner as individuals treat each other as equals consistent with the liberal theory of the state.[41] The departures of the post-colonial state from the Westphalian model have significant implications for the theory of the post-colonial African state. They also have critical consequences for the manner of our exploration of the nature of conflicts in these late entrants into the Westphalian system and the inter-state system constituted by them.

In the analysis of conflict, the state has remained the basic unit of analysis and the major preoccupation has been with domestic factors in relation to the problem of nation building. The thrust of inquiries in this connection has been what factors must be responsible for the failure of the nation building projects in Africa.[42] The impact of the Cold War from the 1960s up to the 1990s after the fall of the Berlin wall on ethnicity and on the interplay of domestic forces constitutes in almost its entirety the analysis of the security calculus of the African state. The religious dimension to conflict, an important source of conflict, is often recognized but is usually left out of serious discourse because of its political volatility. It is thus understated in the analysis of conflict in Africa. The understandings of the sources of conflict in African states generated through such narrow and constrained prisms are thus limited. A significant lacuna exists in our comprehension of the systemic linkages that drive the implosion of the African state and the instability in the inter-state system. The implications of conflicts in the various African states as a possible manifestation of deep seated crisis of the state in Africa deserve further exploration. The structural linkages between failing states that share borders confronted with instability in whole sub regions, have not been adequately addressed. A systematic appreciation of the implications for systemic stability of these interacting elements, especially the role of transnational forces that give rise to the intermesticity of context and the unique character of the environment, has so far eluded analysis of conflicts.

A broader perspective, which treats what is conventionally understood as distinct conflicts in particular states as expressions of structural defects in the regional or sub-regional inter-state system and within the context of an almost stagnant historicity of the state in Africa, is yet to emerge. Conflicts are thus conceptualized as entirely functions of developments within each state. Instability in sub-regions is then interpreted as spillovers to neighboring states.[43] Such unduly statecentric and atomistic frameworks, even as they capture aspects of the sources of conflict in Africa, are ultimately reductionist. They militate against the proper understanding of the intermestic character of conflicts in African states and fail to highlight the structural linkages in the sub-systems that lead to the implosion of whole sub regions. In many respects, this state-centric focus, and its implied atomism, is consistent with the fiction of the state and its sovereignty, including respect for the non-interference protocols that had held sway in Africa until the post-Cold War era. A meaningful exploration of these concerns in a manner that seeks to unravel the trans-national character of conflicts in the African state system should be rewarding. Understanding the often not so subtle sub-regional undercurrents that characterize these conflicts should move us closer to building a more comprehensive profile of forces whose interaction constitute the dynamic of the crisis of the African state and the challenges of instability of the post colonial African inter-state system. As reality imposes, a first step in this discourse is to undertake a structural deconstruction of the post-colonial African state, and by implication, the state system composed by it.

The post-cold War era has made bankrupt hitherto dogmatic pretensions to a sacrosanct sovereignty of African states, especially in relations with other state actors in the regional system. Developments in the post-Cold War period, including outside Africa and particularly in the Balkans and the old Soviet Union, have forced the expansion of the discourse to problematize the concept and concrete expressions of the state itself in multinational societies and the inter-state system constituted by those states. The serial implosion of states in the Great Lakes region, including the adjoining state of Congo Brazzaville, and the difficulties of reconstructing them through success on the battle field or even negotiating them back into existence within the same historical space force on us certain reflection.

The collapse of states in West Africa, Sierra Leone, Liberia, Guinea Bissau raise serious queries on the very conceptualization of conflict, the unit and level of analytical focus, and traditional theorization of conflict in Africa. It is instructive that in the two pivotal state actors in the respective regions, Nigeria and the Democratic Republic of Congo, as well as in Sudan, the state itself has become the major issue. They epitomize the problems of the post-colonial African state. In Nigeria the clamor for restructuring and true federalism has often been interpreted as nuanced calls for the breakup of the country, while the Democratic Republic of the Congo is yet to be reconstituted into a state since Laurent Kabila took up arms against the dinosaur state of Mobutu. Before its final implosion certain regions had virtually ceased to be part of Zaire. Around these pivots revolve a galaxy of unstable satellite states; Sierra Leone, Liberia, Senegal, Guinea Bissau and Guinea Conakry in West Africa; and Rwanda, Burundi, Uganda, and Angola in the case of the embattled Democratic Republic of Congo. In the north, Sudan is a constant poignant reminder of the intractability of the struggle to appropriate the African state as an instrument to, first, advance the internal hegemony of a certain idea and force, and secondly, the hegemony of an external force bent on deploying the state as an instrument in consolidating its global mission. There is indeed pandemonium in post-Cold War Africa.

The Cold War also induced a certain pattern of relations between the post-colonial African state and powerful actors in the global system, such that conflicts engendered by local problems soon bore the imprimatur of the Cold War. These relations cast African states in the role of minor elements, the literature would say proxies, in this larger global playground dominated by hegemonic forces and influences. African states were instruments in the articulation of larger strategic considerations that bore no relevance to their own national interests. The imposition of the dominant themes in global security on African affairs during the Cold War, which incidentally has spanned the total lifespan of these nascent states, made irrelevant the problems intrinsic to the post-colonial African state and its inter-state system. The liberating consequences of the end of the post-Cold War have ironically been to make manifest the complexities of conflicts in the African state and the intermesticity of these crises that were ignored in the Cold War era.

The patterns of security relations between post-colonial African states and extra African elite states and the changing character and patterns of post-Cold War conflicts in Africa, paradoxically, merely highlight not only the ultimate instrumentality of the African state, but also bring to the fore the critical implications of the transnational structural forces and factors for sub-regional stability. The dismantling of global security factors in the post-Cold War has accentuated the play of the full panoply of forces, both domestic, sub-national and sub regional, in the affairs of the respective African states. Religious forces, economic forces, nativist and cultural forces, diverse and sharply divergent ideas and conflicting worldviews all interact to create a very complex security dynamic that may be said to overwhelm the crude institutions of the relatively unsophisticated and almost primordial Westphalian state in Africa.

The post-colonial African state has barely evolved beyond the basic attributes of the nascent state of 1648 in Westphalia. It is thus the failure of the many African states that has captured attention. Economic forces, democratization, sub-nationalism and ethnicity continue to remain the analytical fads, even in the face of developments that direct attention towards more rigorous and sophisticated interpretations of the seemingly unending fractiousness and the chaos that has come to characterize the African state and its inter state system. That the numerous breakdowns of political systems indeed are expressions of the crisis of the African state and its inter-state system is mostly lost or at best treated as outlying factors that are consigned to footnotes. This is understandable as being politically correct. Such approaches fit the preferred paradigms of political status quo, even if they befuddle serious attempts at comprehending the nature of conflicts in Africa.

The relative neglect of the fractious sub-systemic linkages which seem to be critical elements in seeking comprehensive explanations of instability creates serious gaps in the understanding of the sources of conflict in the respective African states and the tendency for whole regions to implode. The domino effect is a pattern well-established in West Africa and the Great Lakes region. Indeed, the transformations of the post cold war world and the radical alterations of the calculus of global security brought in its wake have impacted on the character of conflicts and their management in Africa. The pretensions towards neutrality have given way to partisan interventions that express behavioral transformations in these post-colonial states in relation to their imposed inter-state system.

Like every other state, the post-colonial African state is an artificial creation. Created in an era of more refined sensibilities at the international level, the Westphalian transplant is unable to impose the development of a loyal citizenry and continues to lack organic roots in society. It is thus an imposed aberration that has sought from its very creation to find a raison d'etre to legitimize its problematic existence. The state floats in the absence of any universally acknowledged ideational foundations that hold society together or that define the essences of the peoples forged into the political contraption. The embryonic social and political orders born out of impositions lack legitimacy, since there are no legitimizing principles on which the state is anchored. In fact, there is systemic value dissonance, given the lack of convergence in basic values and worldviews around which any legitimizing principles could evolve. The state must compete with powerful indigenous social and political orders that are organic and are the distillation of the evolution of the various peoples. Paradoxically, the creation of the African state in many instances triggered the rise of sub- nationalistic consciousness following threats of possible subjugation in the new order. Resolving the classic security dilemma becomes the first crisis to be managed by the new state. The evidence of the failure to do this abounds.

A conceptual transplant into this hostile environment, the post-colonial African state , is largely fixated on its crude Westphalian attributes. The post-colonial African state is unable to evolve, that is, grow like an organism, and in a manner that the earliest state of Westphalia has grown. The devolution of sovereignty and the increasing delegation of certain sovereign attributes to supra-national bodies and institutions that have marked the evolution of the post modern state is still unthinkable by the African state. The African state is left out in the development of an international community characterized by a convergence of norms and values by constantly evolving states in Europe. The African state is in a world of its own in which it is seemingly fixated in a time capsule, unable to cope with the rapid transformations in the essential character of the state. The internal processes of the African state, revolving largely on the state capacity for coercion, further undermine its tenuous legitimacy by alienating key stakeholders.

The crude character of the post-colonial state whose structures and institutions have not evolved beyond the original Westphalian conceptions easily collapse in the face of the multi-dimensional crises that are engendered by the vigorous challenges for dominance and hegemony by the competing forces and world views in the state and in the larger inter-state system. The frontiers of the African state are not co-terminus with the boundaries of the various nationalities that constitute the new state. Since the frontiers of the African state do not fit neatly to incorporate these clearly defined major stakeholders in its affairs, there are no conflicts that are strictly internal to any one state. Conflicts in post colonial African states are intermestic in character and easily integrate domino elements implicated in those crises across their immediate frontiers. The conflicts in Angola, linked communities and elicited partisan influences if not interventions in the Democratic Republic of Congo, Congo Brazzaville and Zambia. The crisis in the Democratic Republic of Congo implicates active interested parties in Rwanda, Burundi, Angola, Uganda, Congo-Brazzaville, Namibia, and Zimbabwe. The irredentism in Casamance in Senegal cannot be treated in isolation of developments in the Gambia, Guinea Bissau and Guinea Conakry. These transnational complexities of conflicts that, on the face of it, look internal to post-colonial African states point at the structural incongruities of the post colonial state as well of the inter-state system constituted by those state.

Notes

1.   George B. N. Ayittey, *Africa in Chaos*, St Martins Press, New York, 1998, p. 193.

2.   African Centre for Development and Strategic Studies, *Africa Conflict, Peace and Governance Monitor*, Dokon Publishing House, Ibadan, 2005, Map 2, p. 4.

3.   Mark Doyle, "Sudan's Interlocking Wars," *BBC News*: http://news.bbc.co.uk/1/hi/world/africa/4759325.stm, accessed on December 12, 2006.

4.   "Chad and Sudan Unite over Rebels," *BBC News*: http://news.bbc.co.uk/2/hi/africa/5218064.stm, accessed on July 29, 2006.

5.   "Chad Declares Victory over Rebel Column," *CNN International*: http://edition.cnn.com/2006/WORLD/africa/04/13/chad.ap/index.html, accessed on April 13, 2006.

6.   "Chad Declares Victory over Rebel Column," ibid.

7.   "Darfur Violence Spills into Neighboring Chad", *CNN*: http://www.cnn.com/2006/WORLD/africa/10/18/chad.attacks.reut/index.html, accessed on October 19, 2006.

8.   Christopher Clapham, op. cit.

9.   Mohammed Adow, "At the Frontier", *BBC Focus on Africa Magazine*, October-December 2006, p.24.

10. Mohammed Adow, ibid.,

11. Mohammed Adow, ibid., p. 26.

12. Secession: Bakassi indigenes write OBJ, Biya, UN - New Republic to take off after Nigeria's withdrawal, Nigerian Tribune, Saturday, 1 July, 2006.

13. Ditto

14. Cyrus Sami, op.cit.

15. Henry A. Kissinger, *A World Restored: Metternich, Castlereagh and the Problems of Peace, 1812-1822*, Houghton Miflin Company, Boston, 1973.

16. Anna Simons, "Somalia: A Regional Security Dilemma," in *Africa in the New International Order: Rethinking State Sovereignty and Regional Security*, ed. Edmund Keller and Donald Rothchild, Lynne Rienner Publishers, Boulder, CO, 1996, p. 71.

17. Solomon Gomes, *Africa in the New International Order: Rethinking State Sovereignty and Regional Security*, ed. Edmund Keller and Donald Rothchild, Lynne Rienner Publishers, Boulder, CO, 1996, p. 41.

18. Crawford Young, *Politics in the Congo*, Princeton University Press, Princeton, 1965, p. 296.

19. Crawford Young, ibid., p. 5.

20. Crawford Young, ibid., p. 488-489. Young cites Sepulchire as noting that by 1957 European settlers suggested a federal Congo but were actually in pursuit of the province of Katanga and a "second European dominated state" within a proposed five state Congolese federation. This arrangement was perceived as the best design to function in relative interest of Europeans in the Congo. By June 1960, when all the ingredients of a national crisis were in place, Moise Tshombe was encouraged by the Europeans to declare a breakaway sovereign state of Katanga. Belgian troops collaborated with the Katangese authorities to disarm other Congolese and expel them from Katanga. A 1991 documentary directed by Raoul Peck, *Lumumba: La Mort du Prophete*, provides new information from Mme Peck, Secretary to the Mayor of Leopoldville for over 20 years, spanning the colonial era and early independence, and from retired Belgian officers of the Force Publique in colonial Congo, which attest to the fact that the chaos that emerged at independence was partly orchestrated by Belgian authorities. This backfired leading to attacks on Belgian officers of the Force Publique and the subsequent problems that evolved from this.

21. *West Africa*, no. 4193, 22 June- 12 July 1998, p. 556. The imagery of the dinosaur has been associated with the state under Mobutu by commentators and analysts. In more recent times a number of African regimes, noted for the brutal treatment of the citizens and the personification power have been grouped as dinosaur states.

22. Howard W. French, "In Congo, Province's Dreams of a Better Life Fade," *The New York Times International*, December 10, 1997.

23. Collete Braeckman, "Rebel Official Rejects Secession, Wants Mobutu to leave," March 3, 1997, *Foreign Broadcast Information Service*: http://wnc.fedgov.com. The Alliance was made up of many organizations, sometimes with diverse interests, but mobilized under the immediate common interest in toppling Mobutu. The leadership of the Alliance however had a clear vision about retaining the territorial integrity of Zaire and fighting secessionist tendencies among some of its allies. This fact was highlighted by Bizima Karaha, the Alliance's Commissioner for External Affairs (Southern Hemisphere) when he stated that *"I believe that no Zairian wishes to concern himself about territorial integrity as a question. We strongly*

support a united and democratic Zaire." Kabila observed in this connection that the aim of the AFDL was the immediate task of boosting development by using local resources. He emphasized that most of the developmental program should be largely financed through internal resources without recourse to external aid. Yet some of the Zairoise fighting men were former Katangese gendarmes whose fathers and themselves in their youth had fought for the secession of Katanga. Indeed, these elements in the fighting wing of the AFDL were led by General Vindicien Kiyana, also known as "Mufu" who had commanded the attack on Kolwezi in 1978. Another group in the Alliance fighting force, the UFERI, (the Union of Federalists and Independent Republics) was led by Mr. Mukatshungu. These groups commitment to the unity of Zaire was not so certain. Other major groups in the Alliance of Democratic Forces included the Parti de la Revolution of Laurent Kabila, around which the Alliance was built, Conseil National de Resistance pour la Democracie, le Movement Revolutionaire pour le Liberation du Zaire and L'Alliance Democratique des Peuples.

24. Raymond Bonner, "France Linked to Defense of Mobutu," *The New York Times International*, May 2, 1997, A6.

25. Georges Nzongola-Ntalaja, The Organization of African Unity has since transformed itself into the African Union

26. Bolaji Akinyemi, "Nigeria, a Mere Geographical Expression," Public lecture in commemoration of June 12 and the creation of the Ondo State, Akure, June 21, 2001. http://cometnews.com.ng/20062001/p171901.htm.

27. Bolaji Akinyemi cites Chief Obafemi Awolowo.

28. Ason Bur, "Nigeria's National Conference on Political Reform: Will it Constitute the Laying of the Foundation for a New Democratic Order in the Country?," in Africa Conflict, Peace and Governance Monitor. Ibadan: Dokon Publishing House, 2005, p. 91.

29. David Asonye Ihenacho, "Sharia's Late Nullification a Timely Fight," *Nigeriaworld*: http://nigeriaworld.com/columnist/ihenacho/032302.html, accessed on March 25, 2002, p. 3-4.

30. Dan Isaac, "Nigeria's Turbulent Prospects," *BBC News*: http://news.bbc.co.uk/hi/English/world/Africa/newsid_1753000/1753559.stm, accessed on January 11 2002.

31 IISS (International Institute for Strategic Studies), "Nigeria's Political Prospects," *Strategic Comments* 12, no. 5 (June), 2006.

32. IISS, ibid.

33. IISS, ibid.

34. Ason Bur, "Nigeria's National Conference on Political Reform: Will it Constitute the Laying of the Foundation for a New Democratic Order in the Country?," in Africa Conflict, Peace and Governance Monitor. Ibadan: Dokon Publishing House, 2005, p. 91.

35. Victor E. Dike, "Power Shift and Nigeria's Unity (1)," *Daily Champion*: http://odili.net/news/source/2006/aug/16/608.html, accessed on August 16, 2006

36. Editorial, Africa Conflict, Peace and Governance Monitor, 2006, African Center for Development and Strategic Studies, p 1.

37. Central Intelligence Agency, "Sudan," *The World Factbook 2006*, Potomac Books, Washington, D.C, 2005.

38. "Niger's Arabs to Fight Expulsion," *BBC News*: http://news.bbc.co.uk/1/hi/world/africa/6081416.stm, accessed on October 25, 2006.

39. Ademola Araoye, "Conflict and Cooperation in Central Africa: Explaining Behavioral Transformations of States in the Post Cold War," Ph.D. diss., Claremont Graduate University, Claremont, 1999.

40. "Uganda/Sudan: Opening Broadside," *Africa Confidential* 47, no. 15 (July 21), 2006, p. 2-3.

41. Stephen D. Krasner, *Sovereignty: Organized Hypocrisy*, ibid., p. 14.

42. Dipo Irele, "The Nation State in Africa: A Fresh Look," *Africa Quarterly* 38, no. 2, 1998.

43. Edmund Keller and Donald Rothchild, ed., *Africa In the New International Order*. Lynne Rienner Publishers, Boulder, CO, 1996, p. ix.

Chapter 2

THE NATURE OF THE STATE IN AFRICA

The concept of the state has been straightforward, but, at the same time, not very clear. Although pre-figured in earlier centuries, since the end of World War I the nation state has been the uncontested normative grounding of political independence in the modern states system.[1]

It has been considered as an ontological given and has been taken for granted because the state was understood and treated as a sovereign political entity by other sovereign states. The state has rarely been a subject of investigation.[2] If any differentiation was allowed in the definition of the state, it was in terms of the varying power capabilities of members of the states system. The distribution of power among states defined the structure of the system, for the systemic configuration of power was central to the equilibrium of the interstate system. This structure, in turn, was perceived as the critical consideration in the maintenance of systemic peace and stability. Shifts in the international distribution of power are often believed to create the conditions likely to lead to at least the most important wars, and power is the most important determinant of whether a war will be won or lost.[3] This understanding of the notion of the state, and undue focus on power, derives from the realist traditions, which have dominated the field of international relations concerned with inter-state conflict and cooperation. The exclusive focus on power was relevant in as much as it defined the structure of the interstate system, but not consequential in understanding the nature of the state. Hence, analysts have of late become more and more concerned with various problems relating centrally to the notion of the state. One such problem is to identify the state's basic structural features, and the range and significance of their variations over time or from country to country.[4]

The Montevideo Convention of 1933 elaborated the requirements for statehood and defined the state as "a subject of international law (that) should have a permanent population, a defined territory, a government, and the capacity to enter into relations with other states."[5] The state was conceived of as a unified rational actor with one source of authority. In theory state sovereignty postulates a neat fit between boundaries and politically significant identities, but in practice the two rarely coincide.[6] The internal character of the state, the structure of its society, its domestic processes and the logic of its internal dynamic were of research interests only to the extent that they facilitated broad comparative analysis. The wide variations in the internal contents of states did not alter the almost axiomatic fact of a state being just another state.

There is no agreement on the historical evolution of the system of constitutionally sovereign states, though it is generally understood that the 1648 Treaty of Westphalia codified the principles of the secular state, setting domestic sovereignty above the authority of the Holy See.[7] Domestic sovereignty, the organization and effectiveness of political authority, has thus remained the single most important question for political analysis.[8] Beyond the element of power, the notion of the state is not very clear. The concept of sovereignty, which is core to the concept of the state, has been employed in four different ways. These include international legal sovereignty, Westphalian sovereignty, domestic sovereignty and interdependence sovereignty. The various kinds of sovereignty do not necessarily co-vary. A state can have one but not the other.[9] Stephen Krasner notes in this connection that

> ... the exercise of one kind of sovereignty, for instance, international legal sovereignty -can undermine another kind of sovereignty such as Westphalian sovereignty, if the rulers of a state enter into an agreement that recognizes external authority structures as has been the case for members of the European Union. A state such as Taiwan can have Westphalian sovereignty, but not international legal sovereignty ". A state can have international legal sovereignty , . . . but have only the most limited domestic sovereignty either in the sense of an established structure of authority or the ability of its rulers to exercise control over what is going on within their own territory.[10]

States therefore vary on different dimensions of their most important common attribute. On Westphalian sovereignty, "which refers to political organization based on the exclusion of external actors from authority structures within a given territory"[11], the dependence of many states, especially post-colonial African states, on external aid and technical expertise and the relatively weak bargaining profiles of many of the new states vis-a-vis other elite state actors in the global inter-state system compromises their Westphalian sovereignty.

The 2001 annual budget of $120 million of Guinea Bissau depended 80% on external aid and grants. It is the equivalent of the annual budget of the Fontana Unified School District, an average school district in Southern California. The international donor community has a large say not only in the process of the establishment of national and domestic priorities, it also maintains mechanisms for direct control and management of funds donated. Guinea Bissau is thus vulnerable to external pressures on internal programming and developmental priorities of the state. Since the end of the post-conflict transitional arrangements in that country, Bissau based French experts have overseen fiscal management of such aids and grants received by the government.

From 1980 to the overthrow of the Samuel Doe regime in 1990, Liberia's fiscal management and control were taken over, under agreement, by American experts deployed to oversee the management of the economy, especially fiscal and monetary procedures. Indeed, some analysts have observed that the post-colonial African state is no more than fiction, the show of state that is often propped by important contributions from its metropolitan creators. France is noted to act behind the scene in post-colonial francophone Africa. A network of Franco-African cooperation agreements thus supports the state in a wide range of domains-military, judicial, educational, for example – a special budget in the Ministry of Cooperation provides for the payment of civil service salaries in a range of francophone countries.[12] These tendencies derogate from effective claims to Westphalian sovereignty by post-colonial states.

In the area of domestic sovereignty, which relates "to the formal organization of political authority within the state and the ability of public authorities to exercise effective control within the borders of their own polity" the pervasive prevalence of conflict in post-colonial political entities in Africa and challenges to the power of the central authority clearly reflect a lack of effective control of the national territory by claimants to sovereign powers of the state. In most Third World states there are competing locations of authority; these are usually weaker than the state in terms of coercive capacity but equal to or stronger than the state in terms of political legitimacy in the view of large segments of the state's populations.[13]

On the basis of sovereignty, states vary in the degree of their statehood. It is for these reasons that many of the post-colonial political entities have been described as characterized by lack of adequate stateness.[14] It has been observed that many sovereigns in sub-Saharan Africa have not been interested in emulating more developed states.[9] The contentions are either that post-colonial states in Africa have not been successfully transplanted from their Western origins or that they are in the process of being constructed.[15] Some analysts think of them as being in decline and suffering from dual crises of the state and the economy. The post-colonial African state, it is further observed, belies the validity of the assumptions about the existence and viability of the state, which analysts generally take for granted.[16] The very notion of the 'lame Leviathan' state in Sub-Saharan Africa has been problematized as characterized by state arbitrariness, instability, corruption and high inefficiency. The modal African state has been described

> ...as an organization of domination controlled with varying degrees of efficacy by a ruling group or class that competes for power and sovereignty with other political, economic, and social groups, both internally and externally. It is only partly autonomous, as it seeks to cope with constraints and uncertainties and to manage its dependence internally and externally...Internally the state must concern itself with ethnic, regional, religious, linguistic, and other particularisms, as well as strongly rooted universalistic religions, pluralist groups and emerging class structures. Externally, the state combats major legacies of the colonial state.[17]

Africa, or more precisely, Sub-Saharan Africa, analysts have observed, has been particularly subject to fluctuating truths and flights of interpretative fancy. They note that in no other continent have so many layers of power and prejudice been imposed from the outside. Today everything is subject to controversy; race, ethnicity, language, religion, ideology, all exacerbated by severe economic decline and long-standing and unresolved difficulties of state formation.[18]

The profound qualitative deviations of the characteristics associated with the post-colonial state in Africa from the attributes conventional to the classic modern state reflect fundamental differences among the kinds of state in the global international system. The many deviations of these new states on different dimensions of the core attribute of the state, the fully evolved modern Westphalian model, are significant, even if these differences are overshadowed by the assumed structural monism that had pervaded the discourse of the state. Though strong theoretical reasons have been adduced for this[19], the assumed structural homogeneity of the state has impeded gaining clearer understandings of the workings of the African state, especially its proclivities to implode. It is quite clear that there are a number of paradigms on the institutionalization of power which simply fail convincingly to account for the role of the state in contemporary Africa[20].

The assumed monolithic structure of states in the global inter-state system has therefore retarded in-depth analytical probes into the nature of the post-colonial African state and meaningful problematization and theoretization of this genre of state. This has consequently created significant lacunae in the appreciation of the role of the nature of the state and the character of its society or a lack of it in the pervasive instability afflicting that genre of state and the inter-state system constituted by them. This general theoretical laxity in the treatment of the state is attributable to the legacy of the realist's dominance of the discipline. Against such a background, the theoretical adequacy of deploying the Westphalian model as a representation of all states and its claimed general empirical relevance have been questioned. Unfortunately, there is no easy pathway from the unproblematic notion of the sovereign state to a richer concept and theory of the state, and thus, there is no consolidated body of state theory to build on.[10]

Many questions in relation to the state and the states system remain unanswered. While the formal solidity of the idea of the state has been accepted, the conceptual ambiguities of the state system have, paradoxically, proliferated.[11] The legitimacy of the states system as constituted has been challenged. Oyvind Osterud observes that a substantial number of groups are demanding their own sovereign statehood, or territorial transfer to an adjoining state. Separatism and irredentism along ethnic lines have shaken a multitude of post-colonial states in Africa, Asia, and Oceania. Thus, it is a critical requirement to examine the nature of the post colonial African state and its points of departure from other states in the inter-sate system as a starting block for any realistic attempt to understand the malaise of the post-colonial African state. The goal of this chapter is to locate the post colonial African state within a discernable evolutionary trajectory of the Westphalian state. At the center of this evolution is the crudescent Westphalian state. This facilitates an understanding of the emergence and continuous differentiation of the internal contents and processes among states as an epochal development in the historical continuities of the society. Simultaneously and paradoxically, these developments are also the sources of discontinuities that have distorted the trajectory of the political evolution in many societies that have been dislocated by the intrusion of the Westphalian framework for the political organization of society.

In the proposed evolutionary framework, Westphalia is treated as a heuristic concept. Since 1648, the Westphalian notion of political organization of peoples, also known as the state, has evolved to a point in its development marked by the modern state as we know it today. It is argued that the modern state has advanced in fitful progression in the continuous evolution to the conceptually distinct post-modern state. The post-modern state has a character and a logic of operations that are quite different from that of the modern state. Indeed, the post-modern state essentially begins to repudiate the fundamental axioms that underpin the modern state. A major shift in political culture is thus postulated as a pre requisite to a state's transformation from a modern state to a post-modern one. The path to the modern and post-modern states is predicated on certain fundamental steps beginning with the Renaissance that Western societies first took in the middle of the last millennium. Milton Viorst identifies that the seminal notion that the Renaissance introduced to the West was that mankind, not God, is at the hub of the social universe. It held reason as important as faith, and urged men and women to claim responsibility, free of clergy, for their own lives. These had important implications for the evolution of Western society, the principles governing the organization of this society, including, by implication, the content of the various types of state that have emerged. Viorst observes that

> Under the influence of texts from ancient Greece, Muslims in their golden age considered and rejected these ideas before passing on the texts to Europe. After triggering the Renaissance, the ideas led, over quarrelsome centuries, to the Enlightenment, and the Scientific Revolution, While Islam remained wedded to desert tradition, Europe created a civilization imbued with a sense of individual identity, in which men and women asserted rights apart from those of community. These ideas, for better for worse, became the foundation of the secular culture that characterizes Western civilization today.
>
> Religion by no means disappeared. Instead, it was redefined as a personal bond, a relationship of choice, between the individual and God. The redefinition made Westerners comfortable separating worship from the state. True segments of the Catholic Church, Orthodox Jewry and evangelical Protestantism still question this arrangement. But the secular idea constitutes the foundations of mainstream Western values. Without it, democracy-and the civil society that, along with the press, supports it-would be impossible. [21]

Georg Sorensen provides an insightful analytic scheme to differentiate three main types of state in the present international system. He identifies the contents of the standard modern Westphalian sovereign state and elaborates the distinguishing features of two other kinds of state, which he labels as the post-colonial and post modern-states.[22] Sorensen highlights variations in the internal contents of the various states in the inter-state systems and concludes that these have implications for the theory and analysis of the state. Despite the pertinence of Sorensens's approach, it is imperative to extend his classificatory scheme to reflect the dynamic nature of the phenomenon of states in the inter-state system .

Sorensen's framework implies a dynamic at work, yet it is silent on this process and thus obscures the important source of differentiation between the kinds of state identified by him. The explicitly evolutionary perspective being formulated in this undertaking seeks to account for the continuing differentiations of the internal character of states. The main thrust is to isolate the forces in society and the interaction among these forces that drive the process of continuous evolution of states, the differential paces of the evolution in some states and a lack of it in different kinds of states and the direction in which the evolution is driving society in all states. An interactive dynamic drives the evolution of the different expressions of the Westphalian state.

In this evolutionary lineage of states, the post-colonial state is cited as a mechanical transplant of the Westphalian state to a hostile African environment by the now evolved European modern state. This quasi-Westphalian or post-colonial political entity inherited many of the attributes of the crudescent Westphalian model at its creation. Beyond this, it is argued that the post-colonial state has been unable to keep pace with the evolutionary advance of the modern states that emerged from the impulses of mid C17th. It is a marginalized member of the global inter-states system. The post-colonial state is grappling with the tensions and struggles that characterized if not the formative stages of Westphalia, at least its phase of state consolidation that gave birth to the nation by 1781. Nation building remains a formidable challenge to the consolidation of the post-colonial state. Its fragmented and unpacified society is the biggest threat to its continued existence as a member of the global states system. Conventional wisdom perceives the inter-state system as a state of anarchy in which those states which fail to help themselves, or who do so less effectively than others, will fail to prosper. In this self help system units worry about their survival.

This traditional understanding of the inter-state universe locates the threat to the state in the hostile anarchic external environment of the inter-state system. The double paradox is that the threat to the perpetuation of the post-colonial state is internal as the state is permanently in danger of imploding or disintegrating. Many post colonial African states have lived with powerful proto states[23] within their territory as rival claimants to the sovereignty of that state. A second paradox is that the post-colonial state owes its continued existence to the protocols and myths of the global inter-state system and often to direct patronage of elite state actors in this system. A fourth category of state is the pre-Westphalian state, in which there is a fusion of both the religious and political communities. The secular and the religious realms are not delineated. The legal codes and political processes derive from the holy book and national processes around the state religion.

An interactive dynamic is postulated between state and society. In essence, conventional frameworks for political organization, as we know it today, may not be the end station of the evolutionary process unleashed by the treaty of Westphalia. The modern state, which Sorensen classifies as standard Westphalia, is indeed the product of a long process of evolution of the crudescent original Westphalian state. Gianfranco Poggi traces the origins of the modern state from the creation of the Carolingian empire, as a representation of the feudal system of rule, through the rise of towns and the Standestaat, marked by the creation or political reactivation of centers of solidary action by singly powerless individuals, the development of absolute rule, which ultimately led to the 'making' of the modern constitutional state in the nineteenth century.[24] The post-modern state has evolved into a distinct class from among a select group of elite modern states.

Yet not all modern states can be said to be enthusiastic about acquiring post-modern characteristics. The United States of America, long protected by natural buffers that were only shattered by the Pearl Harbour invasions and consequently with a penchant of being inward looking, is a close approximation of the modern state. The United States is deeply suspicious of and antagonistic to supra-national institutions that would derogate from its sovereign attributes. This is despite its rank as the preeminent power, if not an outright hegemon in the post Cold War era and in the new millennium. Against our theoretical model, Great Britain is located mid way between an entrenched modern state and a post-modern one. France and Germany would come closest as representations of the post-modern state.[25] Thus, when an evolutionary perspective is employed in analyzing the internal contents of states, including entrenched national attitudes adopted by each state member of the global system to a number of developments in relation to the evolved global society, a more complex view of the state of modern Westphalian state emerges.

A whole shift in global political culture is seen to be at work. This political culture shift is driven by a general culture shift in advanced industrial society involving, among other transformations, redefinition of identities through the expansion of narrow nationalities in some modern state. Ronald Inglehart posits that during the past few decades, economic, technological, and socio-political changes have been gradually transforming the cultures of advanced industrial societies in profoundly important ways.[26] The cultural change is reshaping the social basis of political conflict, transforming the vision of society as to what constitutes the appropriate political goals of society and government. The values of Western publics and society have been shifting from an overwhelming emphasis on material wellbeing and physical security toward greater emphasis on the quality of life. One of the profound implications of these changes is that it no longer seems self-evident that the expansion of state authority constitutes progress.[27] Indeed, a large proportion of the public in advanced industrial society is coming to have sufficient interest and understanding of national and international politics to participate in decision making at this level.[28] The elite challenging, in contradistinction to elite directed, style of politics of the mass public gives the public an increasingly important role in making specific decisions, not just a choice between two or more sets of decision makers. These have important consequences for relations between state and society and the internal processes and character of the state. Ultimately, the shift in attitudes, values, and behaviour of the publics of advanced industrial society remains a critical element in directing the evolution of the modern Westphalian state.

In this evolutionary schema, the Westphalian state is deployed as a benchmark to measure the degrees of substantive variations and differentiations; institutional, social, cultural, political, economic, security and attitudinal attributes of states; and the qualitative deviations of the internal dynamic of different kinds of state. Variation in the speed of adaptation in itself is a source of the differentiation in the kinds of state. The sources of variation in states are partly traceable to the antecedents of some of the states. In general, states that are historically parts of the original Westphalian cluster, mainly European states, have continued to evolve based on constant adaptation to the emerging challenges of the inter-state environment. The continuous evolution of the modern state remains unabated. States that were mechanically created or transplanted have been sluggish in acquiring the attributes of a modern state. The mechanical transplant of the Westphalian state into the post-colonial environment has led to stunted growth, as these states are constrained in negotiating the process of modernity successfully. A vast majority of Westphalian state transplants are in fact fixated in the archaic attributes of the Westphalian state while others still have actually degenerated. A few have withered and died only to be resuscitated by the international community. Paradoxically, the great success of the United States as a modern state partly militates against the rapid adoption of the psychological impulses that drive the transformation to the post-modernist era. The United States of America is largely fixated in the early Westphalian attributes of the state.

The framework designed in this work thus conceives of the Westphalia state as in a process of a continuous evolution. Two main conceptually distinct stages of this evolution are identified as the modern and post modern states. The modern state in the present schema corresponds with the Sorensens's standard Westphalian notion of sovereign statehood. The Westphalian state is here adopted as a hueristic and crudescent emergence phase of the state. As Sorensen aptly elucidates, the sovereignty of the state was always contested; the dominance of the Westphalian system did not end all challenges to the authority of states. The observation continues to remain relevant today in post colonial state environments. There is also considerable contention about when to date the emergence of the state system itself. Some analysts link the full emergence of the Westphalia state system to the process that led to the development of nationhood. This process is traced to the Congress of Vienna in 1781. The two processes are different but related developments. Two other states are identified as the quasi-Westphalian or post-colonial state, a mechanical creation or transplant, rather than the product of an autonomous historical process.

Within the context of the unfolding social processes which it truncated, the emergence in the African universe of the concept of the state represented a historical discontinuity of tectonic proportions. The final in the category is the pre-Westphalian state where the political community is a divinely ordained hierarchically ordered society, where the State and the Mosque are fused. Political legitimacy of regimes of governance, mainly monarchical, derived from interpretation of the Quoran. Sovereignty in this context is a moot concept, for the individual is at the mercy of the will of God. This refers to mostly Islamic republics where the secular and the spiritual are essentially fused and mutually reinforcing, despite the trappings of modernity and the sophistication of the material acquisitions which some societies of these states exhibit. The state is an ecclesiastical community of the 21st century in the manner of Iran under the Ayatollah and Taliban's Afghanistan. Saudi Arabia would fit into this category.

We proceed with 1648 as the date of birth of a second new world order. It is generally agreed that the 1648 Peace of Westphalia effectively affirmed the state as the unchallenged guarantor of domestic order and legitimiser of external war. It also consigned the *ancien regime,* a mutually supporting trinity of the monarchy, church and aristocracy, to history. This crudescent state of 1648 has evolved through two major phases.[29] It has continuously metamorphosed, through a process of institutional differentiation and in response to internal tensions and pressures emanating from the interaction of the ruling regime and society that had to be pacified, the national economy that had to be protected and new ideas propelling challenges in the political community. The first major conceptualization of the state was the modern state or the constitutional state of the nineteenth century. The modern state, in turn, responding to an impetus generated by massive cultural transformations, the emergence of an international society and the imperatives of globalised citizenry following the harmonization of universal values and ethics, has, through an incremental process, been altered into the conceptually distinct post-modern state. Four distinct states now exist in the inter-states system.

In constructing ideal typical models of states, the key features of the major evolutionary stations of the crudescent Westphalian state and its transplant in Africa are accentuated and defining empirical variations and deviations in the characteristics of these major points of evolution are synthesized into four conceptually distinct kinds of state. The full emergence of the modern state is conveniently dated to early twentieth century. By the beginning of the first World War, by and large the major features of the modern state were in place. The modern state, in responding to the pressures intrinsic to the gradual development of an international society, and an increasingly globalised citizenry, has infused its elite members with attributes that deviate from those of modern states. Along with this has been the challenge posed by the emergence of powerful transnational non-state actors whose operations transcend the reaches of traditional control mechanisms put in place by sovereign states. In the course of adapting to the challenges imposed by the new realities, some of the elite states have been transformed into what can analytically be established as qualitatively different states from modern states. Paradoxically, the pursuit of ideological consolidation, containment of rival ideology and expansionism of liberal democratic tenets that characterized the cold war laid solid foundations for the eventual birth of the post-modern state.

The Marshal Plan in Europe, the building of islands of capitalist havens in far-flung South East Asia helped to lay the foundations of a global economic process that has forced the redefining of the normative principles of international trade. The United Nations in codifying new principles that should govern relations between the state and its citizens, including group and minority rights, underlined the emergence of universal standards in an evolved international society. This is shifting the locus of moral accountability from the nation to the international society accompanied by the development of supra-national institutions that have challenged traditional notions of the extensive latitude associated with the sovereign powers of the modern state. The dynamic of the international society, technological advances in communications and the consequences of the globalization process, perceived by various domestic interest groups as both positive and negative, have eroded the underpinnings of national economies and national societies and fostered the development of transnational coalitions seeking to advance or even impede perceived threats.

The rapid rise of transnational communities and coalitions defined by limited interests, the workings of supra-national judicial institutions, transnational economic conglomerates with their global complexes and linkages, supra-national legislative chambers and others have been the consequences of a culture shift with seismic impact on the nature of the inter-state system and the axioms undergirding its operations. By 1957, the collaboration by France and the Federal Republic of Germany in coal and steel production was laying the humble foundation for the post-modern state. It is now concretely expressed in the European Union and its supra-national institutions. The institutions of the Union derogate significantly from traditional understandings and practice of domestic sovereignty. Two other kinds of state yet still exist. One of these is the post-colonial or quasi-Westphalian state, mostly in Africa and including such political entities as Haiti, Liberia and Ethiopia that never knew classic colonialism. The last in the category of four kinds of states from this evolutionary perspective is the pre-Westphalian states. A central element in this differentiation is the motivating philosophy and ideational foundations around which each kind of state revolves.

The internal structure of the respective states would, among other parameters, be largely defined in terms of the homogeneity or heterogeneity of the ideational sub-structures and attitudes derived from the values of the dominant groups in society. It would be posited that the degree of convergence or relative dissonance in the contending realms of dominant ideas, attitudes, value systems and the overall worldviews held by major groups that constitute the population of a post-colonial state and immediate extraterritorial stakeholders in developments in that state is a critical element that defines the structure of society based on allegiances to the pre-colonial nations and political communities. The imposition of foreign political control, of which the post-colonial state is a successor, did not destroy the entrenched loyalties, identities and community ties expressed in common languages and, often times, religion of the various communities. The continuities pre dating colonial impositions by intrusive political forces include shared cultures, norms, ideas and world views that define a people. These allegiances defy the territorial confines of the new state.

The post-colonial state is thus superimposed on this incongruous foundation. So resilient have these transnational affinities been that some analysts anticipate that African culture and possibly its pre-colonial political arrangements, may reclaim the ascendancy and help the post-colonial state in Africa retreat to its ancestral authenticity[30]. Ade Ajayi perceives the era of European colonization and its impact on Africa as merely episodic and may turn out to be short-lived in the *longue duree*. Deriving from this perspective, the modern African emerges as part of a shallow impact and merely marks a discontinuity without organic roots in society. It is thus a common assertion that African borders and the states which they encompass are unique in their arbitrary and artificial character[31] in creating tenuous multi-ethnic states without the shared sense of common destiny to hold society together. Nationhood in the African state, Mazrui and Tudy assert, is an ambition rather than a reality.[32]

The problem of nationhood is related to the arbitrariness and artificiality of the borders of the post-colonial state. The charge of artificiality of these borders and states refers to their relatively recent and imposed origins. Saddia Touval clarifies that it is suggested that since they were only recently imposed, African boundaries have not crystallized naturally under the impact and influence of slow social, economic and political developments. The more important criticism of African borders, he observes, relate to the arbitrary manner in which they were drawn. The image has often been that of European statesmen of the 19th century parceling out African territories on inaccurate maps of the continent in total disregard of sociological and political realities.[33] These unilateral borders merely divided territories belonging to one colonial power from those of other rival powers. Hugh Seton Watson describes these frontiers as mere lines on a map that cut across regions which might have formed natural units. This was truer of pastoral peoples, accustomed to drive their herds over enormous distances. Further, Watson cites the examples of divided peoples as including the Yorubas, in the Republic of Benin and Nigeria, the Ewe in Ghana and Togo, and the Bakongo in the two Congos and in Angola[34]. The fragmented tribes and political communities were often forced to switch allegiance across new lines and new colonial administrations and post-colonial states. The determination of these borders, and by implication the construction of the new state, did not involve a process of negotiation between rival sovereign governments to harmonize the interests of the affected communities. Rather, it resulted from the unilateral decision of imperial governments exercising control over these territories.

Obviously, under such circumstances, the bargaining power of African societies was minimal.[35] Furthermore, these new lines that became borders were changed whimsically at the convenience of the new controllers of the territories. In many cases, the indigenous political authorities challenged the jurisdictions imposed by European powers. W. Newbury documents these challenges extensively.[36] He notes that political relations between European and African tribes required the prior sanctions of formal treaties with African chiefs as jurisdiction over British subjects was imposed on the basis of Acts of Parliament. Where treaties were signed, they helped to win general recognition of the primacy of the European power that had made the treaty. The post-colonial state that emerged is thus a product of a historical process involving the primary agency of external actors and propelled by external interests. Multinational states were floated without common understandings of the legitimizing principles underpinning the post-colonial state or a longer-term vision of the longer term essences of the artificially created political arrangement. The post-colonial state is therefore perceived as the successor to a regime of alien rule that sought to forge political entities out of diverse nations and peoples.[37] For Mazrui, Africa is caught between the birth of her modern nationalism and the quest for nationhood. The agonies of the post-colonial state in Africa in the second half of the twentieth century have been ultimately derived from the pain of the intermediacy between nationalism and nationhood.[38]

This problematic character, ultimately, impacts on the nature of the internal processes of the state, including its political processes, which in reality is a struggle between contending value systems and worldviews seeking to appropriate the state to consolidate a hegemony of the dominant systems of ideas. Given that primary loyalties and identities in the post-colonial societies are to ethnic and tribal groups and that no fit exists between the territorial configurations of the post-colonial states and the territorial base of these contending groups, the processes in each of these states have implications across their boundaries. The impact of policies in Rwanda on the Hutu is of paramount interest to the Hutu in Burundi. In the same vein, the fate of the Tutsi in the Republic of Congo is of intense concern to the Tutsi in Rwanda and Burundi. How the Ewes fare in the Togo impacts on the Ewes in Ghana. In West Africa, the Madingo are spread virtually throughout the whole sub-region ranging from Mali, Sierra Leone, Liberia, Guinea Conakry, the Gambia, Senegal (Casamance), to Guinea Bissau. What touches the Yoruba in the Republic of Benin and Togo is closely watched by the Yoruba in Nigeria.

This pervasive lack of fit between nation and state and the sociological incongruity represented by formal boundaries render the boundaries of these states loose and permeable frontiers over which no state has any real control. This is in terms of the legitimacy of the state, which is attributed to traditional institutions and identities which supersede citizenship, and to physical movement of peoples across boundaries with scant regard for the protocols associated with the pretences of state control over its boundaries. Importantly, the affinities of contending groups that straddle the frontiers engender pervasive cross-border osmotic interaction. These osmotic influences have serious repercussion for relations between these ethnic groups or tribes competing as transnational stakeholders in developments in all states in which their members are present. Strictly speaking, therefore, there are no developments that are internal to any of the post colonial states. This scenario imbues in the developments in each state in relation to the stakeholders outside its formal boundaries an intermestic character. Consequently, President Laurent Gbagbo of Cote d'Ivoire would accuse Burkina Faso of backing dissident troops to overthrow his government, while the homes of northern Ivoriennes were burnt by rival ethnic groups because of the ethnic affinity of their northern compatriots with groups in Burkina Faso.[39] Accusation by Bissau Guinean President Joao Bernardino Vieira of his Mandingo Chief of Defense Staff General Ansumane Mane's of supporting Casamancais rebels in Senegal led to a civil war in Guinea Bissau. Senegal and Guinea Conakry intervene militarily in the war in Bissau. President Charles Taylor of Liberia drew attention to the intervention of Guinea Conakry in the invasion of his country by insurgents funded and armed in Sierra Leone and Guinea Conakry. The LURD and ULIMO in Liberia acknowledged diplomatic and armed support from Guinea. This intermestic character of the environment impacts on bargaining in the post-colonial African state of which armed conflict is an integral part. Intermesticity is thus often critical in the trajectory of conflicts in these states.

DISSONANT IDENTITIES, SUB-STRUCTURES AND VALUES

It is thus a major argument advanced in this book that the post colonial African state is an instrumental state to be appropriated in the service of the dominant hegemonic force(s) in the social and political space. What goes for society in these states are in actuality rival contending groups and forces that do not rest on a minimum of universally acknowledged and shared ideational substructures and values systems. The contending groups are, therefore, unable to reach a level of inter-subjective normative understandings that allow for the formulation of a common vision, elaboration of a national order, and development of common ideological guidelines to direct common political action by the diverse and fragmented peoples. In such post-colonial African state environments, intra-societal relation would be intensely conflictual as clashes of diametrically opposed worldviews and value systems constrain the emergence of common identities and the development of a national value system. The opposed values, attitudes and world views are embedded in identities that are professed by the contending protagonist groups.

These identities have often been described as primordial, yet they are the vehicles by which certain worldviews are espoused. The political process is thus effectively in conflict for the appropriation and domination of the total social and political spaces by contending constituent groups in these spaces. The degree of convergence or dissonance of ideational and value substructures within multi-national states is directly related to the degree or lack of domestic peace and stability. In societies where value systems are universally shared, the political process would be relatively stable. States with great value dissonance in society and therefore among its contending groups would be relatively unstable. The wider the value dissonance in the contending groups, it is argued the more violent the internal processes of the post-colonial African state.

Society in post colonial states is structurally heterogeneous and marked by great dissonance between the ideational sub-structures and value systems of the constituent groups. This has created serious problems for the concept and practice of citizenship in the states as Abdulraheem, Nkuna and Odinkalu have observed

> Thousands of Africans daily join the millions of victims of statelessness and arbitrary denial of citizenship in our continent. Although each case of statelessness or denial of citizenship produces unique experiences of victimization, common patterns are clear. These include the stripping of citizenship status and rights resulting in statelessness; forced expulsion or forced population transfers; elimination of minority groups through mass de-nationalization, followed—in many cases—by targeted killings of members of the affected groups; persecution of vocal opponents or critics of incumbent regimes; and refusal to recognize or accord the rights of particular (groups of) citizens in the absence of documentary proof.
>
> In several cases, governments make such proof extremely difficult or even impossible to obtain. For example, Kenyan Somalis

and Nubians in Kenya are required, in order to prove their citizenship, to produce birth certificates of their grandparents, nearly all of whom were born when there were no birth records.

Violations of citizenship rights are truly indiscriminate. Around Africa, there are millions more who are too poor to challenge this violation or too unknown to register in the frightening statistics of the stateless. Affected populations include: a majority of the continent's estimated migrant and pastoralist populations of 17.3 million persons representing the biggest population of persons at risk of statelessness in the world; an estimated 30 per cent of Cote d'Ivoire's 17.5 million people de-nationalized by the Ivoirite-inspired amendments to Cote d'Ivoire's citizenship laws between 1995-2000; more than 1.5 million Banyamulenge (Tutsis) of Eastern Congo, whose citizenship in the Democratic Republic of Congo (DRC) remains disputed, fuelling a bloody war; another 1.5 million Zimbabwean mine and commercial farm workers born of parents descended from Malawi, Mozambique and Zambia whose nationality was arbitrarily cancelled by the government of Zimbabwe in 2001; and hundreds of thousands of Ethiopians of Eritrean-descent who had their Ethiopian nationality cancelled and nationality documents destroyed before their forced expulsion to Eritrea in 1998-1999 and hundreds of thousands of black Mauritanians expelled to Senegal in the 1990s. The list is endless.[40]

The ideologically inspired divisions and tensions of the long Cold War are instructive concerning the consequences and dangers of fundamental disagreements in values and ideologies that spring from those different value systems. The evolution and character of the modern state and its inter-state system were propelled by the internal convergence of ideologies, philosophies, shared ideas and common value systems in each of those states. The major undercurrents of the wars that finally delineated the European state system in the eighteenth century were ideas purveyed by the various protagonist states in the wars. Transcending the calculus of the systemic balance of power, England stood not only for the splendors of empire, but for democracy and the rule of law. Germany was home of a uniquely spiritual culture. France was a historic civilization that united the two factions of republicans and Catholics. America sought to extend democracy and introduce a new international order.[41] The focus on ideas as motivators of the character of the state and the state system is consistent with the perspective adopted by Martin Wight and Rosalyn Higgins.

In building models of the four different expressions of contemporary Westphalian state and one pre Westphalian state, the parameters of four theoretical perspectives, namely; Weberian, realist, constructivist and legal, would be central in guiding us. Debates on the complexion of the African state, it has

been observed, often reflect a priori disagreements on definitions between analysts belonging to different scholarly or theoretical traditions.[42] The model of
each of the four kinds of state would be constructed on the basis of the way they
meet or deviate from the Weberian, realist, constructivist and legal understandings of the state. Proceeding from the Weberian tradition, Chabal and Daloz
note that the modern state is the outcome of a process by which the realms
of politics is gradually emancipated from society and constituted into increasingly autonomous political institutions.[43] In essence, in classical Weberian
states, there would exist a clear demarcation of the public domain in which the
political process plays itself out and a civil society sector, constituted by private
organizations and social networks on which individuals depend to mediate a
wide variety of issues outside the realm of politics and the state. Ideally, then
one parametric variable between states must be the degree of clear delineation
where civil society stands out from the political realm. The model also would
evaluate elements in the various kinds of state that reflect variations in the realist
conventional expectation of the monopoly of the legitimate use of force over a
people in a clearly defined territory that is recognized as such by the other state
actors in the international system. How do different kinds of state vary in their
expressions of this realist conception of the state? This would also be consistent
with the injunction that a paradigm of the post-colonial state that does not
make security its center piece will lack adequate power to explain the domestic
and international behaviour of Third World states.[44]

   A third measure to be adopted in modeling the different kinds of state
would be to convert the Strasner concept of four varying kinds of sovereignty
into a 'Strasner test'. This would imply a critical evaluation of the varying degrees
of the four kinds of sovereignty that is actually enjoyed by the four kinds of
state in the inter-states system. This would include how much of international
legal sovereignty is conferred by the international community on the legitimate
authority of different kinds of state. Are there varying levels of international legal
sovereignty enjoyed by different kinds of states? Is the principle of Westphalian
sovereignty, implying the exclusion of external actors from domestic authority
configurations, adhered to the same degree in relations between state actors
with different kinds of state? How able are the states in assuring their inter-
dependent sovereignty in controlling trans-border movements? Finally, from a
constructivist perspective, the different kinds of states would be assessed on the
basis of the varying degree of normative inter-subjectivity that exists in their
societies. How widespread are shared structures of knowledge and commonal-
ity in values espoused by the constitutive units of its society? What degree of
fundamental value dissonance or convergence across society is associated with
what kind of state?

To borrow Putnam's analytical concept, the question may be put in terms of the varying quantum of social capital available in the national society. Along with these would be an exploration of the different attitudes and policy preferences demonstrated by the various kinds of state on different planes of activities within the global inter-state system. How well do different kinds of state tolerate the diminution of their traditional Westphalian sovereignty in the pursuit of the greater goal of the international community or limited sub regional common welfare? In reality, some of these different conceptual tools refer to only one and the same dimension of statehood. Domestic sovereignty, defined by Strasner as referring to the organization of public authority within a state and to the level of effective control exercised by those holding authority,[45] looks at the realist phenomenon of consolidation of the legitimate use of force by the state.

Thus the models are bi-dimensional. They distil both internal characteristics of the different kinds of state and their relations with and responses to the external environment of the global inter-state system. Careful note is taken of the Weberian definition of ideal types being formed by the one-sided accentuation of one or more points of view and by the synthesis of great many diffuse, discrete, more or less present and occasionally absent concrete individual phenomena, which are arranged according to those one-sidedly emphasized viewpoints into a unified analytical construct. The model thus is a conceptual purity, the mental construct that does not exist empirically anywhere in reality[46].

PROBLEMATIC ANTECEDENTS OF THE POST-COLONIAL AFRICAN STATE

The evolution of pre-colonial African societies toward the grounding of the Westphalian state concept was problematic from its very beginnings. As the eventual end-product of the imposition of Western political power and government, ideas and institutions, economic patterns, customs, religion, as well as moral and ethical codes in pre-colonial African societies, the state elicited diverse reactions.[47] In the face of the rapid changes to society and threat to pre existing institutional frameworks for social and political organization, segments of the nucleus of new westernized pre-colonial elites were seriously concerned about what the future African society would and ought to be. Essentially, the earliest acculturated black and westernized elites were searching for a philosophy that would synthesize into a balanced framework the very best from Europe that is beneficial to Africa, while preserving the best of the traditional African way of life. Those concerned about the wholesale transplantation of foreign institutions, whatever the claims of superiority of the new dispensation over local structures and institutions, espoused that institutions were expressions of the soul of each people, and to kill those institutions was to kill the soul of the

people. It was argued that it was critical for the African to pursue his time-hon-
oured and time-tested philosophies, cosmologies and customary ways of doing
things secure in his knowledge of their intrinsic merit.[48] These were considered
non-negotiable conditions in laying the foundations for the new modernity
being imposed by the ascendancy of new ideas and codes for organizing society.
Robert W. July cites one of the earliest African nationalists, Edward W. Blyden,
as stressing in the late nineteenth century that

> We must start out . . . fully recognizing. . . that the customs of all
> peoples. . . are due largely to the influence of race and culture and
> that while these customs may sometimes be modeled to advantage
> by wise and judicious external agency, they cannot be wholly or
> indiscriminately eradicated without most serious mischief-without
> leaving a void which nothing can supply and in consequence of
> which disintegration and demoralization must take place.[49]

These reservations about the project of wholesale transformation of the
African society in the direction of European society ran counter to the interests
of the new and dominant forces. The state that emerged in post-colonial Africa
is founded on ideational structures that are alien to the African environment.
The major challenge of the state and the process of nation building in Africa
have been how to subvert traditional African structures and institutions and
replace them with imported ideas and structures. These traditional ideational
structures along with the institutions that sprang from them before Western
intrusion have proven to be resilient, and they continue to sustain the psychic
and emotional sense of security of the African communities. In the face of the
radical transformations of society and the introduction of alienating structures
and institutions in the African milieu as expressed in the new African state, the
struggle for a new balance in the newly created political spaces has been disruptive to the evolution of the new state. The harmony of a network of diverse
axioms, ideas and ways of thinking which constitute the ideational foundations
of the Westphalian states are conspicuously lacking in the African environment.
The African state is fixated in time, as much of the energy is expended seeking
accommodation or appropriation of the new forces, including the new state as
instruments in the struggle for hegemony by conflicting forces. The hybrid state
that has emerged from the transplant of the classical Westphalian state into this
environment is a monstrous variant.

This late entrant into the universe of the Westphalian state system is unable
to evolve along with other Westphalian states, so it continues to survive as a concrete fiction. It is aided by the myth of its status as a state in a global inter-state
system that is regulated in a manner tolerant of its own myths and yet pragmatic
enough to assign to weak post-colonial state a subordinate class and role in the

affairs of this system. Expectations of this generic state are not very high among the elite actors. At best, they are handmaidens of the leading elite states in the global system. While, in practical terms, the power coefficient in the cumulative global power pool of the weak post colonial African state is almost nil, contrary to realist theoretical expectations, the major threat to its continued existence as a state are not external forces. The threats are embedded in its internal construction and the problematic character of its intermestic environment. In other words, the major threat to its continued survival is internal, for its society is not pacified. The state lacks internal legitimacy, and its institutions are feeble, Just as its economy is weak and dependent. The claim to sovereign powers by the state, especially in its relations with elite actors in the global system, is merely juridical. The late Westphalian state essentially controls territory. While the pre-existing nationalities have the allegiance of the people, citizenship is considered an accident of birth, and obligations to this alien state are coerced. Of the four classes of state (the post-modern state, the late Westphalian state, the classic Westphalian, and the quasi-Westphalian state), the post colonial African state system is composed of entities that mainly exhibit the classic attributes that can be accentuated in building the model of the ideal-typical late Westphalian state.[50]

THE QUASI–WESTPHALIAN STATE (POST COLONIAL AFRICAN STATE)

Within the state system, each state is a self-originating, self-empowered unit operating exclusively in pursuit of its own interest.[51] The origin of the post-colonial state is different. It also lacks the capacity to operate exclusively in its own interest. The quasi-Westphalian state was an imposition by its external creators on indigenous and pre-existing nations. The post- colonial African state is largely a European import or graft,[52] which perpetuates discontinuities introduced by the colonial process. The first of these discontinuities was the creation of colonial administrative units by imperial powers in near total disregard for the populations' pre-colonial affinities and loyalties. Political boundaries drawn for purposes of administrative convenience or as a result of territorial trade-offs among imperial powers arbitrarily cut across ethnic, tribal, religious, and linguistic ties; dismembered established political units; and linked more than one pre-colonial political entity in uneasy administrative unions.[53] The quasi-Westphalian state is thus an alienating political construct containing trapped peoples within dehumanized political spaces.[54] Basil Davidson laments this alienating impact of the post-colonial states and observes that " instead of building new states from the foundation culture of Africa's pre-colonial states, Africa had tried to build new states from the foundation culture of colonial states, a very different society. So independence had not been able to join Africa to its own history and tradition."[55] A major preoccupation of the newly created post-colonial state is the struggle to gain internal legitimacy in the social space and to concretize its international legitimacy from its very creators. The inhabitants of African states, whether they should be properly designated as citizens or subjects, do not readily regard their rulers as providing legitimate authority, and state power does not rest on a secure foundation of popular belief in the right of rulers to rule.[56] The struggle for intra- and international legitimacy has become the dominant theme of its very existence.

The internal structures and the whole internal processes of the post-colonial state are geared toward achieving hegemony by all the contending forces seeking to appropriate this space. The central challenge of the state is to bring order, coherence, and harmony to an inherited process of consolidating the reconstitution of fractured social and political spaces that had been systematically dislocated by violent intrusions of its external creators. The emergence of the post-colonial state must be seen against the broader context of vigorous and profound historical movements reshuffling the entire global political universe, in which, the peoples and spaces of the quasi Westphalian states have an inconsequential role. In this setting, the leverage of the post-colonial African state for action is constrained by the very structure of the inter-state system, which ultimately must decide the leverage for independent action to be granted the weak and inconsequential members of the inter-state system. The quasi-Westphalian state can only act independently in matters with low salience for modern and post-modern states. Those include matters traditionally judged to be internal to the sovereign state.

On the continuum of the pre Westphalian, Westphalian (heuristic benchmark), Quasi-Westphalian (post Colonial) state, Modern State and Post Modern State that derives from the evolutionary approach adopted in this work, the post-colonial African state is the youngest of the three post-Westphalian states. It was created from a colonial regime almost 300 years after the treaty of Westphalia. African colonial territories were granted independence from about a decade after the Second World War in 1945. The British Gold Coast became independent in the first quarter of 1957 and became the Republic of Ghana. It was sub-Saharan Africa's first successful decolonization in the nationalist era. The Northern and Southern protectorates of the Niger were amalgamated into Nigeria in 1914 and finally granted independence as a sovereign state in October 1960. The former Belgian colony of the Congo became the Republic of Congo (Leopoldville) in 1960. Then followed the British colonies in East and Central Africa and, after anti-colonial guerilla wars, also the Portuguese colonies in 1974, Rhodesia (now Zimbabwe) in 1980 and South West Africa (now Namibia) in 1990. In 1994 majority rule was introduced in South Africa.[57] The ideal typical post colonial African state is thus a late entrant into the global inter-states system and in the early stage of state formation.

The emergence of these states into the international system shortly after the Second World War meant that they were born into the ideologically frozen division of the international system. In the post-colonial African state, consequently, many of the international power concerns displayed on the eve of the scramble for Africa in the late nineteenth century were purposefully perpetuated and accentuated. Africa continued to provide a prime playing field for global actors.[58] The implications are that the leverage for total freedom by action of the post-colonial African state was effectively constrained by the logic of appropriateness that defined relations in the international system. Otherwise, it was often tied by formal agreements to toe the foreign policy, including ideological preferences, of its metropolitan ex-colonial elite creator, at least in the first few years of its existence as an independent state actor. With the exception of Sekou Toure-led Guinea Conakry that in 1958 voted against French proposals to continue with special relations after independence, all francophone countries in black Africa were formally tied to continued collaboration with France in military, economic and cultural agreements. In their relations with the external environment, a concentric principle was applied in organizing their priority in relations with member-states of the state system. The most important circle of relations was with the organization that grouped it with its metropolitan colonizer, then its continental organization in which it defended the interests of its metropole, the Non Aligned movement and the United Nations where it merely showed its flag.

The primary forum for the participation of the post-colonial African state at the international level was within the first circle revolving around the metropole. Shellar Gellar notes Patrick Quantim's observations that following the demise of the French Community, de Gaulle forged the concept of 'cooperation' to redefine the nature of France's relationships with its old Black African colonies and used bilateral cooperation agreements to safeguard its interests and influence in the newly independent states.[59] Toward this end, Gellar elaborates that after the independence of its colonies, France also encouraged the establishment of regional Francophone organizations like the Union Africaine et Malgache (UAM) founded in 1961, its successor, the Organisation Commune Africaine et Malgche (OCAM) created in 1965; and the Communaute Economique de l'Afrique de l'Ouest (CEAO) organised in 1973. These institutions were designed as a Francophone counter weight to Nigeria and to serve as a moderate pro French bloc within the Organisation of African Unity (OAU) in opposition to more radical African states.[60]

The post-+-colonial African state thus first belongs to international organizations that revolve around its metropolitan state. This established, in the wake of these agreements, new subservient relations that have been described as neo-colonial. Post-colonial Anglophone states belong to the Commonwealth of Nations that groups all ex colonies of Great Britain, while the lusophone countries, Guinea Bissau, Angola, Mozambique and Sao Tome belong to the Community of Portuguese speaking peoples (CPLP). These primary fora of international transaction initially mediated the role and policy preferences adopted by the post-colonial African state at bigger and global platforms. Through these organizations, impulses from the international system as a whole are filtered and interpreted, often by the ex-colonial authorities, for action by the post colonial state. In this manner, the postures adopted at the international level by the post-colonial state is largely tied to the interests and perceptions of how these global developments impact on its ex colonizer. The post-colonial African state was a member of the Non-aligned movement in the Cold War and belonged to that agglomeration of poor states that is generally referred to as the Third World.

Approaching the state from the perspectives of the Weberian tradition, Chabal and Daloz argue that a proper understanding of the informalization of politics must be grounded in a more sociological approach. From this view-point, they advance that the modern state is the outcome of a process by which the realm of politics is gradually emancipated from society and constituted into increasingly autonomous political institutions.[61] In a rather restrictive conception, Peter Lewis insists that civil society comprises part of a civic realm, or public sphere in which state and society interact over issues of common concern. In this view, civil society constitutes the domains of associations which are engaged with the state in cooperative or adversarial relations. Civil society extends beyond non-party political opposition, yet it is delimited by the civic orientations of its constituents.[62] A more inclusive understanding treats civil society as a diverse realm of organizations occupying the domain between family and state. From all these perspectives, it emerges that civil society is autonomous from the state and its institutions and structures. Gianfranco Poggi sums up that one might say that the key phenomenon in the development of the modern state was the institutionalization within modernizing western societies of the distinction between the private/social realm and the public/political realm, and that the same process was later carried further within each realm. In the public realm, for instance, the division of powers assigned different functions of rule to different constitutional organs; in the private realm, the occupational system became further differentiated from, say, the sphere of the family.[63]

While these conceptual delineations reflect the reality in advanced political systems, the realm of civil society is not that differentiated from the political in post-colonial African states. Indeed, the concept of civil society presents certain difficulties, as nothing that could be said to be civil per se is allowed to thrive in the state environment. One main reason for this is the totalitarian project of the state itself. A second is the very confining structure of what goes for civil society in the post colonial African state. The state seeks to penetrate civil society, while civil society is fragmented along natural sociological boundaries that constitute the contending forces in the political process. It is against this background that Chabal and Daloz highlight both the failure of the African state to be emancipated from society and its poor institutionalization.[64] Finally, they also argue that the dichotomy between state and society does not reflect the realities on the continent. In effect, such dichotomy or autonomy between the state and society does not exist in post colonial African states. The boundaries are blurred and often times explicitly intertwined.

Several attributes of the construction of society in the post-colonial socio-political space must be understood if we are carefully going to plot the locus of the state in relation to civil society and understand the problematic nexus between the character of society and the travails of the state. Inter-communal relations in post-colonial states may be defined as mutually antagonistic. This antagonism runs through the gamut of processes that constitute national life, including the political, economic and the social. Indeed one of the salient characteristics of the post-colonial African state is that there is no concept of the political outside the realms of the struggle among segments of factionalized civil society. The political process masks the formal interaction between the segments of society or inter-societal contests for the domination of the political space. The political party in the post-colonial African state is not grounded in ideological foundations. Ideological platforms may be presented by political parties, yet parties are not articulators of ideological visions. Political parties in the state are the acceptable mechanisms for conducting formal inter ethnic struggles, as long as they are dressed in the right cloak of a political party. This is a critical distinguishing element in differentiating between the political process of post-colonial states and the political processes of other kinds of states; the pre-Westphalian, the modern and the post-modern state.

Political parties in the twentieth century became the sine qua non of liberal democracy, the means by which a chaotic mass public was transformed into coherent alternatives of both elites and programs. The party became the means by which men could offer alternative policies and alternative administrations.[65] The political party system was not only a device for broadening control, but it was a device for political integration as well.[66] Political parties in post-colonial African states serve opposite ends to these. Rather than broadening control over national society, political parties in young post-colonial African states formalize and fossilize differences of worldviews along ethnic lines and make the lines of cleavages along more permanent ethnic lines. A political party in a post-colonial African state conventionally brings together people of similar ethnic or tribal backgrounds and those who share common myths of antecedence to the struggle for the domination of the political space. It is a parochial mechanism.

To facilitate the articulation of this sectional goal, universal political goals and ideas are espoused to hide this generally acknowledged character of the ethnic grouping. The structure of the political party system is closely aligned to the structure of contending tribes and ethnic groups in society. To comprehend the multi-party political process is to explore the overtly expressed currents of tribal and ethnic interests. There exists a dualism of the formal and informal faces of the political party system. This dualism pervades the whole life of the state and the multi-dimensional processes that constitute the internal dynamic of the post-colonial polity.

In Guinea Bissau, following the post-conflict democratization, in the elections scheduled for November 1999 by the Abuja Accord, 21 political parties emerged. All the political parties presented their formal manifestos and platforms. Yet, most of them were arrowheads of particular ethnic interests. Indeed, the Party for Social Renewal, (PRS), which emerged with a relative majority in parliament and whose Ballanta presidential candidate, Kumba Yala, was also victorious in the first truly multi party elections held in that country, did not hide its desire to entrench a parochial Ballanta hegemony in the country. The search for ethnic hegemony and domination had thus substituted the socialist ideas on which the state was established by the founding father, Amilcar Cabral. This followed the defeat of his liberation movement and party, the Pan African Party for the Independence of Guinea and Cape Verde (PAIGC) at the polls, after years of internal decay that eventually led to the country's civil war. The search for ethnic hegemony has dominated the bloody trajectory of Bissau Guinean national life.

During the period of multi-party politics in Nigeria's First Republic (1960-66), an enduring system of political networks arose, based on ethnicity and the patronage and charisma of individual leaders. The policy preferences of the parochial networks constituted the major subterranean undercurrents of the ensuing northern dominated thirteen years of military rule. They resurfaced in the process publicly in a slightly altered form during the country's democratic experiments of the Second Republic (1970-83) and were at work in instigating General Ibrahim Babaginda's still-born Third Republic.[67] Major political parties have been historically heavily tribal. At independence, the Action Group, cloaked with its socialist ideas, metamorphosed from the Yoruba cultural organization, Egbe Omo Oduduwa. The National Council of Nigeria and the Cameroun (later known as the national Council of Nigerian Citizens) had originally been created in Lagos, the Yoruba coastal metropolis, and led by the Yoruba elite. By independence, however, it had become the stronghold of the Igbo and remained so until the demise of the first republic. The Hausa–Fulani of the north created its own Northern Peoples Congress (NPC) whose agenda was to foist the interests of the northern tribes on the country as a whole. The

Northern Element Progressive Union of Malam Aminu Kano was regarded as a repudiation of the conservative political agenda of the mainstream NPC. The party, unique in the country with its socialist agenda, drew its followership from Kano area, where the leader came from. In the 1970s at the end of the civil war and the long interregnum of military rule, the Unity Party reincarnated the old Action Group, the National Party of Nigeria re-grouped all the major Hausa Fulani political actors, the Nigeria Peoples Party (NPP) was synonymous with Igbo interests, while the Kano-based Peoples Redemption Party (PRP) resuscitated the old northern socialist radicals from Aminu Kano's Kano city and state.

From 1983 to 1993, the northern-dominated military seized the political space to the near exclusion of southern participation at the highest policy making levels. Whatever the look of alliances at the surface, support for individual politicians and political parties tended to be largely defined in ethnic terms. The constituency of each party tended to be regionally exclusive, as illustrated by the fact that the membership in the ruling Northern People's Congress was open only to indigenes of the Northern Region. The Action Group was predominantly Yoruba. Authoritarian regimes have also been grounded in their ethnic constituency. At the height of the General Ibrahim Babaginda administration all members of the Supreme Military Council, with the exception of two, were northerners. When a Yoruba politician finally won the presidential election after a tortuous transition programme, this was annulled because the top brass of the northern-dominated military would not hand over power to a non Hausa-Fulani. The Nigerian military acquired the reputation of being the most potent political instrument of the Hausa-Fulani north.[68]

The last experiment at democratization in Nigeria in the post-Abacha dictatorship has seen the evolution of political parties whose ethnic flavours are largely veiled. Against this background have emerged three powerful ethnic groupings as the preeminent and consequential actors in the political process. They effectively mediate the political process and have demonstrated greater salience than the formal political parties. By attempting to shed their traditional ethnic character, the political parties seem to have lost legitimacy and leverage for effective action on behalf of the various ethnic groups. In their stead have grown powerful tribal umbrella organizations: the Afenifere and the Yoruba Council of Elders for the Yoruba; the Ohan'eze for the Igbo; and the Arewa Consultative Forum for the Hausa-Fulani. These groups have become the mouthpiece of the dominant tribes and their pronouncements reflect the true pulse of the polity. The defence of Hausa-Fulani interests by the Arewa Consultative Council has included a project of consolidating the Islamic faith in the north and advancing it to the whole federation. In 19 of the 36 states of Nigeria, Islam has been raised to the pedestal of a state religion. Such has been the pervasiveness of these parochial organizations that some analysts have lamented the abandonment of any pretences toward nationalism and patriotism. Their activities are seen as tending toward the polarization of the country.[69] Garba Ibrahim notes that

> Indeed, the rot has gone much deeper, as former military leaders, retired top federal civil servants, high flying academics, former progressives and traditional rulers openly attend meetings organized by these parochial groups, where calls are made for sectional candidates for high office, and threats are issued to Nigeria...[70]

The point is more poignantly expressed by Anthony Enahoro, Nigerian elder statesman, who observed that

> The failure of Nigeria so far may be attributed in great part to the perennial tensions and conflicts among nationalities, resulting from mutual insecurity,.... Rather than manage primordial identities, which are our nationalities, positively, successive constitutions have studiously and dismissively ignored them. But as disillusionment with the Nigerian project has grown, it is to these very celebrated identities that the people have begun to look for refuge. Thus the nationalities that the colonial invaders thought that they had buried have forced themselves back into our collective consciousness. No amount of blank repetitions of hollow appeals can change those realities.[71]

In Congo Brazzaville, the Congolese Movement for Democracy and Integral Development (MCDDI) draws its membership from the Bakongo ethnic group of Brazaville, the Union for Progress and Social Democracy (UPDS) is the political arrowhead of a collection of small ethnic groups in the Niari, Boenza and Lekoumou regions, often referred to as the NIBOLEK region. These ethnic groups include the Babembe, Nzambi, Bateke, Bakomi, and Bayela. The former state party, the Congolese Workers Party (PTC), has maintained a veneer of national character, but in reality has transformed into the party of the Mboches and Kouyou tribes from the north of the country. Rather than ideologies and programmes, ethnic and tribal interests are at the core of political groupings and associations in the post-colonial African state.

In Kenya, the complex equation of politics is tribally based. President Moi is observed to have survived by mastering the tribal calculus. In 2001, the opposition was noted to have been

> caught napping when Moi entered into a coalition government – a first for KANU which has been in power since 1963-with the opposition's Luo dominated National Development Party, NDP. Moi's alliance with Raila Odinga, NDP's leader and former leftist

firebrand, seemed to have deftly manipulated the rift between the big Kikuyu and Luo tribes that has been a dominant feature of politics in this nation of 30 million. Both Luo and Kikuyu tribes have languished in political wilderness during Moi's tenure. And a rivalry rooted in cultural and political differences has long prevented them from making common cause and using their demographic weight to unseat Moi. The president, from the small Kalenjin tribe, has maintained control since taking office in 1978 through links to other small tribes, exploiting their fear of being dominated by one or another of the big communities...

Taking a cue from KANU, the opposition has also been engaged in frantic alliances in a bid to capture political power from Moi's party. But the strongest sign of opposition unity emerged in February when five mainstream opposition parties signed a memorandum of understanding as a framework for choosing a single presidential candidate...The deal brought together the Kikuyu, who traditionally vote for the Democratic party and are the largest tribe in Kenya, the Abaluhya (Ford –Kenya supporters and the third largest tribe), and the Akamba, regarded as supporters of the National Party of Kenya and the fourth largest tribe in Kenya.[72]

In Sierra Leone, a multi-ethnic state of some 17 ethnic groups, the political process has been dominated by the Mende and Temne, who, between them, account for 60% of the country's population. The Temne traditionally inhabit large sections of the northern region, while the Mende occupy the south and eastern parts of the country. The two groups dominate their respective regions and have over the years extended their cultural influence and otherwise over other ethnic groups in their respective domains. Before the civil war in March 1991, the political party system and the political process revolved around struggles of the two main political parties associated with the two ethnic groups, the Sierra Leone People's Party (SLPP) and All People's Congress (APC), for dominance. SLPP, which began with an impressive national spread in its ranks, was soon to be perceived by opposition elements and non-Mende party stalwarts as a party representing mainly the interests of the Mende and those with close affinity to that ethnic group. In the midst of turmoil generated by the widening perception of the ethnic agenda of the SLPP, the APC was born in October 1960 under the leadership of Siaka Stephens. Many northern politicians gravitated toward the APC and encouraged other northerners to join the party as the only one that could genuinely protect northern interests. APC received considerable support from the Krio and Koono because these groups felt they could not make much headway in the SLPP. Since independence, political party leaders have often appealed to their kith and kin for support.[73]

In quasi-Westphalian states, tribal and ethnic interests drive the political process and polarize society. Civil society is thus not autonomous from the political process. It is integral to the politics of the state. These considerations form the powerful undercurrents of the political party system in post-colonial African states. Under the formal political structure of African regimes, a unifying perceptual and operational cultural idiom has emerged which is deeply embedded in society as well as in the state.[74]

Society in the post-colonial state is also characterized by a dearth of internal cohesion. This results from systemic value dissonance and the absence of common or compatible worldviews among constituent units of society. The component societies of the state revolve around different cultural sub-systems. Cultural sub-systems are those aspects of collective life which are shared across classes, differentiate a collectivity from other collectivities, are not necessary for species survival, have continuity amid change, provide significance to events, and goals for collective action, rely on the production and use of symbols and become institutionalized into systems of patterned activity.[75] Since the state seeks to amalgamate diverse peoples from different cultural sub-systems into a political community, it started off burdened with a lack of common understandings about morality, social organization, social norms, basic philosophy on which social life may be predicated, sources of law, symbols and their interpretations, and meanings on which the patterned activities of each rested. There is in effect no agreed overarching ideational foundation on which to build the national society.

The ethnic tripod of Nigeria is made up of the Hausa-Fulani, the Yoruba and the Igbo. The Hausa-Fulani are the major tribe of the muslim north, which groups all the northern states that have embraced the Islamic Sharia legal code. The states with sharia legal codes form a political community of contiguous entities whose weltanschauen and normative underpinnings are quite different from those of many societies in the southern states of Nigeria. The Yoruba ethnic group in the west is reputed for its renowned, highly sophisticated and complex religious corpus[76] and belief systems that revolve around a pantheon of *Orishas* and a transcendental force creator, *Olodumare*. Social interactions and rules of morality are founded on this Yoruba religion, even as the concept of *omoluabi* remains at the heart of the norms of social reciprocity. The political evolution of the Yoruba finally spawned a vast number of highly urbanized traditional kingdoms. In the colonial and post-colonial period, Yoruba society and culture absorbed influences from first the Arab world through conversion to Islam, and from the west, through the agency of Christianity. Yet, the Yoruba absorbed these influences without losing the essential Yorubaness. The Igbo in the east developed a complex acephalous political system.

These three communities differ in their worldviews and philosophical orientations. While the early influence of western civilization has somewhat reduced the ideational gulf between the Yoruba and Igbo, the ideational chasm between the Hausa Fulani and the latter two communities appears to be widening. The ideational chasm in Nigeria was reflected in 1976 as Nigerians sought to write a new democratic constitution for the country. Laitin observes that the issue that generated the most heat, both in the press and in the Constituent Assembly during the constitution drafting exercise, concerned the role of the Federal Sharia Court of Appeal in the Second Republic. Many of Nigeria's muslims saw the Sharia courts (which are in principle avenue for justice in the Muslim world) as the symbol of political freedom. Yet these same courts were seen by many Nigerian Christians as the symbol of potential domination in Nigeria.[77] Juxtaposed with widespread Christian and western orientation of the South, the introduction of the Sharia reflected a widening chasm in the ideological-philosophical foundations of society between the North and South.

The implications of the differences in worldviews and value dissonance have been grave for the country. In July 2009, a virtual war broke out across five northern states between members of the Islamic fundamentalist sect, the Boko Haram, and the Nigerian military and police as the group went on rampage. Their immediate target was to assassinate the Commanding officer of the military base in Maiduguri, Borno State. The fundamentalists were opposed to Western education. From Borno state the mayhem that saw over 400 killed spread to Bauchi, Yobe and Kano states. As President Yar'a dua observed, the action of the fundamentalist had long been planned with training and mobilization by the group that sought to foist their extremism on society. The President informed that:

> What we have now is a situation where the leader of the so-called Taliban group is residing and most of them (the militants) have migrated from all the Northern states to go prepare and declare a holy war.
> ...The people have been organizing, penetrating our society, procuring arms, learning how to make explosives and bombs to disturb, confuse and force their beliefs on the rest of Nigerians.[78]

These differences express systemic value dissonance in society, such that the value systems that undergird the ways of life of the various communities are diametrically opposed. Social interaction is largely limited to the platforms offered by the formal institutions of the state, which are in themselves weak and perceived as theatres for the continuation of inter-ethnic struggles for ascendancy. Even social and professional associations have ethnic coloration. The systemic value dissonance is prominently demonstrated in the old Sudan, with the Islamic and arabised north and a predominantly Christian and animist south occupy the same political space.

In Cote d'Ivoire, the Muslim north and the coastal Christian and traditional African societies present a difficult line of cleavage. It has recently affected citizenship rights in that country. In Senegal, the predominantly Catholic community in the Casamance grapples with the reality of a vastly Islamized society in the north. As society is afflicted with a serious dearth of common worldviews and universally shared ideas on which a national way of life could be grounded, no national way of life develops. No agreements exist on national ethics and morality. The President of the Social Democratic Party of Guinea Bissau, Joao Seco Mane, a Mandinge, once wondered aloud on the seeming dissonance in ethic and value systems among ethnic groups in the country, observing that

> Since the advent of the PRS government, stealing and cattle rustling have been on the increase while the Police uncharacteristically have been unable to prosecute anyone of the many apprehended. Is this because the Ballanta have taken over the state?[79]

Society in post-colonial African states is unable to build social capital that is required as an organic glue to hold society together and give resilience to formal institutions and structures. Or better still, social capital exists within factions of the segmented national society. The stock of social capital is not transferred to the formal state as an asset to enhance its legitimacy. Social capital refers to connections among individuals and social networks and the norms of reciprocity and trust that arise from them. It can be simultaneously a private good and a public good. The networks of community engagement that social capital fosters evolve into sturdy norms of reciprocity. These social connections are also important for the rules of conduct that they sustain.[80] Yet, as Xavier de Souza Briggs cautions, the 'kumbaya' interpretation of social capital is not always so. Networks and the associated norms of reciprocity are generally good for those inside the network, but the external effects of social capital are by no means always positive.[81] In societies constituted by diverse cultural subsystems in the context of wide systemic value dissonance, the constituent groups are resistant to integration, as integration often implies domination and the imposition of the strange ethics and values of the dominant group. Social capital is dense within the respective subsystems, but very restricted system wide. Social capital in post colonial states is thus compartmentalized and can be mobilized as political asset by each of the contending communities when it is so required. Against the background of the limited stock of system-wide social capital, there exist only very few networks of civic engagements that, as Robert Putnam advances, "should foster sturdy norms of generalized reciprocity and encourage the emergence of social trust".[82]

Rather, without a truly autonomous civil society domain, there is a throwback to the patterns of historical interaction, predating the emergence of the state, and mostly under colonial authority, among the constituent units. These historical inter-group relations were competitive. They fuelled distrust that mortgaged the very future of the new independent political community. The dynamic of inter-constituent relations, based on historical rivalries, generates insecurity and leads to a classic security dilemma for all engaged in the social transactions in the state. The security dilemma constrains the development of a civil society realm that can transcend the limited interests of the contending forces in the national arena. This is negative social capital. As noted with the structure of political parties, the network of inter-ethnic relations do not facilitate coordination and communication, but helps to entrench prejudices and fossilize cleavages. In such a scenario, the dilemmas of collective action, including security dilemmas remain unresolved. The inability and failure to build social capital have a telling impact in denying the national society, invariably putative, at large a common template for future collaboration. Traditional identities are strengthened as the development of a national community and the growth of a new identity are stunted. These constitute serious constraining undercurrents for the political process led by an elite, both traditional and emergent, that is a hostage and, at the same time, an instigator in perpetuating the illegitimacy of the state.

Post-colonial African states are dominated by a proletarian elite who are recent social emigres from the margins of society to national leadership. The middle class is often alienated from the very turbulent and deadly political process. Often, some in the middle class do try to impact on the process. Leadership is in a state of flux as ethnic chiefs, military officers, traders, trade unionists, journalists, businessmen, academics, all at different times seek convenient avenues to clinch leading roles in the political process. A career in journalism and human rights activism seem to be popular preludes to the declaration of political ambitions. After stints in politics, some often return to their professional base. Many are ruined or often assassinated. The most successful are military officers attuned to the use of violence and often contemptuous of the rule of law or the finesse of legality.

The concept of political class and political elite is therefore diffuse, as there is no clear demarcation between civil society and the political realm. The political class can be thought of as consisting of those individuals who are or have been involved in the pursuit of political office through competitive elections. This group includes those in the military who may be gunning for political office or civilians running for office and those who are in charge of organizing campaigns. In Nigeria, the Gambia, Burkina Faso, Congo Brazzaville, Democratic Republic of Congo, Sudan, Liberia, Guinea Bissau among others, the identity of this class might seem more ambiguous due to the fact that the country has been under authoritarian control of the military class[83]. The military is itself politicized and implicated in the struggle for ethnic hegemony. Thus, in reality, the military in the post colonial African state is first and foremost a political structure. Its internal situation reflects the larger cleavages in society. As the concept of civil society remains problematic in the analytical discourse of post-colonial Africa states, so is the concept of political elite.

No political elites in the classical sense of the concept exist in the post-colonial African state. There are very few leaders in the post-colonial African state who come from a genealogy of two generations of service or leadership to society or community. More often than not, former leaders are haunted by their legacies of blatant abuses of trust. From one state to the other, leaders in post-colonial African states gain access to power through unconventional and dubious means, mostly through the threat or actual application of violence. They also retain power through the same nebulous channels. Frederick Chiluba, a trade union leader who came to power via democratic elections in Zambia, sought to cling to an unconstitutional third term by changing the constitution of the country. General Robert Gueye, the former leader of Ivory Coast, who seized power in a military coup in 1999 and lost in the democratic elections two years after, died fighting to topple the democratically elected president in September 2002. In Nigeria, General Ibrahim Gbadamosi Babaginda who came to power in a 1985 coup d'etat nullified the democratic elections held in June 1993. The general was forced to step aside by his ambitious deputy, General Sani Abacha. Six months later Abacha took over power from a toothless civilian caretaker regime and threw the winner of the democratic elections, Chief Moshood Abiola, in jail, where he eventually died. The power gained by the leadership is a vehicle to escape grinding poverty and achieve social mobility. They achieve the first goal in grand style. General Sani Abacha of Nigeria, ruling from 1993 to 1998, was reputed to be worth over US$5 billion before his death in office in mysterious circumstances. General Ibrahim Babaginda was unable to account for US$12 billion in a consolidated account of the country. The profile of the leadership of post-colonial state is instructive in this wise.

Joseph Desire Mobutu joined the colonial army of Belgium at age 19 following a formal education in missionary schools. He rose to the rank of a sergeant-major. Following independence, Mobutu, now working as a journalist joined the Congolese National Movement of Patrice Lumumba. When Lumumba became Prime Minsiter of Congo, he appointed Mubutu as Chief of Staff, after a stint as private secretary. In the power struggle that ensued between Prime Minister Lumumba and President Joseph Kasavubu, Mobutu, now a colonel, sided with the President. In Sepember, 1960, at 29, Mobutu as Chief of Staff of the Army, suspended the government and placed Lumumba, who was subsequently murdered in January 1961, under house arrest. In 1965, he led a coup d'etat and proclaimed himself President. By 1970, as President, he established a political party, the Popular Movement of the Revolution (MPR) to which all Zaireans were forced to belong. In 1971, he changed the name of the country to Zaire and in 1972, changed his name to Mobutu Sese Seko. He also urged all Zaireans to drop their Christian and western names. Under the guise of a return to African authenticity, Mobutu created a cult that bordered on being worshipped. He amassed a vast fortune, plunging the country into a huge debt. In 1996, following seven years of an unending sovereign national conference which Mobutu routinely destabilized, the decision of the conference to strip Zairean Tutsis of their Zairean nationality, and constant clashes of an emboldened opposition in the new wave of democratization provided an enabling environment for a band of Zairean rebels under Laurent Kabila, supported by Rwanda, Uganda and Angola to rout Mobutu loyalist forces. The Mobutu loyalists were supported by Angolan UNITA forces, Morocco and France. Mobutu died in exile in Morocco.

Liberia had its equivalent in Samuel Kanyon Doe, who staged a coup d'etat in April 1980 to end Americo-Liberian hegemony in the country. Riding on the crest of popular disaffection against the ruling True Whig Party, Doe's brutality riled the country into many antagonistic camps. Samuel Kanyon Doe was born on May 6, probably in 1951, in Tuzon, a small town in Grand Gedeh County, in the south-eastern part of Liberia to poor and uneducated parents. He was of the Krahn tribe. Samuel Doe's formal education was limited to primary education, after which he enlisted in the military to become a career soldier, presumably because of lack of other job opportunities. He rose to the rank of Master Sergeant in the Liberian Army. On April 12, 1980, he and some non-commissioned soldiers assassinated President William R. Tubman, seized power and imposed military rule over the country. Samuel Doe, who was the highest ranking non-commissioned officer out of the 18 plotters, assumed leadership as Chairman of the People's Redemption Council (PRC) that was created to rule the country.[84]

In Nigeria, a country that has over 45 universities did not produce a president with a university education for 47 years. Indeed, two of the most prominent military leaders were high school dropouts.[85] Sergeants in armies that are only a pale above mere ethnic militias have been known to seize and successfully consolidate their power. Many of these leaders barely understood the import of the offices they had seized, beyond the craving for power. These tendencies were personified in General Sani Abacha, who was tagged as the maximum ruler of Nigeria for his totalitarian control of the social, economic and political space. Because of the background of the leadership, the development of political elites or even a real political class is quite limited in post-colonial African states. These time-bound elites from the margins of society are perpetually anchored in their proletarian antecedents, irrespective of how long they rule and how much they loot from the treasury.

Following the menacing profiles of those in political power and dominant in the political arena, well-meaning candidates with impressive credentials for leadership and public service are driven out of the political arena. There is thus a flight of credible leadership material from the national process, including politics. Those from the credible pool of leadership with alternative and progressive visions of the way forward and who are bold enough to venture into the political arena are often assassinated. Political engagement in the post-colonial African state is often the reserved domain of the very tough, many with criminal tendencies. In one extreme instance, the head of state was proclaimed insane by the opposition.[86] Also, power is often personalized. Rulers stay in power for as long as they can, even when they are severely constrained by physical health to rule. Houphouet Boigny dominated the Ivorian political space for over sixty years before he passed away. Cameroun's Paul Biya, at 78 got re-elected in 2011 and has no plan to leave office, not withstanding reports of his ill-health.[87] In Guinea Conakry, the long public absences of President Lansana Conte, who seized power in 1985 and continued to rule in spite of his famed ill-health, spawned an industry of intellectual permutations on the future of that country should he pass away. He died in power in December 2008. Gabon's Omar Bongo Ondimba, until his demise in June, 2009, was Africa's longest running head of state. He had held power for 40 years in power.[88] The longevity of the heads of post-colonial African states is often attained through the neutralization, including physical elimination, of rivals for power and alternative visions.

POLITICAL CAPACITY OF THE POST-COLONIAL STATE

Political capacity refers to the relative ability of the state to function effectively. The aggregate performance of governments can be approximated as political capacity, or the ability of political systems to carry out the tasks chosen by the nation's government in the face of domestic and international groups with competing priorities.[89] Marina Arbetman and Jacek Kugler note that the major reason the process of state building begins at all is that the elites must pay for the military forces that guarantee safety and their right to rule. If this is to be accomplished, political elites must reach the people making up the society they rule, and extract resources from them.[90] In the final analysis, the relative political capacity of the government to rule is indicated by the degree of its success to reach into society and extract resources. Extraction deals with the transfer of resources from the population to the government to allow the government to advance its policy goals and the ability of the government to tax society reflects this success or otherwise. Arbetman and Kugler cite Organski and Kugler who explained the linkage, thus

> Taxes are exact indicators of governmental presence. Few operations of governments depend so heavily on popular support-or on fear of punishment. Revenues affect directly the lives of most individuals in society, and few activities are avoided so vigorously. Without some form of tax revenue, there is no national unity, and no control. Failure to impose and extract taxes is one of the essential indicators of governmental incapacity to obtain and maintain support.[91]

In sum, governmental operation depends on resources extracted from the population. Without such resources governments do not and cannot govern. There is also substantial evidence that supports the contention that politics dominates all other factors responsible for the generation of revenues, after economic controls are applied. An enormous variation is observed in the political capacities of different societies. The strongest societies manage to extract more than 350% of what is expected of them, while the weakest societies extract 12%. In the post-colonial states, the political capacity is very low. For Guinea Bissau, relative political extraction is estimated at 2%. As a result of this weak extractive capacity, the post-colonial state depends largely on royalties from one or two major mineral extraction operations. In Nigeria, the oil sector accounts for over 85% of state revenues. In Mobutu's Zaire, cobalt and other minerals with great strategic import sustained the rulership. No taxes were paid by citizens who operated their informal economies inspite of the state.

The second dimension of political capacity is relative political reach. This signifies the success of the government in penetrating its society and persuading society to work within the framework of official state institutions and the law. The government's incapacity to harness human resources is captured by the extent the unofficial or black market labor force contributes to the productivity of the overall society. Marina Arbetman and Jacek Kugler clarify this

> The general concept of unofficial markets refers to any activity performed outside the control of the government by individuals who may otherwise observe the law. We concentrate on black markets activity of the labor force because it provides a good indicator of how much human activity escapes government scrutiny. The unofficial labour force includes all functions in the economic (sic) where the objective of individual actors is to evade taxes and other governmental regulations[92]

In effect, the relative success of the government to reach society also demonstrates the degree of the acceptance of the legality of the government. A vast proportion of economic activities in post-colonial is undertaken in what is termed as the informal economy. Production is not reported or assessed for tax purposes. Generally, economic activities in African markets are not controlled by political authorities.[93] In virtually all post-colonial African states, the financial market, which is critical for the stability of the weak economies is dominated by the black markets where major currencies are openly traded without hindrance from the political authorities. This weakness of the government is integral to a crisis of resource mobilization in the state. These anomalies revolve around frontal confrontations between constituent groups and societies in whose territories the mineral and agricultural wealth of the state is located and the politically dominant group which seeks to exclusively control the state and, by implication, the distributive policy process. This crisis is further exacerbated by reckless corruption and the waste to which the revenues are put by the dominant group. George Ayitteh observes that:

> In 1993, for example, Ghana's auditor general released a report that detailed a catalogue of corruption and embezzlement by high government officials, costing a staggering 401 billion cedis (about $400 million) over a ten year period (1983-1994) But no one single bandit was indicted.
>
> For six years, 1988 to 1994, Nigeria's military rulers (Babangida's northern Hausa-Fulani dominated regime) squandered $12.4 billion in oil revenue, estimated by the Pius Okigbo Commission to be a third of the nation's foreign debt. A Petroleum Trust Fund set up by former head of state General Ibrahim Babagida 'lost' $600 million.[94]

The petroleum deposits that generate these resources are located in the South-South region of the country. Until February, 2010 when Goodluck Jonathan began to act as president of Nigeria, marginalization in the political process and lack of economic development and opportunities in the resource-ladden South-South and the Niger Delta region have forced the indigenes to declare war on the Nigerian state.

A third dimension related to the relative political extraction and political reach of the government in the post colonial state is the defection rates of the pool of national human capacity from the political system as a whole. The development process is largely a function of the ability of the government to mobilize available human resources to generate wealth. Yet, the post-colonial state is afflicted with the brain drain syndrome, where the national intellectual power is involuntarily exported to other political and economic systems. The paradox is that both the exporting and receiving states do not positively encourage this interaction. Its persistence in the post-colonial state is a reflection of the absolute alienation of the most vital segment of its population from the political process. It represents a significant proportion of those who choose to flee in a flight or fight dilemma which is one dimension of the crisis of participation that characterizes the political process in post-colonial states in Africa.

CIVIL–MILITARY RELATIONS IN THE POST–COLONIAL STATE.

The armies of post-colonial African states are political armies. Kees Konnings and Dirk Kruijt define them as military institutions that consider involvement in –or control over-domestic politics and the business of government to be a central part of their legitimate functions. These armed forces started off as tools for repression and to slow down the agitation for the creation of the post-colonial state. Often, they were used by the colonizers as repressive tools against political dissent from pre-independence activists.[95] The relationship in the beginning was hostile especially, as the political elites considered their compatriots in the military unsophisticated stooges. The application of the concept of civil military relations in the post-colonial era presents clear difficulties and paradoxes. Since independence, the military have become more politically sophisticated and have been co-opted as the pivot of the intra societal struggle for hegemony in the new state.

Two factors are critical to the understanding of these paradoxes in civil-military relations in the post-colonial state. Since society in the post-colonial state is unpacified and relations between the constituent bodies in society can range from deep suspicions to mutual antagonisms, in a Schmittian sense, the continued integrity and autonomy of constituent groups in the state are of paramount concern to those groups contending in the political space represented by the state. This character of intra-societal relations elicits forcefully a security dilemma to all the constituent units in the state. This dilemma, which, against the background of the pervasive disaffection with the political process in the post-colonial African state is real, largely remains unresolved. These tensions in society are reflected in the political contestations surrounding the structure of the military and the turbulence that characterizes its internal dynamic in the post-colonial state setting. The military therefore lack internal cohesion as an autonomous institution, and it is closely implicated and integrated into the broader schisms of civil society. These problems closely replicate the internal incoherence in society.

The colonial origins and legacy of the military in the post-colonial African state greatly constrain its ability to realize its potential as a truly national institution. This legacy carried over by the military into the newly emerging African nations was in accordance with their respective colonial philosophies and was their direct by-product. One of the most distinctive characteristics of African armies is the way they were disconnected from the socio-political environment.[96] Two strands of tendencies are manifest. In one group of post-colonial militaries belong those armies that are barely more than ceremonial outfits. These military formations, mostly in francophone post-colonial state, lack the leverage to mount autonomous operations. They are designed to depend heavily and exclusively on their French mentors for logistical and operational support. They are tied by formal political agreements between their governments and the colonial power to assure the subservience of the post-colonial state as well as incapacitate any political challenges from them to the political dispensation or influence the course of political developments. Thus, the relationship between such militaries and civil society is based largely on a jointly shared role of assuring the perpetuation of neo-colonial domination of the state. The Africanization of the officer corps may have provided opportunities for the hegemonic group to take over command positions in the military, yet being functionally incapacitated, divisions in the military did not alter the calm in relations with civil society. Such militaries were often insulated from the political process. When a perceived need arose to act, French forces often came to change regimes or reinstate those removed by the ceremonial armies. In recent times in Cote d'Ivoire, France armed, kitted and fought along side rebels Forces Nouvelles to remove President Laurent Gbagbo from office. President Gbagbo had tried to roll back the domineering influence of France in that country. It also used its influence to ensure that the deposed President and his wife were handed over to the International Criminal Court at the Hague to be tried for violations of human rights. The pro France rebel forces and Alhassane Ouattara imposed as President by France has been protected by French forces and intelligence services. France has managed to consolidate its strangle hold on its former colonial entities, despite official pronouncement of its intentions to disengage from the internal politics of its former colonies .

Other armies in post-colonial Africa are largely political armies, which were ascribed political roles right from their inception. Kayode Fayemi notes that the British government, in its recruitment policy for the colonial army, promoted the concept of 'martial and non martial tribes' in West Africa. Some ethnic groups were found to be more loyal than others.[97] Thus, from its very foundations, the post-colonial state's military was structured on the basis of political conveniences of their colonial designers. In the post colonial era, contestations around the structure of the military are not internal to the military as the constituent groups in civil society seek representation at the highest levels of the military. It is part of the political struggle of all groups to retain a share of the state apparatus for coercion. This reflects the pervasiveness of the security dilemma that drives the national process at all levels. These concerns aptly reflect the dearth of trust in intra-societal relations in the polity.

Carl Schmit's horrific understanding of politics helps to illuminate the source of the contest surrounding the distribution of military power. His 'fascist and demonic' conception of politics as concerned with the setting and maintaining of boundaries between collectivities, and in particular, with protecting each collectivity's cultural identity from outside threat unfortunately captures the essentials of the delicate centrality of the intersection occupied by the military in a post-colonial state. In this Schmittian understanding, those whose existence or political activity threatens the integrity or autonomy of a community are defined as foes. Flowing from this, the ultimate decision in politics is existential, not normative; it is a response to a condition imposed on us by the Other.[98] Consequently, in the post-colonial environment each group must look out on its own for its own to protect its integrity and autonomy. Thus, the state once appropriated by one dominant group through the coercive machinery of the military, poses a mortal threat to the project of continued integrity and autonomy of the other constituent communities or groups. Each group must ensure that it has enough share of this coercive instrument. As a result of the growing influence of the military, those who felt excluded from the competition for political power also courted the institution.[99]

Conversely, the project for integrity and autonomy by contending forces constitutes a major threat to the tenuous legitimacy of the state. This sets the stage for what Samuel Huntington describes as the politics of order in the post-colonial African state. The impact of these political factors is to render infeasible the concept of non –political army in state. To be sure, like the political party, the military hierarchy articulates its central mandate as loyalty to the state and the protection of national interest and integrity.. The army often repudiates any role in the partisan contestation of power. The politics of its own legitimacy demands these affirmations. The politics of the larger society constitutes a problem for the military. Yet, as Huntington notes and consistent with the dictum of Clausewitz before him, the need for the military institution for each state derives from the permanency of insecurity and the inevitability of war among states. War arises from the intensification of competition among states as they pursue conflicting policies. Two imperatives therefore drive the military institution in post-colonial states: the constant struggle for partisan control of the military by contending groups in society; and the ever present danger of external aggression. Of the two, the internal imperative is far more salient.

It is internal threat, therefore, that is the primary focus of the military in post-colonial states. The preoccupation of the military with internal pacification of less powerful groups poses the difficulties in civil-military relations. Relations between the military and society at large are largely configured by the security calculus of the respective constituent units in the state as they respond to their appreciation of the security dilemma. The military is part of the arsenal of the dominant of the contending groups. Indeed, the manipulations to capture the military is a central part of the political process in post-colonial states, and the struggle for the control of the military is one of the most decisive competitions of the political process. The military institution is implicated in this process and is a pivotal instrument for all the constituent groups. Many who entered via the political route owe allegiance to political forces external to the military institution.[100] Ultimately, the military are transformed to a partisan political instrument, for the career of the soldier is closely tied to the fortunes of his group in the larger politics of the state. The partisanship grows and the dominant group tries to perpetuate its control through recruitment of its own. By definition, recruitment governs composition.[101] Composition determines control. The group that controls the military is dominant in the political system and determines the very direction of the political process. In their numerous political interventions, the military have mostly been a partisan arbiter of the political process swaying political power one way or the other. Finally, the legitimacy of the military is ruined as they are politicized and lose their professional bearing. Nigeria and Guinea Bissau are cases in point.

The political and de-professionalized military are overtly instrumental in the consolidation of a partisan hegemony in the post-colonial state. The long domination of the north in the politics of Nigeria is predicated on the northern domination of the military institution. northern officers, who perceived the Major Nzeogwu's coup of January 1966 as a drive for Igbo political hegemony, overturned the balance of forces within the military in their favour in their own counter-coup of July 1966. Since 1966, the northern political class and military officers from the region have collaborated closely to assure continued northern ascendance in the political process. Northern military officers have staged coup d'etats against northern-led governments to pre-empt a takeover of the reins of power by the south. General Buhari's December 1983 coup against the Shagari regime falls into this genre. The northern-dominated military hierarchy effectively defended the right of the north to rule the country and reneged in June 1993 to hand over power to a southerner who had been democratically elected as president. Another northern officer, General Abacha, took over power as the nation groped for a solution to the crisis generated by the earlier abrogation of the results of the democratic elections. In Mobutu's Zaire, loyalty was to the president, and commanders of units with credible operational capacities were all northerners, from where he came. The military are thus the ultimate political tool of the ruling constituent unit in the political space.

The military are thus not subordinate to the society, for the direction of society is, ultimately, decided by the dominant faction in the military. Political values are thus dominant over military values in the military of post-colonial states. Since the internal process within the military is fluid, reflecting the larger political process, they are unable to maintain internal stability and consistency. Special forces are created to reassure the dominant regime. They serve as the last line of defence of the status quo. Many analysts have therefore disaggregated the military establishment arguing that it does not always act politically in a unified and consistent manner.[102] In post-colonial states, the control of the special forces is exclusively that of the politically dominant tribe. These special forces are apart from the mainstream military. They are better equipped, trained and paid. They are created to reinforce the balance of power in favour of the ruling regime. The military institution is thus an extension of the overall balance of political forces among contending constituent units in the post-colonial state. Power transitions, which are effectively the end and beginning of hegemonies in the post colonial state, lead to crisis that often degenerate into conflicts. As a result, to change the status quo, new rival armed elements are established by the newly disaffected groups in society. They range from ill-disciplined extortionist rag-tag militias to rebels armed with sophisticated weaponry that easily control territory and establish proto states that may realize the political goal of founding a new state or taking over the old one.

In Guinea Bissau, the Pan African Party for the Independence of Guinea and Cape Verde, (PAIGC), has essentially remained a military-dominated party. The political process, up to the 1998 civil war and thereafter, has revolved around the internal dynamics, including schisms, in the military faction of the PAIGC. The fighting cadres of the liberation war retained control of the political machinery and determined the direction of state policy. In almost 30 years of its existence, all but one of its heads of state have had military background. Instability in the political process was derived from instability within the military and many purges, ethnic in character, were traceable to growing alienation among the Ballanta who felt marginalized in national processes. Colonel Paul Correia and six other Ballanta officers were eliminated by the General Joao Bernando Vieira's regime on allegations of plotting a coup d'etat against the state. The civil war of 1998 was triggered by disagreements between President Nino Viera, a veteran of the liberation war who came to power through a coup d'etat in 1980, and his Chief of Staff, Brigadier General Ansumane Mane, also a veteran of the liberation war. The rubber-stamp Peoples National Assembly dominated by the ruling PAIGC watched helplessly on the sidelines as the titans in the military wing of the party fought it out and plunged the country into civil war.

The revolt of a vast majority of the military against the President Vieira, following the intervention of Senegalese and Conakry Guinean troops in the war, led to his ouster.. In the post-war era, the inability of the military junta, among other reasons, to accept the attempt to de-politicize and de-link the military from the political process, led to a three day civil war. The war pitted the self styled Supreme commander of the Junta, General Ansuamane Mane, and his predominantly Mandingo forces against the democratically elected govern-ment of President Kumba Yala from November 23-27 civil war. Following the demise of General Mane, President Kumba Yala significantly altered the power structure in the military to consolidate control and structure of the military in the hands of fellow Ballantas. At the time of writing, of the 12 operational com-mands in the military in Guinea Bissau, 10 are headed by Ballanta. A special force created by President Kumba Yala to protect the presidency is exclusively Ballanta. The Inspector-General of the military, General Tagma Wai, is also Bal-lanta. The ruling Party for Social Renewal is headed by Ballanta. The Secretary-General is Ballanta. A close linkage has developed between the Ballanta in the military and those in politics. A Ballanta hegemony is emerging in the country. Continuing instability in 2009 in Guinea Bissau that led to the assassination of a now democratically elected President Vieira, Chief of Defence Staff, General Tagma Wai, a former intelligence officer and Presidential candidate Baciro Dabo and the arrest of about 30% of the political class for plotting against the state were indicative of the struggle for power by the Ballanta.

In Mobutu's Zaire, the two most reliable corps, the Special Presidential Division and the Civil Guards, were drawn mostly from his own ethnic group, the Ngbandi from northern Zaire. General Likulia Bolongo Lingangi, Mobutu's last Defence Minister is a native of Mobutu's home region. The Forces Armee Zaire, which were once trained by the United States, France, Israel, China and North Korea,[103] were incapable of mounting most field operations. It had degenerated to an ill-motivated, ill-disciplined, extortionist force that pillaged civil society to pay itself.

Donald Horowitz exemplifies the direct nexus of the military and society in post colonial states as follows:

> In Sierra Leone, the cleavage between Moyamba Mende and Kenema Mende played a major role in civilian politics even at the height of a wider North-South and APC –SLPP conflict. In hotly contested election in 1967, some Kenema Mende had left Albert Margai's cabinet and run as independents. These rivalries reverber-ated in the army command.[104]

Horowitz also illuminates the ethnic undercurrents of relations between the military and society in Uganda. He observes that Milton Obote's northern minority regime had to have an unusually sympathetic army and police. He notes that to insure this:

> Obote placed a loyal Northerner in the position of Inspector General of Police. The overwhelming majority of the police had long consisted of northerners. A Lango himself, Obote packed the army

with Langi and Acholi officers and men, and expanded its budget rapidly in the early years of independence. Conservative estimates gave the Acholi, less than 5 per cent of the population, at least one third of the army.[105]

In Nigeria, the structure of the command and placement of the vital logistics of the military have always reflected the political hegemony of the north. By 2003, of the 10 heads of state since independence, eight had come from the military ranks. Seven of these came to power through violent overthrow of the government, often itself a military one. The post-Abacha democratically elected president was once a military head of state. His electoral victory is widely believed to have been funded by another former military head of state, General Ibrahim Babaginda. The political head of the military in Nigeria is conventionally from the north. With the exception of a two year break, 1976-79, the north has always headed the military politically and also maintained control over its leadership professionally. As at 1999 when Olusegun Obasanjo became President, of the 21 officers who occupied the office of the Chief of Army Staff, 17 have been from the north. Control of national intelligence and civilian police have been traditionally exclusively in the hands of the north. The Nigerian Defence Industry, the Nigeria Defence Academy and the National Policy and Strategic institute are based in the north. The North has a monopoly over control of the Ministry of Internal Affairs and has also dominated the State Security Services since independence. The heads of immigration since independence have been northerners. Northern political leaders have indicated that the election of General Olusegun Obasanjo in 1999 was part of an agreement by the north to temporary allocate power to the south. This agreement was contingent on the elected President committing himself to the appointment of a northerner to head the defence, finance ministries and vital petroleum industry. The northern leaders explained their terms for the allocation of political power to the south on the grounds that as northern leaders, "we have a duty to all northerners to ensure that we protect the vested interest of the north as a political entity within the federation of Nigeria".[106]

Yet, it would be misleading to attribute the formal military institution as the only legitimate agent of coercion in the political space claimed by the respective post-colonial states. Since the state itself is under a cloud of illegitimacy and that reality is reflected in its fractured society, conditions in the post-colonial state are conducive to the development of proto states within its space. The proto state, usually revolving around a rebel army, may control territory for long periods of time. The army of the proto state may be an autonomous formation or may be a faction of the national army that has grown strong enough to challenge the army as a rival contesting for a regime change or outright de-legitimization of the status quo. Political crisis have emerged in the old Sudan since the eve of independence in 1955. Since then the exclusive control of Southern Sudan by the forces of the Southern Peoples Liberation Army and its other offshoots for over thirty years and the near institutionalization of government, including the conduct of relations between that organization and neighboring states was as close as it could get as a state within the state. For forty years, the UNITA in Angola maintained a virtual government that was effective in exclusively controlling its capital and the country-side until the demise of its leader, Jonas Savimbi, in 2002. UNITA, acting as a full-fledged proto state dispatched troops to Zaire in defence of the Mobutu regime and its interests. Forces from the MPLA-ruled Angola fought on the side of the Laurent Kabila-led Alliance of Democratic Forces for the Liberation of Congo /Zaire (AFDLC), as the UNITA and the government effectively competed for military and diplomatic allies in the sub-region. In the two cases, the states were in effective alliances with proto states. Charles Taylor's National Patriotic Front of Liberia (NPFL) started off as a rebel movement and consolidated its hold over more than half of the national territory of Liberia. He established the capital of what was referred to as Greater Liberia in Gbarnga.

For over eight years, its territory expanded and contracted according to the ebb and flow on the battlefield. Following the breakthrough in the peace initiatives of the Economic Community of West African States (ECOWAS) in 1995, the NPFL won the democratic election to effectively merge the NPFL proto state into the bifurcated sovereign state of Liberia. This victory had profound impact on the construction of the Liberian regime head by Charles Taylor and radical implications for sub regional balance of forces. A new rebel movement that challenged the legitimacy of the Taylor regime took over the border region in the north of the country. President Taylor blamed Sierra Leone and Guinea Conakry for supporting these rebels. In all these instances, the proto state was accorded a measure of legitimacy by established state actors who had some intermestic interests at stake in the conflict. In Charles Taylor's NPFL was perceived to have received significant diplomatic support from the Ivory Coast. Ethiopia's hosting of SPLA bases and direct military support to the rebel forces helped it to win unprecedented successes in the battlefield and forced Khartoum to the negotiating table.[107] The rebel Lord's Resistance Army in northern Uganda has benefited from liaison with the government in Sudan, while the Sierra Leonean Fonday Sankor's RUF had close relations with Charles Taylor's government in Monrovia. Robin Luckham notes that non-state military formations have become increasingly important in new conflicts in sub-Saharan Africa.[108]

The presence of non-state actors which possess, to different degrees, the attributes of states, is a unique feature of the system constituted by post-colonial states. The attributes of these non-state actors include the possession of territory under their exclusive control, overt quasi-diplomatic recognition by neighboring states and other elite members of the international system and a monopoly of legitimate force in areas under their control. In terms of their military capacity, population and territories under their control, some of them, exemplified by UNITA and the SPLA, are as strong as any other state in the system of post colonial states. They are unlike a state, even if in many respects, they function as one. In any anarchic system with no hierarchical arrangement as the organizing principle, the uneven distribution of power is normal for any system of states. Except that the ability of non-state actors, or better still, proto states, to effectively project force in the system complicates the structure of the system further. For the proto state is a state in the process of being. The presence of proto states impact significantly the policy choices and the outcomes of choices made by full-fledged sovereign states. The presence of proto states is then one peculiar feature of the structure of the system of states constituted by the post colonial states.

On the whole, it might be surmised that the military is deeply implicated in the political process and is not an autonomous institution that is insulated from the tensions and pressures of civil society. Consequently, the military can become a hotbed for ethnic resentment and an instrument for the advancement of ethnic claims to power. In general, the military reflect divisions in society at large.[109] This character of the military institution deepens the security dilemma for constituent groups in society in post-colonial states, and forces all the contending units to show a very keen interest in developments within the institution The military are thus not insulated from the political process. It is central to it. This has significant import for the political process and the stability of the state itself. These factors militate against the entrenchment of the three core values of expertise, responsibility and corporateness by which professional militaries are defined. Subordination to civil society, which is the hallmark of relations between civil society and professional armies, is supplanted. Military intrusion in the political domain has thus become conventional in the post-colonial African state. These regular interventions are described in Nigeria's political lexicon as political aberrations.

The post-colonial Africa state then deviates significantly in terms of four major attributes of the modern Westphalian state. Examined on the degree of its institutional differentiation, the unification of the state through a development of a monistic structure entailing one locus of power, the pacification of society leading to the ascendancy of a common identity that revolves around the state and the emancipation of the political realm from the social domain, the post-colonial African state emerges in terms of its internal development as only a few decades from the state of 1648. In terms of its political capacity, the post-colonial African state is very weak. Qualitatively, the post colonial state is conceptually distinct from the modern Westphalian state and its more recent transformed variant, the post-modern state. In its internal structure and the structure of its inter-state system, the post colonial state is different. It is the "feature of the nineteenth century state for each to operate in its own territory as the sole, exclusive fount of all powers and prerogatives of rule."[110] The post-colonial state system combines elements from the modern state system and features reminiscent of the pre-Westphalian era. These pre-Westphalian character includes the lack of a unitary internal sovereignty, or the inability of the state to attain, in the terminology of David Easton, the authoritative allocation of values at the societal level carried out by a single decision center (the state itself), no matter how internally differentiated and extensively ramified those activities might be.[111] The post-colonial African state may be categorized as a quasi-Westphalian state.

Notes

1. Jennifer Jackson Preece, "Minority rights in Europe: from Westphalia to Helsinki," *Review of International Studies* 23, 1997, p. 75-92.

2. Georg Sorensen, "An analysis of Contemporary Statehood: Consequences for Conflict and Cooperation," *Review of International Studies* 23, 1997, p. 253-269.

3. A.F.K. Organski and Jacek Kugler, *The War Ledger*, University of Chicago Press, Chicago, 1980, p. 4.

4. Gianfranco Poggi, *The Development of the Modern State: A Sociological Introduction*, Stanford University Press, Stanford, 1978, p. ix.

5. James Crawford, *The Creation of States in International Law*, Clarendon Press, Oxford, 1979, p. 48.

6. Jennifer Jackson Preece, op. cit.

7. Oyvind Osterud, "The Narrow Gate: Entry to the Club of Sovereign States," *Review of International Studies* 23, 1997, p. 167-184.

8. Stephen D. Krasner, *Sovereignty: Organized Hypocrisy*, Princeton University Press, Princeton, 1999, p. 4-5.

9. Stephen D. Krasner, ibid.

10. Stephen D. Krasner, ibid.

11. Stephen D. Krasner, ibid.

12. Donal B. Cruise O'Brien, "The Show of State in a Neo-Colonial Twilight: Francophone Africa," in *Rethinking Third World Politics*, ed. James Manor, Longman, London, 1991, p. 146.

13. Donal B. Cruise O'Brien, ibid.

14. Mohammed Ayoob, *The Third World Security Predicament: State Making, Regional Conflict, and the International System*, Lynne Rienner Publishers, Boulder, CO, 1995, p. 4.

15. Patrick Chabal and Jean-Pascal Daloz, *Africa Works: Disorder as Political Instrument*, Indiana University Press, Bloomington, 1999, p. 3.

16. Thomas M. Callaghy, "State, Choice, and Context: Comparative Reflections on Reform and Intractability," in *Political Development and the New Realism in Sub-Saharan Africa*, ed. David E. Apter and Carl G. Rosberg, University Press of Virginia, Charlottesville, 1994.

17. Thomas M. Callaghy, ibid.

18. David E Apter and Carl G. Rosberg, "Changing African Perspectives," in *Political Development and the New Realism in Sub-Saharan Africa*, ed. David E. Apter and Carl G. Rosberg, University Press of Virginia, Charlottesville, 1994. p 1.

19. Kenneth N. Waltz, "Chapter 3," in *Theory of International Politics*, McGraw-Hill, New York, 1979. Kenneth Waltz adduces strong theoretical considerations to maintain this assumption if they application of system level theoretical frameworks would succeed in showing how, among other reasons, the structure of the system affects the interacting units of the structure and how they in turn affect the structure.

20. Patrick Chabal and Jean-Pascal Daloz, op. cit.

21. Milton Viorst, "Why They Don't Want Democracy," *Los Angeles Times*, May 25, 2003, p. M1.

22. Georg Sorensen, op. cit.

23. The idea of quasi sovereign entities with putative powers of the state existing within the post colonial African state and side by side in the same state environment while conducting various forms of informal or formal relations with the states was captured as proto states by Ed Haley, Professor of International Relations at the Claremont McKenna College, Claremont, CA.

24. Gianfranco Poggi, op. cit.

25. The classification is further elaborated in the subsequent chapter.

26. Ronald Inglehart, *Culture Shift in Advanced Industrial Society*, Princeton University Press, Princeton, 1990, p. 3.

27. Ronald Inglehart, ibid., p. 8.

28. Ronald Ingelhart, ibid., p. 5.

29. Michael E. Howard, *The Invention of Peace: Reflections on War and International Order*, Yale University Press, New Haven, 2000, p. 56-57. In this connection, however, Osterud draws attention to Hinsley's argument that historians have traditionally antedated the radici emergence of the new state system. In Hinsley's views the massive developments which transformed the European state system took place in the pre Napoleonic decades. During the eighteenth century, there emerged a new conception of Europe, one that captured the character of the modern state system. His understanding was that the new conceptualization is intrinsic to the workings of the system. Wight and Hingins, Osterud adds, trace the mutual recognition of sovereignty, and particularly the principle of formal

sovereign equality to basically the epoch after the Congress of Vienna. Osterud cites Robert Klein's "Sovereign Equality among States: The History of an idea."

30. Ali Al'Amin Mazrui and Michael Tidy, *Nationalism and New States in Africa: From About 1935 to the Present*, Heineman, Nairobi, 1984, p xii.

31. Saddia Touval, *The Boundary Politics of Independent Africa*, Harvard University Press, Cambridge, MA, 1972, p 3.

32. Ali Al'Amin Mazrui and Michael Tidy, op. cit., p. xii.

33. Saddia Touval, op. cit., p. 4.

34. Hugh Seton-Watson, *Nations and States: An Enquiry into the Origins of Nations and the Politics of Nationalism*, Westview Press, Boulder, CO, 1977, p. 339.

35. Saddia Touval, op. cit.

36. C.W. Newbury, *British Policy Towards West Africa: Select Documents, 1786-1874*, Clarendon Press, Oxford, 1965, p. 34.

37. Ibrahim A. Gambari, "The Role of Foreign Intervention in African Reconstruction," in *Collapsed States: The Disintegration and Restoration of Legitimate Authority*, ed. I. William Zartman, Lynne Rienner Publishers, Boulder, CO, 1995.

38. Ali Al'Amin Mazrui and Michael Tidy, op. cit.

39. "Ivorien Government Accuses Burkina Faso of Backing Dissident Soldiers," *ThisDay News Online* , September 22, 2002.

40. Tajudeen Abdulraheem, Dismas Nkunda, and Chidi Anselm Odinkalu, "Ghana's Golden Jubilee: Africa's Citizenship", *The Gurdian Newspapers*, Lagos, Wednesday, 7 March, 200

41. Michael Howard, op. cit.

42. Patrick Chabal and Jean-Pascal Daloz, op. cit., p. 4.

43. Patrick Chabal and Jean-Pascal Daloz, ibid., p. 5.

44. Mohammed Ayoob, op. cit., p. xiii.

45. Strasner, p 9.

46. Georg Sorensen, op. cit.

47. Robert W. July, *The Origins of Modern African Thought: Its Development in West Africa During the Nineteenth and Twentieth Centuries*, F. A. Praeger, New York, 1967, p. 208

48. Robert W. July, ibid.

49. Robert W. July, ibid. p. 214.

50. Georg Sorensen, op. cit.

51. Gianfranco Poggi, op. cit., p 88.

52. Donal B. Cruise O'Brien, op. cit., p. 145.

53. Mohammed Ayoob, op. cit.

54. Willie Brattenbach, "The History and Destiny of National Minorities in the African Renaissance: The Case for Better Boundaries," in *African Renaissance*, ed. M. W. Makgoba, Mafube Publishings, Cape Town, 1999, p. 97.

55. Willie Brattenbach, ibid., p. 95.

56. Donal B. Cruise O'Brien, op. cit.

57. Donal B. Cruise O'Brien, ibid., p. 93.

58. Naomi Chazan, "Introduction," *Asian and African Studies* 26, 1993, p. 91-94.

59. Sheldon Gellar, "France in Black Africa, 1958-1990," *Asian and African Studies* 26, 1992, p. 101-117.

60. Sheldon Gellar, ibid., p. 106.

61. Patrick Chabal and Jean-Pascal Daloz, op. cit., p. 5.

62. Peter Lewis.(Confirm source on note II)

63. Gianfranco Poggi, op. cit., p. 14.

64. Patrick Chabal and Jean-Pascal Daloz, op. cit., p. 14.

65. Andrew J. Milnor, ed., *Comparative Political Parties*, Thomas Y. Crowell, New York, 1969, p. 1.

66. Andrew J. Milnor, ibid., p.2.

67. John Lucas, "The Tension between Despotic and Infrastructural Power: The Military and the Political Class in Nigeria, 1985-1993," *Studies in Comparative International Development* 33, no. 3 (Fall), 1998, p. 90-113.

68. Nigerian Clarion

69. Garba Ibrahim, "Repositioning of Focus in the NYSC Scheme," address at 2002 NYSC Annual Management Conference, Maiduguiri, June 2002.

70. Garba Ibrahim, ibid.

71. Anthony Enahoro, "The National Question: Toward a New Constitutional Order," lecture delivered at the Yoruba Tennis Club, Onikan, Lagos, July 2, 2002.

72. *BBC Focus on Africa Magazine* 13, no. 2, April-June 2002, p. 6-7.

73. Anatole Ayissi and Robin Edward Poulton, ed., *Bound to Cooperate: Conflict, Peace and People in Sierra Leone*, United Nations Institute for Disarmament Research, Geneva, 2000, p. 21.

74. Thomas M. Callaghy, op. cit., p 206.

75. David D. Laitin, *Hegemony and Culture, Politics and Religious Change among the Yoruba*, University of Chicago Press, Chicago, 1986, p.13.

76. David D. Laitin, ibid., p 36.

77. David D. Laitin, ibid., p. ix.

78. George Oji and Michael Olugbode, "Shoot-out in Maiduguri as Soldiers battle fanatics", Thisday Newspaper, 29 July, 2009.

79. Joao Seco Mane, "Presidential Closing Address," address to 1st Congress of the Social Democratic Party of Guinea Bissau, Farim, March 17, 2002.

80. Robert D. Putnam, *Bowling Alone: The Collapse and Revival of American Community*, Simon & Schuster, New York, 2000, p. 19-20.

81. Robert D. Putnam, ibid., p. 21.

82. Robert D. Putnam, ibid.

83. John Lucas, op. cit.

84. F. P. M. Van Der Kraaij, "President Samuel K. Doe," http://www.liberiapastand-present.org/SamuelKDoe.htm, accessed on December 1, 2007.

85. Generals Ibrahim Babaginda and Sani Abacha did not complete High School.

86. The opposition in Guinea Bissau proclaimed President Kumba Yala insane.

87. "Central Africa: On the Brink," *Africa Confidential* 48, no. 1, 12 January, 2007.

88. "Central Africa on the Brink," ibid.

89. Marina Arbetman and Jacek Kugler, *Political Capacity and Economic Behavior*, Westview Press, Boulder, CO, 1997. p. 12.

90. Marina Arbetman and Jacek Kugler, ibid., p. 55.

91. Marina Arbetman and Jacek Kugler, ibid., p. 18

92. Marina Arbetman and Jacek Kugler, ibid., p. 25.

93. George B. N. Ayitteh, *Africa in Chaos*, St Martin's Press, New York, 1998, p. 102.

94. George B. N. Ayitteh, *Africa in Chaos*, St Martin's Press, New York, 1998, p. 102.

95. Alain Rouvez, Michael Coco, and Jean-Paul Paddack, *Disconsolate Empires: French, British and Belgian Military Involvement in Post-Colonial Sub-Saharan Africa*, University of America Press, Lanham, MD, 1994, p. 20.

96. Alain Rouvez, ibid., p 20.

97. J'Kayode Fayemi, "Entrenched Militarism and the Future of Democracy in Nigeria," in *Political Armies: The Military and Nation Building in the Age of Democracy*, ed. Kees Koonings and Dirk Kruijt, Zed Books, London and New York, 2002, p. 205.

98. Gianfranco Poggi, op. cit., p. 6-7.

99. J'Kayode Fayemi, op. cit.

100. J'Kayode Fayemi, ibid.

101. Donald L. Horowitz, *Ethnic Groups in Conflict*, University of California Press, Berkeley and Los Angeles, 1985, p. 445.

102. Robin Luckham, "Military Withdrawal From Politics in Africa Revisited," in *The Military and Politics in Africa: From Engagement to Democratic and Constitutional Control*, ed. George Klay Kieh and Pita Ogaba Agbese, Ashgate, Aldershot, Hants, England and Burlington, VT, 2004.

103. "Four Faces of a Showdown," *New York Times International*, April 11, 1997 p. A6.

104. Donald Horowitz, op. cit.

105. Donald Horowitz, ibid., p. 487

106. Obasanjo reveals northern Agenda on Power Shift, the Guardian Newspaper

107. Francis M. Deng and Khalid M. Medani, "Civil War and Identity in Sudan's Foreign Policy," *in Africa in the New International Order: Rethinking State Sovereignty and Regional Security*. Lynne Rienner Publishers, Boulder, CO, p. 111.

108. Robin Luckham, "Radical Soldiers, New Model Armies and the Nation-State in Ethiopia and Eritrea," in *The Military and Politics in Africa: From Engagement*

to Democratic and Constitutional Control, ed. George Klay Kieh and Pita Ogaba Agbese, Ashgate, Aldershot, Hants, England and Burlington, VT, 2004.

109. Donald Horowitz, op. cit., p. 444.

110. Gianfranco Poggi, op. cit., p 92.

111. Gianfranco Poggi, ibid., p 92.

Chapter 3

THE MODERN AND POST MODERN STATE

Earlier postulations suggested that the concept "state" has been bereft of critical interrogation. The term has always implied a modern state. Political analysis has largely differentiated states on the basis of their varying capabilities to project force. Central to the logic and operation of the modern state system is power and its internal and external deployment. Internally, the state has the legitimate use of the monopoly of force within a clearly defined territory with a fixed population that was governed by a sovereign so recognized by other states for purposes of international treaties and international life in general. The people and the territorial space under the control of this sovereign constituted an autonomous economic unit and the state often possessed a national currency. The state was the most defining element in the identity consciousness of its citizens. Individuals and groups became building blocks of a national society that shared a common identity built around the state. This society developed worldviews and ways of life that were peculiar to and associated with the people of that state and formed a distinct cultural entity. The state and the nation came to acquire a neat fit and became co-terminus.

The modern state thus at once constituted a political community, a nation and an economic unit as well as a distinct social space. The defense of the collective interest of this society and community called a nation represented the highest challenge of the state. The *raison d'etre* of the state was to perpetuate itself, and by implication, the national interest by securing the general well being of the nation. In its relations within the self help inter-state system, the state was expected to protect itself with all the power at its disposal. The continued survival of the modern state ultimately rested on its power. War, in the apt description of Clauswitz, was understood as the continuation of politics by other means. The modern state system was thus premised on power, and interactions, including diplomatic negotiation among states, were undertaken against the general understanding that war could be resorted to, to resolve any differences. Also, the theories associated with the behavior of the modern state insisted that law could not constrain or regulate state behavior. International law might be created by states to serve their own interests, particularly as a tool for the strong to control the weak; but states would never create laws that constrained them against their own interests, nor would they continue to conform to any law that had once served their interests when it ceased to do so. In short, law was described as at best epiphenomenal in international politics.[1]

The axioms and theories underpinning the monolithic understanding of the modern state have been challenged by new values that have evolved and increasingly governed relations between a number of old Westphalian modern states and interactions between their more and more increasingly intertwined societies. These values rest on a common agreement on the superiority of global and human interests over the state as well as a continuous diminution of the salience of state sovereignty in regulating many facets of international life that otherwise were not subject to external interference. The emerging consensus on values that transcend the state are backed by social constructivist theories which have offered a different type of challenge to the realist rejection of the place of law and norms in international politics. These theories claim to start with the realist presumption of anarchy in the international system, but argue that the outcome of anarchy is not inevitably disorder and conflict: it merely means that there is no supranational authority.[2]

Also, liberal institutionalists often challenge the 'black box' conception of the state promoted by realists, in which state behavior is the same regardless of the domestic political structure.[3] The codification of the initiatives to replace a world of chaos and conflict implied in the operating procedures of the modern state system with a rules-based system that proposed limits on the use of force, promote the protection of fundamental human rights, and enshrine free trade and international economic liberalization dates back to the 1940s led by the United States and Britain.[4] Increasing differentiation among segments of the modern state system is based on differences in attitudes on a wide range of changes impacting on the modern inter-state system that is setting post-modern states apart from modern states whose behavior in the international system are guided by old and conservative notions of sovereignty. Differences between the two genres of state are expressed in their relative adherence to or rejection of new principles resting on a rules-based international society enshrined in a corpus of international law and a system of global rules[5] as well as the acknowledgement of, and respect for, an evolved international society that calls the state into account.

Post-modern states are welded together by a dense network of evolved transnational social capital linking their national societies. Civil society and the private sector have become actively interested in international rules, which have also become the subject of increased media attention.[6] A network of causes, based on shared values that bind civil society across state boundaries and enhance interests in international rules regulating these causes, drives a new transnational political process that assures the acceptance by the states of the new principles which undermine old notions of sovereignty associated with the modern state. The states accept that international law has emerged as a regular feature of modern political life.[7] Notions of sovereignty have changed with growing interdependence, such that to claim that states are as sovereign as they were fifty years ago is to ignore reality. The extent of interdependence caused by the avalanche of international law means that states are constrained by international obligations over an increasingly wide range of actions.[8] By the 1950s there existed an embryonic global constitutional order, with rules that remain in place, albeit rather shakily in some cases, to this day. And the rules, once adopted, take on a logic and a life of their own.[9] This has led to historic transformations and geo-political revolution expressed in the emergence of a New Europe which has all the symbolic apparatus of a unified political entity.[10] In the world of post-modern states, the preeminence of state sovereignty and the associated outpouring of patriotism expected of its citizens is an oddity, as their societies work hard to move away from nationalistic tendencies and toward a supranational union that eviscerates borders and traditional national rivalries.[11]

Thus, the evolving governing principles of the post-modern state system appear to be breaking new ground and instituting new inter-subjective understandings and *grundnorms* in society as well as with the state. These new organizing principles are radically altering the character of the state, its society and the nature of the international system, especially the post-modern state, within this heterogeneous international and inter-state system. The international system in the new millennium is composed of unlike units: the post-colonial entities, the Westphalian modern state and the post-modern state. One may also add the pre-Westphalian political communities of theocratic Islamic societies. As such, the organizing principles of the differential state systems clash as both the new variant of the westphalian state, the post-modern state, and those of the modern state interact within the same space.

The cumulative impact of the increasing alteration of the character of the post-modern state, and of its increasing differentiation from the entrenched modern state as the two kinds of state interact closely in the international arena, has been a pervasive misunderstanding and a climate of mistrust.[12] This climate has continued to erode friendship among allies and led to smoldering resentment.[13] The close juxtaposition and interaction between two genres of state with differing worldviews, policies, philosophies, axiomatic understandings and standard operating procedures have thus created tensions in the operations of the inter-state system.

In the setting of the modern state system, the structure of inter-state relations reflects the configuration of power among state actors. The system was stable, some argued, because of the balance of power among the elite states that dominated it. This balance meant a rough parity in the distribution of power among the major alliances that dominated the state system. The structure of the state system was thus based on an alliance system that grouped state actors in such a manner as to leave no single state actor and its allies with preponderant power in the system. For another group of realist analysts of systemic conflict, the balance of power in the state system may, however, be skewed with a strong asymmetry in favour one state actor. This power had the capacity to impose the defining principles of obligations for the system.

In this conception of the structure of the international order, the state system was understood to be hierarchically arranged with the hegemon at the top followed by other elite states. The pecking order, including the ability of each state actor to influence the system, was based on the power quotient held by each state. The preponderant power was at the top of the league because it held enough power to overwhelm the system. This hegemon, however, had allies who enjoyed privileges based on the structure of obligations imposed by the dominant state actor. For this school, the international system was most stable where there existed a clear hegemon dominating the state system. The system was most unstable in periods when a revolutionary state actor acquired parity or was about to acquire parity in its capability to challenge the regime of inter-state obligations imposed by the hegemon. The process of power transition led to war[14]. Some authorities perceive a skewed structure of the balance of power among states as more stable.

Yet, the system was not consciously designed to sustain peace because as Henry Kissinger pointed out, "whenever peace-conceived as the avoidance of war- has been the primary objective of a power or a group of powers, the international system has been at the mercy of the most ruthless member of the international community".[15] Kissinger further explained the sources of stability in the modern state system as follows:

> Stability, then, has commonly resulted not from a quest for peace but from a generally accepted legitimacy. 'Legitimacy' as here used should not be confused with justice. It means no more than an international agreement about the nature of workable arrangements and

about possible aims and methods of foreign policy. It implies the acceptance of the framework of the international order by all major powers.[16]

The modern state and the operations of its state system are weaned on these axioms. It is, however, by no means certain that the legitimacy of the prevailing order would be acceptable to all state actors, especially as the balance of power in the system keeps evolving. Revolutionary situations arise in which certain state actors are dissatisfied and act to challenge the extant regime. Such revolutionary powers have the courage of their convictions and are ready to use force to establish new principles to govern relations between state actors. Kissinger emphasizes that principles in a revolutionary situation are so central that they are constantly talked about.[17] He stresses that a revolutionary situation develops when a revolutionary power boldly proclaims intentions to recast the existing structure of obligations among states. Such a challenge undermines the legitimacy of the existing order because of profound dissatisfactions with the organizing principles underpinning the extant order.

As such, a revolutionary challenge is a determined repudiation of the structure of the system as well as of the regime of obligations deriving from this structure. Otherwise, the system is marked by clear understandings of the extant operational principles and the continuous spontaneous application of those principles that further reinforce perceptions of the legitimacy of the international order. Within this setting, what passed for international law reflected the dominance of the state over society on the one hand, and the putative character of an international community that simply was an aggregation of member-states of the system. Integral to the operations of this inter-state system, war was a legitimate instrument of policy. The international system was an amoral world. Force was deployed in relations with other states. Sovereignty was sacrosanct and sovereigns did not tolerate interference in their internal affairs.

It is this world of the modern state, of which the United States of America is its most approximate representation at the beginning of the new millennium, and the logic of its operation that have been vigorously challenged by a number of developments in some old modern states. Changes in values and the emergence of a global consensus on these values, are beginning to transform the character of some modern states and are developing new understandings and logic to guide the operations of the post-modern state system. A discernable international community of humanity rather than a community of states has emerged. This international community is distinctly recognized as having interests that are higher than those of the constituent states of the international system. By accentuating the security of the international community, the course of the evolution of the Westphalian state is leading to a conceptually distinct and new form of state that departs from the organizing principles associated with the modern state and its states system. The principles governing the social, economic and political organization of societies and communities in the post-modern state are often opposed to the foundational axioms of the modern state.

These old modern states are transiting to a new genre of political community that may be described as the post-modern state. The emerging post modern state is organized on the basis of different principles, and the post-modern state system is based on new norms and understandings that have their roots in a new and engaged international community. Unlike the modern state driven by power, the post-modern state is driven less by power than by transnational understandings, including moral force of an emergent international society. The decision making process in these states is not entirely internally focused and the conception of citizenship is diffused. These developments have challenged and have undermined the fundamental principles governing the world of the modern state system. The new principles that are evolving in some of these elite states, hitherto modern states, are altering the very character of the inter-state system. It is also gradually leading to the emergence of a new kind of state other than the conventional modern state. Flowing from these developments, the very legitimacy of the organizing principles of the modern state and its state system are now in doubt. While power remains an integral element defining relations between states, its arbitrary and unbridled use by states has been delegitimized.

As a result of the evolution of universal moral standards and the emergence of an international community conscious of itself as such, in contradistinction to the aggregation of states that earlier constituted the international community, states neither enjoy the unquestionable right to the recourse to violence as an instrument of internal coercion, nor, more importantly, in its relations with other states. Indeed, it is inconceivable that some states, mostly post-modern states, would even go to war with each other. The existence of an international community, built around transnational convergences in ideas, values, principles and interests and the complex transnational communal linkages that these relationships have spawned, have altered the very nature and character of international society. Morality has acquired critical salience in the conduct of international affairs. In the world of post-modern states, it has rendered obsolete the instrument of war to regulate relations between constituent members of the system.

Post-Realism

Until now, the legitimate monopoly of the use of force within a defined territory was the hallmark of the modern state. New developments have questioned even the legitimacy of war as the final arbiter in the affairs of mature modern states. Post-modern states abjure unilateral pursuit of military campaigns. While the decision to go to war still remains the prerogative of each state, it has become the responsibility of a larger community to legitimize such decisions as a new norm of the emerging new system of post-modern states. A state cannot simply just go to war, as the international community has insisted on forging a new kind of approach to the use of power in world politics.

In the emerging post-modern dispensation, the incidence of war among states is perceived as more a breakdown of the workings of the inter-state system than the continuation of politics by other means. The incidence of war among post-modern states would be an aberration and not an expectation as conceived within the modern state system. War has become an aberration and the military machinery of powerful states has been deployed more for humanitarian intervention in troubled states than to prosecute conventional hostilities between powerful state actors. [18]

In contrast to the traditional international age, when they were formally declared and formally terminated, wars today are viewed as aberrant behavior much like domestic crime. To declare war in the post-modern era, the most powerful states cannot act at will, they are constrained to seek international legitimation for their acts. This includes even glaring cases of provocation such as the war unleashed by the United States against the Taliban in Afghanistan following the unwarranted Al-Qaeda attacks of September 11, 2001. The war in Iraq (opposed by large popular majorities in every EU country, even nations like Britain, Spain, and Poland, which the United States counted as allies in the war) exacerbated the split between the United States and Europe. Indeed, Spain's Jose Maria Anzar, who supported Bush in Iraq, paid a high price for his pro-war stance. In the spring of 2004, in the wake of a terrorist bombing, the voters of Spain dumped Aznar's Popular Party and handed the government in Madrid to the strongly antiwar Socialists.[19]

The legitimation of any use of armed force in difficult transactions between states, especially when a major power is involved, is only conferred by supranational institutions such as the United Nations. Such is the de-legitimization of power and force in inter-state relations that the outbreak of armed hostilities between states is enough for the United Nations to convene a special session of the Security Council. In general, there is revulsion to war and a commitment to the pacific resolution of differences in the affairs of states. Ninety per cent of Spanish citizens rejected the invasion of Iraq in 2003 led by the Bush administration of the United States, although the Spanish government failed to respect the wishes of its people. In spite of strenuous manipulation of intelligence in respect of the alleged acquisition of chemical weapons by Iraq, only 50% of Britons supported British participation in the war in Iraq. Later an inquiry was conducted to determine whether the former prime minister, Tony Blair, and his government were drawn into the conflict — over the objections of Britain's defense, intelligence and foreign policy establishments — by an eagerness to please the United States.[20] In the international community, there would appear to be preference for alternative instruments, including sanctions, to force compliance by states.

In general, the United Nations engagement of military force has almost always been guided by the norm of humanitarian military intervention. The United Nations and regional and sub-regional institutions interpret and reflect the mood of the international community and make judgments regarding the proportionality of provocation and courses of action and consequences proposed by powerful states. This generally facilitates the resolution of conflicts through negotiations and other courses of action short of war. Such is the altered structure of interactions between states, as noted by Jonathan Power, that when powerful states go on their own, either in war or in regulating some international crisis situation their own way, they inevitably humbly return to the international community for legitimization and help.[21] He further observes that even though the United Nations is everybody's whipping boy, the big powers can run to it and find a solution short of war or revolution. He exemplifies this with the "desperate return of the United States to the United Nations following difficulties encountered in the aftermath of its invasion of Iraq and the overthrow of Saddam Hussein and the destruction of his Baathist party". Power asserts further that the crawl back of the United States to the United Nations in the aftermath of the removal of Saddam Hussein was consistent with the pattern of behavior of powerful states as they seek to escape the horrors that confront them. In summation, Jonathan Powers reveals the benign dependence of powerful states on the moral leverage of the United Nations to extricate themselves from complications that emanate from self-imposed crises, including war. In all these, he hoped that Washington, perceived as a principal culprit, would learn from experience.[22] Indeed, the United Nations has become the bulwark against arbitrariness by the most powerful states in the system and the universal moral clearing house of the emergent international society.

The universal principles that are emerging in the post-modern era, including the transformation of national societies and the emergence of an international community, expressed in the organizing principles of the post-modern state system, have come to the fore at a critical juncture when the configuration of global power has undergone a radical transformation. These monumental changes in the structure of the international system following the demise of the Soviet Union have impacted global developments, both at the political and economic levels. The end of the cold war led to a transition from a multi-polar structure of the international system to a unipolar world. The end of the cold war also had a catalytic impact on the post-modernization process of some elite states by freeing the allies of the leading modern state to pursue new political directions that do not always converge with those of the hegemonic power. This, in turn, has infused a certain momentum in the globalization process as small states in the orbit of the old COMECOM were sucked into the expanding reach of the economic frontiers of Western Europe.

The United States has emerged as a clear hegemon that is dominating world affairs in the post-Cold War era. The United States has conducted its world affairs and imposed an international regime founded on the fundamental principles governing the modern state system: the aggressive articulation of national interest through unbridled threat and actual use of force. These organizing principles of the post-cold war world order represent attempts to consolidate the classic principles of the modern state system. This process has played out within the context of an evolved international system populated not only by modern states but also by post-modern states who operate on the basis of new understandings of evolved principles that identify the post-modern state. In this new understanding, power and force are no longer the ineluctable instruments driving state policy and the organization of the inter-state system. This evolution of state and society, both at the level of the state and the global system, has broken down narrow worldviews associated with modern states and in its stead has enabled the growth of a dense network of transnational social linkages that connect societies across hitherto impregnable state frontiers.

POST-STATISM

The phenomenon of a post-modern state can thus be interpreted as an unfolding process and the wholesale shifting of political culture at the global level. It may also be seen as a further evolution of the Westphalian state system as the modern state begins a certain long decline. This development has entailed the subversion of the axiomatic foundations of the modern state and has accentuated the redefinition, through expansion of nation-state identities that include the progressive breaking down of institutional barriers that had resulted from national, linguistic, ethnic, and cultural identities. In its place are new institutions of post-modern states that recognize the differences but that also transform them into powerful elements of a transnational new political community. This has been followed by the institutionalization of universalizing norms and values, including the growth of international society and the increasing legitimatimization of international law and institutions to enforce those laws. The impact of these post-modern features on the state has been the increasing repudiation of the foundational principles undergirding the modern state and the rise of the supranational political entity. A historical shyness to subject the state and developments related to the character of the state to rigorous analytical attention has resulted in a dearth of interrogation on these developments within the context of the continuous evolution of the Westphalian state. This has obscured the recognition of the emergence of a new kind of state, the post-modern state that is profoundly different in its fundamental assumptions from the conventional Westphalian modern state.

The principles associated with the modern state system have become archaic. As such the classic modern state operating on the basis of these principles has become a revolutionary state within the context of the emerging global understandings of the character of the international community and the norms that govern the acts of state actors in that global community. The character of the international community has effectively changed. The international community is no longer the aggregation of sovereign states but rather the increasing integration of national societies and communities on the basis of moral and normative standards that are becoming universally acknowledged. These principles promote the welfare, aspiration and the dignity of humanity as a whole. The birth of non-governmental agencies all over the world and the dense network linking thousands of these organizations reflects this reality. Non-governmental organizations have taken on the central role of monitoring the pulse of humanity through their reports on the state of human rights, good governance, conditions of the health of humanity, flow and administration of international aid, the conduct of war and treatment of prisoners of war, and in many other domains relating to the welfare of international society. Through these activities, international society in effect has been emancipated from the stifling domination of the state.

The modern state is being effectively put in check. Through the building of a dense network of transnational values and interests that has given rise to the evolution of powerful international value-based societies and transnational communities, respective national societies have effectively been transformed into integral constituent elements of a global community. The continued application of the norms of the classic modern state system in this new environment may be perceived as a subversion of the emergence of new principles that alter or deviate from controversial norms associated with the operation of relations within the modern state system. It is within such a context that the United States, particularly the administration of George W. Bush, may be said to be a classic status quo modern state defending the legitimacy of an old order. It is simultaneously a revolutionary state dissatisfied with the emergence of a new regime redefining the structure of obligations associated with the evolution of the post-modern state system. President Bush has made the argument that the world legal order that has emerged is not working.

Faced with constraints on the exercise of its sovereignty, the US has sought to side-step those rules, particularly where they provide no direct economic benefit. In its first term the Bush administration embarked on a course that threatened significant damage to the rules-based system which was put in place after the Second World War, but proposed no viable alternative.[23] This depicts the United States as a selfish, individualistic society devoted to commerce, profit, and the despoliation of the planet. It is perceived as uncaring about the poor and sick and indifferent to the rest of humankind. As a result, the US is seen as riding roughshod over international laws and treaties and threatening the moral, environmental, and physical future of humanity. It is seen as a bull in the global china shop.[24] A conclusion can be drawn that there is no agreement on the principles that should govern the structure of obligations in the international system in the first two decades of the post-cold war era. Some have referred to the gap in values between states.[25] Against the backdrop of these developments, Robert Kagan's fashionable thesis that Europe and the United States were two tectonic plates inevitably moving apart seems irrefutable.[26] This is symptomatic of the fissiparous legitimacy of the regime governing the modern state system and a reflection of the constraints faced by the emerging new principles to entrench themselves immediately.

The logic and fundamental principles of the evolving system of post-modern states are different from those of the modern state system. The evolving principles of the post-modern states essentially revolve around the continuous diminution of sovereign powers of the modern Westphalian state, including the redefinition and interrogation of the fit between the state and nationality. In this wise, the notion of expanding layers of the identity of the individual and the evolution of transnational societies based on clearly defined albeit narrow interests and maxims, including the moral and ethical, are a significant deviation from the monolithic structure of state-centric national societies that revolve around complete allegiance to the national cause or flag that is associated with the modern state. Puritanical patriotism is fading and giving way to trans-national communities of shared values, visions and interests in the post-modern state and across the system of post-modern states. American expressions of patriotism seem to annoy Europeans.[27] This has raised the consciousness of national societies to their obligations towards international society and has established a moral barometer to measure the acts and policies of their respective states in its relations with the international community. This sensitivity is acute in societies of post-modern states. Mary Kaldor has observed this phenomenon and argued that the post-Cold War moment offered a new kind of international possibility based on the emergence of the global society. She has attributed this development to the fact that at the heart of this possibility were the revolutions of 1989 and the new currents of international dialogue and exchange they enabled. However, she has further observed that the new phenomenon belonged to Western and Eastern Europe - certainly international, but manifestly not global.[28]

This evolved consciousness of the existence of international morality and sensitivity to this at the individual level was poignantly expressed in the hurried withdrawal by the state in the State versus Katherin Gun case. Katherin Gun, an employee of Britain's General Communications headquarters, the intelligence agency which intercepts and deciphers communications around the world for the British government, was arrested in March 2003 and scheduled to be put on trial on charges of divulging state secrets. Her assertion that she had "acted out of conscience to expose what she regarded as an attempt by the United States to 'undermine' the debate at the United Nations" during a critical international crisis over the insistence of the United States and Britain to go to war in Iraq resonated all over the world[29]. Gun argued that she was compelled to leak secret code cables by the belief that both the American and British governments were acting outside international law.[30] Mark Leonard sums up the mood of the international community in relation to their expectation of the conduct of their states with international institutions, when he observed that for the first time since the Cuban missile crisis, dramatic presentations at the United Nations during the Iraqi crisis dominated the media, and international public opinion rallied to its cause. Leonard concludes that the United Nations, which was sidelined and mocked, has begun to restore its sheen even in the United States, where UN bashing had become the staple of mainstream politics.[31] The war in Iraq would seem to have so consolidated the delegitimization of war as an instrument of inter-state relations that when future generations of analysts look back on the Iraq war, they may see it as a decisive turning point in international history, as the beginning of a post-Clausewitzian era in which it became all but impossible to use force to achieve political goals.[32]

Jonathan Power captures two salient differences between the United States, an entrenched modern state, and European countries, most of them with attributes of post modern states, thus

> In practical terms, Europe cannot bridge the gap with an America that spends 3% of its gross domestic product on the military compared with Europe's 2%. Likewise, there is no way that the United States, whether led by Republicans or Democrats, is going in the foreseeable future to match European spending on non military side of foreign policy. European countries contribute three times as much aid to developing countries and twice as much to the UN budget as the United States. European countries contribute 10 times as many soldiers as the United States to peace keeping and policing operation.[33]

Policies of the classic modern state flow from an institutional framework of domestic power and from a highly centralized process of decision making.[34]

These translate into a unilateralist posture as the modern state seeks to project more and more power in the inter-state system. The modern state is driven by a grand strategy to acquire and consolidate its preeminence in "power, position and prestige" among states and acts to ensure the limitation of any exercise of sovereignty by states that might interfere with this global design.[35] The end of the cold war was envisioned as the beginning of another defining epoch as the United States rejected its organic alliance, most notably with Western Europe, which had given rise to the notion of the West. The post-cold war epoch is marked by the emergence of the United States as the global hyperpower, freed from the Soviet threat, unconstrained by any alliance, able to explore and define its own interests unfettered and uncluttered by other considerations.[36] Jacques Martins notes that the classic entity of the new post-cold War American empire is the sovereign nation-state and that the American doctrine in the new epoch was based on war without end.[37] Noam Chomsky characterizes it as the philosophy of the new norm of nationalism.[38] In this connection, Noam Chomsky notes that the primary principle of the foreign policy of the United States, rooted in Wilsonian idealism and carried over from Clinton to G. W. Bush II is

> ...the imperative of America's mission as the vanguard of history, transforming the global order and, in doing so, perpetuating its own dominance," guided by "the imperative of military supremacy, maintained in perpetuity and projected globally.[39]

Consistent with the operating principles of the modern state system, the overwhelming American military dominance is designed to discourage and intimidate the three main threats to its global supremacy from, among others, other major powers - China, Russia, Japan and the European Union. At the same time, American military might is designed to discipline and intimidate all nation-states.[40] This hegemonic agenda and vision of the classic modern state clash with the normative foundations of the post-modern state and the evolved international society that seeks to move away from war. This difference in attitude to war can be adduced to be one of the elements driving the emergence of a new sense of European identity among ordinary Europeans.

The evolution of the post modern state is consistent with the demystification of the Westphalian concept and the repudiation of the attributes of the state and the international arena deriving from the Westphalian myth. Richard Ned Lebow queries the axioms surrounding Westphalian foundation of understandings of the nature of the Westphalian state as well as the nature of the state and the international environment deriving from that theoretical tradition. He observes that the concept of sovereignty, which is at the heart of the Westphalian state, has diverse and murky origins. He attributes to nineteenth and twentieth century century jurists and historians, many of them Germans influenced by Kant and Hegel, the development of a narrative about sovereignty that legitimized the accumulation of power by a central government and portrayed the state as the sole focus of a people's economic, political and social life.[41] These theoretical impositions were without empirical justifications:

> Without empirical justifications, they described the 1648 Treaty of Westphalia as ushering in a novel, sovereignty-based international political order. The ideology of sovereignty neatly divided actors from one another, and made the binary of 'us' and 'others' appear natural, if not progressive, development, conferring a similar status on conflict and warfare among states...There was no concept of the 'international' until late eighteenth century, and its development reflected and facilitated the transformation of the European system into an international one in the course of the following century.[42]

The seeds of the on-coming destruction of the Westphalian myth lay in its own edifice. Twentieth century international relations developed against the background of the Westphalian myth. This myth made interstate war the norm, and enduring cooperation an anomaly that required extraordinary explanation. This Westphalian edifice propounded that the international arena was distinct from the domestic and that anarchy and warfare were it norm.[43] Developments at the end of the millennium gave a lie to these propositions that had taken on a life of their own. The self-fulfilling prophecy of war interminable among states had only raised questions about the tenets that were supposed to govern the anarchic international environment. The brutality of the theory in practice set the stage for the demystification of the sovereign scourge. The historical roots of the European Union lie in the killings and destruction of the First and Second World War and the determination to ensure that horrors of that war never happened again. In the years after World War I, as European leaders looked back in horror on the four years that had virtually eliminated a whole generation of the continent's young men, the Idea of Europe had considerable appeal. Also, amid the smoke and splinters of the blasted, impoverished continent that emerged from World War II, a group of visionaries from several countries took up anew the dream of a united Europe. This gave birth to the loose aggregation of government leaders, academics, business leaders, and writers, known collectively as the European Movement.[44]

The processes of the emerging post-modern state reflect the repudiation of war as central to relations among states as held by modern states. To the extent that there is an entity called Europe, with a distinguishable identity, culture and world view, many young Europeans characterize it only in anti-America terms. To a young Pole, the rudimentary European identity he has formed is against the United States, against the image of America as the new imperialist superpower that regards everything that happens in the world in the context of its own national interest.[45] To some Czechs, American patriotism, particularly in the Bush era, is perceived to be uncomfortably reminiscent of Soviet rhetoric of old.[46] Newly elected Spanish Prime Minister Luis Rodriguez Zapatero affirmed that it was unacceptable to "organize war with lies" and called the United States invasion of Iraq and its subsequent occupation a disaster. He also conditioned the continued deployment of Spanish 1300 troops in Iraq with the United Nations taking political control of Iraq from the United States. Spain, Zapatero vowed, would be more pro European than ever.[47]

The conservative Popular Party of Prime Minister Jose Maria Aznar became the first European government that backed Washington in the invasion of Iraq to be voted out of office. Andy Eckardt observed that ever since Germany and other European nations refused to support the US-led military intervention in Iraq, a trans Atlantic rift had been evident. One year after the war, a majority of European Union citizens still believed that the US led invasion was wrong. Eckardt reports that in January 2004, 75 percent of Europeans described the mission as unnecessary, 72 per cent said that they had a bad opinion of President Bush, and only 7 percent of respondents thought of the President as good. Eckardt further cites the observations of Nicole Renvert, director of the Future of Transatlantic Relationship project at Germany's Bertelsmann Foundation that

> For the past ten years, we have been seeing an emerging of different views and different approaches toward certain issues on both sides of the Atlantic. Even though the new European generation is very much influenced by the United States in everyday life, a general misunderstanding and new rhetoric is fueling certain stereotypes about the United States.[48]

As a result of these developments, Europeans' faith in US global leadership has been fading, Eckardt concluded.[49] These differences highlight some major departures of post-modern states from the modern state. Post-modern states work less and less on the basis of power and more and more through the building of supranational institutional frameworks for the harmonization of multiplicity of interests among states.

The Copenhagen criteria, passed by the European Council on 12 and 13 December 2002, established that membership of the Union requires that the candidate country has achieved stability of institutions guaranteeing democracy, the rule of law, human rights and respect for, and protection of, minorities, the existence of a functioning marker economy and the capacity to cope with competitive pressure and market forces within the Union. Membership presupposes the candidate's ability to take on the obligations of membership including adherence to the aims of political, economic and monetary union. In its practical expressions, adherence to the accession requirements of the European post-modern state system requires a certain transformation in the institutions of state and society. These transformations reflect the entrenchment of certain universal principles that have become axiomatic in this universe. In this regard, member-states of the European Union must have instituted administrative changes that aim at smoothening the interaction and cooperation between national institutions and those of the Union. The Copenhagen criteria explicitly demand that all candidate states must fulfill these terms.[50]

In March 2004, the European Parliament in Strasbourg adopted a resolution harshly critical of Romania's bid to enter into the Union. The Parliament voted by 374 to 10 (with 29 abstentions) to tell Romania to deal with corruption, ensure the independence and proper functioning of the judiciary, guarantee freedom of the media, and stop ill-treatment at police stations.[51] Romania's unsuccessful application highlighted the sensitivity of the European Union to its core values. Its real problem with the European Union was the adoption of 105 Romanian presumed orphans by Italian families pushed through by its Prime Minister Adriana Nastase, under political pressure from Rome. The deal angered the European Commission because it broke a three-year moratorium on international adoptions of Romanian children. The ban had been imposed because the adoption of orphans had become a highly profitable business which ignored the welfare of children and their natural families.[52]

The difference between a post-modern state and the modern state is further reflected in the value dissonance in their two societies. This is reflected in the differences in the dominant attitudes towards same sex marriages between European societies and the United States of America. Today, for the majority of the French, even homosexuality poses no profound problem. Polls released in the first quarter of 2004 by the Ipsos polling agency showed that 57% of those under 35 believe that gay couples should be allowed to marry. That compares with only 24% in the United States. Yet, France is comparatively more conservative than much of the rest of Europe. In Denmark, 82% approve of same sex marriage, and in the Netherlands 80% approval, just as in Luxembourg, Sweden, Spain, Belgium, Norway, Switzerland and Germany.[53] This contrasts with the United States where conservatives see gay marriages as "the end of western civilization" and Americans favour a constitutional ban on gay marriages and youngsters oppose it by a margin of two to one.[54]

In practice, accession to the European Union implies the ceding of parts of the sovereign attributes of each member to the supra-national institutions that have been invested with powers to evaluate developments in domains where the respective states hitherto had unlimited powers of control. The oversight powers of the supra-national institutions confer on them the right to override national institutions in their areas of competence. The areas of competence of supra-national institutions are quite extensive ranging from human rights protection to litigations on varied subjects, in which the European-wide institutions and regulatory bodies have the ultimate say. In this way, the post-modern state is founded on the rule of law that overrides the political expediency that often characterizes the dispensation of justice in the modern state system. In both its internal workings and the operating procedures of the post-modern state system, the rule of law is predominant.

In its relations with the global system of Westphalian states, the post-modern state is constrained by its commitment to certain universal standards, including the imperative to respect the declared wishes of the majority of its people. The principle of the higher interest of the state that is associated with statecraft in the classic modern state has been whittled to its barest influence, given the powers conferred on European supra-national institutions. These European institutions can arbitrate between the European citizen and his primary state of origin. The position of the European Ombudsman was created by the Treaty of European Union (Maastrict) in 1992. The ombudsman acts as the intermediary between the citizen and the EU authorities. The EU deals with many other subjects directly relevant to the day to day lives of its citizens. These include citizen's rights, ensuring freedom, security and justice, job creation, regional development, environmental protection and making globalization work for all.[55] Noam Chomsky observes that in the two major European countries, Germany and France, the official government stance on the American invasion of Iraq in 2002 corresponded with the views of the large majority of their populations. In Britain, the population was split roughly fifty-fifty on the war, but the British government was alsoconstrained to maintain the stand of a junior partner.[56]

The modern state imposes a rule of force as against the rule of law that is increasingly preferred by post-modern states. The United States of America, especially George W. Bush's strident, nationalistic America that is sometimes woefully ignorant of what lies beyond its Eastern Seaboard,[57] comes closest to the approximation of a modern state. Noam Chomsky notes that high on the global agenda of the United States by fall 2002 was the declared intention of the most powerful state in history to maintain its hegemony through the threat or use of military force, the dimension of power in which it reigns supreme. He cites the official declaration of the National Security Strategy as

> Our forces will be strong enough to dissuade potential adversaries
> from pursuing a military build up in hopes of surpassing, or equal-
> ing, the power of the United States.[58]

Greenway observes reaction to this strategy by other state actors, mainly the post-modern states in close interaction with the United States. He states that even among America's friends there is something about the trumpeting of America's exceptionalism, especially when wedded to what appears to many to be a desire to make the world over in America's image, which is profoundly off putting.[59] In explaining the source of some of the distrust in the international system, Greenway adopts the standard medical description of narcissistic personality disorder as put forward by Dr. Bandy Xenobia Lee as follows

- Has a grandiose sense of self importance e.g exaggerates achievements and talents, expects to be recognized as superior without commensurate achievements
- Is preoccupied with fantasies of unlimited success, power, brilliance,
- Requires excessive admiration
- Has a sense of entitlement, i.e unreasonable expectations of especially favorable treatment or automatic compliance with his or expectations
- Shows arrogant, haughty behaviours or attitudes.

He observes that, in light of current events, Dr. Lee thought the diagnosis might at times be applied to nations[60]. In essence these represent the personality profile of a classic entrenched modern state as perceived by a mature modern state that has repudiated some of the foundational principles on which inter-state relations had been anchored only some two centuries ago. It would appear that the personality profile of the modern state is narcissistic.

The picture that emerges of the community of post-modern states is exemplified by the unification of Europe

> The unification of Europe has played a key role in the continent's corporate renaissance. The emergence of borderless, tariff-free supranational state with uncontrolled movement of goods, services, and workers has given European companies a home market that is bigger and richer than the United States. The single currency makes formerly complicated sales transactions more efficient. The uniform regulatory apparatus across twenty-five markets has permitted developments of uniform sizes, packaging, and technical standards that mean a product designed for one corner of Europe will work for the entire European continent and its half billion consumers.[61]

POST-MATERIALISM

The post-modern state has evolved, through an incremental policy process, as small mature modern states adapted to changing realities of a transformed international society, international economic forces breaking down antiquated conventions about the assumed fit between the borders of sovereign nations and their economies, and the structure of the inter-state system itself characterized by the rise of the United States as a hegemon. The impulses for transformation have thus been both internal to the state and external to it. Internally, the inter generational culture shift of a post-materialist era of the post-war generation created a more liberal generation that was conscious of a multi-layered identity in an ever widening web of community outside their immediate national universe. Guy Coq underscores the implication of this liberalism for society in the debate over symbolism and headscarves in France and relates this to social transformations in Europe as a whole

> Meanwhile, more and more, there is talk of a Europe wide laicite. More and more, European democracies are multi religious. They no longer have a base of common religious tradition. Instead, they are constructing social guidelines built around ethical, universal values like justice and liberty of conscience.[62]

Catherine Field stresses the seismic changes of the perceptions of most European Union citizens over the past 20 years from a view that is almost parochial to one that leaps across borders. She attributes these changes to learning of foreign languages, especially the spread of English by the scrapping of border controls, tax barriers and economic protectionism, by the weaving of cultural and social contacts across borders and by simple, but important, things such as the lowering of postal charges, telephone tariffs, and price of airline tickets. These have facilitated the development of a European society based on the emergence of a European identity consciousness and notions of European citizenship. She asserts that the development of a European society is based on mutual respect, trade ties and cross border friendships that are at the very foundation of a real European identity. Field observes that

> In the 15 EU states more than 50 percent of the population can speak at least one European language in addition to their mother tongue, while 26 percent say they can speak two foreign languages. At grassroots level, more than 7,000 'twinning associations' link towns inside the European union. The French German Youth Office, set up as part of the Elysee Treaty between France and Germany in 1963 has led to more than 6 million students benefiting from exchange agreements. The number of marriages between nationals of different EU states increases annually, as does the number of families who travel to other member states either to buy second homes or simply to holiday... Put together, this force from below can provide a powerful moment for change.[63]

The wholesale transformation of national societies into constituent elements of an ever expanding web of larger political identities and bigger transnational communities in the post-materialist era is expressed in the emerging rise of Europe-wide political parties based on shared beliefs and ideology. These parties are beginning to think in terms of the leverage for action at the continental level through enhancing their fortunes in elections to the European parliament. On 20 February 2004, about 1000 Green party leaders from across Europe gathered in Rome to launch a continent-wide party to boost their chances in coming European elections. The meeting was motivated by the increasing realization that European politics could not be the result of 25 national politics.[64] Implied in this development is the emergence of a European political process and dynamic distinct from the political process of the constituent post-modern states of the European parliament. The center of this European political process is the 626 seat European parliament that grew to 732 members after the admission of 10 new states into the European Union in May 2004. Millions of citizens now vote in direct elections to the European parliament. The reality of the emergence of an autonomous European political process is underlined by John Palmer's demand that the President of the European Commission, the supra national executive charged with the day to day running of the European Union, should be directly elected by the citizens of the Union. Palmer notes that currently

> The power to appoint the president lies with the European Council, comprised of heads of government; the European parliament only has a right to use its 'nuclear' option of vetoing a president formally proposed by the heads of governments. European citizens have no role in deciding who will head the commission. Members of the public have great difficulty even finding out what deals are being done behind closed doors to select a president in their name. [65]

The platform of the European Green party best reflects the post-materialist character of the post-modern state. The Green campaign focuses on food safety, sustainable development, the fight against nuclear power and genetically modified organisms, and support for the Kyoto Protocol on emission limits. Other issues in the manifesto of the European Green party are the call for further European integration, support for women's rights, plus traditionally socialist themes like job security.[66] The expansion of Europe means the transformation of Europe. This transformation has been intuitively understood in the founding states of the European Union, as well as those that have since become full members.[67] The members of the European parliament do not sit in national block but as members of Europe-wide political groups whose similar programmatic orientations reflect ideological similarities and affinities.

As at 1 April 2003, the 624 members of the European Parliament were distributed among seven constellations of European political parties and groups. These include the European People's Party (Christian Democrats) and European Democrats (EPP-ED), Party of European Socialists (PES), European Liberal, Democratic and Reformist Party (ELDR), European United Left/Nordic Green Left (EUL/NGL), Green/ European Free Alliance (Greens/EFA), Union for Europe of the Nations (UEN), Europe of Democrats and Diversities(EDD). Thirty-one members of the European parliaments were unattached. Since 1979, members of the European parliament have been elected directly by citizens that they represent. Parliamentary elections are held every five years and every one of the 374 million registered European voters is entitled to vote. Palmer highlights that the encouraging gradual emergence of transnational parties in Europe will have a crucial role to play in creating a true European democratic polity. Palmer notes that the European Union cannot function effectively without offering voters real choices in European elections. As such, under the proposed new constitutional treaty, EU political parties will have legal identity and clearer cut financial status.[68]

The attributes and operations of the European Union are neither those of a federation of states nor simply an organization for cooperation between governments. It is a unique evolution among certain old Westphalian states. These states pool their sovereignty in order to gain strength and world influence none of them could have as individual states and also create an economic unit that is more competitive against other forces acting in the world economic system. Pooling sovereignty means that member-states delegate some of their decision making powers to shared supra-national institutions they have created so that decisions on specific matters of joint interest can be democratically made at the European level.[69] State members, in practice, have voluntarily given up aspects of their sovereignty to a new supranational entity that exercises the will of the people of Europe rather the interests of the member-states. The European Parliament exercises democratic supervision over the other European institutions.

These European institutions also have oversight responsibilities over national institutions of member-states. The domains in which the supranational European Union institutions have powers that override those of the members keep growing and widening as the Union consolidates. The European Commission is the politically independent institution that represents and upholds the interests of the European as a whole. It is the driving force within the Union's institutional system: it proposes legislation, policies and programs of action and it is responsible for implementing the decisions of the Parliament and the Council.[70] The European Commission has the principal responsibility of enforcing European law. It is described as the "Guardian of the Treaties". This implies that

...the Commission, together with the Court of Justice, is responsible for making sure EU law is properly applied in all member states. If it finds that an EU country is not applying an EU law, and therefore not meeting its legal obligations, the Commission takes steps to put the situation right. First, it launches a legal process called the 'infringement procedure'. This involves sending the government an official letter,... If this procedure fails to put things right, the Commission must then refer the matter to the Court of Justice, which has the power to impose penalties. The Court's judgments are binding on the member states and the EU institutions[71]

William Pfaff draws attention to the centrality of moral considerations in the evolution of the European Union. He notes that the initial impetus for the creation of the Franco-German Coal and Steel agreement was perceived as a "matter of morality" by both Robert Schuman, the French Foreign Minister who sent Jean Monnet to Germany, and Chancellor Konrad Adeneaur of Germany in 1951. He notes that initial moral commitment did not wane as the expansion of the European Union to Greece in 1981 and Spain and Portugal in 1986 was driven by moral convictions that Europe had to include the nation at the source of European civilization, Greece, and the two countries that had just awakened from rightist dictatorships. Further, Pfaff observes that

...the moral argument for incorporating the former Soviet states of Central and Eastern Europe has been: How can we exclude them after all that they had been through?[72]

This highlights the changing character and ground rules of the post-modern state. Unlike its modern-state counterpart which continues to operate on the assumption that states exist in an amoral environment and prey on each other, the environment of the post-modern state is mitigated by emerging moral imperatives that often significantly influence policy and relations between constituent units of that sub-system of post-modern states.

THE IMPACT OF CULTURE SHIFT

The radical transformations of state and society resulted from what Ronald Inglehart has described as inter-generational culture shift. Indeed, rather than narrow national identities which are associated with the modern state, the new generation is conscious of its trans national identities as Europeans, rather than as only French or German. Inglehart has postulated that following unprecedented levels of economic and physical security achieved in the most industrialized societies, the values of affluent communities began to move away from concern about material security to higher post-materialist values.

The post-war phenomenon rested on the different environment and material conditions under which the younger generation was brought up. The values of this generation thus shifted away from materialism. Society has also become more liberal. Culture shift and the multiple identities it spawned have impacted on the state by weakening the nation-nationality-state nexus as the individual and society are increasingly conscious and approve of a multiplicity of widening identities. These are translated into a readiness on the part of society to trade in the large aspects of state sovereignty to concretize their new identities. Paradoxically, the trade-ins are promoted by the state which sees this as a form of adaptation in the new global system. Therefore a harmony of interest exists between the evolving post modern state and the expanding consciousness of its societies and individuals.

GLOBALIZATION AND THE EVOLUTION OF THE POST-MODERN STATE

At the economic level, the process of globalization has rendered small markets constituted by the modern state relatively unviable. States as economic units that have large markets and enjoy economies of scale have advantage over small political and economic spaces in the competitive world of a globalized economy. There is thus the pressure on mature modern states to integrate their economies, widen their markets and create monetary zones, and adopt policies that secure the interests of their widening societies. The development of multinational business conglomerates across state boundaries has raised the issue of control to protect international consumers and international society that form the bulk of their clientele. Indeed, no one single state is powerful enough to regulate the activities of these economic behemoths. The average modern state is thus fast losing its claims to being a viable economic unit. Many of them, especially in Europe, have opted to increase the powers of supranational institutions as regulatory mechanisms in the globalized world. Three of the most important bodies of the European Union focus on economic matters and the protection of the workplace and work-related rights of its citizens. These are the European Economic and Social Committee which expresses the opinion of organized civil society on economic and social issues: the European Central Bank which is responsible for monetary policy and managing the euro currency; and the European Investment Bank that helps to achieve EU objectives by financing investment projects.[73]

In a world evolving through increasing convergence of common interests and the evolution of an international society and a clearly discernible corpus of norms, values and principles on which there are common universal understandings, war as a policy instrument in the hands of the modern state to force a solution of its own on other states is not perceived as a legitimate enterprise. Many mechanisms have been put in place by the international society to check the unfettered use of war by as an instrument of inter-state intercourse by the modern state. Above all, unbridled use of force or the external deployment of power is no longer amoral. Power is perceived positively as an instrument to consolidate the morality of an emergent international community of the global community and the international society, rather than an international community of an aggregation of states.

The deployment of the instrument of war by states that insist on going to war is expected to be moderated by moral considerations for the welfare of the societies of the belligerent states. The protagonists, especially the power with the upper hand, must give bread to and arrange shelter for the victims of their bombing campaigns as the United States was forced to acknowledge in dislodging the Taliban hosts of the Al Qaida movement from Afghanistan. International politics of the state has ceased to be amoral in an international community conscious of itself as a global village or an emerging conglomeration of human societies. The cumulative implication of these developments is the evolution of a post-realist post-statist global environment that is driving the acquisition of new traits by certain mature modern states. In the post-materialist, post-realist, post-statist, globalized world, the social construction of the state is being redefined and perceptions of the construction of the mature state is along the lines of the post-modern states, whose contours have been highlighted above. These states that combine attributes that essentially repudiate the fundamental assumptions of modern statehood are conceptually identified as post-modern states.

Against the dictums of the modern Westphalian state is the emergence of new elements that are driving the radical transformations of the character of some mature modern states into post-modern states. The implications of the voluntary diminution of state sovereignty are revolutionary. These include the rise of multiple centers of authority, the widening of political boundaries, the building of larger political units that are co-terminus with the expanding economic spaces, the broadening and deepening of the powers of supra national institutions with legislative, judicial and executive functions, as ell as the increasing cultivation of a consciousness and acceptance of different identities at varying levels instead of the single national identity associated with societies in the modern state. The aggregation of state and national interests as common policy of a new collective entity implied in this new arrangement reflects the progressive transformation of the modern state into a post-modern state at another level in the continuing evolution that began with Westphalia. This revolutionary character of the transformations involved is underlined by the changing nature of mature modern states as power, the most potent symbol of national sovereignty, is being surrendered to a new supranational authority. Humanitarian military interventions have become one of the central tasks of the armed forces in the era of the post-modern state. To back this commitment, emerging post-modern states in Europe are seeking to develop a military establishment with a European central command and control to consolidate the birth of a "European public consciousness".[74]

It would appear that the modern state, impelled by certain imperatives, including the unending competition in the inter-state system, the unfeasibility of relatively small and medium-sized political and economic units in the global competition and evolving geo-strategic considerations, seek to adapt to the new situation through the acquisition of certain new characteristics in order to survive the emerging challenges in the global inter-state system. These factors have forced many states, mainly in Europe, that are also the oldest of the early states that had evolved from Treaty of Westphalia, to progressively surrender chunks of their sovereignty to the common cause so that Europe can act as a powerful distinct voice in global politics.[75] In adapting to the challenges and pressures of the global system, a new form of state has evolved, with distinct characteristics that are qualitatively different from the modern state. This is the post-modern state.

Yet, not all modern states have demonstrated the willingness to follow the evolutionary advancement to post-modernism. The impetus has been a collection of factors and opportunities that are presented by the history and geo-strategic and political circumstances of each state. In the least, a community of post-modern states must share certain attributes and a long history of an intertwined fate of its peoples. In a sense, the emergence of the post-modern state in Europe is another systemic reform in the search for systemic equilibrium. Against this background, it may be postulated that the most powerful of the modern state system, the hegemons of the system, have resisted the forces propelling transformation into post-modern states. These are the entrenched modern states represented by the United States of America and the Peoples' Republic of China. The United States of America, under George W. Bush, exhibits all the defining elements of the modern state. France, Germany, Belgium, and to some extent, Britain as the pivots of the 15-member European Union, would reflect the classic characteristics of a post-modern state.

MODERN VERSUS POST-MODERN STATES

The qualitative aspects of the post-modern state include the transformation of societies. The continuous evolution of the Westphalian state has produced two conceptually distinct genres of the state. These are the modern and post-modern states. The former represents the classic notion of the state as it is generally understood by political analysts. The modern state is the closest approximation of the state as elaborated by the Montevideo Convention of statehood. The modern state is defined by the consolidated nature of its sovereignty located in one sole authority within the territorial confines of the state. The post-modern state is an evolved genre of the modern state. As such, it has begun to repudiate some of the defining characteristics of the modern state. Sovereignty is whittled [76]down as the state willingly begins to accept the emergence of complementary centers of power outside its territory that participate in elaborating and enforcing policy in areas that traditionally had been defined as exclusively internal affairs of the sovereign state. Catherine Field has characterized the impulses of the transformation of modern states into post-modern political entities as seismic in nature, as parochial perceptions give way to visions that leap across borders. The emergence of the post-modern state has resulted from a massive culture shift in society.

The adaptations leading to transformation to the post-modern state are expressed at the level of state institutions and the shift in culture in society. Indeed, the continuous evolution of the Westphalian state has been driven by emerging new and harmonized understandings on a whole range of philosophical concerns that underpin the organization of society and an expanding identity consciousness, including the enlarged horizons of societies and the radically altered world views of international society. As highlighted by Catherine Field, it is the increasing widening and density of transnational social networks traversing traditional national boundaries, which are strengthened by the development of common economic, political, and military institutions that develop around these expanding worldviews that drive the transformation of the modern state into a post-modern state.

In essence, while the modern state remains largely relatively autonomous, inward looking, narrowly focused on its geo-political and economic space, the post-modern state is cultivating strong social capital across international frontiers and cultures and working on the basis of more universalizing principles. There exists one locus of sovereign authority and power in political and economic decision making in the modern state. In the post-modern state, there is a hierarchy of centers of power to which the state has voluntarily relinquished important elements of its sovereign authority. There are thus diffused centers of power in the post-modern state. The United States is an entrenched modern state. The hallmark of this is its unilateralist inclinations[77] that reflect the undiluted pursuit of its national interests and consideration for its reputation for power as a state in its relations with other members of the state system. The neo-conservative bloc in the Bush administration, exemplifying the prominent articulators of these principles, held multilateral organizations such as the United Nations in deep contempt and suspicion as they sought to pursue national strategic objectives of the US administration unrestrained by international opinion and sensibilities. The unrestricted projection of national power was seen as the most effective route to achieve American national strategic goals, which in 2003 focused on achieving regime change in Iraq. Neo-conservatives in the Bush administration defined national interests as extending beyond geographic security and material concerns to the spread of democratic ideology. Another strand of hardliners, categorized as "exceptionalists" - ideologues, idealists, and intellectuals- under the broad rubric of neo-conservatism, believed that America's power and 'rightness' gave it both the authority and the responsibility to set the rules for the rest of the world.[78] In short, the neo-conservatives sought to remake the world in the image of the United States and reserved the rights to pursue that agenda as it suited the hegemon of the post Cold War World. The neo-conservatives saw the world exclusively through the lenses of American interests. What has been described as the Bush Doctrine essentially identifies

> ...the first duty of the United States Government remains what it always has been: to protect American people and American interests. It is an enduring American principle that this duty obligates the government to anticipate ad counter threats, using all elements of national power, before the threats can do grave damage. The greater the threat, the greater the risk of inaction-and the more compelling the case for taking anticipatory action to defend ourselves, even if uncertainty remains as to the time and place of the enemy's attack.

> ...To forestall or prevent such hostile act by our adversaries, the United States will, if necessary, act preemptively in exercising our inherent right of self–defense.[79]

The Bush doctrine was perceived by some as controversial and a dangerous deviation from the foreign policy of the United States. Its proponents justify this by arguing that an America that is scrupulously deferential to international rules, studiously avoiding flexing its muscles in economic areas of special interests to major segments of its electorate, is obediently ready to limit its own sovereignty, and is prepared to place its military under international legal jurisdiction might not be the power of the last resort to prevent global anarchy.[80] Yet, it is precisely for these reasons and particularly the rationalizations implied in the justifications that the United States remains an entrenched modern state.

The emergence of the post-modern state is marked by the increasing regulation of hitherto internal affairs of the state by supranational regulatory mechanisms over which none of the contracting members of the wider community has a determinant control. As such, one distinguishing difference of post-modern state from the modern is the narrowness of the worldviews of the modern state which contrasts with the expansive social and political identities that are dominant in the post-modern state. This makes the post-modern state integrationist and accommodating. The post-modern state system revolves around increasing collaboration among its members, unlike the modern state that is focused on war without end. The emergence of the post-modern state thus began to challenge, if not outrightly repudiate, traditional conceptions of the iron-clad sovereign rights of the state. In this way, modern states, under certain conditions, give up their sovereign rights in exchange for other benefits that strengthen a new pluralist political identity and an increasingly widening of the economic space. This follows the advanced shift of cultures in society leading to a wholesale shift of political culture in certain adjacent societies that encourage the expanding identities that are coterminous with newly emerging larger geo- political and economic spaces. It is this pressure from below that drives the policy process in a manner that is unfamiliar within the setting of the modern state.

As a result of the evolution of the core values underpinning the operation of the post-modern state system, there have emerged clear differences between the modern state and the post-modern state about leadership required in the global system. Many analysts argue that the European Union is unable to offer world leadership and that this leaves the United States on its own to make the big decisions.[81] Yet, it would appear that the profound questions of the moment revolve around the kind of leadership the global system requires in the epoch of the post-modern state. From the perspective of the post-modern state, the principles on which the modern state is founded are anachronistic at this point in the evolution of the Westphalian system. A leadership based on that regime would be problematic not only to post-modern states but also to the international societies in post-colonial and pre-Westphalian states. The turbulence of the long march of the Westphalian state system up to the end of the cold war would appear to have forced a reappraisal of the concept of statehood and its underlying axioms by the earliest and oldest members of the modern state system. This is partly responsible for the repudiation of the principles that turned the last century into years of horrible wars in Old Europe. That regime is perceived as unable to make or sustain peace among states and societies in the new millennium. Paradoxically, consolidated modern states in their tenacious refusal to acknowledge the lessons of Old Europe have become revisionist actors within the context of the emerging new dispensation. Post-modern states and their societies, characterized by their integrationist and widening orbit of layered identities, have moved beyond the single-minded focus on power of the era of the modern state.

IMPLICATIONS OF THE EMERGENCE OF THE POST-MODERN STATE

In this manner the post-modern state would appear to be continuing the unceasing long march of the Westphalian state system to a new destination. For now, the struggle of the organizing principles of the old modern state and emergent post-modern ideologies on the organization of state, society and economies is bound to reflect itself in stormy trans Atlantic relations for some time to come. This raises some profound questions about the validity of the very framework in which the modern state and the post-modern state are condemned to live and work together. Few indicators in the past offer clues on the nature of the difficult processes that lie ahead in the continuing evolution of the Westphalian state system into a new form. The state system is undergoing revolutionary transformations without the agency of a revolutionary power of state per se. It is a revolutionary epoch driven by the very force of ideas and universal principles that are organic and that have rendered long established principles and axioms that drove the modern state system obsolete, if not dangerous. As Henry Kissinger notes, whatever else a revolutionary power may achieve it tends to erode, if not the legitimacy of the international order, at least, the restraint with which such an order operates.[82] At the beginning of the new millennium, the revolutionary transformation affects the very conception of international order and the nature, if not the structure, of the international system or the state system itself.

Principles are central to every revolutionary situation and discourse because the extant regime defines the sets of implicit or explicit principles, norms, rules and decision-making process around which actors' expectations converge in given areas of international relations at a given period. The revolutionary principles governing the management of the internal affairs and its integrationist response to the impulses of the external environment are recasting international order in peculiar ways. In challenging the validity of the old governing principles of the sovereign both in its internal affairs and setting stringent constraints on the external deployment of the powers of this old sovereign, the emerging new principles are eroding the convergence on the fundamentals in the unrestrained exercise of sovereignty by the modern state. As a result, the units of the inter-state system in the post cold war are not similar. They are not like units.

The emerging post modern state is thus conceptually distinct from the modern state, even if they both belong to a common Western civilization. Disputes in this international system would now revolve around the validity of the defined ends of the various kinds of Westphalian state that have emerged, and particularly the legitimacy of the ends and means of the modern states vis a vis other states that have repudiated those ends and those means associated with Old Europe and inherited and defended by the modern state principally expressed in the United States of America. The struggle between the modern state and the post-modern state is already doctrinal. The unending clashes of Germany and France with their closest ally, the United States, and the dramatic opposition over the legitimacy of the Iraq war demonstrated the incompatibility of the guiding principles and frameworks that drive policy in the post-modern state and the modern state. Historically acting in the relative margins of the sanguine horrors of Old Europe brought about by the organizing principles of the modern state, the United States is fixated and entrenched in its narrow nationalism and its unbridled pursuit of power and a hegemonic agenda. The United States, a classic modern state, is untouched or unfazed by the new doctrine that has evolved as Europe works out new doctrines and principles of state and society that must assure it the long-term peace that has always eluded it.

The post-modern state is work in progress that reflects the task of constructing a new international human order based on universal moral truths that are perceived to be far superior to the cold abstractions on which the claims of the centrality of the sovereignty of the modern state in human affairs rest. The post-modern state promises to be the vehicle for the concretization of a new global order. The ideals of the evolving post-modern state are by now well familiar. The evolution of its principles has thrown into bold relief the fragility and proneness to war of the organizing principles of the modern state. It is early nineteenth century again. Henry Kissinger would probably observe that time has finally accomplished the labours of Metternich as Europeans, with the emergence of the post-modern state, have institutionalized the deeper consciousness that the things that they share are much more fundamental than narrow parochial labours conferred on the little modern state. In the European post-modern state system, differences are recognized, but the contemporary European state is basically a vessel holding local variations of a widening and expansive greater and universal whole. In this new world, the old conception of state glory and power infused into the sovereign modern state has lost its relevance, vitality and validity.

The modern state is hard pressed to justify the continued legitimacy of its operative axioms. Notwithstanding the spirited efforts of the United States, which was a late entrant into the world of the modern state system, and indeed a transplant of sorts or a mechanical recreation of the modern state in the new world, the future of the Westphalian state system, it would appear, belongs to the post-modern state. Leadership in this direction is being provided by those old and mature polities that derive their statehood from the original Westphalian historical process.

Notes

1. Chandra Lekha Sriram, "International Law, International Relations Theory and Post-Atrocity Justice: Towards a Genuine Dialogue," *International Affairs* 82, no. 3, May 2006, p. 469.

2. Chandra Lekha Sriram, ibid., p.470.

3. Chandra Lekha Sriram, ibid., p.470.

4. Philippe Sands, *Lawless world: America and the making and breaking of global rules from FDR's Atlantic Charter to George W. Bush's illegal war,* Viking, New York, 2005, p. xi.

5. Philippe Sands, ibid., p. xvii.

6. Philippe Sands, ibid., p. 13.

7. Philippe Sands, ibid., p.1.

8. Philippe Sands, ibid., p.xvii.

9. Philippe Sands, ibid., p.10.

10. T. R. Reid, *The United States of Europe: The New Superpower and the End of American Supremacy*, Penguin Books, New York, 2004, p. 3.

11. T. R. Reid, ibid., p. 16.

12. H. D. S. Greenway, "The Diagnosis: Narcissism," *International Herald Tribune*, February 3, 2004, p. 6.

13. Noam Chomsky, *Hegemony or Survival: America's Quest for Global Dominance*, Metropolitan Books, New York, 2003, p. 3.

14. A.F.K. Organski and Jacek Kugler, *The War Ledger*, University of Chicago Press, Chicago, 1980.

15. Henry A. Kissinger, *A World Restored: Metternich, Castlereagh and the Problems of Peace, 1812-1822*, Houghton Miflin Company, Boston, 1973, p. 1.

16. Henry A. Kissinger, ibid.

17. Henry A. Kissinger, ibid., p. 3.

18. Zbigniew Brzezinski, *The Choice: Global Domination or Global Leadership*, Basic Books, New York, 2004, p. 15.

19. T. R. Reid, op. cit., p. 23.

20. John F. Burns, Panel asks how Britain Got Involved in Iraqi War, The New York Times (Europe), November 4, 2009.

21. Jonathan Power, "United Nations: Much maligned, but much needed," *International Herald Tribune*, February 26, 2004, p. 6.

22. Jonathan Power, ibid., p. 6.

23. Phillippe Sands, op. cit., p. xix.

24. T. R. Reid, op. cit.., p. 15.

25. Sergei Karaganov, "The Perils of Pressuring Russia: Brussels vs Moscow," *International Herald Tribune*, February 25, 2004, p. 6.

26. Mark Leonard, "One Year Later: Europe's Debt to Rumsfeld," *International Herald Tribune*, February 28-29, 2004, p. 6.

27. T. R. Reid, op. cit., p. 16.

28. Martin Jacques, "Divided We Stand," *The Guardian*: http://books.guardian. co.uk/print/0.3858.4871153-99793.00.html, accessed on March 3, 2004, p. 1.

29. Patrick Tyler, "Britain Drops Secrets Case against Linguist," *International Herald Tribune*, February 26, 2004, p. 1.

30. Patrick Tyler, ibid.

31. Mark Leonard, op. cit., p. 6.

32. Richard Ned Lebow, "Fear, Interest and Honour: Outlines of a Theory of International Relations," *Intenational Affairs* 82, no. 3, 2006, p. 438.

33. Jonathan Power, "Europe Shouldn't Compete with the U.S.," *International Herald Tribune*, January 22, 2004, p. 6.

34. Noam Chomsky, op. cit., page 15.

35. Noam Chomsky, ibid.

36. Martin Jacques, op. cit., p. 1.

37. Martin Jacques, ibid., p. 2.

38. Noam Chomsky, op. cit.

39. Noam Chomsky, ibid., p. 47.

40. Martin Jacques, op. cit., p. 2.

41. Richard Ned Lebow, op. cit., p. 444.

42. Richard Ned Lebow, ibid., p. 445.

43. Richard Ned Lebow, ibid.., p. 445.

44. T. R. Reid, op. cit.

45. Sarah Lyall, "For Young Europeans, Identity Questions," *International Herald Tribune*, March 5, 2004, p. 10. Lyall quotes Adam Pulchart, a student of European Studies at the Charles University in Prague.

46. Sarah Lyall, ibid.

47. "New Spanish Leader may pull out of Iraq," *The Associated Press*: http://www. msnbc.msn.com/id/4522638, accessed on February 16, 2004.

48. Andy Eckhardt, "Old Europe Unrepentant," *MSNBC*: http://www.mnsbc.msn. com.id/4379560, accessed on March 14, 2004

49. Andy Eckhardt, "Old Europe Unrepentant," *MSNBC*: http://www.mnsbc.msn. com.id/4379560, accessed on March 14, 2004.

50. Report of the Copenhagen Council of The European Union of 12-13 December 2002, Brussels 29 January, 2003.

51. *International Herald Tribune*, March 12, 2004, p. 4.

52. *The Economist*, February 7, 2004, p. 29.

53. Elaine Sciolino, "Same-Sex Marriage Ties the French in Knots," *International Herald Tribune*, May 21, 2004, p. 3.

54. "Another thirty Years War in the making?" *The Economist*, May 22 –28, 2004, p. 45-46.

55. Europa, "The EU at a glance" http://158.169.50.70/institutions/index_en.htm

56. Noam Chomsky, op. cit., p. 131.

57. Catherine Field, "Wrangle over EU Constitution Masks a Seismic Shift," *International Herald Tribune*, October 31, 2003.

58. Noam Chomsky, op. cit., p. 11.

59. H. D. S. Greenway, op. cit.

60. H. D. S. Greenway, ibid.

61. T. R. Reid, op. cit., p. 125.

62. Guy Coq, "Why France Values its Religious Neutrality," *International Herald Tribune*, February 2, 2004, p. 12.

63. Catherine Field, op. cit., p. 4.

64. "Greens Meet to start up a Europe Wide Party," *International Herald Tribune*, February 21-22, 2004, p. 3.

65. John Palmer, "Let Europeans Help Choose EU Leaders," *International Herald Tribune*, March 6-7, 2004, p. 8.

66. *International Herald Tribune*, February 21-22, 2004, p. 3.

67. William Pfaff, "Expansion Jeopardizes EU'S Founding Vision- Redefining Europe," *International Herald Tribune*, February 21-22, 2004.

68. John Palmer, op. cit.

69. Europa, "European Union institutions and other bodies," http://158.169.50.70/institutions/index_en.htm, accessed on March 12, 2004.

70. Europa, "European Union institutions and other bodies," ibid.

71. Europa, "European Union institutions and other bodies," ibid.

72. John Palmer, op. cit.

73. Europa, "European Union institutions and other bodies," ibid.

74. Jonathan Power, "Europe Shouldn't Compete with the U.S.," op. cit., p. 6. Power attributes the phrase to Valery Giscard d'Estaing, former President of France and President of the European Convention.

75. Catherine Field, op. cit., p. 4.

76. Catherine Field, ibid., p. 4.

77. Jonathan Power, op. cit.

78. David Rothkopf, cited in Karen de Young, Soldier, the Life of Colin Powell, (Alfred A. Knopf New York, 2006) p. 322.

79. National Security Strategy of the United States, 2006.

80. Zbiniew Brzezinski, op. cit., p. 94.

81. Andy Eckardt, op. cit., p. 5.

82. Henry Kissinger, op. cit., p. 3.

Chapter 4

THE SOURCES OF CONFLICT IN THE POST-COLONIAL AFRICAN STATE SYSTEM

Conflicts inhere in the multiple instrumental character of the post-colonial African state. At one level, the post-colonial African state is a vehicle for the articulation of the parochial interests of contending groups within the socio-economic and political space who act in concert with respective affiliated trans-national groups in the intermestic environment in which the state is located. The goal of the struggle is to dominate the space. At another level, the post-colonial state is an instrument for the advancement of the hegemonic agendas of powerful elite forces in the international state system. These powerful forces collude with internal forces whose strategic interests are served by this coopera-tion, to determine the direction in which the post-colonial state should evolve. Through the joint actions of the international forces and their allies within the state and its intermestic environment, the hegemonic force imposes its vision on the post-colonial state. The interaction between these multiple forces, either as separate elements or acting in concert, evolves into conflict. This interaction also determines the dynamics of the conflict that is so generated and impacts on its outcome.

Conflicts in the post-colonial state may thus result from competition at the first level around the struggle for domination by internal forces and their transnational allies. It may also emanate from or be compounded by the actions of second level systemic actors struggling to consolidate their historical control over that state. In either case, the dynamics and trajectories of conflicts that are generated in the post-colonial state are determined by the interaction between the forces at the two levels, variously in collaboration, or in opposition, to achieve certain strategic outcomes in that conflict. Finally, the struggle implicates the people who create leaderships as agents that at one level articulate the political goals of the protagonist groups and at another level define those partisan political goals in an interactive process between the people and their leaders.

The sources of conflict in the post-colonial state are thus first found in its peculiar internal structure and, by implication, the structure of its intermestic external environment. This environment is constituted by the state system in the immediate sub-region, the collection of contending forces made up of groups whose territorial spread traverses the boundaries of the states in the system and their loyalties are primarily to the group than to the state, as well as the proto states that may periodically exist within the various post-colonial states. The post-colonial African state lumps together and attempts to superimpose an order on disparate groups that are distinguished by wide cultural and value dissonance and often traditionally hostile to one another. The internal construction of the post-colonial state and the ordering principles elicited by this peculiar construction impact on the structure of its inter-state system and the definition of the critical ground rules of inter-state relations. The immediate consequences of the problematic structures of both the post-colonial state and its state system are the existence of objective, transnational and extraterritorial stakeholders who perceive legitimate interests to protect in the outcomes of the strategic interactions of its domestic processes. These interests include the emergence of a configuration of power that is favorable to this transnational community from the conflict(s) that rage for the control of the political space by contending internal forces within the state and its immediate inter-state system. The structural attributes and the internal processes of the state therefore impact on the nature of relationships generated in the inter-state system constituted by such states. The nature of relationships elicited by the structure of the inter-state system and external environment also impact on the internal characteristic of the post-colonial state in an interactive process.

Strategic interaction among groups is characterized by competition for control of the state as the state sets the terms of competition among groups. Accordingly, the pursuit of particularistic objectives often becomes embodied in competing visions of just, legitimate, and appropriate political orders.[1] The political process becomes rivalries of contending groups to control resources and dominate state policy as the communal agenda of the competing entities, incorporating ethnic cousins outside the territorial demarcations of the post-colonial state. This generates clear security imperatives that drive the struggle of the constituent groups for the appropriation of the state. It is imperative that the political process is a struggle without safeguards for all the forces implicated. The zero-sum struggle without safeguards is unending. Armed hostilities, which often break out, represent the most intense stage of the struggle.

At this first level, the security dynamic is also an interactive one between the post-colonial state and its immediate external environment. This interactive dynamic implicates not only constituent groups in the states, but also allied stakeholders in the intermestic external environment who are directly and actively engaged in the struggle. Conflict in the post-colonial state is thus a clash of interests among various transnational cultural forces and their communal blocs whose activities transcend its borders and challenge the civil order of the post-colonial state. Conflicts in the post-colonial state are thus hardly internal to the state entity. This process leads not only to the weakening of the post-colonial state, but also undermines the very state system in the immediate neighborhood. Yet, collective fears of the future arise when the weakened state loses its ability to arbitrate between the constituent groups or provide credible guarantees of protection for groups. As David A. Lake and Donald Rothchild show

> State weakness, whether it arises incrementally out of competition between groups or from extremists actively seeking to destroy ethnic peace, is a necessary condition for violent ethnic conflict to erupt.[2]

The political system in the post-colonial African state environment is most prone to violence when one constituent group perceives an opportunity to bring to an end the domination of another group. This is often the case at the end of a one-party state system, or through the death of the charismatic leader or the imposition by external forces leading to a sudden opening of the political space for truly competitive democratization of the process. Deprived of the overwhelming influence of the often cultic and charismatic sway of the old leader that drove the system, the stage is set for competition unlimited in scope by all the contesting groups. Often the single party, the instrument for the old leader, begins to implode through its internal contradictions as well as its inability to harmonize the parochial interests of all the contending forces that begin to publicly show dissent to established principles and modes of thinking that were considered sacrosanct. Often a conjuncture of factors may simply unravel the myth or delegitimize the old leader and his regime and open the political space to competitive contests.

In the ensuing post-one-party one-man state system (POPS/POMS), especially within the context of an incipient democracy, the political power of groups is often determined by the size of its population. Demographic structure acquires significant political importance in determining what groups have the population to win elections. This is exemplified in Congo Brazzaville's post-Marxist civil war that began with the delegitimization of the Sassou Nguesso-led Parti Travalleurs Congolaise (PCT) by the country's national sovereign conference, the Kabila war in Zaire that began with the demystification of Sese Seko Mobutu by the sovereign national conference, the crisis of succession in Cote d'Ivoire in post-Houphouet Boigny that degenerated into a civil war and the emergence of an Ivorian proto state, the two and half decades of war in post-hegemonic Liberia following Samuel Doe's April 1980 coup d'etat that toppled the True Whig party that had been in power since the founding of the Republic in 1847, as well as the crisis generated by the ascension to power of Faure Eyadema in Togo following the demise of his father, Gnassingbe Eyadema. The leaders of these countries had ruled for over a decade and half before being forced out of office mostly through death. Before then, access to power was determined by historical factors, including the disposition of the colonial power toward the various contending groups. The leadership of virtually all francophone states in sub-Saharan Africa were validated or put in office by France.

As a result of the unending pervasive contest for control of the post-colonial state, regime changes are very unstable for the political process because they are invariably transitions of power from one contending group to another. The struggle for control may also lead to the consolidation of an old hegemony. The two outcomes are often violently contested. The process of regime change has often sparked the start of violent conflicts as contending forces see the process as a unique opportunity to wrest power and control. These changes may be ushered through revolutionary means such as a coup d'etat. Such coups are designed to dislodge the dominant group from power as in the September 2002 attempt of the Forces Nouvelles in Cote d'Ivoire to usher in a northern-dominated regime. It may also be through democratic means in which elections are required to legitimize the consolidation of the rule of the dominant forces or the power transition to another power-contending group or force in the political system as the experience was with the President Pascal Lissouba in Congo Brazzaville. President Lissouba who hails from the NIBOLEK region of the south overthrew a hegemony of the northern-dominated Parti Congolaise du Travaslleur (PCT).

In the nominally democratic scenario in the post-colonial political process which is marked by the absence of commitment to any social or ideological principles, the population structure, especially along group lines, becomes a critical indicator of the potential configuration of power between the constituent forces. The political power of groups is determined by demography, the resources available to each group, and their capacity to organize effectively. More powerful groups have a larger say in setting the terms of the contract.[3] The struggle for the appropriation of the state among contending forces leads to the weakening of the state and undermines its capacity to function to protect the interests of all. This breeds pervasive insecurity in the political process and leads the constituent units to factor the ensuing security dilemma into their strategic calculus as they interact with other contestants for the domination of the social, political and economic space. The national process becomes a zero-sum game and the state a totalitarian one.

In the face of the weaknesses of the state in the post-colonial state system and the complex linkages created by the intermestic character of the external environment, a domino effect is set off when any one state in the sub-region implodes as the violence, in time, spreads across adjacent borders. The complex linkages between the contending domestic forces and their transnational allies across international borders and the perceived legitimacy of the stakes of these transnational forces in the affairs of the various states in which they are represented imply that there are no affairs strictly internal to and limited to each formally demarcated sovereign state whose communities are inextricably linked. The conflicts in Sierra Leone, Liberia and Cote d'Ivoire, Guinea Bissau and instability in Guinea are all linked and constitute a wide orbit of instability in the sub-region. The linkages reflect the sub-regional flow of sociological affinities across state boundaries, and the alliances of the peoples in the various states do not necessarily mesh with the policy of the state.

As the orbits of conflicts in West Africa and Central Africa have amply demonstrated, post-colonial states do not just implode, whole sub-regions or sub-state systems are ultimately engulfed in violent political hostilities. The conflict which began in Liberia in December 1989 through the invasion of Nimba county by the Charles Taylor-led National Patriotic Front of Liberia eventually engulfed Sierra Leone with the rise of Fonday Sankor's Revolutionary United Front (RUF) in 1999, the war in Guinea Bissau in 1997 and an insurrection of the Patriotic Movement of Cote d'Ivoire (MPCI) led by Ibrahim Coulibaly in September 2002.

At another level, the potential for domestic conflict also inheres in the nature of the relations of the post-colonial state with elite state actors in the global state system. These powerful state actors seek to sustain a determinant role in the domestic and external affairs of the post-colonial state for their global economic and security interests.

At both levels, the post-colonial state is deployed as an instrument for the articulation of narrow interests of contending partisan domestic units and as a satellite actor and proxy in the service of the interests of elite actors in the international system. These two factors interact in a myriad of ways to generate instability or conflict, and determine its trajectory, manner and outcome.

The concrete reality of the transnational character of the affinities of autonomous communities of power juxtaposed with the post-colonial state within the same geo-political space underpins the evolving governing principles that define interactions in the post colonial state system. In a conventional international system constituted by modern states, the ordering principle is characterized by its decentralized and anarchic nature because it lacks order and organization. The inter-state system is formed by the co-acting of the units and maintained on a principle of self help[4]. In this scenario, a state is conceived of as a single rational actor with undisputed control over the territory it claims and uncontested sovereignty and legitimacy of rule. The interactions of these states form the structure of the inter-state system. The structure is also determined by the functional differentiation and the extent of power capabilities of the respective states. The structure of the system changes with changes in the distribution of power across the system's units. These changes in structure alter expectations about how the units will behave and the outcomes that interaction among them will produce. Kenneth Waltz highlights this definition of structure accordingly

- Structures are defined, first, according to the principle by which a system is ordered. Systems are transformed if one ordering principle replaces another. To move from the anarchic realm is to move from one system to another,
- Structures are defined, second, by the specification of functions of differentiated units. Hierarchic systems change if functions are differently defined and allotted. For anarchic systems, the criterion of systems change derived from the second part of the definition drops out since the system is composed of like units.
- Structures are defined, third, by the distribution of capabilities across units. Changes in this distribution are changes of system whether the system be anarchic of a hierarchic one[5]"

STRUCTURE OF THE POST-COLONIAL AFRICAN STATE SYSTEM

As Patrick Chabal and Jean Pascal Daloz observe, the acuteness of Africa's crisis is such that defies the usual parameters of current political analysis[6]. The post colonial state is formally hierarchically ordered. Yet, the legitimacy of the state is perpetually contested and in many instances many loci of power exist side by side with the formal state. The existence of proto states at various levels of stateness within the post-colonial state and their demonstrated capacity to participate in international life are important radical departures from the conventional structure of the inter-state system and indeed, the state itself. These departures determine the contours of the external environment in which the inter-state system is embedded. The external environment is thus conceptually distinct from the interstate system. The inter-state system is however the central constituent of the structure of the external environment, yet the character of this environment is mainly defined by the presence of proto states and the flow of transnational interest groups across the formal frontiers of the state. These distinctions in the internal structure of the post-colonial state systems have radical implications. The formal state seeks the perpetuation of its structure as constituted, while the goal of the proto state is either to transform the structure of the state or to carve out a new autonomous political space from it. In instances, the proto states have been able to mobilize more powers of coercion than its challenger, the post-colonial state.

For the structure of the inter-state system, this means that the post-colonial African state system is constituted by functionally unlike units. A second implication is that the constituent units of this system, the post colonial state, are not hierarchically ordered all the way, since the supremacy of the central power, the formal state, is contested by embryonic states. These proto states are also effectively power-based non-governmental actors in the external environment of the post-colonial state. The state is also not a single rational actor. Owing to the informality of engagements defining relations between proto states and post-colonial African states in this external environment, the ground rules of the inter-state system and the external environment are not codified. In fact, the rules governing these engagements are often repudiated in public because their practical expressions often violate conventional international norms governing interaction among sovereign states. Nevertheless, they foster interactions that have critical implications for conflict in the post-colonial state and the inter-state system constituted by it.

The post-Cold War era has been marked by profound behavioral transformations that reflect increasing willingness of states in the post-colonial state system to be explicit with the informal rules governing inter-state relations. An essential character of conflicts in the post-colonial state since the end of the cold war has been the increasing deployment of cross-border partisan intervention by governmental and non-governmental units alike in these conflicts. Proto states in the post-colonial state system have also been emboldened to stake their claims and relevance in the Hobbesian inter-state environment. Proto states have entered into alliances with state actors on the basis of their permanent interests. They have deployed military force across international frontiers to fight on the side of government troops. The implications are that the structure of the post-colonial states system and its external environment, which proto states are part of, undermine the legitimacy of the post colonial state. The overt and unfettered participation of proto states in the external environment is grounded in the conflicting political goals of different transnational communities of power within the post colonial inter-state system. The danger posed by the transnational affinities of constituent units contesting the control of the state has a great influence on the behaviour of the post-colonial African state.

This character of the external environment thus influences the security calculus of the post-colonial state.

INTERMESTIC ENVIRONMENT

Qualitatively, the constraints posed by the intermestic external environment of the post-colonial state is different from those posed to the modern state by the structure of the normal Westphalian inter-state system. In any case, the structure of their respective state systems is different. The interplay of all these elements, namely the incongruity of the structure of the post-colonial state, its peculiar state system and external environment and the nature of relations between the post-colonial state and powerful elite state actors in the global inter-state system, gives conflicts in the post-colonial state their intermestic character. This intermestic character challenges the notion of conflicts in post-colonial states as simply civil war, for these wars have large currents and under-currents of participation by transnational stakeholders in the neighbourhood and external forces from the larger state system. Conflicts in post-colonial states are an expression of internal structural deficiencies as much as the problematic structures within their immediate sub-system. What many analysts have per-ceived as spill-over effects are indeed expressions of the intrinsic sub-systemic linkages to the violent conflicts that flare up in the various post-colonial states. Both the post-colonial state and its inter-state system are at once anarchic and hierarchically ordered.

Intermesticity thus refers to two qualitative attributes of the environment of the post-colonial state. It alludes first to the character of the external environ-ment that is created by the close juxtaposition of proto states and post-colonial states within the same geo-political space. Secondly, it captures the implication of the character of the external environment for the rules or governing prin-ciples of the post-colonial state system. It draws attention to the fact that while conflict in the state may play out within a discernible political space or the ter-ritory of one state, legitimate stakeholders and parties to the conflict can be found across its immediate frontiers. These extra-territorial stakeholders may or may not be direct participants in the ensuing armed hostilities of the conflict. Such direct engagement would depend on a host of other factors including the configuration of power and other structural considerations pertinent to the conflict. In extreme situations, the war may spill over into the territory of a neighbouring state and the armed hostilities fought outside the territorial con-fines of the post-colonial state objectively at war. In October 1997, one of the major subplots of the Laurent Kabilla-led rebellion of the Alliance of Demo-cratic Forces for the Liberation of the Congo (AFDLC) against the Mobutiste state of Zaire was the continuation of the Rwanda civil war in northern Zaire.

This war pitted the Tutsi-led Rwandese Patriotic Front government forces against the Rwandese Hutu militias (ex-FAR), the Hutu Interharamwe, constituted from the old Hutu government army, the Forces Armee d'Rwanda. The conflicts are, however, conventionally territorially contained within a delimited political space, but the interests at stake in the conflict are often not confined to one particular state.

The entanglement in these civil wars of fighters from neighboring countries has added a further layer of complexity and violence[7] to the character and structure of conflict. Harsch notes that West Africa was one region where multiple groups operated repeatedly across national borders. He illustrates as follows

> In 1989 rebel forces entered Liberia from neighbouring Guinea and Cote d'Ivoire. Then from Liberia, Charles Taylor, initially as warlord and later as President, backed the Revolutionary United Front (RUF) in its attacks against the government of Sierra Leone. At various times combatants from Liberia, Burkina Faso and other countries fought directly alongside the RUF. Later two new rebel groups opposed to Charles Taylor launched a second civil war in Liberia, initially striking from Guinea and Cote d'Ivoire and eventually prompting Mr. Taylor's departure in 2003.[8]

Citing the conclusions of a report of the UN Office of the Special Advisor on Africa, Harsch stresses that foreign fighters and armed groups that operate across borders are significant threats to regional stability in all areas where they exist in significant numbers.[9]

Conflict is thus inherent in the existence of competing informal power communities (outflows of constituent units of the post-colonial state across international frontiers) that transcend national boundaries along with formal power communities (formal states) where sovereignty is presumably located. The central authorities seek to project the power of autonomous sovereign political communities based on the objective power configuration in the formal states. Fragments of domestic and transnational communities of power occupying the same and adjacent political space or jostling within the same political space occupied by a system of power communities seek to articulate partisan interests of the entities of which they are a part of. The flow of transnational communities of power across the formal boundaries of the post-colonial state implicates many other interested groups outside the state, who represent problematic historical continuities, in the domestic affairs of the state. For these communities of power, the post-colonial African state is a myth and its boundaries fictional. This configuration of communal entities across international frontiers has practical implications for the evolution of political developments in the post-colonial African state and the immediate state system. These consequences are manifest in external interventions in so-called domestic conflicts in the state.

Filip De Boeck asserts that traditional actors are caught up in wider national and supra-national political and economic events and power games. Local cultures and their representatives seem to be sandwiched between, and made use of in, larger power struggles and interests that transcend the regional level. He asserts that these traditional forces are not just passive victims of larger forces imposed on them, but rather, in reality, a complex dialectics of power is at play in which both sides take part. De Boeck illustrates the impact of transnational communities in conflict situations through a personal experience in the Angola civil war. He narrates that in

> In the 1970s, the actual Luunda title holder, not yet enthroned and still living in Angola, openly supported Roberto Holden's FNLA, and after its disappearance from the Angolan political stage, started backing UNITA. When the MPLA killed one of his sons, and the future title holder himself got into trouble with the MPLA, because of his UNITA sympathies, he moved across the border, settled in Zaire, and was enthroned in 1984. Since his enthronement, he has grown into a strong and powerful chief, capable of not only strengthening traditional ties with other sub-regional titleholders, but also able to create contacts with administrative and political scene on a regional and trans-regional level.[10]

Anarchy is seen as one end of a continuum whose other end is marked by the presence of legitimate and competent government.[11]

John Mearsheimer has amplified the implications of anarchy for the behavior of states in the system. He writes:

> Add to this, the assumption that there is no central authority that a threatened state can turn to for help, and states have greater incentives to fear each other. Moreover there is no mechanism - other than possible self-interest of third parties- for punishing an aggressor. Because it is often difficult to deter potential aggressors, states have ample reasons to take steps to be prepared for war.... Political competition among states is a much more dangerous business than economic intercourse; it can lead to war, and war often means mass killings on the battlefield and even the mass murder of civilians.[12]

All states are constrained to operate in the inter-state system with these dangers in mind. Kenneth Waltz illuminates that anarchies are marked by the exact likeness of units and the determination of relations between units would be based on capabilities alone. No mechanisms of control of the activities relating to interaction between the units are expected. In hierarchies, the complete differentiation of parts and the full specification of their functions would produce a realm wholly of authority and power[13]. Although these are pure conceptual delineations, yet they capture the normative essences of the modern state and its state system. As earlier observed, there exists a good measure of anarchy in the post-colonial state leading to its perennial implosion. Its civil society is unpacified leading to the rise of proto states within the claimed territorial boundaries of the state. The hall mark of hierarchy, which is expressed in the differentiation of parts and the required specification of functions under a legitimate controlling authority, eludes the post colonial state.

THE POST-COLONIAL STATE AND ITS PROTO STATES

One critical element of differentiation in the post-colonial state is based on degrees of access to the center of power in the state. A series of rings that revolve around direct relationships to the group that has consolidated its appropriation and instituted its hegemony at the center constitutes the core of the state. The locations of the various groups on those concentric rings indicate the proximity and distances of contending groups to and from access to the state. The further away the ring is from the core, the more distant groups on those rings are from the state until the margins of the state are reached. Proto states are located further away from the rings that delineate the margins of the state into a zone of alienation that may also mark the beginnings of zones where rebellions are most likely. When a rebellion is proclaimed, armed hostilities commence and a rebel movement seizes control and begins to establish some semblance of administration in areas within national territories under its control, it has transformed itself into a proto state. Such rebel movements often enjoy overt or covert support from the communal entity from which it was launched and or, complicity from sympathetic state actors in the inter-state system.

In the post-Cold War era, proto states have been overtly engaged as allies of post-colonial regimes in conflict. The Sudan Peoples' Liberation Army (SPLA) /Sudan Peoples' Liberation Movement (SPLM)and other southern liberation movements in the Sudan, Jonas Savimbi's UNITA within Angola, Charles Taylor's National Patriotic Front of Liberia with its capital at Gbarnga and Odumegwu Ojukwu's Biafra are celebrated proto states. Before the Laurent Kabilla-led overthrow of the regime of Sese Seko Mobutu in Zaire, East Kasai province had advanced its fledgling statehood through an autonomous administration, which managed its own currency, promoted its own development projects and had just opened a new university outside the institutional framework of the state of Zaire. These proto states all managed to build putative administrations and effectively entered into the diplomatic mainstream within and outside their sub-regions. In the case of the SPLA/SPLM, it is inconceivable to think of it in any other way other than a government perpetually at war with the sovereign state of Sudan.

These proto states are therefore non-state actors who to different degrees have attributes of states, even if they do not possess formal recognition as sovereign states. They however possess a large degree of domestic sovereignty in the political space under their control. These actors have territories virtually under their control, with populations, informal economies in their zones and enjoy virtual monopoly of coercive apparatus in their enclaves. Sometimes proto states can project force outside the territorial confines of states in which they are embedded. Above all, they conduct foreign relations to a limited extent and challenge the supremacy of the states in which they operate as parallel governments or states. In terms of capabilities, the state actors are not necessarily superior. These non-state actors are proto-states, who are very much a part of the overall structure of the post-colonial state system. Their activities impact on the policy options available to state actors, either as allies or as impediments to the articulation of policy preferences of state actors.

Yet, there is a large measure of coordination and structured interaction among the transnational communities of power and proto states that are integral parts of the construction of the inter-state system and the external environment. A large measure of hierarchy exists within the international environment, while despite the many sectors of hierarchy internally, anarchy is a defining attribute of the internal process of the post-colonial state. This is because the social contract has unravelled. Emerging from these observations is the understanding that the inter-state system is constituted by transnational societies, including proto states, whose presence in the post-colonial inter-state environment has tremendous impact on the character of the inter-state system and have important implications in defining the constraints posed by this environment on the post-colonial state. The nature of constraints on the behavior of the post-colonial state posed by such an environment are qualitatively different from the nature of those imposed on the modern state by the inter-state system of modern and post-modern states. In this environment, the dominant contending unit in the respective post-colonial states is quite keen that their legitimate interests, implying the interests of its residual or major segment of its communities of power, in the neighboring state, are taken care of. These elements, who are autonomous actors in the adjacent state, are clearly transnational allies in the post-colonial states who share borders. In crisis, these groups can intervene in the internal affairs of each other. The Rwandan –Burundi Hutu-Tutsi scenario exemplifies this complexity. This complexity is, however, better illustrated with the unconventional configuration of alliances of states and non-state actors interacting to prosecute the war declared by the Alliance of Democratic Forces for the Liberation of the Congo(ADFLC) against the Mobutu regime beginning in October 1996.

BEHAVIORAL TRANSFORMATIONS IN THE POST–COLD WAR PERIOD

Article III of the charter of the Organization of African Unity forbade member states from meddling in one another's internal affairs. With a few exceptions, African states had abided by this rule, at least overtly. The behavior of states in Central Africa in intervening militarily in the Zairoise crisis, and so overtly too, was thus novel in African diplomatic experience. The military intervention by Uganda, Rwanda, Angola, Morocco, UNITA, the Hutu Inter-haramwe and the SPLA/M marked the first time that African state and non-state actors would overtly collaborate and, in a partisan manner, interfere in the domestic crisis of another African state. All the above-named actors were militarily engaged in battles on one side or the other of the conflict. Troops from Uganda, Rwanda, and Angola fought on the side of the Alliance of Democratic Forces for the Liberation of the Congo/Zaire.

The overt partisan military intervention by a coalition of neighboring states in the domestic affairs of Congo was unprecedented. Apart from the unusual response of these neighboring state and non-state actors, France's first policy choice of bankrolling Serbian mercenaries in support of forces allied to its friend Mobutu[14] was unusual. Its later policy option which was to mobilize its trusted French-speaking African states to facilitate negotiations ran counter to its conventional responses to domestic conflicts in states considered to be inside France's exclusive zone of influence in Africa. France almost always deployed troops to quell such challenges, especially if a friendly regime in good standing was threatened. The role of non-state actors such as UNITA and the SPLA/M was unprecedented in committing their troops to fight in a war across international borders in the sub-region.

The seven-month 'Kabila war' that overthrew the Mobututiste state, by unleashing the full potential of the interaction of proto states with state actors, was unprecedentedly multi-dimensional and complex. Firstly, there was the transformation in the behavior of states that overtly joined sides with proto states in a war in military engagements to define the structure of power within another post-colonial state. Secondly, the alliances forged between state and non-state actors on both sides of the divide indirectly conferred legitimacy and recognition on the rebels as important actors in the sub region. The alliances publicly associated state actors with the causes of their non-state actors. These developments were intriguing. Further was the rapid evolution of what was assumed as the initial limited objectives of the Alliance of Democratic Forces for the Liberation of Congo. This was to mobilize disaffected Zairoise Tutsi to fight for their rights as citizens of Zaire and to challenge the purported denaturalization of their citizenship by the provincial authorities in Kivu and Kasai. After they had been denaturalized of their Zaroise citizenship by the provincial governments, the Zairoise Tutsis, along with Rwandan Tutsi who had fled the genocide in Rwanda in 1994, were under attack in the Kasai region.

The initial primary military objective of the Rwandan Tutsi elements in the Alliance's fighting force was to neutralize the security threat posed to the Tutsi-dominated Rwandan government by armed Hutu militias in United Nations refugee camps in northern Zaire. The Tutsi formed the bulk of the army of the Alliance at the beginning of the war and remained critical to its successes throughout the war. As the war progressed southwards and Westwards, units of Tutsi in the Alliance army and reinforcements of the Rwandan Patriotic Army (RPA) linked up to engage ex-Forces Armee Rwandaise (ex-FAR), who were massed in northern Zaire and in United Nations refugee camps. However, as the Forces Armee du Zaire (FAZ), the national army loyal to Mobutu, fell apart from one battle to another, the phased schedule of operations by the Alliance of Democratic Forces evolved into a more ambitious program. The ADFL decided to pursue the total liberation of the Congo from the Mobutiste regime within an accelerated time frame.

Sub-plots in the war included the battles of the AFDL against separatist elements in Shaba (the old Katanga). In the Masisi area of Kivu Province, the Alliance had to militarily engage Mai Mai militia, who interpreted the prominent Tutsi representation in Kabila's army as the extension to Zaire of a perceived threat of Tutsi hegemony in Central Africa. South of Kivu in the Fizi area, another rebel movement of guerrillas led by Charles Simba, a former comrade of Kabila, confronted forces of the Alliance, which it also saw as a Tutsi foreign invasion of Zaire. These Babende guerrillas in Fizi were autonomous from, and not associated with, the Forces Armee du Zaire of the Mobutiste state. They were also not in alliance with the Etienne Tshisekedi-led Sacred Union which had been attempting to play the role of a constitutional opposition against Mobutu from the national sovereign conference. The national conference had been meeting intermittently for seven years in Kinshasa.

Another major operation within the larger civil war, analytically distinct from the anti-Mobutu rebellion, was indeed a Rwandan civil war of regular Tutsi-led Rwandese Patriotic Front government forces against the Rwandese Hutu militias constituted from residues of the old Hutu government army, Forces Armee d'Rwanda (ex-FAR). These elements and Hutu Interaharamwe militia were mingling among Hutu refugees in United Nations-run camps in northern Zaire. The confrontation between the two Rwandese sides in Zaire was, in effect, a continuation of the Rwandan civil war on Zairoise territory. This second war was fought away from the international spotlight, which was focused then nearly exclusively on the main advance of the Alliance forces to Kinshasa. Further still were the tensions within the Kabila group, often escalating to fights.[15] Thus even, within the Democratic Republic of the Congo, the heavy involvement of neighbors in the internal affairs of the country had presented clear problems to the Alliance of Democratic Forces for the Liberation of Congo/Zaire. These developments violated established principles on which conventional inter-state systems rest.

ORGANIZING PRINCIPLES OF THE POST-COLONIAL AFRICAN STATE

The organizing principles of the post-colonial African inter-state environment are based first on established international norms that are applied mechanically and, more critically, on the informal solidary codes of interaction between transnational communities and formal governments representing the dominant group in the post-colonial African state. As a result of the pervasive anarchy in both the post-colonial African state and its external environment, unilateral overt and covert interventions in armed hostilities have increasingly become a policy instrument. Why states decide to unilaterally intervene in civil conflicts remains an elusive question, yet it is possible to postulate that in the post-colonial state environment, it is much easier to discern that structural factors, both domestic and in the external environment, encourage such interventions. These interventions are generally military deployments that are aimed at least to change the balance of power in favor of a particular protagonist group in the civil war. In other cases, military interventions are undertaken to counter the designs of other external forces interjected into the civil war. A complex two-level interaction is thus generated by the structure of the post-colonial state and its inter-state system.

The second level of the sources of conflict refers to how state capacity for power and influence, or a lack of it, by the post-colonial state affects its capability to insulate itself from the designs of powerful external actors that seek to undermine its autonomy of action. In the self-help international system, elite state actors possess tremendous capacity to influence weak post-colonial states and to willingly align or force them to align their policies in a direction favorable to their declared interests. This is done even in the face of opposition and conflicting aspirations of the weaker members of the global state system. The real capacity and reputation for power of the post-colonial African state is very weak. For most of these states, decolonization and the end of the Cold War did not entail the end of domination by exogenous forces, especially by entrenched former colonial powers such as France, Great Britain and Portugal. As Prof Jean-Pierre Cot, former French Minister of Co-operation, has noted, "independence was not conceived of as a clean break but rather as the innovation of a complex network of all kinds of connections between the metropole and the new African states."[16] Competition to dominate the post-colonial state and its environment among elite actors may express itself in the form of domestic conflict pitting domestic proxies of external forces in the target state against each other. An important dimension to the quest for total control of the new post colonial state by the metropole is highlighted by Jean Pierre Cot when he asserts that in the kinds of arrangement that was forged between the metropole and the client state, third parties have no place. This implies the determination of the neo-colonial forces to maintain total control of the political space that they deemed was rightfully theirs. The practical implication of this policy for European ex-colonial forces was to directly engage, whether overtly or covertly, in the internal processes of the post-colonial state. The dynamics of this foreign engagement for domination and control impacted on the internal struggle for control by the constituent and contending forces through alliances with, and support from,these foreign interests. As a result, since independence, African states have been linked to their former colonial powers by close security arrangements.[17]

At the level of external forces, another powerful external actor that is a critical factor in the security calculus of post-colonial African state is the continuing agenda and struggle for the consolidation of western worldview on the one hand and challenges to this by Arabic and Islamic values and way of life in the heterogeneous environment of the state. Each of these forces has its established constituency that in many cases also coincide with ethnic and regional divisions. Relative to ethnic identity and class, religious affiliation has been muted in its disruptive potential in the post-colonial state. Yet, with increasing radicalization and politicization, Islamic fundamentalism has challenged the legitimacy of the post-colonial state order and its largely Western *weltanschauen*. The dominant worldview and order have been questioned as forms of externally imposed hegemonic order by which the hegemonic group controlling the state, and thus the state, have become instruments of its propagation. Peter Woodward observes that religious affiliation has proved generally less contentious as a basis for political action and, in much of Africa, of limited relevance. He notes that "one major exception is in Islamic Africa, though elsewhere, too, religious organizations did play a role; the juxtaposition of Christian and Muslim communities in the same state came to be an explosive combination."[18] This is more so where ethnic identities and religious differences are fused.

As Alain Rouvez[19] asserts, sub-Sahara Africa proved to be particularly vulnerable to unwholesome external influence. Independence has made no difference to the exploitation of Africa's wealth by European colonial powers. He explains that as poor countries, independence created a power vacuum to be exploited by those who cared enough to initiate attempts to graft Black Africa into their security agenda. Rouvez attests that the ex-colonizers learned to convert remnants of imperial liabilities into post-colonial assets[20]. The colonial forces retain varying degrees of control over their erstwhile colonies. These forces have policy preferences in the policy process of the post-colonial African states and they construct their relations and domestic allies to assure that political, social, security and economic, policy outcomes in the states are consistent with their larger political goals at the global level. The declared and undeclared interests of these former powers impact on conflicts and the evolution of such conflicts once they have begun. Towards this end, they retain and build new friends and allies among the contending forces in the political system. They are directly implicated in old and new conflicts, as they seek to retain their leverage for action and influence in the states and in the immediate state system. They interact strategically with domestic forces contending in the geo-political space. In the final analysis, the activities of external powers militate against the development and organization of systems of domestic, regional and continental order. As William Zartman highlights, conflict can be expected to increase until Africa is obliged to achieve exactly the aforementioned goals[21].

The internal structure of the state generates the first aspect of its double instrumental character. The state is conceived as a political system, and its vital elements may be verified in conceptually variable amounts[22]. These varying elements of the state operate as variables which determine the degree of stateness, autonomy of action, and indeed, the very legitimacy of the political system. In adopting the post-colonial state as a political system, the concept of national society or the emergence of a nation would connote success in the building of integrated and inclusive institutions which have given birth to a pervasive sense of nationalism and near universal sense of belonging in the political system. This ideal, as noted in our earlier chapter, remains an ambition. Society in the post-colonial state is mostly fragmented and the political process merely camouflages intra-society schisms or struggles. Where religious and ethnic lines converge, they make more difficult the process of the distillation of various identities into one dominant nation. What goes for civil society is no more than an amalgamation of diverse interests groups that have a close fit to ethnic and tribal construction of the political system. Competition is the norm rather than collaboration in the national project. Patrick Chabal observes in this connection that though the discussions about African politics have largely been concerned with the state, states have not operated in a vacuum, and it is ultimately their action in relation to civil society which determines their complexion and the fate of their policies. Chabal posits that civil society matters because the state seeks to act upon it and in so doing provokes self-conscious or even spontaneous reaction. Successful states, he adds, devise modi operandi which adapt to and respond to civil society. Unsuccessful states either dissolve, absorbed piecemeal by civil society, or they turn to absolutism and tyranny in opposition to civil society[23].

CIVIL SOCIETY—STATE RELATIONS

Civil society state relations are critical factors in the analysis of politics in Africa. especially in regard to the security imperatives of the post-colonial African state. In this systematic framework, the state is defined as the government or the totality of all institutions by which control, which is often considerable but not absolute in view of the presence of proto state(s), over the territorial space is achieved by the government. The state is primarily viewed as the arena within which economic interest groups, normative social movements, religious interests and different ethnic groups contend. Yet, the structure of the state is such that these interests have ethnic and tribal connotations. The outcome of interaction within the partisan blocs of consolidated group interests, in contra-distinction to civil society in the modern state that is built on diffused networks of criss-crossing personal interests, tends to be sharp and absolute because the stakes are very high and unmitigated. The desired outcome of interaction is to appropriate and dominate the policy process and in effect, the state. The functionary of the state in the African political process is cast as an agent of a clearly discernible interest group and the state itself an instrument to be dominated by the dominant of the mutually antagonistic constituent groups. Once the state is captured by a constituent part of the system, Claude Ake observes that

> ...it continues to be totalistic in scope...It presents itself as an apparatus of violence, has narrow social base, and relies on compliance on coercion rather than on authority.[24]

The post-colonial state is thus not end in itself, but an instrument to be deployed by competing interests within the state. This instrumental character of the state motivates the search for domestic hegemony by contending constituent units in the state. This search expresses itself in a vigorous struggle for appropriation of the state. Once a dominant force emerges among the various competing constituent groups, it seeks to consolidate its hold on the state and to create a long-term hegemony. The post-colonial African state is constructed to assure this evolved hegemony through various institutional frameworks until conditions, both internal and external, are ripe to effectively challenge it. The national processes, including the politics of the post-colonial African state, are all about partisan appropriation, consolidation and hegemonic control of the state. Regime changes thus effectively represent hegemonic transitions that lead to radical transformations in the configuration of domestic power and institutional framework of the state.

The state operates on the basis of affinities that define what groups to include at what varying levels and those to exclude. Since the stakes are so very high, only a zero-sum attitude emerges among the actors. Coercion, rather than persuasion, is the conventional rule of the game. Violent conflicts and the implosion of the post-colonial state peak at periods of hegemonic transitions. In many of these states, proto states, constituted by alienated groups outside the margins of the state, emerge and live side by side in competitive relations with the state until one or the other is able to appropriate the political space and seek to consolidate its new hegemony. These proto states form part of the external environment and interact in the inter-state system.

NORMATIVE AND VALUE DISSONANCE AS ROOTS OF CONFLICT

This first source of conflict is from the incongruity of the multi-national construction of the post-colonial state. The state was constructed by its colonial architects through a process of indiscriminate cobbling together of its colonial holdings without regard for the cultural proximities and distances of the communities involved. Besides, the final structure of the state and the state system that emerged was determined by a politics of domination and appropriation. Adekeye Adebajo describes the politics surrounding the formation of the post-colonial francophone states and notes that it was marked by leadership ambitions and rivalry between Cote d'Ivoire's Houphouet-Boigny and Senegal's Leopold Sedar Senghor. In this connection

> The roots of the rivalry go back to Senghor's support of the continuation of the pre-independence French West African Federation, which had been broken up before independence in 1960 at Houphouet–Boigny's instigation. Dakar had been the capital of the federation, which had helped it to attract investment, services, and infra-structure. Houphouet Boigny distrusted the Senegalese and accused the federation of devouring Ivorian resources as Abidjan's wealth subsidized other West African territories. After Senghor established the putative federation with Mali, Upper Volta, and Dahomey in November 1958, Houphouet Boigny used his personal friendships, economic muscle and political prestige to lure Upper Volta away to join his own entente in 1959.[25]

The constituent units of the new states are therefore marked by absolute value dissonance. These ideational distances are often expressed in diametrically opposed worldviews and ways of living, such that the peoples are unable to elaborate a basic minimum understanding of the ideational premises of their new state. The lack of normative consensus, paucity of face-to-face social interactions and greater difficulty of mutual surveillance all preclude effective social control at the regional and international levels.[26] Such ideational differences are

131

well exemplified by sharp divisions in Nigeria and Cote d'Ivoire. The fault lines ran from East to the West across the breadth of the two countries separating a north with an Islamic world view and compatriots with different ideas on the principles of how society and the state should be ordered. In northern Nigeria, the deepening of the Sharia legal code as the foundations of the organization society has further widened the chasms between the north and the south. The situation has been exacerbated by the rise of Boko Haram that seeks to violently impose Islam throughout Nigeria.

A common vision of the state or universal understanding of the organizing principles of the state is lacking in the new state. Where attempts are made to formulate this vision, it represents mere caricatures that have no bearing on the existential realities of the respective communities. In this setting, compromises are hard to forge without a threat to the fundamental principles and understandings that have governed the lives of the respective communities now trapped in the new post-colonial state. In the absence of harmonized visions that faithfully capture what the respective communities consider the essences of their lives, a multi-dimensional crisis is set off for all actors and the state itself. As a result and also because of these crises, a struggle among the constituent units for domination is set off. It is the hope of all the contending groups to win this struggle and create a hegemony that will impose its values, attitudes and world-view, as well as its material interests, on all others. The competition that is generated threatens the integrity and autonomy of all constituent units. For the state, coercion becomes the norm and violence assumes currency in the national process. This vicious cycle accentuates the security dilemma which remains unresolved as long as the state is unable contain its fragmented civil society. The struggle between groups for the conquest of the state is intensified. As we observed earlier, the functionary of the state in the African political process is cast as an agent of a clearly discernable interest group. Horizontal policies are employed by the post-colonial state to retain the absolutism and arbitrariness of power inherited form the colonial state. Claude Ake characterized this situation as not unlike Hobbes' pre-political state.[27]

The undercurrents of the situation are elucidated by Jean Francois Bayart that in Africa,

> ... a heterogenous state, either imposed by colonial rule or created by revolutionary will (often modeled on other states), has been deliberately set up against civil society rather than evolved in continual conflict with it.

> The African post colonial state is undoubtedly of that nature. Underlying the ideologies of national unity there is a hegemonic

imperative which drives the state and the self proclaimed dominant social groups to seek to control and to shape civil society.[28]

On the dynamics of the conflict, Francois Bayart notes that the first task of the dominant group in the post-colonial state

> ... is to define the basis on which others can gain access to the political system. Most regimes severely restrict such access by preventing the autonomous and pluralistic organization of subordinated social groups. Instead, rulers either attempt to integrate the various social forces into single movements or set up intermediary and indirect means of control. Their objective is to enlist the dominated social groups within existing space of domination and teach them to be subject to the state. The aim is to administer society, even against itself, and to order it according to the explicit, ideal canons of modernity. Thus, the African post colonial state is 'well-policed' state, (policeystaat), relatively close in conception to the enlightened despotisms of the seventeenth and eighteenth centuries[29]

Thus, the post-colonial African state, Stuart Kaufman concludes, is caught in conflict in which ethnic groups act much like states in the international system where the dynamics of conflict are seen as "international relations without safeguards"[30]. The state becomes an instrument to be used by the dominant interest, ethnic, or sub nationalistic group or coalition of groups to outflank rival contending forces in the political system. The structural heterogeneity of the system therefore has an inherent security dilemma, which may be real or perceptual.

The struggle for internal hegemony is rendered more complex by the structure of the inter-state system constituted by quasi-Westphalian states. This second structural concern refers to the alignment of the traditional affinities of peoples in the state across international borders in the immediate sub-region. The boundaries of pre-existing nationalities criss-cross newly demarcated state borders. In effect, communal loyalties, which reflect primary identities and loyalties, transcend the borders of the state. The territorial boundaries of the state do not neatly fit into the boundaries of preexisting nations. This structure of states with boundaries that defy cultural affinities among peoples in the immediate sub-region creates a crisis of identity for the state and its constituent groups. Which of the numerous identities represented internally would the post-colonial state acquire? What identity would its constituent units adopt?

The constituent units often prefer to retain the old traditional identity and all that it implies. This has implications for members of the old identity group excluded outside the frontiers of the new states. Both those within and outside the new frontiers instinctively remain inside the old identity group. They are legitimate stakeholders in the affairs of the new bounded territories, at least, in as much as developments in them impact on the group in which they share membership. The implication is that the structure of the inter-state system constituted by quasi-Westphalian states elicits cross-border interventions in developments that conventionally would be considered internal to the new post-colonial political entities.

Peter Schwab illustrates these principles with developments in Côte d'Ivoire, considered a country of wealth that only recently "metamorphosed into an ethnically perilous space,"[31] Where he observes that:

> By late 1999 troops overthrew the unpopular president due to what they claimed were unpaid wages, widespread corruption, unemployment, and government sponsored ethnocentrism aimed at separating Christian southern Ivorians from northern Muslim 'outsiders"... Within months, however, despite international opprobrium, he inflamed the anti-northern atmosphere and resolved to run for presidency in 2000. The military coup d'etat, along with ethnic and religious discordance, had arrived in the Ivory Coast (Côte d'Ivoire). A new and more threatening politics was now in the offing as the country began its course....[32]

To further explain these developments, Schwab observes that

> In a country whose politics have been dominated by Christian ethnic groups, Ouattara's popularity and his northern/Muslim heritage were seen as threatening to supporters of Guei. By October the Supreme Court, intimidated by the general, ruled that Ouattara and eight Muslim candidates were ineligible to run for the presidency. Five Christian nominees, including Laurent Gbagbo, leader of the third largest party, the Ivorian Popular Front, were allowed on the ballot. Gbagbo, a so-called socialist, had also organized his campaign around Christian ascendancy and his representation of ethnically pure Ivorians [33]

Following the election of Laurent Gbagbo, the intermestic dimension of the Ivorian crisis of identity came to the fore when, in September 2002, dissident troops attacked the presidential palace in a new round of armed conflict that had become a full blown civil war. The rebel forces occupied the northern part of the country for over nine years. President Laurent Gbagbo accused neighboring country to its north, Burkina Faso of backing the dissident soldiers.[34] Burkina Faso is predominantly Muslim and has traditional ethnic affinity with the ethnic groups in the north of Ivory Coast.

The security situation in the Sene-Gambian basin poignantly illustrates the artificiality and complexity of formal inter-state relations in the face of dominant transnational communities that spread across international borders. In this sub-region occupied by Senegal, Guinea Conakry, the Gambia and Guinea Bissau, a Diolla-Mandinge irredentist movement, the Movement of Democratic Forces for the Liberation of the Cassamance (MFDC), had since 1983 challenged the sovereignty of Senegal over the southern province of that country which goes by the name of Casamance. The Portuguese colonial administration had ceded the region to France in return for the annexation of the French-held province in the south of Guinea Bissau then being administered as part of Guinea Conakry. The Diolla-Mandinge community is strongly represented in Guinea Bissau, the Gambia and Guinea Conakry. The rump of this political transnational community is Gabou in northern Guinea Bissau. As a result of this affinity, the community was in the forefront of the liberation struggle of Guinea Bissau.

The Diolla and Mandinge constituted over 60% of the fighting cadres of the Amilcar Cabral-led Pan African Party for the Independence of Guinea and Cape Verde from 1963 to 1974. Guinea Conakry, which shares the border with Guinea Bissau effectively provided a rear base for the PAIGC guerilla forces in their attacks on the Portuguese colonialists in Bissau. Lansana Conte, later President of Guinea Conakry, indeed fought along with PAIGC liberation forces in the southern sectors of the war. Senegal turned its back on the Front for the Liberation of Guinea Bissau (FLING) the first liberation movement in Guinea Bissau, as the movement tried to radicalize its liberation struggle. At independence many of these cadres, who came from villages and towns in Senegalese territory, acquired Bissau Guinean citizenship. Prominent actors in Guinea Bissau such as General Ansumane Mane were equally at home in the Gambia, Guinea Conakry and in fact, in the Casamance. In the Gambia, there is a strong fear of Wollof hegemony in the sub-region at the expense of the Diolla and Mandinge and Aku. These inseparable bonds of peoples across international frontiers have generated security conundrums which have given conflicts in that sub-region a delicate intermestic character. The Mandinge community and its various ethnic variants indeed are spread all over West Africa including Sierra Leone and Liberia.

In the first Liberian civil war (1989-1997), as often is the case in post-colonial states, the United Liberia Movement (ULIMO) was formed to advance the interests of the Mandinge in Liberia, in the face of brutality by the Charles Taylor-led NPFL. The movement was launched in Sierra Leone and was supported by Guinea Conakry throughout the war and after. The Mandinge factor thus partly explains Liberia's Taylor's involvement in the war in Sierra Leone and his persistent suspicions of Conakry. Intermestic connections largely influence the course of conflicts once they break out, but as would be demonstrated in the case of Guinea Bissau, it could also be the immediate trigger of the implosion of the post-colonial African state.

A third force afflicting the post-colonial African state is the structure of the global inter-state system, of which the quasi-Westphalian state is a young and vulnerable part. At this level are the constraints posed by the structure. It has been observed that many of the main state actors in the global system are predatory states. These states see their interests located outside their own territory, which they euphemistically refer to as their sphere of influence.[35] Africa, particularly the sub-regional inter-states system of quasi-Westphalian states, is one of the main playgrounds of strong predatory state actors in the global system. In order to protect those interests, the predatory elite states intervene to change the course of internal developments in the post-colonial states. To attain this end, they seek allies internally and constrain the policy choices of the actors within the state. These structural problems generate violence in the post-colonial state and also destabilize its immediate inter-state system.

At the foundation of violence in the post-colonial African state is a paradox. The internal processes of the state are dominated by the turbulent and over heated struggle for the appropriation or the acquisition of sole ownership of the state and the imposition of exclusive ownership rights on all other constituent forces in that political space by the hegemonic force that emerges to take control. This presumed internal process may however elicit direct and indirect interventions from extra-territorial forces with which the state may share borders who perceive a stake in its affairs. Yet, the state, even against the backdrop of the struggle for its appropriation, merely floats because none of the constituent groups or contending forces in its fragmented society identifies with the state. In fact, the constituent groups are alienated from the state.

The struggle for the appropriation of the state is a means to consolidate the domination of one of the contending forces over all other groups for ascendancy in that political space. The welfare of the state, which is then identified with the interests of the ruling regime, or the consolidation of its legitimacy, that is, the legitimization of the values, attitudes and the worldview of the ruling group, is not the priority goal of the groups who are the primary actors in the struggle for monopolistic control. Bargaining is very limited by the totality of the political agenda of all groups, which agenda underpins a security dilemma in which all the constituent groups in the political space are caught. Conflict is the expression of the systemic dissonance of the interests, values, attitudes and worldviews of the contending forces within the post-colonial state. Once triggered, the trajectory in the ensuing conflict is determined by the manner of interaction of all the three structural forces highlighted: the internal, intermestic, and the global.

At the first level of its instrumentality, the post-colonial state is an arena for the continuous struggle for ascendancy of often irreconcilable opposing and contradictory interests. These interests include value-systems, attitudes. foundational ideas and overall world views that are represented by, associated and identified with, the diverse protagonist constituent units that occupy the artificially bounded political space. The conflictual process forms the permanent undercurrents of the internal dynamics of the state. Violence, in one form or the other and to different degrees, is constantly present in the limited interaction among the constituent groups in the national process. It is often directed by the group in control of the state against competitor-groups. The dominant regime often fails to subdue those who continue to challenge the legitimacy of the status quo. Each group retains some capacity for violence within the state apparatus or outside of it. Violence may be initiated by any one of the subordinated groups against the state, which, in any case, merely represents only the most repressive and dominant group among the contending forces in the state.

At critical junctures, the use of massive violence is triggered and accentuated by all parties and for prolonged periods. That leads to a full-blown civil war, in which violence is instituted as the main currency for political intercourse between various and contending forces in the state. This may be to achieve a limited goal of regime change in a coup d'etat. At other times, violence is deployed with the broader goal of creating a new and permanent political space in the form of secession. Each group perceives its ultimate vision as a sovereign state to rid itself of the constraints imposed on its developmental aspiration as a people by its antagonistic compatriots in the anachronistic post-colonial creation.

Evidence abounds that control of the state is a central ethnic conflict objective.[36] Against this background, there is no form of insurance sufficient to forestall the dilemmas that produce collective fears and violence.[37] The main articulators of vision in the quasi-Westphalian state are groups and peoples. The main units in the drive for power in this state are competing groups, not individuals. The emotion generated by security issues gives rise to the emergence of aggressive ethnic and groups leaders.[38]Individuals are role actors in the name of the group. These individual actors embody group political goals and spearhead the drive for power for the group. Their actions and policy choices are legitimated by their fit into the goals of the group. These individual political actors have some latitude in choosing particular tactics or approach to achieve clearly defined goals of its natural constituency. They may act in unison within a formal institution such as a political party, which must be under its control. But their tactics must pass the litmus test of advancing the ultimate political goal of the group. The group constitutes a natural constituency of unquestioning allegiance and support for the actors in the arena of the state. This arena includes the political, the economic and the social.

Power is, of course, often an instrument to secure other tangible goods and benefits, including benefits for members of an ethnic group. But power may also be the benefit.[39] In the quasi-Westphalian state, the pervasive systemic material and ideological dissonance and the search for domination lead to mutual insecurity for all. This results in incessant competition for power. Everywhere the word domination is heard. Power is equated with political control. The central concern is the question of who are the real owners of the country and who would rule over whom.[40] The resulting politics is a politics of exclusion. Short of eliminating ethnic diversity in the physical sense, exclusionary groups seek to impose a homogenous identity on the state and to compel the acknowledgement of their prominence.[41] Flowing from this, the integrity and autonomy of each and every group is threatened by each and every constituent unit. The strategic choices of each group are constrained by this security dilemma facing all contending units in that political space.

At the second level, the post-colonial African state remains an instrument for the articulation of interests that are extraneous to its corporate interests. These interests are derived from its post-colonial status in the global inter states system. The internal weaknesses of the state make it perpetually vulnerable to be willingly adopted or imposed upon as an instrument of the conflicting interests of elite state actors. The interests of its super-ordinate ally in the global system are imposed on it. Alain Rouvez points out that the relations between the sub-Saharan state in Africa and its metropolitan center does not depend only on the latter's strength and motives but also, by definition, on the former's weakness. He cites the success of medium powers like France and Britain, or even a small power like Belgium, to invest parts of Africa and contend that this can only be made possible either because the member nations of the zones are willing to cooperate or because they are too weak to consider alternate options.[42]

The interests of the metropolitan elite state actors in relation to the post-colonial state are predicated on many factors. It may revolve around historical rivalry with competing elite actors, strategic factors, a sense of global mission, a need for the revalidation of a national sense of its worth and role in world affairs, ideological and a myriad of other considerations. These all summed up in the creation of spheres of interest in the quasi-Westphalian states system by neo-colonial forces. Of all the former colonial powers, France undoubtedly has been able to preserve the largest influence in its African ex-colonies. The remarkable aspect of this influence is that it has been mainly unchallenged for over half century. In the early 1960s, France usually intervened to protect newly established post-colonial regimes against domestic uprisings; later it would engage in both open and covert operations in defense of these regimes or to undermine the influence of rival European and African powers (Biafra 1969), or to reinstate an established head of state (Gabon, 1964), or to remove one (the Central African Republic, 1979).[43] Now French forces fight alongside rebel movements to topple regimes that seek to undermine its control of its old colonies. The peddling of influence by predatory states in Africa has continued in the post Cold War era, with slight changes in tactics involving more subtlety than hitherto.

In effect, the competition to build spheres of influence also entailed a process of appropriation or consolidation of neo-colonial ties with the post-colonial states. The external force may also be expressed in a global mission of a certain idea, such as a religious force seeking to consolidate its hold on a people or a new extraneous idea.

The deleterious consequences of the implication of powerful external forces in the internal processes of the post-colonial state have been aptly distilled by the dependencia and global systems school, deploying such concepts as structural violence arising from the exploitative centre–periphery relations to underline the global and systemic linkages to conflict in contemporary times.[44] Johan Galtung, in reframing the study of conflict, explained how embedded relationships within the system constitute structural, as opposed to conjunctural, violence.[45] He posits that the relationships that are forged between the centers of the north and those in the post-colonial states revolve around the economy, adding that

> The broader systemic theory argues that the global economic dimension is critical in the making of economic policy, that though African states are formally sovereign, they do not have the same degree of realistic options as do developed countries in making their economic policies. They are, in reality, takers rather than makers of their economic policies, under policy frameworks and theoretical paradigms set by the developed countries...[46]

Yet, beyond economic relations with post-colonial states, there are demands of sustaining entrenched international status as elite actors at the global level that are imposed on powerful metrolpolitan states. Such demands of national psychological aggrandisement are met by demonstrating control over the cultural security and political policies of some of these post-colonial states that are indeed creations of the hegemonic members of the global system. It entails complete access and domination of the cultural spaces through the control of the proletarian elites that emerge within a specific and limited historical context in the post colonial state. The allies in the peripheries are expendable by virtue of their proletarian status. They ultimately fall from grace to grass. Sese Seko Mobutu, Sani Abacha, Jean Bedel Bokassa, Hissen Habre and Charles Taylor exemplify the precarious claims of political leaders to elite status in the post-colonial state. Their proletarian credentials are too strong to be wished away by a temporary sojourn in the corridors of power. Just as with economic policy and relations, which is one (even if a dominant one for that matter) dimension of a complex exploitative scheme, powerful external forces manifest a vested interest in determining the evolution of the internal processes, including the cultural and political, if only to demonstrate their elite status among global powers.

The global status of France, for example, is tied not only to its economic and technological prowess, but also to France's international political reach through sustained capacity to sway critical political decisions in many francophone states, particularly in Africa. Portugal can compensate for its lack of high profile international status by retaining control over the handful of Lusophone states in Africa. Thus, following the tradition of the British Commonwealth, France instituted its Franocphonie while Portugal created its Community of Portuguese Speaking States. These bodies complement the direct bilateral engagements of the metropolitan states in the affairs of their respective post-colonial state entities created by virtue of their will. The vast majority of the membership of these institutions is African post-colonial states.

Whether the external hegemonic force is expressed in a state or by a religious idea, to articulate its interests, it requires local allies. These allies have often times already been put in place by the colonial force or already well entrenched in the case of a religious idea. New domestic friends may also be cultivated following radical restructuring in the post-colonial state that may have altered the balance of forces in the state. The internal politics of these friends must coincide with or advance the perceived interests of the intruding elite state actors. The post-colonial space is largely perceived as areas where dissemination of new ideas and philosophy are relatively cheap. These two levels of the instrumentality of the quasi Westphalian state revolve around its structural weaknesses, internally in relation to the structure of the inter-state system that enfeebles the post-colonial quasi-Westphalian state. The post-colonial African state is thus embroiled at one and the same time in two concrete projects of consolidating its statehood, on the one hand, that is strengthening its internal sovereignty, while at the same time protecting its international legal sovereignty.

The immediate triggers of war are mostly related to the internal processes of the state. Yet, the internal processes often mask unwholesome influences of structural forces impinging on the evolution of developments in the state. A third level that has come to the fore in the character of conflict in the quasi Westphalian state environment in the post-Cold War period is the increasing overt implication of transnational stakeholders in developments in the internal affairs of the state. Trans-national stakeholders may be communities across the frontiers that have historical or cultural affinities usually with one of the groups involved in the political developments in the state. There are also proto states controlling a significant portion of the territory of the post-colonial African state and rebel armies. These participate as active protagonists in conflict and, even more importantly, are often accorded diplomatic recognition by other states in the immediate sub-region. This has given wars in the post-colonial African state an intermestic character.

In the post-Cold War period, wars that are purely internal to states have become a rarity in the post-colonial state environment. In developing a rule of the thumb in relation to secession in the post-colonial state, Horowitz notes that

> whether a secession movement will emerge is determined mainly by domestic politics, by the relations of groups and regions within the state. Whether a secessionist movement will achieve its aim, however, is determined by international politics, by the balance of interests and forces that extend beyond the state.[47]

These developments are challenging the adequacy of pure state-centric tools traditionally deployed in our analytical explications of conflicts in the post-colonial African state and the implosion of whole sub-regions. The interaction between this matrix of forces determine the way which armed hostilities evolve and their impact on the sub-regions.

At all levels of interaction within its political space and its contents, the post-colonial state is alienated. The internal processes of the quasi-Westphalian state are defined by multiple crises that are at best contained by a dominant group or a winning coalition of groups. The interlinked multi dimensional crises, revolving around divergent values, worldviews, religion, identity, participation, integration, legitimacy, penetration, distribution and development are never resolved. The crisis in the dominant ideas and value system is reflected in the absolute levels of systemic value and ideational dissonance in the state. This reflects a total lack of agreement among constituent groups on the structure of ideas and value systems on which the state should be predicated. The differences in value systems and ideas often coincide with identities. These values and ideas are implicated in the various primary and secondary identities that the people claim. Such coincidences fossilize the lines of cleavages and conflicts in the system and further polarize intra-societal distances. Its internal society is marked by absolute and very high levels of ideational dissonance.

Consequently, there are no sovereign national worldviews, values or interests per se that are universally acknowledged by all constituent groups in the post-colonial African state. The national interest is the interest that the dominant group has imposed on society and state. It is therefore the short term and fleeting interest of the ruling hegemony. By the rules implicit in the game, these interests must change with power transition or changes of regimes in the state. As a crude variant of the Westphalian system of states, the post-colonial African state is characterized by the lack of a unitary sovereign vision. This encourages each constituent group to develop mechanisms to protect the survival of its way of life, including building structures and mechanisms to resist the state. This results in the inability of the post-colonial African state to develop a monistic structure entailing one locus of power. Interaction among the contending forces is geared toward appropriating the state to impose their respective ideas, worldview, religion, identity, material as the national interests. The state is thus in a state of permanent crisis. Clashing interests identified with competing powerful units in the post-colonial states struggle for hegemony as a response to the pervasive security dilemma. As a product of mechanical and arbitrary fiat, the state was neither constituted on the basis of any form of contract between it, its peoples as corporate entities and individuals as prospective citizens, nor was it underpinned by any grand or overarching philosophical vision that was universally acknowledged by all its constituent units. Violence only lurks just beneath the façade.

States were not created to bring peace to the world, but to satisfy the 'national interests' as defined by their elites, and if necessary by war.[48] Since the state is perceived as illegitimate by its internally contending units, including the emerging hegemons in the domestic political system, the value of future returns for the present rulers are marginal. As Margaret Levi's shows, in such scenarios, the rulers have high discount rates

> Rulers discount rates-that is, how much present value future returns have for them- are another major factor in the calculation of the costs and benefits of a policy choice. Rulers with high discount rates care little for the future. They will be less concerned with promoting the conditions of economic growth and increased revenue over time than with extracting available revenue even at the risk of discouraging output... Rulers with high discount rates will encourage agents to extract all there is from constituents but will try to ensure that they get the lion's share of the take [49]

The political process in the post-colonial African state is thus fraught with tension because the high discount rates translate into massive deployment of force to enforce the hegemony of the winning group. Secondly, the winning group equates the process of consolidating its hegemony with the process of state and nation building. The latter is often more accentuated in political discourse. In the predatory state, what is clear is that from Hobbes to modern day anthropologists, political sociologists, and economic historians, the first step in the process of state creation is to build a monopoly of organized violence.

In the multi-national structure of the quasi-Westphalian state, Carl Schmitt's vision of politics, generally found shocking and unfortunate, underpins the interpretation of the internal processes by constituent groups and their leaders, including the political. In this perspective, Schmitt defines the political realm by the distinction between friend and foe. For him,

> ... a collectivity's quintessential political function is to decide which other collectivities are its friends and which are its foes. In the confrontation between Us and the Other, we define as friends those collectivities whose own definition of all other collectivities, including Us, as friend or foe appears compatible, in the given circumstances, with our preservation as an autonomous, integral society, we define as foes those whose existence or political activity threatens our integrity or autonomy.[50]

Thus politics involves a continuous preparedness for possible conflict with inimical others.[51] Intra-societal relations are mutually antagonistic. Cooperation is at best antagonistic collaboration. In this setting where the legitimacy of the state is very much contested, rival constituent units mount challenges to any initiatives by anyone group or a coalition of groups which seeks to mobilize and monopolize the instruments of organized violence of the state or has indeed taken control of the military forces of the state. It is well understood that the instruments of state violence would ultimately be deployed to establish an internal hegemony. At the material level, the spatial and geographical distribution of vital natural resources, which the state must extract to sustain its hegemony and especially pay to oil its monopoly of violence, is disparately distributed. At the level of values and ideas, the state seeks to impose its worldviews on the total cultural space occupied by what other competitors perceive as an illegitimate state.

In this scenario, identity has to be altered by all to conform with the identity of the rulers of the new state. In the conspicuous absence of a sense of nationhood in the state, resentment grows with increasing extraction and expropriation of resources by the hegemonic group, particularly when those resources are located outside the traditional territorial expanse of this group. The putative institutional arrangements of the quasi-Westphalian state are designed to facilitate what is perceived by subordinated groups as plunder of its 'national resources' by the hegemonic force. It must be highlighted that the term 'national resources' refers to the patrimony of not only the constituent group internal to the state in question, but also includes the stakes of transnational groups with cultural affinity to the land where the natural resource is located. A threat to the cultural heritage of any group within the post-colonial state reverberates as a threat to the integrity and autonomy of the culture of the subordinated group including its members outside of the state. The boundaries of these groups are contiguous with the borders of the state.

It is to counter these challenges that in the predatory state that emerges

> Rulers aim to develop a sufficient coercive capacity to defeat rivals and maintain control over the countryside defined as their territory.[52]

The rivals include transnational stakeholders, who may be the dominant group in the adjacent state sharing borders with the state in question. The intermestic character then develops into antagonisms between two regimes dominant in the two states, thereby fuelling and rendering the conflict more complex.

The new national order that is elaborated superimposes a partisan world-view and sometimes, religion and language. It acquires absolute control of material resources which are put at the service of the dominant force of the new order. Against this background, leadership entails collective action by individuals and groups who share absolute and a high level of value convergence to confront other groups with diametrically opposing material interests, vales systems and world views. A ruler must be legitimized by at least one of the powerful groups or a coalition of groups. Levi affirms that the sole political goal for all groups is the appropriation of the state

> A process of collective action underlies the acquisition and mainte-
> nance of rule. To become ruler requires first coordinating a group
> of individuals who face a common enemy or problem, but rule ulti-
> mately rests on control of resources necessary to enforce participa-
> tion in dominant group by individuals who agreed to become its
> members. Successful rulers are those able to maintain the group,
> able to maintain relative dominance over the opposition, and be able
> to build sufficient power to block rivals.[53]

These conditions are almost classic real-life representations of the elements for building a paradigm for a conflict theory of the genesis of the state.

In the quasi-Westphalian state, the ruler has to build his coalition within his natural constituency. This natural constituency, within the larger context of national politics, is narrowly defined in terms of ethnicity and religious groups that have claims to clearly demarcated geographical space. When ethnicity and religious identity coincide, they produce absolute convergence of norms, values and worldviews in the constituent groups. When they traditionally lay claim to clearly demarcated part of the national territory, this becomes the ruler's de facto power base. However, a coalition becomes imperative, if there is relative dissonance in norms, value systems and worldviews in this natural constituency, maybe because values and norms of one of the primary identities, the tribe, has relative dissonance from the values of the other important identity, religion. Thus, if the worldviews promoted by either of the two identities conflict, coali-tional politics becomes inevitable to sustain the dominant worldview of the majority in the ruler's natural constituency. The ruler may have to suppress a faction in his own constituency, if incentives fail to convince them to subscribe to the political agenda of the fold. They are denounced as traitors. It is in this context that in the dominant group of the multi-national quasi-Westphalian state "… all rulers are part of a contract".[54] The contractual circle is, however, severely constrained by the logic of the political process. The contract in this case is with those within the natural constituency who accept the dominant worldview of the group and the political goals of the group championed by the ruler. As Margaret Levi posits, bargains made with constituents and agents on whom rulers depend underlie the acquisition and maintenance of rule.[55]

Conversely, the opposing group will form an alliance to counter the new hegemony personified by the ruler. However, in the logic of the internal processes in this setting of antagonistic collaboration, building political alliances are not given. Though a common foe is created by the rise of a hegemon, the feasibility of an alliance depends on a host of other considerations, including relative convergence of norms and values. The political goals of each are paramount and since these relate to appropriation of the entire political space, they are conflictual. In this setting it is rulership that counts. Power is indivisible among allies. It is a zero-sum game, where the winner takes all. Since those who opt out of the political strategy of the mainstream group are seen as having defected from the group, and given the backdrop of the security dilemma of the political process, extremism grows among the groups out of power. Coalition among the contending groups from their subordinate positions are usually shortlived, if they are ever forged. In a democratic environment, the coalitions survive until election time, when each group goes its way in search of the prime prize of rulership to facilitate the goals of state appropriation. In a military regime, alliance formation is declared as treason against the state. The ascendancy of the ruling group does not end the competition.

The resources of the state, notably its coercive instruments and agents, are easily deployed by the dominant group or a coalition of groups on attaining a favourable balance of forces once the state has been appropriated. The ruler settles in a patrimonial fashion the narrow coalition in his natural constituency but increasingly consolidates his personal control of the state apparatus of violence. He creates new military formations around his person and informal mechanisms, that is, intelligence, to control minor dissent in his natural constituency. Through such acts, the ruler consolidates his hold on power at the national level. The excesses of the ruler are largely rationalized by his natural constituency. These excesses however polarize the already fragile intra-societal relations. This radicalizes the responses of the opposing groups, who are not acting in unison because of the mutual antagonisms underlying the political process. War is the expression of the intense struggle for the appropriation of the state by two or more groups as they seek to destroy the integrity and autonomy of other competing interests and frustrate the ruling group from consolidating its hegemony in place. The political process is thus always violence-prone as it is only one step away from massive use of force.

Though the struggle, including armed hostilities, is conventionally confined to a particular state, active protagonists in the struggle include trans-territorial stakeholders in the affairs of that bounded political entity. The participation of transnational vested interests, mainly extensions of ethnic groups straddling the artificial borders of the state, imposes an intermestic character on conflicts in post-colonial state in Africa. This intermesticity has been accentuated in conflicts in the post-Cold War era. The nature and intensity of the participation of the legitimate stakeholders located across the frontiers, which is the intermestic calculus, in the struggle for appropriation and hegemony have a critical import for the trajectory of conflict, once they are triggered. The alignment of the primary loyalties of the peoples across the boundaries of quasi-Westphalian state also impact on the structure of the quasi-Westphalian state system. These alignments make viable the proto states that dot the political landscapes of the post-colonial African state system. The communities in the adjacent states provide havens and safe rears across international frontiers for forces in military operations across international borders. The structure of the immediate inter-states system has profound implication for choices by states constituting these quasi-Westphalian states. These interests converge and diverge to varying degrees. The sources of conflict in the post-colonial African state are embedded in the structure of the state, and, by implication, in the structure of its interstate system.

SECOND INSTRUMENTALITY OF THE POST-COLONIAL AFRICAN STATE AND ITS IMPLICATIONS FOR CONFLICTS:

As highlighted in the early part of this chapter, the post-colonial state is instrumental to the articulation of interests by foreign forces that dominate and control the weak state. These are mainly the interests of ex-colonial forces that seek the appropriation of the political space and its control to advance their economic, cultural and political agenda Post-colonial relations between metropoles and post colonial states have three dimensions. These are the sustenance of linguistic and cultural affinities built over years of unrivalled domination, geostrategic interests, and economic exploitation of the post-colonial state. These elements constitute the trinity of interests that to different degrees drive policy and underpin relations between the metropole and post-colonial dependencies. On the part of the post-colonial state, the state, in other words, the hegemon among the contending domestic forces must submit itself to this subjugation. In return it is assured protection and legitimacy. The metropole plays the role of an assurance broker and the guarantor of last resort. The substance of French policy in post-colonial Africa into the post-Cold War and in the wake of the post sovereign conference democratic wave remains unchanged, even if some of the major actors have been replaced and the operational environment has been altered by the behavioral transformation of the post-colonial states themselves.

The internal processes in francophone states have become more dynamic since the advent of national conferences and the democratic wave that followed it as represented by the political violence in Cote d'Ivoire, which hitherto had been considered an oasis of tranquility and a sub-regional economic engine house. Internally, as in Cameroun, Congo Kinshasa, Congo Brazzaville and the Central African Republic, coup d'etats are giving way to rebellions as mechanisms to effect radical structural changes within the post-colonial African state. Along with this has emerged overt and increased covert intervention in these rebellions in post-colonial states by neighboring states and the overt participation of proto state in the external environment of the post-colonial state system. Liberians and Sierra Leoneans were deployed to fight alongside the rebels in Cote d' Ivoire. In Cote d'Ivoire, Nigeria and Ghana were the first state actors to deploy military help on the side of the state. Burkina Faso has been accused of supporting the Mouvance Patriotic du Cote d'Ivoire (MPCI) which was the first of the rebel movements to take up arms against the Laurent Gbagbo-led state on 19 September 2002. In the wake of the military uprising, the government of Laurent Gbagbo accused foreign countries of being behind the rebellion and of there being a 'rogue state' responsible for supporting the rebels. Keith Somerville reported

> ... that the rebels had been successful in holding the north and center of the country and appear to have support form many of Ivory Coast's Muslims has increased the suspicion on the part of the government and many Ivorians that their mainly Muslim neighbour is to blame.[56]

The complex linkages of conflicts were further acknowledged by the Ivorian Prime Minister when he observed that

> ... if we don't stop war in Cote d'Ivoire, it is certainly going to continue moving on- to the east there is Ghana, Togo, a little further Nigeria. It is going to keep moving. No one thought there would be a war in Ivory Coast. So, why has there been a war-because there was war in Liberia, Sierra Leone and Guinea[57]

Other rebel movements in Cote d'Ivoire include the Movement for Justice and Peace (MJP) and the Ivorian Popular Movement of the Great West (MPIGO). External predatory state actors engaged in the post-colonial state system are thus forced to take these imperatives into consideration in mapping out strategies to sustain their traditional super-ordinate/subordinate relationship with the state.

The Republic of Gabon is presented as an exemplar of the continuity in policy between post colonial state and its metropole. Lucy Ash observes that Gabon:

> ... is the quintessential French client state. Its leader for more than three decades, President Omar Bongo, was handpicked by advisers of De Gaulle. French troops were sent in twice to put down rebellions- a reward for unwavering loyalty to Paris. Recently, he had to submit himself, only for the second time, to a general election. The first time, in 1993, he lost. He went to Paris to seek help. He was told to disregard the results form Libreville, the capital, and count votes only from the countryside. The right result was secured[58]

The dynamics of economic dependency are well documented and theorized.[59]

The dynamics of the struggle for control are at two levels for ex metropolitian forces. At one level, the neo-colonial force must first ward off other western competitors in their target spheres of exclusive influence. Underpinning the whole structure of relations between France and the satellite post-colonial French speaking states are military and technical agreements. These agreements constitute the basis of the construction of French preserves between Senegal, on the Atlantic coast, and Chad, in the sub-Saharan interior. In these preserves, notes Craig Whitney, live 160,000 French citizens and where ELF, the big and once state-owned French oil company, benefited from powerful patronage from Paris.[60] When these French preserves are threatened by other elite actors that are acting directly or in support of a coalition of actors, state and non-state, in a manner perceived to be undermining the status quo, it leads to panic. Such threats have come to the fore only in the aftermath of the end of the Cold War. In this period, the disappearance of the threat to common western interests has revealed divergences in national perceptions of objective interests in various post-colonial states. In the last days of Mobutu, France's confused policy response to the alignment of forces against him may be explained by this threat perception. According to this hypothesis in relation to the transformed behavior of state and non-state actors in the Zairoise civil war, entangling ties among state and non-state actors, if not full alliances, observed in the Zairoise civil war suggested the possibility of developing 'polarity' -'axes of shared perception' and interest' – in the relationship among the myriad armed of factions in the sub-region.

Central to one of the blocs, the dominant status quo power in the sub-region was France and its pre-eminence in Zaire and in the sub-region could be toppled in the event of a reconfigured post-Mobutu post colonial state. France supported Zaire and its ally Sudan in the conflict. This bloc was pitted against a coalition of Rwanda, Burundi, Angola, and Uganda, the Southern Sudanese (SPLA/SPLM) proto states. This coalition was said to have the support of the United States of America.[61] Another version of the thesis was advanced by French analysts of events in Central Africa. In April -May 1997, shortly after the victory of Kabila over the forces of Mobutu, Jean-Michel Demetz observed that for French diplomacy, the ascendance of Kabila in Kinshasa had generated panic. With Kabila's triumph, he asserted that France had registered a more humiliating defeat in the dark continent than the rejection of de Gaulle's vision of a French Community by Sekou Toure's Guinea in 1958.[62]

François Soudan echoed the same sentiment and recalled the helplessness of francophone leaders in Africa, who watched from the sidelines at the Pointe Noire summit which sought to negotiate an end to the Zairoise civil war under South Africa's good offices.[63] The French view was further elaborated by Albert Bourgi who claimed that on reaching power the lieutenants of Nelson Mandela of South Africa, Museveni in Uganda, Aferweki in Eritrea, Meles Zenawi in Ethiopia, Sam Nujoma in Namibia, Kagame in Rwanda, and Dos Santos in Angola had found an ally in Laurent-Desire Kabila which enabled them to reconfigure East, Southern and Central Africa in a new African order. The whole project, supported by Washington, he wrote, was a post- Cold War geopolitical restructuring of the sub-region to enable the United States to supplant France as the foremost power in Africa. He warned that the siege of Francophone Africa by Anglo-Saxons occasioned by this would have serious repercussions on the allies of France in West and Central Africa.[64]

One essential element in France's African policy was to create divisions between French-speaking Africa and non-French-speaking areas. France also fostered the development of a perception of a distinct community of Francophone interests based on this divisive policy, while it simultaneously worked to undermine non-francophone black African states. One of France's most controversial initiatives in this regard was its covert action in Nigeria under de Gaulle in 1968 in the form of shipments of French arms to support the Biafran insurgency. It encouraged its proxies in Africa to extend diplomatic recognition to Biafra as a prelude to France's recognition of the breakaway region. Alain Rouvez observes that

> President de Gaulle's private view was that the breakup of Nigeria, a potential African great power was in the French interest. As a potential African regional power, a strong Nigeria could make France's policy difficult to implement.[65]

France subtly introduced rivalry among states along the lines of their colonial heritage as it built up its power in Africa and, especially, in Central Africa.

It also imposed and supported local despots according to its evaluations of how well they served French interests. This French project and plans in Africa had repercussions for internal cohesion among the continent's peoples and states. By imposing and encouraging bad leadership in francophone Africa, France had alienated not only the internal opposition in the various Francophone states, but had also generated great animosity against itself and its power outside these countries. In spite of its pretensions to the contrary, more perceptive African leaders and radical intellectuals could see through policies which France has perpetuated since its colonial adventure in black Africa.[66]

The French in delimiting their exclusive zones of influence gave an injunction to the leaders of francophone post-colonial states to coordinate their responses to Anglo-phone states. France was urging the building of a fortress mentality between the French-speaking post-colonial states and their Anglo-phone counterparts. Adebayo Adebajo, in this connection, reports the statement of French President Georges Pompidou that

> ... it is appropriate that the French speaking countries should harmonize their views and coordinate their efforts, vis-a-vis English speaking Africa and Nigeria in particular.[67]

The ex-colonial powers and other predatory global state actors, just as they seek to ward off invaders from their perceived zones of influence in post colonial states and their sub-systems, also seek opportunities to extend their influence into the traditional spheres of influence of rival powers. The French, in this connection, in successfully co-opting Mobutu's Zaire into its zone of influence, successfully edged out the Belgians in the Democratic Republic of Congo. In the post-Cold War era, American decisiveness in the Democratic Republic of Congo was responsible for the eventual negotiated overthrow of the Mobutu regime despite a spirited diplomatic effort on the part of France to rally friendly French speaking governments to save it. The war and diplomacy, against the backdrop of the dwindling fortunes of the Mobutu loyalists and his foreign allies in the battle field, highlighted some of the unrecognised assumptions and the limitations of ex colonial forces in complex intermestic conflicts on the continent. The pertinent question arises as to why France failed to send troops to engage the Laurent Kabila-led Alliance of Democratic Forces for the Liberation of Congo?

Eventually, France was excluded from the American/South African brokered negotiations that finally formally toppled Mobutu. France refused to acknowledge that the Alliance invasion of Zaire was an internal affair, citing the massive presence of Tutsi in the force as a reason for its engagements and diplomatic initiatives on the civil war. Paris wanted to see the conflict defined as a foreign invasion in order to justify foreign intervention to stop the advancing Alliance forces and to prop up the pro-French Mobutu regime.[68] France's international campaign to build an international Zaire force to intervene was snubbed by other western countries, especially coming so soon after France's controversial role in Rwanda and the Hutu genocide against the Tutsi. France was perceived as having lost its moral leverage to initiate the kind of humanitarian intervention that could save the Mobutu regime and, by implication, strengthen its slippery hold on Central Africa.

The marginalization of France and post-colonial francophone states in negotiations on the South Africa boat underlined the complexity of the transformation that the emerging political imperatives in the post-Cold War era in the post-colonial state system for the metropoles. Before then, France had pulled out from Rwanda under a pall of universal opprobrium for alleged complicity in the ethnic genocide in that country. France had effectively, in seeking to elevate its relations to pre- eminent influence in Hutu led Rwanda, undermined Belgium in that country. In so doing, the alleged complicity of France—unwittingly or not—in the ethnic genocide in that country underlined the potential catastrophic dimensions of realpolitik in the fragile environment of the post-colonial state. These developments bred fear for the continued hegemony of foreign powers traditionally known to determine the direction of political process and policy in post-colonial states. French fears, for example, were exacerbated by what seemed to be a new-found enthusiasm about Africa in the United States State Department. Lucy Ash explains that further to the overt challenge to its claims to exclusive rights in these domains

> ... American exports to Africa were rising, some years by up to a quarter. Corporations were looking for new investments. French companies like Elf and Total were finding increasing competition in countries like Gabon that they regarded as their own. This discovery of Africa reached new heights during President Clinton's visit...[69]

This fear was also highlighted by ex-President Pascal Lissouba of Congo Brazzaville when he accused the French oil company Elf of complicity in his violent overthrow by his predecessor in office, Denis Sassou Nguesso, and fanning the civil war in the country by funding arms purchases for ex President Sassou Nguesso.[70]

In Guinea Bissau and the Sene-Gambian basin in general, French influence and competition against the Portuguese provide a problematic undercurrent to the rebellion in the Casamance region of Senegal and continuing internal instability in post-civil war Guinea Bissau and the pervasive instability in that sub-region. In Guinea Bissau, the civil war of 1997/1998 between Joao Bernandino Vieira loyalists and the General Ansumane Mane-led Military Junta was more the violent implications for internal politics of the intense competition for the control of Guinea Bissau by French interests than any disagreements on any domestic policy. In November 2000, the country came to a standstill following three days of standoff between loyalists of democratically elected President Kumba Yala and officers loyal to Ansumane Mane. This was a continuing violent expression of the direction of policy in relation to relations with both France and Portugal. These internal conflicts were direct results of Franco-Portuguese determination to control Guinea Bissau. From the centralism of the colonial period to the apparent flux of the present day, France has exercised a strong and abiding influence on the continent.[71]

At a second level, the metropolitan power must perpetuate regimes that are amenable to control in their various post-colonial holdings. This control has become critical in the post-Cold War era when traditional ideological rationalizations for maintaining blatant support for unpopular hegemonies in post colonial states have dissipated. The end of the Cold War delegitimized the social, political and economic stranglehold of post-colonial states by their metropoles. The post-cold war democratic wave with the attendant radical opening of the political space in post colonial Africa was predicated on this transformation at the global level. This new opening has translated into regime transitions underpinned by democratic values in the post-sovereign national conference era, which came in the wake of the end of the cold war. In this period, against the background of the tumbling authoritarian regimes that had been put in place by France in French-speaking post-colonial states in Africa or other post-colonials regimes that had enjoyed cozy relations with metropoles, the strategies of neo-colonial control have been altered. The new strategies, which are still emerging, appears to be to survey the spectrum of political actors and pitch camp with those who have the potential to protect the continued economic and political interests of the ex-colonial power. Lucy Ash cites French President Jacques Chirac's emphasis of the permanent presence of France in post-colonial and post-Cold War Africa at the Franco- African summit

> France is not one of those countries which from time to time rediscovers Africa. We just don't pop in for a visit or when there's a disaster. France-for a very long time- has been your friend. We have a common history and we're always there, day in day out. Make no mistake about it: France will not abandon Africa, we are in for the long run.[72]

In post-sovereign conference Congo Brazzaville, France had earlier abandoned its long-time ally, Denis Sassou Nguesso, in favor of Pascal Lissouba, especially since Mitterand's France was then reluctantly waking up to new moral and ethical standards for its protégé which he espoused at the meeting of the

Francophonie at La Baule in 1990. The patronizing culture and cronyism of the leadership in its post-colonial dependencies remain the essential French policy instrument of control. Craig R. Whitney draws attention to this character of relations between France and its post-colonial dependencies when he observes that

> ... democracy and human rights were not the main standard by which French presidents measured their African policies. However, it was loyalty, a word that crops up often in French histories of the post colonial era. What it meant was that French governments would support African leaders who remained loyal to France, which depended on French Africa for much of its oil and $10 billion a year in trade.[73]

Yet, this is not uniquely French, for it has remained the strategy of choice for Arab and Islamic states in seeking to penetrate further the post-colonial state in black Africa.

A second force is constituted by disparate religious affiliations and contra-pulling worldviews which seek to consolidate their influence in society and their unrelenting expansionism in society and in the post-colonial state. Christianity and Islam, per se, pose no problem. The disruptive potential lies in the close juxtaposing of the so-called major religions within the same political space. The worldviews derived from foreign religions and bequeathed to the post-colonial societies are mutually antagonistic. Colonial policies and administration tended to reinforce a perception of differences among the various groups. Indeed, in West Africa the broad ethno- religious cleavage runs from East to West. Up to a point roughly 150 to 200 kilometers due north from the coast of the Atlantic are Christians. Even when they have managed to protect their traditional outlooks in the face of the assault and propagation of Christianity and Westernization, the worldview has been heavily influenced and basically Western. Even among the Yoruba with a significant proportion of Muslims, the worldview is basically Western. In the north, colonial administrative practices, such as the indirect rule of Lord Lugard in northern Nigeria, reinforced emerging value dissonance with the Christian south, which was later to be amalgamated with the north into one political entity. Thus, the Islamic and Arab worldviews and values that are intrinsic to them predominate in the north of the country. This has led to sharp divisions in the country that generated a lot of tensions and impacted on national processes. The declaration of the Sharia as the legal code for many states in the north that share borders has posed serious problems, as many have dubbed the declaration an act of secession from the Nigerian federation. Differences in the sources underpinning social mores and values are noticeable in virtually all post-colonial states, including, Ghana, Cote d'Ivoire, Togo, Benin,

Sierra Leone, Guinea Bissau and Senegal. In Senegal, Casamancaise in the area of Zuguinchor often put accent on the fact that, owing to their more recent excision from the Portuguese-controlled territory of Guinea Bissau, they have greater affinity to Catholicism, while Muslims from that province relate less to the dominant Mouride traditions that is dominant in northern Senegal.

The value dissonance arising from the close juxtaposing of peoples with differing worldviews has proven to be a major source of violence in the post-colonial state. This close proximity, especially when they coincide with ethnic identities, reinforces the sense of unity of communities across international frontiers and their sense of separateness from compatriots with whom they are trapped in the political space of the post-colonial state. The question arises as to from which of the competing religious traditions the vision and philosophy to underpin the raison d'etre of the state are to derive. In Côte d'Ivoire, the substantive contents of authentic Ivorite proclaimed under Konan Bedie and reinforced by Laurent Gbagbo was to deny northerners and Muslims the citizenship of the state. The state belonged to the Christian ethnic groups indigenous to the coastal South of the country. In Côte d'Ivoire, the implication of the declaration of Ivorité was the communal violence that preceded the civil war in that country. Keith Somerville observes that

> ...the main northern political leader, Alassane Ouattara, was excluded from taking part in elections for several years when the government said that he was of Burkina origin and so not an Ivorian citizen. The action against him angered Muslim Ivorians and there was considerable sympathy for him in Burkina Faso
>
> ... In July 2000, Burkinabes living in the central town of Daloa were caught up in violence between southerners and northerners in the town of Daloa. This increased the feeling among President Gbagbo's supporters that Burkina Faso backed the political ambitions of their opponents in the north. The success of the rebels in holding the north has only intensified this perception. Recent years have seen growing connections between the political and military problems of neighbouring states in West Africa-notably in the wake of the Liberian war that overthrew Samuel Doe and eventually brought Charles Taylor into power.
>
> Burkina Faso was accused of arming factions in both Liberia and Sierra Leone during their civil wars.... The attacks on immigrants in the immediate aftermath of the uprising and the increasingly strident attacks by the government and the state media on Burkina Faso and Burkinabes in Ivory Coast are creating an unstable situation that threatens wider communal violence and the possibility of inter state conflict[74]

In effect, both forces represented by Christianity and Islam and their worldviews seek to expand, acquire political control of the machinery of the post-colonial African state. The two forces are indeed rivals. They both seek the appropriation of the state and hegemonic influence in its affairs. Behind each of these foreign forces are identifiable external actors.

In Guinea Bissau, the November 1999/January 2000 democratic elections that ended the post-conflict transition were fought, on the face of it, on party lines. Yet the dominant influence on Malam Bacai Sahna, the interim president and the candidate of the PAIGC, were external Islamic countries in North Africa and the Middle East seeking to expand Islamic influence in the country. Malam Bacai's presidential campaign was financed by these countries. On being elected, President Kumba Yala appeared to have taken his cue from this. He courted the Muslim community in political moves that fused ethnic and religious elements to consolidate the hegemony of the Ballanta that had evolved under his leadership of the country. He took the Muslim name of Mohammed and openly antagonized everything Portuguese, a part of a grand political strategy that pits Christianity against Islam and realigned the Foula Muslim community. In concert with his Ballanta ethnic group, President Kumba Yala decided to wade into an internal Islam debate by prohibiting the Ahmadiya sect from Guinea Bissau. Through this ban, the president gave prominence to a relatively obscure problem within the Muslim community in Guinea Bissau and raised his own profile as a defender of orthodoxy in Islam in relevant capitals in the Middle East.

Kumba Yala's exploitation of the situation exemplifies one of the modes of expansionism of religious faith that is a veritable source of conflict. Through him, a new alliance was forged between international Islam and the political project of reconstructing the post-colonial state of Guinea Bissau that would revolve around a hegemony of the Ballantas ethnic group. In time, that hegemony would become synonymous with the protection of Islamic influence against perceived Western interests identified with Lisbon. The focus of external propagators of foreign interests and faith is usually on key persons in the political process. They form the bridge to various contending forces interacting in the political spaces of the post-colonial state. Many African leaders are known to have changed faith and names after receiving heavy gratification from Middle Eastern rulers and old rich emirates. Many Christian heads of state have also resorted to the use of Christian symbols to shore up their position. President Olusegun Obasanjo of Nigeria conveniently leaves no one in doubt of his born-again status. In the April 2003 presidential election, General Muhammadu Buhari was tagged a candidate of Islamic fanaticism for his support of the introduction of the Sharia legal code. As president, Olusegun Obasanjo was an enthusiastic born-again Christian who flaunted the idea that he sourced his inspiration from Jesus Christ. Each of the two was also clearly identified with the ethnic domain that constituted his primary constituency.

In all, the major goal of external actors in the internal affairs of the post-colonial African state, the competing metropoles and foreign worldviews, is to appropriate the social and political spaces to advance their own global interests. In the case of metropoles, these goals are cultural, geo-political and economic. With religious forces, the goals of propagation of their faiths for new converts are more than just exercises in religion. The expansion of the religious community, especially into new communities, facilitates global expansion of that faith, and the incorporation of new social and political spaces into the system of worldviews and values remains unabated. It increases its global weight, especially in a dangerous age when civilizations are perceived to be clashing. This agenda of the global forces that motivated policy toward post-colonial states during the Cold War remains relevant and is equally valid in the post-Cold War era. The alterations in structure in the international system and the emerging dynamism of the intermestic external environment of post-colonial state system, includingproto states, , have impacted to delegitimize traditional policy instruments of choice for the articulation of the strategic goals of the external forces.

To advance their strategic goals in the transformed environment of the post-Cold War, these global forces need to consolidate their hold on society, especially the local hegemonic groups, and also ally with those dominating the political process. It is a more nuanced policy. They are thus compelled to constantly probe national societies in post-colonial states for opportunities to penetrate them. These penetrations lead to the consolidation and further opportunistic cultivation of domestic constituencies that are willing to stake their internal political goals of appropriation and constructing local hegemonies by deploying their assets to the benefit of the external force. In return, the external actor assures the longevity of the hegemony of the local ally. Often times, these agents are no more than individuals with great leverage in the political process. At times they are old-time despots whose services are even more readily available, given the increasing internal challenges that post-Cold War democratization has unleashed on traditional hegemonic regimes in post-colonial states. The interests of all parties engaged are constant, in probing for internal allies as proxy, the policy instruments may be modified.

Partisan military interventions by metropolitan forces, such as those conventionally associated with France in the Cold War era, have limited utility in the new era of full-blown civil wars with intermestic character in the post-colonial external environment. That would appear to be the central lessons of the war in the Congo and to a limited degree in Côte d'Ivoire and the Central African Republic. The critical breaking point is at the imminent transition of one hegemony to another. The range of possibilities includeds democratic change that guarantees peaceful transitions, self-succession, coup d'etat, and finally rebellion. At the end of this spectrum of violent transitions of hegemonic regimes is the total implosion of the post-colonial state and its immediate state system in violence. All changes portend important implications for both domestic forces and their external agents as they may usher in new hegemonic regimes that are consolidated through radical structural realignments of the state unfavorable to all other forces left out in the cold. As demonstrated in Congo Brazzaville in the case of Sassou Nguesso, an overthrown hegemony has access to its powerful external allies that can help to mobilize resources and logistics to commence a war to return the country to the status quo ante. The external force, whether an elite predatory state or a set of beliefs or an externally inspired faith, is always willing to use its local proxies to advance its parochial interests in the target post-colonial state. The interaction generated in this complex play of external and domestic forces determines the outbreak of violence, its trajectory and the manner of its resolution or management. In the final analysis, the post-colonial state and all its institutions are primed as instruments for the achievement of goals that are extraneous to the corporate interests of the state. The instrumental character of the post-colonial African state is the source of the conflict among its internal and transnational contending forces acting in concert to appropriate the state. The transnational engagement and intermesticity of the environment renders the post-colonial African inter-state system unstable and conflict prone.

Notes

1. David A. Lake and Donald Rothchild, "Containing Fear: The Origins and Management of Ethnic Conflict," *International Security* 21, no. 2 (Fall), 1996, p. 41-75.

2. David A. Lake and Donald Rothchild, ibid.

3. David A. Lake and Donald Rothchild, ibid.

4. Kenneth N. Waltz, *Theory of International Politics*, McGraw-Hill, New York, 1979.

5. Kenneth N. Waltz, ibid.

6. Patrick Chabal and Jean-Pascal Daloz, *Africa Works; Disorder as Political Instruments*, Indiana University Press, Bloomington, 1999, p. xv.

7. Ernest Harsh, Setting foreign fighters on the road home, Africa Renewal, United Nations Department of Public Information, Vol 23, No 2, July 2009, p.6.

8. Ernest Harsh, Setting foreign fighters on the road home, Africa Renewal, United Nations Department of Public Information, Vol 23, No 2, July 2009, p.7.

9. Ernest Harsh, Setting foreign fighters on the road home, Africa Renewal, United Nations Department of Public Information, Vol 23, No 2, July 2009, p.7.

10. Filip De Boeck, "Postcolonialism, Power and Identity: Local and Global Perspectives from Zaire," in *Postcolonial Identities in Africa*, ed. Richard Werbner and Terence Ranger, Zed Books, New Jersey, 1996, p. 80.

11. Kenneth N. Waltz, *Theory of International Politics*, McGraw Hill, New York, 1979, p. 114.

12. John J. Mearsheimer, "False Promise of International Institutions," *International Security* 19, no. 3 (Winter), 1994, p. 5-49.

13. Kenneth N. Waltz, op. cit.

14. Raymond Bonner, "France Linked to Defence of Mobutu," *The New York Times International*, May 2, 1997, A6.

15. Complex Emergency Report on the Great Lakes by the United States Aid for International Development of October 9, 1997 reports fights between a newly organized 10th Brigade of Katangese loyalists of Kabila and Tutsi units in Goma during September 4-8 leading to several deaths.

16. Edmond Kwam Kouassi and John White, "The Impact of Reduced European Security Roles on African Relations," in *Europe and Africa: The New Phase*, ed. I William Zartman, Lynne Rienner Publishers, Boulder, CO, 1993.

17. Edmond Kwam Kouassi and John White, ibid.

18. Peter Woodward, *Sudan, 1898-1989: The Unstable State*, Lynne Rienner Publishers, Boulder, CO, 1990.

19 Alain Rouvez, Michael Coco, and Jean-Paul Paddack, *Disconsolate Empires: French, British and Belgian Military Involvement in Post-Colonial Sub-Saharan Africa*,University of America Press, Lanham, MD, 1994.

20. Alain Rouvez, Michael Coco, and Jean-Paul Paddack, ibid., p. 5.

21. William Zartman, "Regional Security and Changing Patterns of Relations," paper presented at conference, "James Coleman African Studies Center Conference on the End of the Cold War and the New African Political Order," University of California, February 17-19, 1994.

22. J. P. Nettl, "The State as a Conceptual Variable," *World Politics* 20, 1968.

23. Patrick Chabal, "Thinking about Politics in Africa," in *Political Domination in Africa: Reflections on the Limits of Power,* ed. Patrick Chabal, New York, Cambridge University Press, 1986.

24. Claude Ake, *Democracy and Development in Africa*, Brookings Institution, Washington D.C., 1996.

25. Adekeye Adebajo, *Building Peace in West Africa: Liberia, Sierra Leone, and Guinea-Bissau*, Lynne Rienner Publishers, Boulder, CO, 2002, p. 27.

26 Richard Ned Lebow, "Fear, Interest and Honour: Outlines of a Theory of International Relations," *Intenational Affairs* 82, no. 3, 2006, p. 443.

27. Claude Ake, op. cit.

28. Jean Francois Bayart, "Civil Society in Africa," in *Political Domination in Africa: Reflections on the Limits of Power*, ed. Patrick Chabal, Cambridge University Press, New York, 1986.

29. Jean Francois Bayart, op. cit.

30. Stuart J. Kaufman, "An International Theory of Inter-Ethnic War," *Review of International Studies* 22, 1996, p. 2.

31. Peter Schwab, *Africa: A Continent Self-Destructs*, Palgrave MacMillan, Basingstoke, 2002, p. 32.

32. Peter Schwab, ibid, p. 33.

33. Peter Scwhab, ibid, p. 34.

34. "Ivorien Government Accuses B/Faso of Backing Dissident Soldiers," *This Day News*, September 22, 2002.

35. Johan Galtung, C. G. Jacobsen, and Kai Frithjof Brand-Jacobsen, *Searching For Peace: The Road to Transcend*, Pluto Press, Sterling, VA, 2000, p. xiv.

36. Donald L Horowitz, *Ethnic Groups in Conflict*, University of California Press, Berkeley, Los Angeles 1985, p. 188.

37. David A. Lake and Donald Rothchild, "Containing Fear: The Origins and Management of Transnational Ethnic Conflict," *International Security* 21, no. 2 (Fall).

38. David A. Lake and Donald Rothchild, ibid.

39. Donald L. Horowitz, op. cit. p. 186.

40. Donald L. Horowitz, ibid., p. 189.

41. Donald L. Horowitz, ibid., p.199.

42. Alain Rouvez, op. cit. p. 17.

43. David R. Smock, ed. *Making War and Waging Peace: Foreign Intervention in Africa*, United States Institute of Peace Press, Washington, D. C., 1993, p. 5.

44. Yash Tandon, "Economic Policy and Conflict in Africa," *Journal of Peacebuilding and Development* 2, no. 1, 2004, p. 6-17.

45. Yash Tandon, ibid.

46. Yash Tandon, ibid.

47. Donald Horowitz, op. cit., p. 230.

48. Johan Galtung, C. G. Jacobsen, and Kai Frithjof Brand-Jacobsen, op. cit., p. xiii.

49. Margaret Levi, *Of Rule and Revenue*, University of California Press, Berkeley, 1988, p. 32.

50. Margaret Levi, ibid., p. 6.

51. Margaret Levi, ibid., p. 8.

52. Margaret Levi, ibid.

53. Margaret Levi, ibid., p. 46.

54. Margaret Levi, ibid., p. 46.

55. Marageret levi, ibid., p. 47.

56. Keith Somerville, "Burkinabes in Ivory Coast Firing Line," *BBC News*: http://news.bbc.co.uk/2/hi/Africa/2306087.stm, accessed on October 7, 2002.

57. Paul Welsh, "Ivory Coast: Who are the rebels?," *BBC News*: http://news.bbc.co.uk/2/hi/Africa/2662655.stm, accessed on January 15, 2003.

58   Lucy Ash, "France- Superpower or Sugar Daddy," in "France's New Mission," special issue, *BBC News*: http://news.bbc.co.uk/1/hi/special *report/1998/12/ French_in_Africa/235589.stm*, December 23, 1998.

59.   The works of Johann Galtung, Shivji and Mahmoud Mamdani refer.

60.   Craig R. Whitney, "Paris Snips Ties Binding It to Africa," *New York Times International*, July 25, 1997.

61.   David Smock, report from conference "Crises of War and Governance," United States Institute of Peace, January 16, 1997, http://www.usip.org. This represents one strand of the configuration of power thesis that was advanced at the conference on The International Community and the Post Mobutu Transition organized by the United States Institute of Peace on January 16, 1997.

62.   Jean-Michel Demetz, "The Shadows of Kabila," *L'Express*, no. 2394, April 22-May 20, 1997, p. 99-102.

63.   Francois Soudan, "Humiliation Francophone," *Jeune Afrique*, no. 1896, May 7-13, 1997.

64.   Albert Bourg, "Un Yalta Africain," in "En Verite," *Jeune Afrique*, no. 1896, May 7- 13, 1997, p. 6-7. Albert Bourg asserts that '*Aujourd'hui parvenus au pourvoir, les lieutenants de Mandela au sein de l'ANC, les Museveni, Aferweki, Zenawi, Nujoma, Kagame et Dos Santos ont trouve en Laurent -Desire Kabila l'allie leur permittent de dessiner, en Afrique orientale, australe et centrale, les contours d'un nouvel order africain.——Ayant opte deliberement pour un strategie de mouvement qui, de soucroit, s'inscrit dans la logique de leurs interets strategique, economique, commerciaux et financier, les Etats Unis sont passe de supplanter definitivement la France dans son role de 'chef d'orchestre' multiforme en Afrique. Indeniablement, ce reflux de la Francesur un 'pre-carre' en etat de siege pourrait avoir de repercussion sur ses allies rancophones d'Afrique de l'Ouest et d'Afrique centrale.'*

65.   Alain Rouvez, Michael Coco, and Jean-Paul Paddack, op. cit., p. 48.

66.   Vaiju Narawane, "The Stakes in Africa," *Hindu Newspaper*, November 10, 1996. Narawane observes that 'the second challenge to traditional French policy in Africa comes from enlightened Africans themselves. Newspapers in those countries in black Africa where a semblance of a free press exist contend that French presence in black Africa has essentially to do with perpetuating Paris' dominance in an area considered its zone of influence'.

67.   Adebayo Adebajo, op. cit., p. 31.

68.   Chris Mcgreal, "French calls for Zaire Force is Spurned," *Mail and Guardian*, March 14, 1997. Jan Pronk, Dutch Minister of Cooperation, after a visit to Zaire in the first week of March 1997, accused Paris of denying reality in its attempt to halt the imminent victory of the Alliance of Democratic Forces for the Liberation of Congo/Zaire. He is quoted as saying that 'the French refuse to allow any talk of the Zairean conflict as an internal' affair because Paris only wants it discussed in terms of a foreign invasion. That way it can justify foreign intervention to prop up what it sees as a pro -French government'

69   Lucy Ash, op. cit.

70. Le Petrole, "veritable cause du differend Tchad-Central afrique" *Minister*: http://www.izf.net/izf/AFP/francais/topics/tchad/021105201340.qqjecyc1.html, accessed on November 6, 2002.

71. Lucy Ash, op. cit.

72. Lucy Ash, op. cit.

73. Craig R. Whitney, op. cit.

74. Keith Somerville, op. cit.

Chapter 5

POLITICAL INSTABILITY IN GUINEA BISSAU

We would now explore recent political evolution of Guinea Bissau as a case study of the conceptual precepts discussed in the foregoing chapters. The conflicts in Guinea Bissau have their sources in the abandonment of the Cabralian concept of the cultural unity of all Guinean identities. The consequence of the repudiation of the Cabralian concept was the degeneration of the political process into a struggle by the major cultural groups in society for the total appropriation of the political space of the Guinean state. The extreme violence that has characterized the Bissau Guinean national process has reflected the intensity of the partisan search for absolute control of the state. The concept of the cultural unity of all Guinean identities was the foundational principle that underpinned the vision of state founder Amilcar Cabral of Guinea Bissau as a homogenous union of diverse cultures. This vision mobilized the indigenous peoples of Guinea Bissau, and those of the adjourning Bijagos islands and the Mullato (referred to as the *mesticos* locally) of the Cape Verde islands under the homogenizing crucible of a common struggle for liberation from Portuguese 'shameful colonialism'. Cabral's foundational principle also guided Guinea Bissau's liberation war that is reputed to be the most successful armed liberation struggle in black Africa. The powerful vision of one people forged by the harsh privations of a brutal common liberation struggle had propelled the unique liberation process of the two colonies of Guinea Bissau and Cape Verde islands against Portuguese colonialism that was jointly executed under the common platform of the Pan African Congress for the Independence of Guinea and Cape Verde (PAIGCV). Following the assassination of philosopher and statesman Amilcar Cabral in Conakry 1973 at the imminent end of the liberation war, his philosophy and vision provided a guiding worldview that motivated and directed the national process, including social, economic and political policy, from 1973 to 1980 under the leadership of Louis Cabral, a Mullato and half brother of the state founder. The 1980 coup d'etat of General Bernadino Vieira, one of Cabral's comrades-in-arms, essentially repudiated the foundational concept of the cultural unity of all Guinean identities that drove the revolution of Bissau Guinean peoples and on which the Bissau Guinean state was founded. In exploiting public misgivings about the domination of the state by the minority and elite Mullato, General Vieira's 1980 coup d'etat marked a watershed in the political evolution of Guinea Bissau. It set in motion a process of delegitimizing and unraveling a nascent national consciousness forged during the liberation war. It also instigated the derailment of Amilcar Cabral's vision of the political union of the Cape Verdean archipelagos, with its significant mulato population, and mainland Guinea Bissau into one state. The repudiation of this key principle by the anti-Mullato coup d'etat of 1980 changed the tenets of inter-group relations among the major groups in Guinea Bissau. It thus laid the foundation for the struggle for cultural ascendancy and the consequential violent search for partisan control of the political space and total state appropriation, which has been the dominant imperative of the national processes of Guinea Bissau since the end of the Civil War of 1998 and the continuing attempts at inaugurating a durable post-conflict democracy.

Amilcar Cabral was responsible for the revolutionary and nationalist orientation of the PAIGCV under his leadership until his assassination at the virtual defeat of Portuguese colonialism in Guinea Bissau and Cape Verde. Adherence to Cabral's vision legitimized policy in Guinea Bissau up to the mid 1980s. In the 1990s, the tumult against the one-party state in the wake of the end of the Cold War, the decay and schisms in the PAIGC stemming from its obsolete revolutionary methods, and the wave of democratization in post-colonial African states imposed a new litmus test for regime legitimacy. The test of regime validation shifted away from revolutionary rhetoric against abstract imperialism to the electoral process and empowerment of the population in the democratic process as well as the attainment of concrete social and economic development. The continued linkage and dominant role of the military faction in the ruling PAIGC in the political process also became anachronistic in the context of the emerging international environment of the late 1990s. Democratization of country's militarized political system that was steeped in, and operated on revolutionary principles presented formidable challenges for the status quo regime, for continued internal coherence for the PAIGC and for national cohesion of the Bissau Guinean state and society that had, by this time, developed many poles of diverse approaches and orientations to social, economic and political development.

The imperatives of democratizing Guinea Bissau, in the context of its formidable economic challenges, raised considerable questions about the continued validity of its historical strategic engagements in the immediate sub-region. This posed clear problems for continued validation and the manner of the expression of its relations with intermestic forces, mainly the Movement for Democratic Forces of the Casamance (MFDC) of Senegal that claimed major stakes in the direction and the outcome of the political evolution of the country. By 1998 Guinea Bissau and the MFDC were firmly locked in a relationship that was given birth to by the full engagement and sacrifices of the Casamancaise in Guinean Bissau's revolutionary anti-colonial struggle. Since then, Bissau Guinean forces have been implicated in the operations of the MFDC in the Casamance in the south of Senegal. The demands of democratization and the attendant reconfiguration of the internal structure and balance of power among disparate forces in the nascent democracy in Guinea Bissau elicited new strategic considerations that polarized stakeholders in the state and society, the political forces, and the military that was now riled by ethnic interests. The new strategic thrust radically altered the calculus of national strategic stakes by states in the sub-region and impacted on the undercurrents of the competition between Portugal and France that sought to expand its zone of influence in the sub-region and, working through Senegal, to integrate Guinea Bissau into its orbit of control. These have constituted the major elements of the complexities that have fed into the dynamics of the violent Bissau Guinean political process.

Without the clear ideological compass of the Cabralian worldview and the associated concept of cultural unity now jaded, the management of the contradictions thrown up by the process of democratization in Guinea Bissau in the early 1990s proved beyond the capacity of a PAIGC now divided into factions. A dominant faction that perceived itself as defenders of the Cabralian traditions emerged in a military junta that sought to retain the integrity of state policy, in particular in relation to the struggle of the Casamancaise in Southern Senegal, most of who trace their antecedents to Gabou in Guinea Bissau. This struggle fed into the undercurrents of the continuous search of ascendancy by major cultural groups, including a new third political force represented by the rise of the Mandingue and their affiliated cultural groups as a major political force in the country. This search translated into a heightened struggle for the control of the political space, notably by the Balanta, that had begun since General Nino Vieira removed President Louis Cabral from power. The struggle exacerbated the historical competition for ascendancy between the Balanta, who claimed the majority of the population of Guinea Bissau, and the elite minority mulato that had found its way back into dominant role in the public sphere. It reiterated the Balanta and the question of the mulato as the enduring challenge of Bissau Guinean politics. The political evolution of Guinea Bissau in the post-

Civil War era has been dominated by the violent currents of the struggle of the Balanta to dominate the state.

Tensions and conflicts in Guinea Bissau thus revolve around the continuing struggles between defenders of the vision and ideals of Amilcar Cabral, the founding father of the Bissau Guinean state and Cape Verde, against political forces that have deviated from these conceptions. The two forces, the defenders and defectors, however have their roots in the Cabralian tradition. In the development of a national consciousness, Amilcar Cabral highlighted the important role of the political and moral unity of the liberation movement through the preservation of the positive cultural values of every well defined social group, of every category, and to achieve the confluence of these values to give a new national dimension. This unity is achieved on the one hand by total identification with the environmental reality and with the fundamental problems and aspirations of the people; and on the other hand, by progressive cultural identification of the various social groups participating in the struggles.[1] There was an emphasis on the economic, social, political and cultural reality of Guinea Bissau.[2] Conflicts in Guinea Bissau have resulted partly from attempts to reinstate Cabral's foundational principles of the Bissau Guinean state and to sustain the integrity of historical relationships of one people in a diversity of cultures forged during the liberation war against forces bent on repudiating these principles. Continued bloodshed in the post-conflict Guinea Bissau has also resulted from the determined thrust of the Balanta to take over the Bissau Guinean state, with all necessary means and at all costs. The entrenched dominant role of the military in the political process, which dates back to the years of the liberation struggle, has militated against the development of a civilian democratic culture. The incapacity of the Bissau Guinean political system to effectively delink the military from political control and the various attempts to transform the military into an instrument of partisan political control remains an embedded structural conflict factor in the Buissau Guinean political system. All the regimes after the overthrow of Louis Cabral in 1980, Bernandino Viera, Kumba Yala as well as the General Ansumane Mane-led military junta have sought to use the military to advance their parochial ethno-religious political agendas. Given the inextricable link between the military and the political process, the political process has been characterized by recourse to revolutionary violence.

The betrayal of the political vision of Amilcar Cabral that directed the liberation struggle for the independence of Guinea Bissau has plagued the entire history of the country. This has been expressed in cycles of political violence that, since 1980, has escalated into intermittent civil wars and continuing political violence. These wars have been motivated by the pursuit of political ascendancy by those who perceive themselves as the true indigenes of Guinea Bissau vis-à-vis the mulato as well as violent schisms by the Balanta, who have demographic superiority over various other indigenous groups that constitute important minorities in the population. The dislodgement of the mulato from the commanding heights of the administration and economy, and schisms between major constituent groups in the country to dominate the political system have had deleterious impact on stability. It is within this context that the internal political process in Guinea Bissau has been dominated by the search for control of the state by the Balanta. This has engendered a new dynamic that repudiates the nationalist unity that marked the years of the liberation struggle and which was the foundation of the visions of Amilar Cabral. It all began with the assassination of Amilcar Cabral in Conakry. Meanwhile, the planned union of the Cape Verde islands and mainland Guinea Bissau was repudiated. The Cape Verdean state dissociated itself from the new political course being charted on the mainland and renamed its faction of the Pan African Party for the Independence of Guinea and Cape Verde (PAIGC) as the Pan African Party for the Independence of Cape Verde (PAICV).

The assassination of the soldier, philosopher and statesman Amicar Cabral in 1973 at the virtual defeat of the Portuguese colonial army in Bissau laid the grounds for the derailment of his vision. The 1980 coup of General Joao Bernadino Vieira, who overthrew the government of Louis Cabral, Amilcar's half brother, finally concretized the long-term designs of the Portuguese imperial interest to sever the Cape Verdean islands from the mainland Guinea. Toward this end, Portuguese PDE (secret service) operatives had sown the seeds of animosity between mainland Guineans and Cape Verdeans, first to eliminate Amilcar Cabral and ultimately to break up the planned union of the two peoples who had jointly fought a war of liberation. Secondly, the historical linkages between the people of Guinea Bissau and their kith and kin in the Casamance assured that the insecurity in the adjacent Senegalese province of Casamance would impact on the evolution of internal struggles among various groups in Guinea Bissau. This intermestic impact brought to the fore the complexities of the immediate environment in which the country is situated.

The changes that have emerged with the transformations in Guinea Bissau have made more complex the two unresolved historical cleavages around which political instability, since independence, has revolved. These are the problems of the domination of the state by the mulato (known as the mestisco in Guinea Bissau) and the marginalization of black indigenous population, particularly the Balanta, who constitute the largest single ethnic block in the country, in national life. The former is considered largely responsible for the violent overthrow of Louis Cabral in 1980, which, in turn, also disrupted the steady move to unify Guinea Bissau and Cape Verde. The Balanta question was at the heart of the violent suppression of officers of that ethnic group in the military in 1986. It also lay behind the façade of the insurgency on November 2000. At the same time, internal strife within Balanta political circles in the context of the evolving hegemony has contributed profoundly to political instability since the end of the post-conflict transition in 1999.

Continuous outbreak of armed hostilities in Guinea Bissau since May 1998 reflects the final unraveling of the revolutionary and exceptional character of Guinea Bissau as an expression of the vision of its founder Amilcar Cabral. This unraveling resulted directly from the gradual decay of the PAIGC, following Cabral's assassination by Portuguese agents in January 1973,[3] independence of Guinea Bissau in 1974 and the ethnically motivated coup d'etat of 1980 that brought into the open tensions between the largely Cape Verdean mulato and the indigenous black population of mainland Guinea Bissau.

In the wake of the assassination of Amilcar Cabral, the immediate and vital problems of the survival of the party and the transition to the post-colonial period were overcome effectively. Nonetheless, Cabral's role as party thinker and organizer was not fully assumed by anyone else and it is clear that the PAIGC would have continued to benefit greatly from his leadership.[4] As a consequence, the political process in Bissau Guinea acquired the traditional characteristics of post-colonial states to be dominated by the violent struggle for the appropriation of the state by the major constituent and contending groups within and outside the state. This situation was rendered more complicated by the activities of powerful elite state actors, Portugal and France, whicht sought to keep Guinea Bissau under their hegemonic control. Domestic forces in the struggles in Guinea Bissau are directly or indirectly aligned to either of these two external players in Bissau. They also cultivate allies in the immediate sub-region who serve as proxies to their interests.

An important undercurrent which provided the immediate spark to the armed hostilities and struggles in Guinea Bissau is the continuing competition between Portugal, the former colonial metropole of the country, and France. The latter is seeking to consolidate its influence in the ex-Portuguese colony, in the wake of the opportunistic opening offered by President Joao Bernadino Viera's decision to join the France controlled CFA monetary zone (Monetary Union of West Africa in West Africa) in 1997. The difficult sub-regional sociological, historical, security complexities that drew transnational forces in the region, including from Senegal, Gambia and Guinea Conakry into, first, the liberation struggles under the PAIGC, have also lately implicated the three countries in the conflict and the political processes in Guinea Bissau. These same factors have also entangled Guinea Bissau in the over two decades of Diolla irredentism in the Senegalese southern region of Casamance. The conflicts in Guinea Bissau are also directly related to the fortunes of the Diolla dominated MFDC that is fighting for the independence of that region from Senegal.

The conflicts in Guinea Bissau are thus rooted in the struggle for domestic hegemony by the major constituent groups in the country. This is compounded by the struggle between Portugal and France to dominate the social, economic and political space of the country. By implication, Senegal, Gambia and Guinea Conakry have large stakes in the outcome of the struggles in Guinea Bissau. Political instability in Guinea Bissau can therefore be attributed to its double instrumental character. This follows the decay of the revolutionary fervor that gave the country its peculiar place as the product of the most successful nationalist movement in Black Africa and the first to achieve independence through armed struggle.[5]

SOCIETY IN GUINEA BISSAU

The exploration of the rivers of Guinea and the islands of Cape Verde was among the earliest undertakings of Portugal in Africa. Portugal claimed Guinea in 1446, but few trading posts were established before 1600.[6] Portuguese Guinea, as it was defined by the 1886 agreement between France and Portugal, is a small territory of some 32,000 square kilometers wedged between the former French colony of Senegal to the north and Guinea (Conakry) to the east and south.[7] Before the agreement, there had been considerable rivalry and competition between Portugal, France and Great Britain over portions of the territory of modern day Guinea Bissau claimed by each of those powers. In this connection,

> Portuguese conquest and consolidation of the interior did not begin until the latter half of the 19th century. Portugal lost part of Guinea to French West Africa, including the center of earlier Portuguese commercial interest, the Casamance River region. A dispute with Great Britain over the islands of Bolama was settled in Portugal's favor with the involvement of U S President Ulysses S. Grant.[8]

Meanwhile, the process of pacifying the interior of the country was difficult. Notwithstanding the collaboration of the Muslim population to conquer other indigenous African tribes, the interior of Portuguese Guinea was pacified only after more than 30 years of fighting. The Bijagos islands did not come under effective Portuguese control until 1836. In 1941 the administrative capital was moved from Bolama to Bissau, originally established as a military and slave trading post in 1765. In 1952, by constitutional amendment, the colony of Portuguese Guinea became an overseas province of Portugal.[9]

Guinea Bissau, at the same time, was once part of the old Kingdom of Gabou, the southernmost reaches of the old Mali Empire. Its territory covers nearly 37,000 square kilometers (14,000sq miles). It is bordered by Senegal to the north, Guinea (Conakry) to the south and east. The Atlantic Ocean is to the west. The population of Guinea Bissau is estimated at 1.6 million people. It's ethnically diverse population replicates the problematic structure typical of post-colonial African states. The population can be divided into three main ethnic groups: Foula and Mandinka speaking people to the north and north-eat, the Balanta and Papel in the southern coastal region, who constitute the largest ethnic group; and the Manjaco and Mancanha in the central and northern coastal areas. The ethnic groups in Guinea Bissau are often small communities of larger ethnic groups that flow across international boundaries in the sub-region. The remainder of the population is made up of Mesticos of mixed Portuguese and African descent, including a small community of Cape Verdeans. The Portuguese population left following the loss of the liberation war by Portugal. There are also the Diolla and Fuola, who are a minority of the larger stock of these communities in Guinea Conakry, Southern Senegal (Casamance) and the Gambia. The Mandingo, who live in islands of communities in Fuola country, are spread across West Africa with a bigger ethnic community in Guinea Conakry that flows into Guinea Bissau and through the north into Senegal. The Madinka, Diolla and Fuola community in the immediate sub region trace their origins to Gabou and consider this provincial town as their spiritual home. The Balanta form the largest single stock of ethnic group in Guinea Bissau and are traditionally found across the central western part of the country up to the north on the border with Senegal. Other major groups include the Peul, a sub group of the Fulbe group in West Africa, Fellupes, Biafadas and the Nalus. In the islands are also the Bijagos.

The population of Guinea Bissau is young. In 1991 40% of the population was less than 15 years old. The population of young people; that is less than 25 years, increased from 51% in 1960 to 63% in 1991. Women represent 52% of the population with 25% within childbearing ages. The ratio of men to women is 93 to 100. Each woman of childbearing age is expected to have 5.4 children. Death rate is very high at 18 to 20 per 1000. Infant mortality is at an alarming rate and life expectancy at birth is 45 years. The literacy rate in 1995 was 54%. The population of Guinea Bissau is unevenly distributed over 3500 towns and villages across the national territory. Bissau, the capital of the country, has a concentration of socio-economic infrastructure, facilities and administration. The availability of formal paid employment is also concentrated in Bissau. These confer on Bissau the advantage of being the center of national life and processes. More than 30% of the population lives in urban centers (1991 census) because of its strong pull of people from rural communities. This state of affairs reflects the absence of balance in the development policy. The eight other administrative provinces, apart form the capital Bissau, are Bafata, Cacheu, Bolama/Bijagos,

Gabu, Oio, Quinara, and Tombali. This multi-ethnic population is divided between Muslims, who may be said to constitute about 40%, Christians, 35% and 25% practitioners of indigenous faith and traditional religion.

CABRAL'S FOUNDATIONAL PRINCIPLES

The African Party for the Independence of Guinea and Cape Verde (PAIGC) was founded in 1956 by Amilcar Cabral and Rapheal Barbosa as a clandestine organization to engage in a revolutionary struggle for the liberation of Guinea Bissau and the Cape Verde. Before then, the Front for the Liberation of Guinea (FLING) based in Dakar had unsuccessfully sought the acquiescence of the Senegalese government to launch an armed engagement against the Portuguese colonial administration in Bissau. With the support of President Sekou Toure of Guinea Conakry, the PAIGC moved its headquarters to Conakry, Guinea, in 1960 and started an armed rebellion against the Portuguese in 1961.[10] The presence of over 35,000 Portuguese forces notwithstanding, the PAIGC steadily took control of most of the country. The failure of the Portuguese military had profound consequences, as its Governor and Commander in Chief from 1968 to 1973, General Antonio de Spinoza, returned home and led the movement that brought democracy to Portugal and independence to its colonies.[11] Meanwhile, Amilcar Cabral was assassinated in Conakry in 1973 and Aristides Pereira assumed the leadership of the movement. The National Assembly organized by the PAIGC as it controlled most of the territory met in Boe in the southeastern region and declared independence on 24 September, 1973. Portugal granted formal independence to the country on 10 September, 1974 following its revolution of April 1974. Louis Cabral, Amilcar Cabral's half brother, became the first President of liberated and independent Guinea Bissau.

The anticipated character of independent Guinea Bissau evolving from the liberation struggle was to deviate from the norm of the post-colonial African state. This expectation derived from the very process and principles that were integral to its liberation struggle. The evolution of the policies of the PAIGC reflected the objectives of Amilcar Cabral.[12] The specific conditions of colonialism in Guinea Bissau and on the Cape Verde islands were instrumental to the political development of Amilcar Cabral. Portuguese colonialism meant a stagnant existence coupled with the absence of personal dignity and liberty Cabral observes that in the early 1970s, More than 90% of the population could not read or write. Sixty percent of the babies died before reaching the age of one year. Forty percent of the population suffered from sleeping sickness and almost everyone had some form of malaria. There were never more than 11 doctors for the entire rural population, or one doctor for every 45,000 Africans.[13]

In the face of these privations, Cabral did not define the Portuguese as the enemy. The enemy was seen neither simply as poverty, disease, or lack of education nor as the Portuguese people or whites; rather it was colonialism and its parent, imperialism. For him, "Bissau Guineans were forced to take up arms in order to extirpate from the soil of our African fatherland, the shameful Portuguese colonial domination."[14]

Patrick Chabal observes that some of the most significant party policies were:

> ... the maintenance of political control over the armed struggle and the development of a guerrilla war based on popular mobilization; the achievement of nationalist unity inside the country by co-opting rather than excluding serious nationalist rivals and by neutralizing those who chose a pattern of exile politics; the attempt to transform Guinean society during, rather than after, the struggle; the determination to achieve party policies by revolutionary democratic system in which party rule and popular aspirations could be balanced...and collaboration with Portuguese democratic opposition.[15]

Cabral's definition of the enemy was central to the political, moral and humanist principles which characterized the liberation struggle. It reflected a policy of fighting a clean revolutionary war which repudiated the use of terrorism as a tactic and was constantly demonstrated in his refusal to maintain party unity by means of physical elimination of those with dissenting or alternative opinions. More significantly, Cabral had an almost obsessive desire to rehabilitate party members who had been convicted for personal or political misconduct.[16] This set the basis for the creation of a truly democratic space in the liberated zones and that was expected to be consolidated throughout the national territory on attaining full independence.[17] Finally, Cabral's principles reflected pragmatism over ideological dogmatism or rigidity. He sought a convergence of views to forge durable unity of purpose which derided from existential realities and experiences rather than from universal political doctrines.[18] These foundational principles that had proven instrumental to the profound successes of the war of liberation, have since constituted in the collective minds of Bissau Guineans the test of legitimacy of policy and action of successor leaders.

VIERA'S 1980 COUP D'ETAT AND THE DECAY OF THE PAIGC

Joao Bernandino Viera's coup d'etat of 1980 was a watershed and marked the effective derailment of the hope that independent Guinea Bissau would be directed by the visions of Amicar Cabral. The coup and the subsequent policies of the government effectively marked a break from the Cabral injunctions of the imperative of a continuing search for cultural harmony between the various cultural groups in Guinea Bissau and the humanistic tenets that guided the liberation struggle. Significantly, the coup d'etat resonated with the operations orchestrated by the Portuguese secret police, the PIDE-DGS, since 1971 to exploit a perceived racial split between Cape Verdeans and mainland Guineans to prepare the grounds for the elimination of Amilcar Cabral and also frustrate the declared goal of the emergence of one united state comprising the peoples of Cape Verde and mainland Guinea Bissau. The immediate task in 1971 was to assassinate Amilcar Cabral under the guise of disagreements over policy within the PAIGC, followed by the pursuit of Portuguese strategic interests, which lay in severing Cape Verde islands from mainland Guinea. It was to this end that the Portuguese secret police engaged in massive anti-Cape Verdean propaganda campaign in mainland Guinea Bissau.

The 1980 coup thus reflected the success of the long-term strategic goal of Portugal to severe Cape Verde from the Guinean mainland through the exploitation of an orchestrated discord on racial lines in the Guinean mainland. The Portuguese establishment considered mainland Guinea Bissau as of no value and sought to retain direct control of Cape Verde, given its strategic significance, should Guinea Bissau declare its independence.[19] Nino Viera's coup d'etat was the final betrayal of the visions of Amilcar Cabral that helped to concretize the Portuguese designs on the two peoples. The PAIGC in Guinea Bissau, from which the Cape Verde side had withdrawn to create the African Party for the Independence of Cape Verde (PAICV) in 1981, was in steep decline following the open disavowal of the true Guinean nationality of the mulato "counterfeits" and the insistence of the "original copies" to remove the mulato from commanding sectors of the national process. Many mulato age-long residents of the Guinean mainland emigrated to Cape Verde, Portugal, Boston area in the United States as well as the Netherlands.

The initial removal of the mulato from day-to-day administration opened a pandora's box among the indigenous peoples who began to assert their relative rights to political power on the basis of their demographic strength and being indigenous to the country. The Balanta, who constitute about 40% of the population, were most prominent in this restiveness. President Viera soon discovered that the pool of technical and administrative expertise available outside the mulato circles was quite limited and was, therefore, forced into rehabilitating those who were still interested in retaining their positions in the administration. Against the background of the successful anti-mulatto campaign on which Nino Vieira's rode to power, the rehabilitation of the mulato by him almost immediately after gaining power smacked of inconsistency or opportunism. The continued prominence of the mulato in national life and administration exacerbated anti-mulato sentiments. General Viera in overthrowing the regime of Louis Cabral had also rendered more complicated a potential crisis of national identity that had simmered from the very beginnings of the liberation struggle in 1963. The coup of 1980 thus amounted to a repudiation of the central pillars of Amilcar Cabral's theory of achieving nationalist unity through progressive cultural identification of the various social groups participating in the struggles. The coup therefore opened a difficult chapter separating the era of a unified nationalist struggle underpinned by the philosophy of Amilcar Cabral from the beginning of an internal struggle within the PAIGC. The two tendencies were forces determined to salvage Cabral's legacy and those whose political activities tended to undermine that legacy.

The state establishment, under President Bernandino Vieira, was perceived as representing threats to the legacy of the Amilcar Cabral group by the anti-establishment group. As a consequence of the dubious legitimacy of any project that tended to assault the integrity of the philosophy and memory of Amilcar Cabral, the Viera regime survived through coercion and political patronage for as long as possible. To consolidate his increasingly unpopular government and against the ground rules established by Amilcar Cabral, Nino Viera executed countless opponents and uncovered numerous attempts at coup d'etat. Victims included Vice President Paulo Correia and Attorney General Viriato Pam, along with 20 others who disappeared in 1985, for attempting to topple his regime in 1984. Following the overthrow of Vieira's government, the 22 bodies exhumed in 1999 from unmarked mass graves in Mansoa, 60 km north east of Bissau, were later identified as those of Nino Viera's Vice President, his Attorney General and 21 others who were accused of plotting to overthrow the government. Many other unmarked graves were discovered by the Procurer General Amin Saad in 1999 which he presented as evidence to buttress a request to Portugal, where Nino Vieira had taken refuge, for the nullification of his status as a political exile. Political opponents had been executed despite the fact that, in line with Cabral's principles, the constitution of Guinea Bissau forbids the death penalty.[20]

By 1991, General Bernnadino Viera, responding to internal pressures and external demands, began the project of the liberalization of the political space. This culminated in the conduct of popular elections in 1994 to shore up the legitimacy of his continued hold over power, given rumors of imagined and real coups d'etat. The outcome of the elections confirmed the disenchantment of the population with his rule. In the elections, a fledgling and harassed opposition Party for Social Renewal (PRS) led by Kumba Yala, a former seminarian radically opposed to any orthodoxy, won 62% of the popular vote against the PAIGC that continued to assert itself as the liberation party. However, by a peculiar method for calculating representation in parliament, the PRS which won 62% of the popular vote was awarded 48% of the seats in the 102 Peoples National Assembly. Though the PAIGC allocated to itself a majority in parliament and controlled its leadership, the party had in fact lost the first multi-party elections in Guinea Bissau. In the run-off of the presidential election, Kumba Yala won 48.2% of the popular vote. Many observers note that he had in fact won a majority vote in the presidential elections[21].

These developments underlined the serious internal crisis within the PAIGC as well as the clear mandate to alternative political formations to lead the country. Bernadino Vieira's government, having repudiated the legacy of Amilcar Cabral and now sanctioned by the electorate in the 1994 elections, became more repressive and depended largely on coercion to suppress internal dissent. The verdict rendered by Bissau Guineans in the elections and the clear dangers posed to the Vieira presidency informed strategies adopted by Nino Viera in preparation for the 1998 elections. These new policies entailed initiatives to shore up the weak Bissau Guinean economy by integrating it into a broader sub-regional economic framework. This had become imperative with the imminence of the need to consolidate the democratic openings achieved in 1994. Besides, the Bissau Guinea economy was helpless against hyper-inflation and the virtual loss of value of its currency, the peso, which was backed by Portugal.

In May 1997, Bernadino Viera switched the nation's currency, the peso, for the French-backed CFA. The integration of the Bissau Guinean economy into the Monetary Union of the West African States (UEMOA) had serious implications for continued bilateral relations with Senegal, in the light of the historical collaboration between the Bissau Guinean military and the MFDC in its irredentist struggle in the Casamance. This change also had significant implications for relations with Portugal which remained apprehensive over the increasing encroachment of French influence in Guinea Bissau. The implications of President Vieira's new strategies designed to shore up the legitimacy of the government through economic liberalization and far-reaching realignment of Guinea Bissau's foreign and security policy ultimately tore the last shreds that held together the powerful political wing of the PAIGC and the Nino Viera presidency.

The alienation of the military, which traditionally has controlled the political process since independence, from the Nino presidency, along with key PAIGC members in politics, led to open denunciations between the two blocs of the PAIGC. By 1997, the decay of the PAIGC was expressed in serious disharmony and policy divergencies between the political establishment around Nino Vieira and defenders of the legacy of Amilcar Cabral located with the military, led by General Ansumane Mane, with the support of radical elements within the political system, including Francisco Bernante, key members of the party, Malam Bacai Sahna as well as prominent activists in civil society such as Amin Saad. These schisms were heightened by policy differences over the economy and continuing support for the MFDC, which President Nino Viera had repudiated. The heightened political tension beginning from early 1997, which culminated in the civil war in June 1998 and the overthrow of President Viera in May 1999, represented the last struggles for the protection of the integrity of the vision of Amilcar Cabral by the military against those who were perceived as using his legacy as a manipulative instrument to remain in power and legitimize their actions.[22]

THE PROBLEM OF TRANSNATIONAL FORCES: SENEGAL, THE MFDC AND CIVIL WAR

The link between Guinea Bissau and the separatists in Senegal's Casamance province runs deep. The people on both sides are mostly of the same ethnic group and the two regions had been one territory under the Portuguese until Casamance was ceded to France in 1888. More important, Casamance fighters helped the Guineans win their bloody war of independence from Portugal in 1974.[23] For Senegal, the conflicts in Guinea Bissau and in its Casamance province are really one.[24] One of the enduring legacies of the struggle for liberation was the close alliance formed between the Diollas and Mandigues of the Casamance, Guinea Conakry and the Gambia with the PAIGC. They were found among the ranks of the PAIGC cadres during the war of liberation and many saw themselves as citizens, or, in the least, as members of their larger community that spread as far as Guinea Bissau. Prominent among these was Ansumane Mane, who was acknowledged to be Gambian as well as Bissau Guinean. Many Casamancaise were automatically integrated into the Bissau Guinean military at the end of the liberation struggle and held command positions. The Bissau Guinea military as well as the state was therefore sympathetic to the cause of the Casamancaise. The sympathy translated into both military and diplomatic support for the MFDC that was engaged in a struggle to carve that province out of Senegal. The radical re-alignment of policy undertaken by President Nino Viera elicited stout opposition from the military, led by Chief of Defence Staff, General Ansumane Mane, a Madingue with roots in the Gambia.

The practical implication of the policy realignment was for President Vieira to repudiate support for the MFDC in order to achieve a status of good standing in the francophone UEMOA in which Senegal had considerable political weight and the support of France. France stood to gain from the Guinea Bissau integration into the French-backed CFA zone because it strengthened in-roads already made and also reduced by one another potential recruit into the Economic Community of West African States (ECOWAS), that France was determined to make ineffective, if not completely derailed.

France perceived and consistently promoted the idea of the sub-regional political and economic grouping ECOWAS as a rival to francophone UEMOA. It had kept the two apart in order to ensure its continued control over the francophone states in its orbit of influence in the sub-region. Apart from the problem of the Casamance which was a source of irritation between Guinea Bissau and Senegal, significant off-shore oil reserves have been an important source of conflict between the two countries over the years. Guinea Bissau continued to protest the formulae adopted in sharing revenue derived from the oil fields under the control of Senegal. Senegal paid Guinea Bissau 10% of the receipts generated from the oil field. Several disputes in relation to the demarcation of the territorial waters of the two countries arose and were lodged with the International Court in the Hague[25]. It was, however, well known that President Nino Vieira had entered into an understanding with Elf Aquitaine for his personal profit.

Finally, against the backdrop of the widening influence of France and French-speaking informal businesses in Guinea Bissau which resulted largely from Bissau's dependence on Senegalese ports and markets to supply the markets, General Ansumane, with strong roots in the Gambia, remained suspicious of the agenda of Senegal and France in his country. These were elements that fuelled the profound divergence of views within the PAIGC. This was expressed in personal affront between General Ansumane Mane and President Bernadino Viera who both personified the two poles of this policy difference. In May 1998, President Viera relieved General Ansumane Mane of his position as the Chief of Defence Staff on allegations of complicity in gun running in the Bissau Guinean military for the MFDC. The President followed General Mane's removal with the appointment of a new Chief of the National Armed forces on June 5. A Parliamentary Investigation Commission on Arms Sale concluded that President Vieira and a large group around him were responsible for the arms trade with the Casamance. The report called for the trial of the president.

General Ansumane Mane's defiance of the President resulted in a military face-off between loyalists of Ansumane Mane and President Vieira. On 7 Jun, 1998, shooting began in military installations at Santa Lucia and spread quickly to the military bases in Bra. On 9 June, a spokesman for General Ansumane Mane announced the formation of a military junta which called for the resignation of the President in order to create conditions for the holding of democratic elections within sixty days.[26] As early as June 9, the very day of the rebel's initial declaration, 1300 troops from Senegal were already in place in Bissau on the demands of President Vieira to support few loyalist troops. They were joined by 400 soldiers from Guinea the next day. Thus the conflict was almost immediately regionalized.[27]

The military Junta, composed of Mane loyalists, took over the main military bases and arms depots, as well as Radio Pidjiguity in Bissau. Under the battle cry of "*hora tchiga*" (time for change) , the military junta in radio broadcasts demanded an improvement in the living conditions of soldiers and national heroes of the war of liberation and accused the president of ineffective governance marred by corruption. Significantly, the military junta emphasized that its goal was not a coup d'etat and had no plans to take over power. The military, overwhelmingly in support of General Mane, reminded the President that they were comrades in arms who had fought together for the liberation of the country and accordingly called for dialogue with their "Camamrada Presidente Vieira". The junta was supported by a vast majority of the civilian population and its demands on the president were popular. Appeals to the president by civil society groups, including from the Catholic Bishop of Bissau, as well as the delegation of the People's National Assembly to negotiate with the rebellion were unheeded. President Vieira argued that as a democratically elected head of state, he could not negotiate with criminals. Vieira insisted that the Bissau Guinean military was providing a sanctuary for MFDC rebels within the territory of the country and was undermining regional security through its collaboration with the irredentist Senegalese movement[28]. After the first day of the war, President Vieira appeared politically isolated and abandoned by most of his army.[29] By the 6th week, the junta had consolidated its military hold over the capital, Bissau, and in all military formations throughout the country. President Nino Vieira and his government remained confined to the more central parts of the city and totally dependent on foreign troops.

The Bissau Guinean military was thus nearly unanimous in the request for negotiations with the president. They were joined by elements of the MFDC to defend positions held by the junta forces. Mamadou Krumah Sane, deputy leader of the MFDC, explained that his movement joined in the war to fight against the neo-colonial adventure of Senegal in Guinea Bissau. He added that their main "objective was to liberate Casamance from Senegalese control (it's never been a part of Senegal either before or after the French came) and then to create the Federation of Gabou with Guinea Bissau and Gambia"[30]. The invasion of Senegalese forces galvanized a united national resistance that quickly isolated President Vieira and the forces under his command. The Senegalese military in launching its "Operation Gabou" in Bissau, a name resonant with its sarcasm to crush the ambition to create the republic of Gabou through the secession of Casamance and a subsequent re-grouping with Guinea Bissau, Gambia, believed that its intervention was going to be a quick intervention. The radical wing of the MFDC saw the creation of a federation of Casamance, with Gambia and Guinea Bissau as the ultimate goal of the struggle.[31] This undue sarcasm and overconfidence of Senegal proved to be a gross underestimation as the Senegalese forces were defeated from battle to battle. As its casualties mounted, Dakar urged Vieira to seek the intervention of ECOWAS[32]. As the Senegalese army got embroiled in Guinea Bissau and closed its borders, the MFDC resumed attacks on Senegalese forces based in Zuguinchor, the Casamance capital. A small French military technical contingent stationed in the French Embassy in Bissau was overpowered by the junta forces. In spite of its domination of the military situation, the military junta reiterated that its plan was not to take over power and repeatedly called for foreign facilitation of negotiations with their former comrade, the president.

THE ABUJA ACCORD OF NOVEMBER 1998

In the absence of any meaningful engagement by the international community in the early days of the Bissau Guinean crisis, the sole diplomatic action to ensure a temporary truce and to facilitate negotiations was undertaken by the Swedish charge d'affaires, a.i. in Bissau, Ulla Andrein, representing one of the traditional development partners of the country. Ulla Andrein contrasted the openness on the side of the junta to her mediation with the complete lack of transparency of the Vieira camp during the conflict. She also observed the involvement of France in the presidential palace where President Vieira was holed in. "Nobody knows what is going on behind the wall of the presidential palace, except for the fact that they have constantly been hindering the peace process".[33] Throughout the early days of the conflict, Sweden's diplomatic chancery remained open and accessible to the embattled people of the country. At this critical time, Sweden provided an important window to the outside world, interpreting developments and urging a humane appreciation of the unfortunate events unfolding in the country. Indeed, Swedish diplomats in Bissau, in direct contacts with the protagonists in the civil war, provided the most visible, if not the only, international moral force on the ground that unrelentingly worked to achieve a negotiated settlement of the political crisis.

Just as no military solution was in sight, efforts at mediation by the Bishop of Bissau, and the foreign ministers of the Gambia, Portugugal and Angolan acting together also failed to bring the belligerents together. The rebels declared themselves for talks, but demanded the withdrawal of Senegalese troops, the number which had increased by some hundreds since the first days of their deployment in Bissau. The President still insisted that the rebels would have to lay down their arms without conditions[34]. Portugal, in providing the rebels with communications access to the outside world, helped to break their isolation. It also led members of the Community of Portuguese Speaking States (CPLP) to broker a formal truce on July 26. The agreement called for the withdrawal of Senegalese forces and Guinean troops from Guinea Bissau and their replacement by military observers from Lusophone countries.[35] This was followed by a meeting in Praia, Cape Verde, which led to a signing of the formal ceasefire on 26 August, 1998.

The intervention of ECOWAS began with a meeting of foreign and defence ministers of member states in Abidjan, the capital of Cote d'Ivoire, on 3-4 July. They decided that ECOMOG, the regional peacekeeping force deployed to Liberia and Sierra Leone under Nigerian leadership, would have its mandate extended to Guinea Bissau. The diplomatic intervention of ECOWAS was undertaken against a difficult backdrop of schisms between it and the CPLP, on the one hand, and internal problems within the Community itself along the francophone-Anglophone divide. CPLP mediation initially generated reservations from the ECOWAS. On the other hand, Portugal was, like General Mane, suspicious of the mediation of francophone countries, including Senegal. The invasion of Bissau by Senegal and Guinea Conakry on the side of President Vieira and the clear interests of Senegal because of the involvement of the MFDC and the Casamance problem added additional complexities to the war in Bissau. The Senegalese were probably making a negotiated settlement difficult and were using the ceasefire brokered by the CPLP to strengthen their military positions. Senegal insisted that the ECOWAS was better suited than the CPLP to lead negotiations, and wanted a regional peacekeeping force to take over.

For Portugal, the problem was that two of ECOWAS members, Senegal and Guinea, were already engaged in the war.[36] Portugal was also aware of the French interests in the evolution of the crisis in Guinea Bissau, and it put its stakes as the ex-colonial power of the embattled country, in direct opposition to France's design to usurp the political control of post-colonial state. According to Portuguese sources, Senegal was pushed to go to help Mr. Vieira by France. But pushed or not, Senegal had good reason to fear the rebels taking over Guinea Bissau. They are sympathetic to Senegal's own rebels in the Casamance, a region that borders Guinea Bissau and, until 1888, was part of it. The people on both sides of the border are of the same ethnic origin[37]. France also had significant leverage within the ECOWAS to move the mediation process in its favor. The CPLP was thus directly involved with the ECOWAS in negotiating the agreement between President Vieira and General Mane in Abuja, Nigeria. To counter-balance increasing French influence over the mediation process under the auspices of the ECOWAS, Portugal dispatched a strong delegation led by the Portuguese Secretary of State for Foreign Affairs, Luis Amado, in March 1999 to Bissau, and Togo to stress the Portuguese new African policy which was no longer focused solely on its former colonies, but expanded to undertake dialogue with such countries as Mali and Benin. It also dispatched during Easter in 1999 its minister of foreign affairs, to West Africa to "underline that that zone has space for initiatives from Paris, Lisbon, London, Washington or Berlin"[38]. That is to say that it intended to challenge the presumed hegemony of France in the West Africa sub region. The diplomatic tug of war between ECOWAS and the CPLP led to some ambivalence in the mediation process itself. It was also feared that France was implicated behind the scenes in manipulating the incipient ECOWAS mediation through its influence in francophone capitals in the sub-region. These fears later proved to be well founded.

Against the early condemnation of the Junta by the ECOWAS foreign and defence ministers and the body's affirmation of support for the constitutionally elected President Vieira[39], when ECOWAS entered the scene, it was largely perceived as partisan by the junta and was thought to be on the side of President Vieira. A deployment of a large force by the sub-regional organization would in practice be to occupy the country and defend the interests of a President Vieira that the majority of the population thought had become delegitimized. Yet, it was also clear that the image of a simple mutiny against the legal, democratically elected government was very far from the whole truth. Legality and political legitimacy appear in this case to be far apart[40]. Within ECOWAS, there remained some apprehensions about the unilateral engagements of certain francophone leaders in relation to the Bissau Guinean conflict. It was within this context that on 1st November 1999, President Vieira and General Mane for the first time made personal commitments to a formal framework for peace contained in an Agreement signed in Abuja, the Nigerian capital. The Abuja Accord reaffirmed the ceasefire agreement earlier signed in Praia, Cape Verde, on 26 August 1998 and agreed to the withdrawal of all foreign troops from the country simultaneously with the deployment of an ECOMOG interposition force. The ECOMOG force would be responsible for security along the Guinea Bissau-Senegal border to the north and also keep the warring parties apart. The two sides agreed to immediately put in place a government of national unity, which would include representatives of the military junta. They also agreed to the holding of a general election not later than the end of March 1999.

Following the signing of the Abuja Accord, subsequent meetings between President Vieira and General Mane agreed to the appointment of Francisco Jose Fadul as the Prime Minster during the transition to a new democratically elected government. In early February 1999, observers noted that the military force around President Vieira was reinforced as his forces became provocative and eventually commenced a new round of fighting. It was also observed that new French 155 mm artillery was used by loyalists of President Vieira during this round of fighting. In obvious reference to the quasi-legitimacy acquired by General Mane and the junta by virtue of their designation as co-president during the transition in the Abuja Accord, President Vieira again reiterated his status as a democratically elected president[41].

International intervention by the larger international community, especially the critical donor countries of the European Union, was constrained by the campaign of France to keep the Bissau Guinean crisis off the agenda. In the European Union, a Swedish initiative in the Africa Working Group to send a demarche by member-state to Conakry and Dakar calling for the withdrawal of foreign troops from Guinea Bissau consistent with the Abuja Accord was stalemated. The proposal was stoutly supported by Portugal and equally rejected by France. France strongly supported the Sene-Guinean intervention in Bissau and adopted a hostile attitude toward the Mane junta, suspending aid to the transition government in Bissau[42]. Roy van de Dwight suggests that "during the first six months of the conflict, France succeeded in keeping Guinea Bissau away from the agenda. Later on, when the EU first made mention of the "importance of withdrawal of foreign troops from Guinea Bissau", the French text talked about the "the importance to assure progressive withdrawal"[43].

THE ABUJA PEACE PROCESS

The implementation of the Abuja Accord was marred by distrust on all sides and laid the foundation for further instability in the post-transition era. The legitimacy of the process was undermined early by the overthrow of President Vieira. However, most of the problems encountered derived from the plans for the future of the country mapped by General Mane and his loyalists and the exploitation of these ambitions by political forces determined to settle old scores and position themselves in good stead for the anticipated democratic dispensation. The process was marked by continued jostling by internal forces for supremacy which, eventually, split loyalists of General Mane, both civilian and military, into two camps. There was marked incoherence in the government as the two camps continued to be directed by their political allegiances until May 1999. The open and subterranean engagements of France and Portugal with their allies in the conflict as well as at the international level foreclosed a unified international intervention and direction on the way forward. Senegal and the Gambia also influenced local political actors in opposite directions. Finally, the General Mane camp designed a two-track strategy to derail the holding of the democratic elections postponed to November 28 to end the transition. Failing in this, through a compact, the Magna Carta, he attempted to impose on the political class, he sought guarantees for a uniquely powerful political relevance well into the post-conflict democratic dispensation that was envisaged. In effect, General Mane wanted to institutionalize a supra-political position of moral guarantor of the political process for his person after the transition.

The deployment of ECOMOG III was disjointed and uncoordinated against the backdrop of mutual suspicions of the contributing states. Adebayo Adebajo notes that

> Togo deployed 110 troops to Guinea Bissau between 26 December and 2 January, without the knowledge of the ECOMOG commander in Freetown, General Shelpidi of Nigeria. Shelpidi had heard about the deployment on the BBC's African service. Having submitted his assessment report to ECOWAS executive Secretary Lansana Kouyate, Shelpidi had heard nothing further until news of the Togolese deployment. Eyadema had apparently secured French support for this deployment during a visit to Paris, having previously garnered the support of the leaders of Benin, Mali, and Niger for a sub regional force in Guinea Bissau[44]

Given the peculiar circumstances in which the force was formed and funded by France, there were doubts as to whether the forces being deployed were truly ECOMOG forces. Also, unlike previous ECOWAS initiatives, the first deployment in Liberia and the second in Sierra Leone, where deliberate efforts were made to include forces from both Anglophone and francophone countries as well Lusophone states where possible, the core of ECOMOG III that was deployed to Guinea Bissau was composed from exclusively francophone countries. Traditionally, the loyalties of the countries involved were to the UEMOA rather than ECOWAS. They were also more susceptible to pressure from France. Only the contingent from Gambia broke the francophone character of the interposition force. This composition posed a serious problem in the light of the reservations about suspicions of ECOWAS mediation in Guinea Bissau earlier expressed by the junta and the CPLP. This was particularly in relation to the known agenda of France and its ex-colonies in the UEMOA in Guinea Bissau, including the fact that the immediate spark of the conflict was related to President Vieira's decision to join the UEMOA and to abandon the country's traditional policy of support to the MFDC in the Casamance. President Vieira's decisions had effectively taken Guinea Bissau to the margins of the Lusophone community and integrated it into the orbit of French control. Since the francophone character of ECOMOG III had become an issue, General Mane refused permission to strengthen the ECOMOG forces to 4000 men as demanded by President Vieira. The ECOMOG deployment in Guinea Bissau therefore remained at 750. Meanwhile, a Government of National Unity comprising representatives of both President Vieira and the junta was inaugurated on 20 February 1999.

General Mane routed the residues of the forces of President Vieira on 7 May 1999. He seized on the refusal of President Vieira to follow through with the disarmament process agreed to in the Abuja Accord, the departure of Senegalese and Guinean troops, his foreign allies, and the weaknesses of the ECOMOG forces on the ground in form of enormous logistical, financial and other difficulties. In torpedoing the Abuja Accord on which the transitional arrangement was based, General Mane left no one in doubt that he had assumed extra-constitutional responsibility for the country. This confounded the situation in the country even more, since the only source of legitimacy in the transitional period, the Abuja Accord, had many disturbing legal precedents. Many cited the concept of co-presidency in that agreement as one such unfortunate precedent. Meanwhile, the country was operating on the residues of the institutional frameworks left over from the Vieira government. This included an atrophied National Assembly, whose membership was split between the loyalists of the Vieira presidency and the stout supporters of the military junta. The Abuja Accord's concept of a co-presidency left General Mane with the impression that he was a co-head of the state of Guinea Bissau. The November 28, 1999 presidential and legislative elections threatened that status and his newly acquired title of "Supreme Commander".

Following the final ouster of President Bernandino Vieira, the Ministers of Foreign Affairs who met in Lome on 24 and 25 May condemned the coup d'etat that had taken place in Guinea Bissau. Despite protests by the Government of National Unity, the ministers also agreed that, in the light of new developments in that country and given the financial difficulties encountered to sustain the ECOMOG interposition force, the force should be withdrawn. With the negotiated exit of President Bernandino Vieira to exile, Malam Bacai Sanha, President of the National Assembly, consistent with the provisions of the constitution, was designated President in the transitional period. The transitional period up to the elections of November 28 was characterized by maneuvers by General Ansumane Mane to take charge of the direction of the evolution of the political process. This was expressed in many of Mane's policy disagreements with the president and in his insistence on vetoing the decisions of the prime minister.

Events on May 6 and 7 had culminated in the deposition of the constitutionally elected President Nino Vieira, aggravated the existing problem of internal stability and earned the reproach of the international community for the violation of the Abuja Accord. In a statement, on 18 May 1999, the European Union condemned the outbreak of violence in Guinea Bissau leading to the deposition of President Vieira in violation of the Abuja Accord. The Union expressed its expectation that the country would return to the process of democratization based on its constitution and, in that context, take the necessary measures to lead to free and fair presidential and legislative elections in November. The Central and Eastern European countries associated with the European Union, the associated country of Cyprus, the European Free Trade Association countries and members of the European Economic Area aligned themselves with the declaration of the European Union.[45] The Secretary-General of the United Nations described the scenario as a regrettable turn of events and firmly condemned the transfer of power by unconstitutional means, which, he observed, was tantamount to a coup d'etat. The violation of the Abuja Accord also led to the withdrawal of the ECOWAS interposition force.

By June 1999 in Guinea Bissau, the elections proposed for April of that year had been effectively derailed, the military establishment held on to political prisoners and to property of the international community commandeered during the two-day event in May, and there were contentions between the international community and the transitional administration regarding the continued validity of the Abuja Accord. Tension along the borders with Senegal was mounting as a result of the increasing insurgency in the Casamance Province of Senegal, while there was acrimony and bitterness in Guinea Conakry following losses suffered in the intervention in Bissau. Meanwhile, the outward flow of armed pro-Vieira sympathizers continued and the number of internally displaced persons escalated. There was also the threat of long term severance of cooperation with donor states and the possibility of sanctions from the European Union.

AMENDMENT OF ARTICLE 5 OF THE CONSTITUTION ON ELIGIBILITY TO HIGH STATE OFFICES

Yet in the face of these, the political class presented its unique challenges to the implementation of the Abuja Peace Process. On 7 July, 1999, barely two months after the events of early May, the People's National Assembly, through a two-third majority, passed a controversial bill to amend constitutional provisions for eligibility to occupy high state offices. The amendment barred all whose two parents, mother and father, are not indigenous to Guinea Bissau. The parliamentarians claimed that they had improved on earlier constitutional provisions that had indeed required the grandparents of office holders to be indigenous to the country. Hitherto, the rules governing eligibility for high state offices excluded Cape Verdeans and children of emigrants. The affected offices included the office of the President, the Speaker of the House, the Premiership, Chief of Defence Staff, and Attorney General. This immediately raised tension in the country, since this amendment foreclosed, the head of the military junta, the three military service chiefs, the attorney general and a host of prominent Bissau Guineans from holding high state offices. Even the founder of the state, Amilcar Cabral, would not have met those conditions.

The easy and sudden passage of the amendment in parliament revealed the extent to which ethnic consciousness was rooted in the psyche of political actors. The initiative was explained as motivated by the Balanta in the House, with the connivance of other ethnic groups, to send signals and hoping to consolidate the political aspirations against perceived competition from more popular Bissau Guineans who were perceived to be less than original Guineans. Specifically, the goal of the Balanta was the presidency and the resuscitation of the controversial provision of the constitution was to elbow some powerful candidates out of contention. The pursuit of hegemonic agendas had thus begun and was accentuated by President Kumba Yala later. On 7 July, Prime Minister Fadul, who woul be disqualified from any high state office by the provisions of the new eligibility, addressed a letter to interim President Sanha protesting the proposed changes to the constitution. He noted that the stipulation of Bissau Guinean parentage to contest or hold the specified high state offices was discriminatory and degrading to the ideals of national liberation and called upon the president to veto the constitutional amendment. Though the constitution grants the president 30 days within which to veto a parliamentary decision, interim President Malam Bacai Sanha, a Balanta, affirmed that he was not in a position to veto the decision of the Peoples National Assembly because of his tenuous legitimacy. And as only recently he was the president of the parliament, he did not want to be perceived as undermining the integrity of the institution. The controversial amendment indeed represented an improvement on the constitutional provisions that the bill tried to change. Finally, as a Balanta, it was not a prudent political move to veto what essentially was seen in some quarters as a Balanta-inspired bill to enhance the chances of a full-blooded black native of Guinea Bissau, particularly a Balanta, to seize control of the state.

Advocates of the amendment of Article 5 of the constitution pointed out that the resuscitation of the eligibility provision was a reaction to the entrenched marginalization of black indigenes of the country to the advantage of their mulato compatriots. The situation was compounded by the experience of purely black communities during the colonial era which had ingrained a sense of inferiority in the blacks and superiority in the mulato. They noted that independence had not in any way ameliorated the conditions of indigenous Bissau Guineans or removed their relative political obscurity in the management of the affairs of the state. It was observed that only two blacks held responsible positions during the rule of Amilcar Cabral. Nino Vieira had also consolidated the marginalization of blacks, even though he was a Papel, an indigenous ethnic group. Thus, the real concern of the indigenous Bissau Guinean was to have access to opportunities open to the mulato and be a full partner in the control of the most strategic and pivotal institutions of the state. The mulato were perceived to be of questionable loyalty to the country. It was claimed that most of them exploited the country and spirited their money out of the country to Portugal or Lebanon, and consequently, their control of government had not been beneficial to the country. The amendment was thus borne out of the frustration of the vast majority of full-blooded black Bissau Guineans. It was suggested that the PAIGC was solidly behind the amendment of the constitutional provision, even though the amendment was popular. When the amendment was put to the vote, 85 deputies were present. Rather than commit political suicide by voting against it, the mulato members among them simply disappeared during the roll call. Of the remaining 72 parliamentarians, 70 voted for the amendment, one parliamentarian voted against, and one abstained from voting. In effect, the amendment was passed by more than the 67 votes required for it to pass. All PAIGC deputies voted for it.[46]

The parliamentary decision elicited reactions from the mulato. About the same time, the Attorney-General, Amin Saad, of Lebanese descent, arrested 15 prominent personalities in business and politics for various offences committed during the one party rule under President Nino Vieira. He further requested the assembly to lift the immunity of 7 parliamentarians, including its Vice President, Carlos Gomes, and the parliamentary leader of the PAIGC, Alhaji Mane, for questioning in connection with what he described as certain criminal activities in the past. Most of these persons were supposedly full-blooded Bissau Guineans. The arrested persons were detained and later put under house arrest. Dr Saad's move, just as the controversial amendment in the parliament, exposed the depth of divisions within the political class in the PAIGC and the coalescing of adversarial camps as well as opened new lines of cleavage in the political system. A prominent camp in these divisions revolved around General Mane, head of the junta, who was incensed at the amendment that seemed to suggest to him that the sacrifices of those Bissau Guineans who had only one parent indigenous to the country, like him, were not appreciated. A sub-set in the Mane group gravitated around Prime Minister Fadul, also of mulato extraction, who was satisfied to see the so-called full-blooded Bissau Guineans arraigned for economic crimes against the country. A third element consisted of minority parties in the parliament, particularly those belonging to the Mouvance para Mudanca (Movement for Change- UM) of the attorney-general who were supportive of every initiative to undermine the powerful hold of the PAIGC on the parliament. Across the divide on the opposing side were Ballanta groups whose drive for political ascendancy in the political process was uncompromising. Yet another splinter faction of the PAIGC was the embattled group of supporters of deposed President Nino Vieira to whom the junta and its allies were a mortal threat.

Meanwhile in July 1999, relations with immediate neighbors, especially Guinea Conakry, remained problematic. President Malam Bacai Sanha of Guinea Bissau visited Dakar, Senegal, to normalize relations following the support of

Senegal for deposed President Nino Vieira. The visit yielded the anticipated warming up of bilateral relations and led to the return of exchange of ambassadors. Lansana Conte of Guinea Conakry did not react favorably to overtures from Guinea Bissau and kept Bissau wondering what the next course of action would be. This sustained tensions that had been generated by the involvement of Guinea Conakry in the war on the side of President Vieira. General Ansumane Mane also prevailed on the government of Guinea Bissau to refrain from any actions that might be interpreted as seeking normalization of relations with Guinea Conakry. So, Guinea Bissau mobilized and massed troops along its borders with Guinea Conakry to the west, further escalating tensions between the two countries.[47]

With the larger international community, relations were characterized by confidence building initiatives from Guinea Bissau directed at its major international co-operant partners such as France and the European Union (EU). Aided by Netherlands, Portugal and Sweden,[48] Guinea Bissau sought understanding for the unique internal circumstances that led to the armed deposition of President Vieira and to explain the unfortunate treatment suffered by some members of the international community during the national crisis. It undertook to retrieve missing properties and restore them to their owners. On 24 July 1999, Prime Minster Francisco Fadul led a high-powered delegation to Brussels within the framework of the Lome Conventions Article 366 revised. The visit helped to put on an even keel relations with the EU. As a direct result of the visit, the EU agreed to release EU 2 Million earmarked for elections in the country and also agreed on the mechanism to pay UE 850,000 in arrears owed by Guinea Bissau to the World Bank by the EU from fishing revenues[49]. The Union also launched an appeal to all member states that had made pledges at the Geneva Round Table to redeem them. The consolidation of relations with the EU, including a special appeal to France by Prime Minister Fadul, led to the resumption of engagement by the donor community, whose participation in the Abuja process was critical to the success of the implementation stage, during which the prime minister as well as the President had to tackle the difficult challenge of steering the process towards the of November 1999 and achieve national reconciliation. The EU also decided not to impose sanctions. Austria undertook to finance the construction of facilities for 200 beds in the hospital at a cost of U$ 23.4 million, while Italy committed to finance the repair of seven health centers.[50] Resulting from these relative successes, on 28 July 1999, the Portuguese Airline (TAP) resumed is stopovers in Bissau, effectively breaking Bissau out of complete isolation from the outside world.

GENERAL MANE'S MAGNA CARTA

After the defeat of President Bernandino Vieira, General Ansumane Mane's strategies, based on perceptions of a messianic role and as the guardian of the legacy of Amilcar Cabral, were aimed at instituting for himself a transcendental apolitical position which would guarantee him the power to control political developments in the country for as long as possible, the emergence of a democratic system not-withstanding. This messianic mindset implied that the junta must take on itself the role of a final arbiter in a political dispute. This self-imposed mandate was, however, confronted with the reality that the international community was focused on developments in the country and had clear and unambiguous democratic tenets for ascertaining the legitimacy or otherwise of mandates and political processes. To achieve this goal, he planned to build up tensions domestically create sub-regional insecurity as an alibi for his determination to remain in charge of affairs in the country, should the November 28, 1999 elections hold. Finally, he remained suspicious of international intervention in Guinea Bissau and opposed attempts to deploy international observer forces in the country, principally to monitor the tense situation along the border with Senegal, where the MFDC continued its sporadic attacks against Senegalese forces. In practice, the strategy implied a destabilization of the transitional process as well as undermining the democratic institutions even before they were put in place. The tensions generated by the agenda of the general dominated the Abuja Peace Process and also constrained the consolidation of the powers of the new democratic institutions. These principally culminated in the events of November 2000.

The military junta's attempt to subvert the democratic process became a major political preoccupation, especially as General Ansumane Mane unilaterally proposed an addendum to the constitution in the form of a Magna Carta that would govern the political class and process after the November elections. In a meeting of heads of political parties, at his headquarters early in November 1999, he spoke sternly to the political leaders and proposed the document for their signature. The preamble and sixteen articles of the Magna Carta sought to retain the military junta in the post-democratic era for another 10 years, with powers to oversee the government, ratify the decisions of the elected president and the National Assembly, and nominate the prime minister.

The Magna Carta sought to undermine the constitution and reduce the November elections to a mere process bereft of real substance. The political class described it as a subtle coup d'etat. It took the intervention of the international community with the military establishment to facilitate negotiations between the transitional government and the military to abort the Magna Carta. Meetings with between Prime Minister Fadul, the Chief of Army Staff, Colonel Verismao Seabra, and Commander of the Air Force, Col Zamura Induta (the spokesman of the military junta) revealed that the document did not reflect the views of the military junta.

The meeting reaffirmed the full commitment and support of the military to the presidential and legislative elections to be held on November 28, 1999 and to the sustenance of the momentum of the ongoing democratic process. It also reaffirmed commitment of the military to their proper and professional role in a democratic system, and to stay out of politics and remain in the barracks. Finally, it was agreed that the Magna Carta be officially withdrawn. However, the meeting conceded that the military would make inputs into policy matters related to security and service matters in the new democratic dispensation. Institutional arrangements to facilitate this role were agreed to. The measures announced in this regard included the establishment of a security structure, subject to approval by the National Assembly, to be chaired by the elected President and comprising the Minister of Interior, the Minister of Armed Forces, the Minister of Justice, and ten members of the military junta. Also, it was announced that the appointment of the Chief of Defence Staff would be in consultation with the military and that a $20-million project spanning three years would be established to address the problem of high ranking officials of the armed forces and ex-servicemen.

The arrangement was announced at a press conference by Col Verismo Seabra and the prime minister. It was also the subject of an interview granted by Col. Induta that was transmitted on the national television. The resolution of an emerging crisis helped Mr. Fadul, who was a civilian member of the military junta, to regain some ground in his relations with the junta. These agreements were arrived at in the absence of General Mane, who was undertaking an official visit to Cape Verde. The success of the negotiations reflected serious differences in perceptions of the continued role of the military in the democratic dispensation that was expected to emerge from the November elections. It however brought into the open simmering disagreements within the junta. These disagreements were central to the events of November 2000 that led to the death of General Mane.

On a visit to Lisbon in October, General Ansumane Mane raised serious questions regarding the intentions of the military when he declared that the junta would not disband itself after the 28 November 1999 presidential and legislative elections. The military junta, he categorically asserted, will not dissolve itself even after the elections that were envisaged to end the political transition to an elected democratic government. He did not indicate for how long more he thought the junta would be in the political process. He said that the Junta, as then constituted, would remain in the political arena as the moral guarantor to ensure the stability of the state. Though it posed a clear danger to the democratic process anticipated in the post-transition period, Mane's declaration was consistent with the activities of a faction in the military that had preoccupied itself, under his leadership, with churning out demands that they insisted had to be met before November 28, 1999 before the military could disengage. Given the tone and nature of those demands and against the backdrop of the limited time left to meet them, discerning observers of events were left with the impression that that the main aim was to stall the democratic process. Other analysts saw the demands as no more than blackmail of the political class, especially the truly democratically inclined among them. Many believed the blackmail was to buy time for General Ansumane Mane to settle political scores or outrightly scuttle the movement toward orderly government. The Lisbon declaration was, therefore, interpreted in political circles as a realization by the anti-democratic faction of the junta that in the face of the difficulties that the general had contrived, the momentum toward democratic government was too powerful to be derailed. The new role of moral guarantor of the state that the junta was arrogating to itself was another phase of resistance to the de-coupling of the military from the political process.

At the end of October 1999, General Ansumane Mane issued a stern warning to Prime Minister Fadul over the proposal for the deployment of a small observer force by the United Nations in Guinea Bissau to monitor the situation along the borders with Senegal. Incessant border closures resulting from perennial attacks by the MFDC against Senegalese troops deployed in the Casamance had forced interim President Malam Bacai and Prime Minister Josez Fadul, acting in concert with other top military officers, including Chief of Defence Staff, Col Verissimo Seabra, to request such a deployment. Mane demanded of Prime Minister Fadul to retract the request of the government for deployment made to the Secretary-General of the United Nations immediately. The government's request for the deployment of a 200 to 300-man military observer group was to help monitor the internal security situation and assure a safe and stable domestic environment leading to and during the elections planned for the end November, 1999. The group was also to stabilize the tenuous border with Senegal in the wake of the upsurge in the insurrection in its Casamance region as well as to dissipate apprehensions caused within Guinea Bissau as a result of the assumed large presence of armed elements sympathetic to ex-President Nino Vieira across the frontiers with Guinea Conakry. It was believed that the armed elements had the support of President Lansana Conte which explained the silence of Conakry to a proposed visit by interim President Malam Bacai Sanha to the Guinean capital. The military observer group was also envisaged to provide technical advice in the demining exercises taking place in Bissau and its environs.

Finally, there were apprehensions within government circles and political parties that the military may attempt to control the outcome of the elections or jeopardize its conduct. General Ansumane Mane's opposition to the deployment appeared to be aimed at keeping arms imported from China which were arriving in batches at this time from public and international scrutiny. Some of these arms were also destined for the Casmancaise rebels who had escalated their attacks along the borders of Senegal. Given General Mane's expressed anger against Guinea Conakry for its intervention in the Guinea Bissau conflict, it was not very certain what his plans were in respect of that country. The presence of international military observers would stand in the way of General Mane's preparations of whatever enterprise he planned.

A second track in the attempt to derail the elections was pursued by the Attorney General, Dr Amin Saad, General Ansumane Mane's closest public figure. Working in concert with the general, he began a campaign to prolong the transition for another six months[51]. The attorney-general argued that the military junta was in control in the barracks, the cities, the intelligence services, the local government and indeed all the strategic institutions in the country. Concluding that it was therefore important to dissolve the military junta first in order to create an atmosphere in which the elections could be held, he proposed that elections into the local government could be conducted on 28 November. Thereafter, he began extensive disinformation and sent signals designed to elicit panicky reactions from the international community, in the hope that these will be transmitted to the international community and provide tenable alibis for the scuttling of the democratic process through a prolongation. He haunted the general's political opponents with unremitting doggedness. He began to exhume bodies of victims of political assassinations committed by President Bernandino Vieira, ostensibly to secure evidence for his prosecution.

Yet, the political uses to which he put his gruesome findings put the whole enterprise under suspicion. On August 6, 1999 Amin Saad unilaterally established a commission to start inquiries into financial misappropriation by the previous regime. The inquiry appeared to be more of an attempt to defame perceived political opponents of General Mane than the search for truth in respect of the allegations against the ex-state officials. The attorney general did not coordinate these investigations with the minister of justice or with Supreme Court, as required by law. The other arms of the judiciary were wary of the political motives of the attorney general. With the imminence of elections, the interim president and prime minister and indeed the political class were beginning to assert their independence. This new assertiveness put General Mane in an uncomfortable political situation. With his allies in government asserting themselves and with the elections irrevocable, the general and his military backers could not contrive any more subtle scenarios to abort the movement towards November 28, 1999. Even though the cumulative impact of the activities of Mane and his sympathizers such as the attorney general succeeded in heating up the political process, their plans to derail the elections failed.

Under the given circumstances, the power of the post-conflict National Assembly was already being constrained by the general's declaration and his Magna Carta. It would perpetuate the historical domination of the military over the political class in the country. How democratic forces within the political class reacted to this proposed truncation of the mandates of democratic institutions in the post-conflict era would determine what kind of peace and the nature of the demilitarization of the political system. Should the post-conflict democratic dispensation be encumbered by an alternate state headed by General Mane, the country would be resuscitating the concept of co-presidency that had been conveniently introduced in the Abuja Accord to achieve temporary stability while the country rearranged itself for a new democratic beginning. It was certain that the concept of "moral guarantor" was another dangerous game of political brinkmanship that would spin out of control in the struggle between democratic and constitutional state institutions and undemocratic elements bent on retaining their self-proclaimed oversight responsibilities over the elected representatives of the country.

The Magna Carta may also be seen as the desperate attempt of three disparate political forces with diverse agenda to retain control of the political process after the November 28, 1999 elections. This trinity of forces included the anti-democratic elements within the Military establishment, especially a core of three or four elements within the military junta; elements within the PAIGC who had convinced themselves that Malam Bacai Sanha, the party flag bearer, would not win the November presidential elections and that such a loss would represent an unwelcome watershed in the political process and signify the end of the hegemony of the party. This second group was led by Francisco Bernante, the Minister of Defence. The third group comprised forces within civil society who were constrained one way or the other to compete effectively in the electoral process and who saw an alliance with the anti-democratic elements in the military and the PAIGC as a solution to their handicap. Led by Dr. Amin Saad, the Attorney-General, this group included those potential victims of the amendment of Article 5. They counted on the anti democratic faction within the military to keep them relevant in the political process. While the agenda of these three groups were disparate, the group converged in their fear of an uncertain future, should real democracy begin to take root in the country. The Magna Carta was thus another of a last-minute desperate effort to derail the democratization process.

In the face of the persistent assault on the political class by the military junta for over two years, the political class was dispirited and weak. This was compounded by collaboration with the junta by a faction of the political class that hoped that such association would boost their political fortunes in the post-transition political process. This constrained the capacity of pro-democratic forces to execute concerted action against the anti democratic forces in the military and within the political class itself. They found the game of political brinkmanship that had been imposed by General Mane too delicate. General

Mane's Lisbon declaration was therefore not a bluff. The declaration, paradoxically, represented a major victory for the pro democratic forces because the general and his military an civilian allies had finally accepted that the November elections could not be stopped. Within the prevailing volatile situation, this was no mean victory for democratic forces and the international community that was overseeing the transition to post-conflict democracy. At another level, the international community had become subtly engaged in a running battle of wits and symbolism to complement the local efforts of the intimidated democratic forces in the political class to ensure the triumph of the democratic option as the best way forward in the post-conflict era. The declaration then represented the beginning of a new phase of a struggle designed to undermine the powers of democratic institutions that would emerge in the post-democratic era. General Mane's goal was to preserve the privileges of a few military officers and to remain a transcendental institution with the final political authority in Guinea Bissau.

There were the other accompaniments to the general's intimidation of the pro democratic faction of the political class as well of officers that had fought on the side of the deposed president in the three-day war. General Mane routinely humiliated pro-Nino Vieira officers who had been put in jail since the 7 May overthrow of President Vieira. On 9 July, 1999, the military authorities formally handed over to the judiciary all the remaining 378 political prisoners, including pro-Vieira military officers taken 'prisoners' during the 7 May events. Before then, 225 detainees had been released from custody.[52] This resulted from international pressure on the junta that, despite its claims that the officers had been taken during war, it could not take the laws into its own hand, particularly as the detainees were defending the legitimate authority at the time of their arrest. What remained of the judiciary was elated by this seeming respect for the law and constitution. The newly appointed President of the Supreme Court, Justice Emiliano Nosolini, assured that the detainees would have access to legal representation and due process of the law. Yet, while the military claimed publicly that these officers had been handed over to judicial authorities, the prisoners were being used as objects to demonstrate to the public who was the real master of Guinea Bissau. Senior-pro Vieira officers were treated like common criminals, thereby humiliating them and their families. They were forced to march barefooted in the hot sun with their hands bound behind them in the provinces and in the cities alike.[53] They were made to walk considerable distances from the prisons in the public glare to fetch water in Bissau city. They cleared the road and were deployed to provide very menial services. They were locked up in their overcrowded prison cells for long hours and, sometimes, just allowed enough time to gobble down what went for their prison meals. Many developed skin diseases. At this point, the judicial authorities in the country merely referred to the person of Dr Amin Saad, General Mane's appointee to that position. The

Minister of Justice, M. Carlos Domingo Gomes, a businessman who nominally played his official role, denounced the activities of the attorney-general. He described him as no more than the errand boy of the military, meaning the General Mane faction. The President of the Supreme Court was exasperated and opted to calmly remain on the sidelines, unable to wade into the murky political waters without compromising his political neutrality and the dignity of his high office.

Against this background, it was feared that the concept of the military as the moral guarantor would imply in practice that the supreme authority in the land would not be the president. The elected president would be less than the Supreme Commander of the Armed Forces, because that position would not be vacant by virtue of General Mane's announcement. The National Assembly could not be the law making institution, because their decisions would ultimately be mere recommendations that will be subject to the veto through a process of ratification, even if informally, by the military junta. Besides the obvious undermining of democracy entailed in this bizarre arrangement, it had implications for sub-regional insecurity.

In view of the established association between the Bissau Guinean military and the MFDC in the Casamance, the concept of moral guarantor of the state of Guinea Bissau personified in the General had consequences for sub-regional stability, involving Guinee Bissau, Guinea Conakry, Senegal and the Gambia. A direct outcome of the unending struggle for preeminence by General Mane and the campaign instituted by Attorney General Amin Saad was the resurgence of ethnic consciousness among the Ballantas who were the most affected by the purges undertaken by President Vieira and among the Mandigue who now openly supported the irredentism of the Diolla and Mandinge in the Casamance. General Mane's declaration was most likely to heighten anxiety in Conakry and Dakar in view of what it portended for these states. It was expected that Senegal and Guinea Conakry would be more inclined to deal with a new civilian administration in Bissau, not encumbered by the burden of the sour events of the previous two years and which would be represented by a moral guarantor personified by General Ansumane Mane.

Relations with Guinea Conakry remained cold as General Mane blocked the initiatives of the transitional government to begin a process of rapprochement with neighboring states.[54] The same logic applied to the general's directives to the prime minister to formally decline the invitation of President Conte to visit Conakry. The international community involving President Chirac, President Bongo and President Eyadema had all appealed to President Lansana Conte to extend the invitation as an ice breaker in the frozen relations between the two countries. The expected thaw in relations arising from such a visit did not fit into General Mane's game plan. While inspecting the border regions of

Guinea Bissau in October, 1999, he had gone one step further to undermine any possibility of rapprochement by unilaterally crossing into the territory of Guinea Conakry and assuring the Guinean local authorities at the border of his good intentions[55]. Thereafter, he offered drinks and biscuits to the Guineans as a gesture of his goodwill. The border authorities replaced the border guards who had fallen for the gestures at the international frontier on the Guinea Conakry side. Under those circumstances the unilateral goodwill mission of General Mane across the border into Guinea Conakry was interpreted as a provocation of the Conakry government. In the context of the position he had proposed for himself in the envisaged democratic dispensation, a new civilian administration with the mandate of the people was required to help the countries in the immediate sub-region to transcend the hard feelings of the immediate past. Should the military retain control in Bissau, it would constrain the pursuit of policy changes necessitated by the state of affairs in the area.

The choice of Lisbon by General Mane to declare his intention to retain the military junta after the November 28, 1999 elections had disturbing undertones. Was Lisbon sympathetic to this concept? What did that import for Franco-Bissau Guinean bilateral relations? These were not very reassuring issues in the last days of the transition as the democratic process reached its crescendo in the presidential and legislative elections on November 28, 1999. Paradoxically, while General Mane's induced instability of the political process was presented as an alibi for a postponement of the November 28 elections that would terminate the beleaguered Abuja process, his strategies made the conduct of the election imperative if Guinea Bissau was to emerge from the problematic constitutional uncertainties created by the Abuja Accord. This situation was made worse by the overthrow of President Vieira who, despite the tenuousness of his legitimacy, represented constitutional legality in the country. It was against this background that preparations continued for the holding of presidential and legislative elections on 28 November, 1999.

THE PRESIDENTIAL AND LEGISLATIVE ELECTIONS OF 28 NOVEMBER 1999

The elections remained the cornerstone of the democratization process that was envisaged to bring to an end the Abuja Peace Process. The formal recognition of thirteen political parties, besides the African Party for the Independence of Guinea and Cape Verde (PAIGC), enhanced the movement to a truly pluralist democracy. The electoral census began in Bissau on 22 August and closed on 2 September 1999. Twelve candidates contested the presidential election and thirteen political parties presented candidates for election into the People's National Assembly. In general, apart from the PAIGC, which had a national outlook, and arguably the Resistance Guinea Bissau-Movement de Bafa-ta (RGB-MB) led by Helder Vaz, the political party system was organized around ethnicity. Some of the parties represented no more than vehicles to perpetuate the political ambitions of individuals who contested to register continued intentions to remain relevant and available in the political process. Other minority parties, exemplified by Joao Tatis Sa's Guinean Peoples Party, unregistered for the elections, reflected attempts at constructing a national forum and platform by elites in the Diaspora. The Alliance of Socialists, under the leadership of the former chairman of the Guinean League of Human Rights, Fernando Gomes, brought together only a strand of a larger ideological group that was badly splintered in Guinea Bissau. The Uniao para Mudanca (UM) of Attorney General Amin Saad and interim Prime Minister Francisco Jose Fadul was perceived as a party for the mulato. All 13 political parties contested the elections, with the exception of the PAIGC, on only one platform of *mudanca* or change. The Party for Social Renewal (PRS) flaunted its ethnic agenda in the electoral campaigns and demanded that the changes required in the country included the recognition that the Balanta had been marginalized in the past and badly treated by the Nino Vieira regime, which it equated with the PAIGC. The party therefore deserved to win and a Balanta given a chance to rule the country.[56]

Although the PAIGC remained defensive about its achievements and the predicament that its internal troubles had brought the country , it maintained a formidable showing. It resuscitated what was left of its mobilization machineries throughout the country to remain a serious player in the elections. Many however observed that funding for the campaigns of the presidential candidate of the PAIGC was sourced from the Middle East. The internal struggles within the party between the traditionally dominant military faction under General Mane and an opposing civilian wing that sought to keep the party distant from the fate of the military junta came to epitomize the broader questions of the direction in which the party should take. It came to a head when General Mane forced the party to cancel its convention slated for August 12 to elect a new leadership and to decide on its flag bearer for the elections. General Ansumane Mane imposed Francisco Bernante as the new chairman of the party.

Prominent presidential candidates in the elections were interim President Malam Bacai Sanha as the flagebearer for the PAIGC, Koumba Yala for the PRS and the intellectual Faustina Imbalo. Other candidates included Antonieta Rosa Gomes, Fernando Gomes, Mamadu U. Balde, Salvador Tschongo, Bubacar R. Djalo, Abubakar Balde, Joaquim Balde, Jose C. Mendes and Joao Tatis Sa. As a result of internal disagreements over the outcome of the congress of the RGB-MB of 26-30 August 1999, the party did not field a presidential candidate. The stalemate revolved around the legality of the congress itself and which of the two candidates, Salvador Tschongo or Helder Vaz, had been appropriately nominated as the party's flag bearer.

In the first round of elections, Kumba Yala had 139,738 of the popular vote representing 38.6% of the total of 363,319 votes cast. The PAIGC candidate Bacai Sanha was in second place with 23.42%, that is, 85,086 of the popular votes. The overall results are presented as follows:

First Round of Presidential Elections November 1999

Candidates	Total Votes Received
Malam B Sanha	85.086
Salvador Tchongo	6.679
Faustino F Imbali	29.668
Joaquim Balde	8.38
Bubacar R Djalo	11.797
Abubacar Balde	19.975
Jose C Mendes	5.404
Jao Tatis Sa	23.884
Kumba Yala	139.738
Fernando Gomes	26.183
Mamadu U Balde	3.492
Antonieta R Gomes	3.033
Total Votes	**363.319**

Source: Department of Statistics and Information, National Elections Commission, Bissau

In the second round of the presidential elections held on 12 January, 2000, Koumba Yala won a landslide victory of 72%.

In the legislative elections, three parties were dominant. These were the PRS, which was won 37 seats, the RGB acquired 27 seats and the PAIGC which elected 25 deputies into the 102-seat post-transition parliament. The distribution of seats in the Assembly is presented below.

Legislative Elections 1999

Party	# of Seats Allocated in Parliament	Leader of Party
Union for Change (UM)	2	Manuel Rambaut

Guinean Civic Forum/Social Democracy (FCG-SD)	0	Antonieta Rosa Gomes
Guinean League for Ecological Protection (LIPE)	0	Bubacar Dialo
United Party for Social Democracy (PUSD)	0	Augusto Barai Mango
Social Democratic Front (FDS)	2	Rafael Barbosa
Alliance for Democracy (Party for Democratic Convergence PCD and Democratic Front FD)	5	Victor Mandinga/Amadu Djamanca
Guinea-Bissau Resistance (RGB)	27	Helder Vaz
African Party for the Independence of Guinea and Cape Verde (PAIGC)	25	Francisco Benante
Social Democratic Party (PSD)	3	Joaquim Balde
National Union for Democracy and Progress (UNDP)	1	Abubacar Balde
Independent Front for National Liberation of Guinea (FLING)	0	Jose Cantengul Mendy
Party for Renewal and Progress (PRP)	0	Mammadu Uri Balde
Party for Social Renewal (PRS)	37	Ibraima Sori Balde
TOTAL	**102**	

Source: Department of Statistics and Information, National Elections Commission, Bissau

The outcome of the democratic elections of 1999/2000 profoundly transformed the entire political configuration of Bissau Guinean politics. For the first time, political power shifted from the PAIGC, which had produced the founding father of the state, elaborated the ideology and political values that conferred legitimacy on the policy process and political choices made by the state, ruled the country from its very incipient stages to independence in 1974 and also for the first time, power was taken away from the military or those directly allied to the military. The implication was that the powerful and dominant military constituency, which had played a major role throughout the life of independent Guinea Bissau was to be shunted aside. The state was transformed from a one-party state to a truly multi-party political system, with at least six parties represented in parliament. No one party had won a simple majority and a two-third majority in the House required the assent by at least two of the three biggest parties and one smaller party, if deputies voted on strict party lines. Throughout the history of Guinea Bissau, the PAIGC had always managed to dominate the political process, as it controlled at the two-thirds of the majority required to pass the more serious bills in parliament. The parliament was a mere appendage at the behest of the party, the president and leader of the party. Above all, the transformation implied the emergence of a new political elite concretely expressed in a vast majority of the parliamentarians who were new to politics and, much more challenging, not familiar with parliamentary procedures or the experience required to harmonize policy and build coalitions through negotiations. Out of the 102 deputies, 75 were being elected into parliament for the first time. The relative triumph of the PRS in the democratic transition marked the emergence of a new center of power in national life concentrated within the Balanta political circles that remained unappeased by perceived marginalization and alienation from the national process by the ruling elites since independence.

This evolved situation gave rise to a new dominant winning force and a possible new winning coalition of forces, the emergence of pro-democratic forces in and out of government, in and out of the winning party, in opposition parties, as well as in organized civil society groups that had emerged during the transition and made more conscious of their responsibilities as a result of the suffering of the last war. More significantly, though, there was a coalition of powerful political actors in society and within the military that had been dispossessed of power and had remained antagonistic to the democratic process as well as to the newly emerged political elite and their ethnic jingoism. The new balance of power among political forces also implied the loss of access to state rent for the losers. The challenges of managing these radical shifts remained the central concerns of the political process throughout the post-conflict democratic dispensation.

The new assembly, composed of 102 deputies, was inaugurated on 28 January, 2000, and it elected its officers. The election into the office of president, between Jorge Malu, 3rd vice president of the PRS and Helder Vaz of the RGB-MB, generated a lot of tensions following arguments over technical accuracy in the nomination papers submitted by the latter. The issues were resolved in the afternoon session to enable voting take place. Jorge Malu won 66 votes against 34 for Helder Vaz. two deputies abstained. The 11 votes of the minority parties, including 5 from the PAIGC, were for Vaz. Voting was thus on party lines, with the exception of the PAIGC where 5 of the 25 deputies voted against party instructions. The minority parties explained their votes in terms of assuring the stability of parliament given that it was the first in the post-transition era. They observed that this was imperative in light of the problems emerging between the PRS and the RGB in working out some pact of cooperation that they believed was required to move the country forward. The tension in parliament over the election of the President of the House therefore was not just a test of the relative balance of strength in parliament between the potential coalition partners who were in the process of negotiating the formation of a government.

The tensions underscored the fact that the President of the National Assembly was next in line to the President. However, the PRS was a wholly Balanta party and all its nominees for national offices were Balanta. In effect, there was the possibility of a Balanta head of state and the executive branch of government, a Balanta president of the legislature, as well as a Balanta president of the Supreme Court. This possibility was not lost on the other parties and there appeared to be no way to effectively counter that possibility. The signs emanating from the Political Committee of the PRS were not reasuring in this regard. The committee, which had nominated Jorge Malu, a Balanta, to head the National Assembly, had also backed another Balanta for the office of 1st Vice President of the House. The same committee had already proposed Caetano N'tchama, a Balanta non member of the party and personal friend of president elect Kumba Yala who had served in the transitional government as the Minister of Interior, as its first nominee for the Office of Prime Minister. These developments provided a difficult backdrop in the negotiations for a government of unity that the president-elect professed that he preferred. The difficulties in negotiations over the terms of a coalition government were reflected in the inability to broker agreements on the structure of the leadership of the National Assembly before its formal inauguration on 28 January. They were ominous signs for the future of the new democracy.

Since the election of Kumba Yala as president-elect, the PRS began weighing its options in respect of a coalition partner. A coalition with the PAIGC presented a problem of credibility, given the vitriolic attacks on the party during the campaign and the fact that the elections was fought on only one platform of change from the traditions of the PAIGC. Also such an association would constrain the choices of the president in resolving sensitive national questions relating to many members of the PAIGC who may be indicted by probes, the future of ex-President Joao Bernadino Vieira, the process of national reconciliation, foreign relations and sub-regional security. PAIGC was also likely to bring into the government liabilities arising from its own internal squabbles that could hamper effective and just resolution of problems that the government was bound to be confronted with.

Against the foregoing, the inability of Kumba Yala, the president-elect and his party to enter into a working accord with the RGB-MB was interpreted as a disturbing sign. The situation was compounded by the open tensions between the two parties in parliament over the leadership of the House, which, ideally, should have been part of a comprehensive working agreement.

EMERGENCE OF A PRS/RGB ACCORD FOR A COALITION GOVERNMENT

It was not until the 15 February 2000 that an accord for a coalition government was agreed to between the PRS and the RGB. In the accord, the PRS was to nominate the Prime Minister and Deputy Prime Minister and to occupy 9 cabinet positions. The party conceded four of the thirteen cabinet positions (one more was created) to the RGB. It reserved the prerogative to fill strategic positions such as Defence, Internal Administration, Foreign Affairs, Finance, and Justice. Others on the PRS slot included Social Solidarity, Reintegration of ex-combatants and Struggle for Probity, Education, Science and Technology, Social Infrastructure and Agriculture and Forestry. RGB would fill the four Ministries of Regional Economic Development, Health, Natural Resources and Environment, and Public Administration and Work. Eight secretary-of-state position, lower than cabinet level, were taken by the PRS. The party clarified that those positions allocated to the PRS might not necessarily be filled by its card-carrying members. This was the case of the Prime Minister elect, Caetano N'tchama, and his designated deputy, Dr. Faustino Imbali. A few of the cabinet positions were destined to go to independent candidates or even non-politicians with relevant expertise. The same applied to the RGB. On the insistence of the RGB, the PAIGC was not accommodated in the coalition.

The preamble to the accord recognised the multifaceted crises facing the country and the need to restore hope to the people of Guinea Bissau, guarantee conditions of social harmony and construct foundations for the socio-economic and cultural development of the country. It envisaged that the coalition would remain in effect until the next elections in 2004. The coalition was seen as the optimal scenario for radical changes and consolidation of the new democratic beginning that was ushered in by the 28 November, 1999 Presidential and Legislative elections. The sidelining of the PAIGC was explained in terms of not diluting the spirit of change that the electorate voted for. It was in this connection that the accord stipulated that the programme of the government would be negotiated and agreed to by consensus between the two parties. Priorities set include national reconciliation, social cohesion, Justice, the Rule of law, reorganisation of state organs, struggle against corruption and social exclusivism, economic growth, good governance and reduction of poverty. Though the signatories to the accord recorded 15 February, 2000 against their signatures, it was only actually signed on 17 February, 2000. The preferred date was in deference to the president, who did not want to be seen playing a partisan role as the leader of his party, after his formal investiture as president of the country.

At a ceremony on Thursday, 17 February, 2000 at the September 24 Stadium in Bissau, President Kumba Yala was sworn in as the fourth President of Guinea Bissau in the presence of President Yahya Jammeh of the Gambia. The hierarchy of the military junta present remained unmoved despite the deafening salutations of the new President to the junta and its Supreme Commando, Ansumane Mane. The military brass hesitated to rise at the arrival of the president-elect and neither gave the traditional salute nor demonstrated any recognition of the emergence of a new Commander in Chief. President Kumba Yala's investiture was thus eventful for its numerous disturbing symbolisms. By presidential decree No 3/2000 of 19 February 2000, President Kumba Yala announced the appointment of Caetano N'Tchama as Prime Minister and Faustino Imbali as the Vice Prime Minister. The president also approved the recommendations of Prime Minster N'tchama to form a 23 man government. Notable members of the government included Helder Jorge Vaz Gomez, leader of the RGB-MB as Minister of State for Regional Economy and Development and Col Verissmo Seabra, Chief of Staff and member of the military junta as Minister in charge of National Defence. The government also contained PAIGC nominees who were in government in their individual capacities.

This was the broadest based-government cobbled together in the history of independent Guinea Bissau, both in terms of the number of parties represented in the government and ethnic distribution. However, it was a relatively inexperienced cabinet as none, except the prime minister, had served in the capacity of a cabinet minister before. It was also a government of young people as most members were in their early forties with a few in their thirties. There were two women. However, there were indications of the direction in which the political process was heading as the president, prime minister and vice prime minister, president of the Peoples National Assembly as well as a deputy vice president, the minister of Internal Administration and other key state offices were all Ballanta. Meanwhile, the locus of the military junta in the new democratic dispensation soon engaged the attention of President Kumba Yala.

THE CHALLENGE OF THE MILITARY JUNTA IN POST-CONFLICT DEMOCRACY

The immediate challenge facing the new president came from General Mane and the military junta that was determined to assert their self proclaimed role of moral guarantor of the state. In the light of this claim and the seriousness with which the junta was pursuing this perceived extra-constitutional role, the struggle for the assertion of the powers of the constitutionally elected president and new democratic institutions posed the immediate challenges facing post-conflict democracy. This was pronounced in difficult relations between the president and the pro-democratic political forces, on the one hand, and and the general and the forces allied to him within the military and the political class, on the other hand. The military junta came under severe stress that culminated in the open break in the junta by officers who believed that the historical domination of the political process by the military had to give way to the truly democratic system that had emerged from the transition. Many however were motivated by considerations of personal welfare, including their career advancement, to remain loyal to Generall Mane whom they perceived to be still capable of overriding the president. The struggle between the new democratic dispensation and the junta was expressed in many ways: an assortment of investigations into corruption and trials orchestrated by the attorney general against senior members of the PAIGC and pro-Vieira military officers on charges of treason without consultations with the minister of justice or even the president of the Supreme Court; and control of the military including promotion of senior military officers as well as appointments to command positions. General Mane contested the decisions of the new president on appointments in the military as well as on foreign and security policy. Yet, President Kumba Yala avowed that he planned to be a ruling president.

The week immediately following the investiture of President Kumba Yala was marked by intense maneuvers for political ascendancy by the Presidency and General Ansumane Mane, the supreme commander of the military junta. While acknowledging the heroic role of the Junta in redeeming the country from the PAIGC, President Kumba Yala sought to assert his authority as the ultimate political power in Guinea Bissau. In counterveiling steps, General Mane and a loyal residue of the Military Junta moved to retain the perceived role of the military establishment, now personified by him as the moral guarantor of the state. First, Mane ordered the chief of staff to reject the cabinet position of minister of national defence offered him by the president. He contested the right of the President to make such an appointment without consultations with him.

The president began to address the problematic notions of whether the events of the last two years that propelled the military into national prominence had conferred on General Mane and his junta any transcendental pedestal from which they could determine the legitimacy of the policies of the democratic government and the direction of state policy in general. This had become an issue because the military junta was not formally dissolving itself and was appropriating for itself continuing presence in the post-electoral scheme of things. These appeared to be the practical implications of the role of guarantor of the state that General Anusmane Mane arrogated to for himself in Lisbon in October 1999. On Sunday, 27 February, 2000, the president repudiated any ideas of a grandiose role for Mane when he formally offered him the office of Counselor on Military Affairs in the Presidency. An incensed General Ansumane Mane rejected the offer and walked out of the formal ceremony where the president had made the pronouncement. Mane rebuffed the president's signal that the era of co-presidency, assumed by him during the transition, had come to an end and that he could function in the presidency under the leadership of the popularly elected president.

The seemingly contradictory imperatives of national reconciliation and the search for justice were exploited by the junta to test the resolve of the new president. The test came in the wake of what was seen as a tactical victory of the junta over the president, when General Ansumane Mane and a retinue of his loyalists, in full military uniform, visited the president and the prime minister to call for an appraisal of the cases of all those in detention before a proposed presidential conditional release of the detainees could be effected. In effect, the junta disagreed with the decision of the president to release the prisoners conditionally and to confine them to the country pending formal charges in court and the pronouncement of judgment after due process of the law. General Mane and his pressure group persuaded the president to agree to a comprehensive review of the files of their colleagues that they saw as prisoners of war, even though President Kumba Yala had made a public pronouncement a few days earlier to release all but 50 of the prisoners provisionally. In his announcement, the president explained that his first major policy decision on a sensitive national concern was on account of the inability of the state to provide for the medical care of the prisoners and appalling prison conditions. The inability of the state in these two areas could only lead to abuse of the rights of the prisoners and detract from their dignity as important members of society.

The challenge to the president's decision seemed to have signaled that a test of resolve between him and Mane might have just begun. Before this subtle confrontation, the main theatre for the expression of this struggle had been the trials of Avito Jose da Silva, a former Minister of Agriculture, Capriano Soares Cassama, former Minister of Information, Baciro Dabo, Director of State Information and Conducto Jose da Pina, a PAIGC deputy in the National Assembly. All the four were standing trial for treason for alleged complicity with ex President Nino Vieira in inviting and facilitating foreign troops to invade Guinea Bissau during the civil war. The trials were being conducted through the seemingly proper judicial process unfolding in the courtroom, as well as on television, orchestrated by pro-Mane political actors, including some anti-Vieira forces in the PAIGC.

The courtroom trials examined the role of the accused in advising and facilitating the intervention of Senegalese and Conakry Guinean troops in the last civil war in Guinea Bissau. Most analysts have observed that the men on trial, paradoxically, were then acting on the side of constitutional order, even if Nino Vieira had become very unpopular as a president. Questions were raised about the legitimacy of the treasonable charges against those who fought on the side of constitutional order against mutinous elements in the military represented by the military junta. The trials were thus perceived as a sort of victory parade of the military junta, determined to ruin the reputation of pro-Vieira forces. The political nature of the drama was demonstrated by the fact that the Procurer General had sustained a media campaign against the accused. The media onslaught was preceded by a public denunciation of all those who had counselled that the human rights of the prisoners be respected[57] and that the judicial process be open and transparent, especially to the international community. After this, the television turned its attention to the accused standing trial. On the first day of the report of the trial treated the viewing public to an extensive reminder of the savagery of the last war. The television documentary was a melange of the tragic images of the war and its dead victims spiced with assassinations that had taken place long before the civil conflict.

Among its emotional, even if controversial, scenes, it showed the attorney-general supervising the exhumations of the skeletons of Viviato Pa, a well-known and respected Ballanta intellectual believed to have been murdered by the former regime, Colonel Paula Correia, Braima Bangura and N'fom. Pictures of these victims of the intolerance that marked the years of the PAIGC were mounted intermittently, while the heavy grief of wailing relatives of the victims served as a permanent backdrop to the gruelling images being telecast into homes. It was a documentary that seemed to be part of a campaign to convince the country that it was not yet prepared and could not move on without resting, one way or another, the cases of these dead. The ominous implication of the message was clear that the men on trial bore responsibility for the agony of the people of Guinea Bissau. Yet, observers noted that the prisoners of the junta had no responsibility for the assassinations displayed on the television. The documentary was evidence produced by the procurer-general in collaboration with elements known to be loyal to the Brigadier General Mane in the Radio Television Guinea Bissau (RTGB). The fact that most of the bodies exhumed were Balanta was exploited as evidence of the persecution of the Balanta by the PAIGC as the political situation in the country evolved.

The court proceedings yielded no new revelations, except for the testimonies of the accused Baciro Dabo, who appeared to be friendly to the prosecution by implicating all others with his details of the war decision-making process under Nino Vieira. He also provided information of how the intervention of foreign troops in the war was facilitated. He laid most of the decision at the doorstep of Avito Jose da Silva. The defence attorneys did not raise issues with the legitimacy of the constitutional order that their clients had defended and the illegitimacy of the acts of the junta as no more than the mutiny of a group of officers. This apparent legal oversight was significant because soldiers often pledged to defend the constitution and constitutional Order, their politics notwithstanding. The trials implicitly tested the integrity of the claims to be the moral guarantors of the state; a role which appears to transcend the constitutional prerogatives of the elected president as the sovereign of the people of Guinea Bissau.

It was against this background that the offer of Counsellor on Military Affairs at the Presidency offered General Ansumane Mane by President Kumba Yala may be seen. It was a first signal to the general that the president did not recognise his claim to some transcendental role in the affairs of the state. The junta was now divided, first by the humiliating trials, and to the embarrassment Col Verrismo Seabra the unilateral decision of General Mane to decline the ministerial position offered the Chief of Staff, Col Verrismo Seabra on his behalf without any consultation. These developments had eroded internal cohesion and undermined the leverage for autonomous action on the part of Mane. His hold on the military was not as formidable as it was in the previouspast two years. He appeared to have squandered his political capital in political miscalculations that cumulatively rendered him relatively weak. But there were allies within the PAIGC and actors in society such as the Attorney General who lined up behind him. With the well-timed absence of the president, the general was left to nurse the implied diminution of his political stature by the offer and to work out his next counter-move. But he had to wait for the return of the president to the country to do this. The inevitable test of resolve between the president and the self-styled supreme commando of the military junta had begun.

The face-off between President Kumba Yala and General Mane always played into the internal dynamic of the junta, as hitherto key Mane loyalists disagreed with the anti-democratic postures adopted by the general, in the name of the junta. This had come to the fore in his decision to overrule the offer of ministerial position to the Chief of Army Staff, Col Verissimo Seabra. The nomination of a replacement for Col Seabra by General Mane was turned down by the president. As a result, General Mane unilaterally put Col Seabra on the reserve list, effectively relieving him of any command or influence in the military. In these tussles, high-ranking military officers were compelled by the sheer logic of the situation to declare a clear stand. The Minister of Defence, Colonel Verissimo Seabra, emerged as an alternative or rival pivot to General Mane within the junta and the military. He had the support of Colonels Emile da Costa, Bobo la Djoto, Watame Lai and Manuel Mina. General Mane's loyalists had dwindled to only a small circle of Madingue and Diolla, including Chief of Naval Staff, Navy Captain Lamine Sanha, Colonels Yahya Kane, Musa Djata and Allanso Vaz. President Yala announced the appointment of Colonel Emile da Costa as the new Chief of Staff while retaining Colonel Seabra as the defence minister. With this appointment and the effective implosion of the junta, General Mane effectively seized to be the head of the military.

On 29 April, 2000, with the encouragement of rival officers in the military, President Yala relieved Navy Capt Lamine Sahna of office as Chief of Naval Staff. This followed an alleged complicity in setting free Russian boats detained on the high seas for illegal fishing in Guinea Bissau's territorial water. Col Emilio Costa, on behalf of the Chief of Defence Staff issued a statement to publicly reiterate the support of the military for, and subordination of the army to, the political class and the democratically elected President Kumba Yala. Despite the encouragement of General Mane to the deposed naval chief to resist the order of the president, he was effectively removed from office. In explaining the decision of the government in respect of Navy Captain Lamine Sahna, Prime Minister Caetano N'Tchama observed that although there was a democratically elected government in place as part of the new constitutional order, there were, if not *de jure*, but *de facto*, two presidents in Guinea Bissau. He observed that it was expected that the junta was going to dissolve with the conduct of elections and the setting up of democratic institutions, but some elements of the Junta still acted as though the country was still going through the post-conflict transition.[58] Between the inauguration on 17 February, 2000 and end of August, the political process had gone full cycle to the removal of General Mane as head of the military. However, the extenuating political circumstances that galvanized the unity of the military and the support of the population for the insurrection of General Mane and the formation of the junta were absent.

GENERAL MANE AND SUB-REGIONAL STABILITY

Meanwhile, the activities of General Mane continued to destabilize the northern borders with Senegal, where there had been a dramatic increase in attacks in the Casamance. In mid-April 2000, while President Kumba Yala was away in Havana, Cuba, a Senegalese military aircraft on a hot chase of MFDC operatives into Guinea Bissau bombed the town of Farin. Before then, skirmishes between Senegalese forces and MFDC operatives along the Senegalese border had been reported in Bissau. Reports in Bissau claimed that the Senegalese bomb left 14 dead. Accounts of Senegalese troops at the border posts claimed that they had repelled an attack on the post by regular Bissau Guinea forces and that the attacking force had left one of its dead behind. The facts as they emerged from partisan accounts on both sides were that a major attack was launched from across the frontiers of Guinea Bissau into Senegal. The attack was repulsed and the retreating attackers were pursued into Guinea Bissau. Though the full identity of the attacking forces could not be established, at a minimum, it involved some elements from the Bissau Guinean military. What was not certain was whether these were rogue elements sympathetic to the Casamancais rebellion or troops acting probably the under instructions or possibly illegal orders of senior Bissau Guinean military officers operating outside the control and authorities of the government, alongside radical rebel MFDC forces.

Most keen observers of sub-regional security seemed certain that the MFDC had bases in Guinea Bissau. The Senegalese Air Force admitted bombing the border towns in the territory of Guinea Bissau in hot pursuit of retreating Bissau Guinean forces. At least one Bissau Guinean soldier was killed, and there were civilian casualties. But whatever political sympathies or motives were involved, the incident set back the process of normalisation of bilateral relations between the two countries initiated by President Yala. It also raised serious concerns on how much control the new government in Bissau had over its military forces. Also, it generated among democratic forces anxiety over the ultimate cost, to the country, of the current ambivalence of the military in Guinea Bissau and its clear indications of repudiating its subordination to civil authorities.

Meanwhile, tensions mounted all across the frontiers. The population in Guinea Bissau was discussing the matter, which was considered grave, especially against the backdrop of the intervention of Senegal to support the embattled President Nino Viera. Bissau Guineans perceived the Senegalese intervention as an invasion of their country. In the absence of the president, Bissau Guinean forces mobilized heavy and long-range guns across the border and also reinforced its frontiers with Senegal with more troops. There were good grounds to suspect that the unfortunate events were, most probably, orchestrated by vested military interests either in Bissau or Dakar. The greater likelihood was that the culprits were the Bissau military establishment. It would appear that the main aim of precipitating this new round of limited and controlled hostilities was to reinforce the dwindling political leverage and influence of the Bissau Guinean military in the emerging democratic system. From the vantage point of critical observers, it appeared that this was part of the military's negotiation to influence the character of the emerging constitutional order as well as define an unusually large role for itself in the nascent democracy.

In the face of the emerging unfavorable light in which the national security apparatus, proposed by the former junta as a compromise to the Magna Carta was being cast within relevant circles of the Legislature, it was not far-fetched to imagine that the military establishment would go to any length, including the play of its most important card, to reaffirm its pivotal relevance. It therefore sought to create an alibi in a contrived heightened insecurity in the immediate sub-region to achieve its domestic goal of retaining the military as a critical actor in the political process. It was in this context that General Mane had stoutly resisted President Kumba Yala's initiative to visit Conakry to kick off the process of rapprochement between the two countries. President Yala's visit to Senegal to witness the swearing in of President Abdoulaye Wade offended the anti0demo-cratic faction of Bissau Guinean military establishment, which had every reason to escalate tension.

On the other hand, based on the conventional wisdom that every war or conflict, especially when protracted, produces its own vested political and economic interests and dividends, it was possible that in Senegal, hawkish elements within the military or vested economic interests that had evolved from the long-drawn low intensity war, felt threatened by the declared pacific intentions of the two new administrations, especially the categorical statements by President

Wade to seek a solution to the Casamance problem as a priority. A conflagration on any of the frontiers posed a threat to the gains so far made in internal stability in Guinea Bissau, the emerging democratic system and the peace process as a whole. In a worst case scenario, it could derail the democratisation process, should the ex-junta, which seemed to act as though they were indeed the "moral guarantors of the state," begin to allege indecisiveness on the part of the democratically elected political authority. This could be grounds to put an end to the emerging constitutional order, ostensibly to protect the country from its neighbours. An immediate fallout of the skirmish was that it gave the military in Guinea Bissau a higher profile in dealing not only with military issues, but also the important political questions raised by the infractions on the border with Senegal.

Meanwhile, the retrieval of the corpse of the Bissau Guinean soldier was a subject of negotiation between the two governments. The Chief of Staff, Col. Verissimo Seabra, wrote a letter to the Minister of Defence to request the retrieval of the corpse. By the end of the month, the situation had deteriorated into full-blown sustained guerrilla attacks and pitched battles between the Salif Sadjoe wing of the MFDC and Senegalese troops in the Casamance region, the fighting was, however, dangerously close to the Guinea Bissau borders. Both countries mobilized heavy troop concentrations on both sides of the border. The Senegalese were determined to cut the supply lines of the rebels, which were well known to originate from Guinea Bissau territory. In September 2000, border crossings across the whole stretch of the northern frontiers remained closed to traffic, especially to trucks carrying merchandise from Senegal to Guinea Bissau. These closures were being effected by a self-styled Commission for Vigilance on both sides of the border. The democratically elected political authorities in Guinea Bissau were in a bind. While they would readily be rid of the burden of the MFDC bases in their territory, MFDC elements in Guinea Bissau were under the protection of General Mane and the hardcore elements in the junta. The political authorities could not execute any decisions on the MFDC, in particular as relations between Guinea Bissau and the movement had been the main instigator of the civil war. MFDC had many sympathisers in the armed forces of Guinea Bissau.

The border with Senegal, the lifeline to the outside world and channels of continued supplies from the ports of Dakar and Banjul in the Gambia, became unsafe and was intermittently shut ostensibly by local communities. These incidents set back the gradual movement toward the normalization of relations between the two countries. On his return to Bissau, President Yala expressed serious concerns about the activities of the radical wing of the MFDC on Bissau Guinean territory. General Mane's activities not only undermined internal stability and the efforts of the democratic government to consolidate its powers, they also posed a grave problem for the much-needed rapprochement with Senegal and Guinea. It was only a question of time for the tussle to blow open. These issues were taken up during a one-day visit to Bissau by President Wade of Senegal on 1 May, 2000.

President Wade's visit again brought to the fore the linkage between domestic stability in the respective states and general stability and peace in the immediate sub-region comprising Senegal, Gambia, Guinea Bissau and Guinea Conakry. It also demonstrated the reality that, in spite of the sovereignty and territorial integrity of states, the sociological structure of sovereign African states and the structural alignment of the interstate system are critical elements that have to be taken into account in solving problems of internal instability in these states. President Kumba Yala explained the difficult circumstances of his government in reining in the junta, and especially General Ansumane Mane to his guest. He implied that he did not yet have full control of his military and their deployment and that any attempt at that time to achieve that crucial goal might derail the evolving democratic and constitutional dispensation. While not formally admitting the obvious that Guinea Bissau was host to a number of rebel bases and that the ultra-nationalist wing of the MFDC, led by Salif Sadjoe, was being protected by hardcore elements in the former junta, President Kumba Yala made it clear that the rebels were undesirable elements who not only posed a serious threat to stability in Senegal, but had also become a menace to the democratization process and the emergence of constitutional order in Guinea Bissau. In sum, peace in the sub-region depended on finding solution to the radical MFDC. It was within the context of this visit that the internationalization of the Casamance issue was becoming a fact, requiring multi-lateral contribution to its solution.

President Wade's visit, on the other hand, represented a new realism in Dakar's policy on the Casamance. Since the inception of the armed conflict 18 years earlier, Senegal had maintained that this was an internal affair and had to be treated accordingly. President Wade's visit to Bissau and also Gambia, mainly to raise the issue of the Casamance somewhat tacitly implied a policy review and a recognition that, indeed, its neighbouring states were implicated, whether covertly or overtly, directly or indirectly, in the conflict in the Casamance and that these complications accounted for the demonstrated resilience of the radical wing of the MFDC. The implications of the common views held by the two presidents were given public expression by President Wade in Dakar where he publicly declared Ansumane Mane a villain. In Bissau, despite President Kumba Yala's concerns about the activities of General Mane with only occasional subtle airings of these misgivings, he maintained a cautious attitude, especially in not openly dismissing the general. He sought time to whittle down the political leverage for mischief and damage by the leader of the junta in order to safeguard

211

the evolving democratic and constitutional order. It was by no means certain that he had consolidated his power and the emergent constitutional order was too fragile to openly confront General Mane, especially in relation to the Casamance problem.

In spite of avoiding open and direct engagement on the issue of the MFDC, President Kumba Yala would appear to have made up his mind about repudiating the historical ties between Guinea Bissau and the MFDC. Despite the evolving changes in his attitude to the continued presence of the MFDC on Bissau Guinean territory, he was constrained by the influence of General Mane to respect the status quo in the bilateral relations of the country with the movement. More problematic was the fact that ultimately the MFDC fighters, mostly Mandingue linked to Mane as well as to the PAIGC, posed a threat to his rule and Guinea Bisau's fragile post conflict democracy which he as president symbolised. As a result of these constraints to effective policy realignment, the shared borders with Senegal continued to pose security problems. This began to hurt the fragile economy as border closures on the Senegalese side became the norm. The poor state of bilateral relations began to impact at the community levels as inter communal differences led to continued border closures.[59] The permanent commission of the Bissau Guinean National Assembly at its session on 18 September 2000 devoted to the problems at the border with Senegal passed a resolution calling on the government to accelerate the development of alternative outlets to international markets and to facilitate the importation of goods into the country through other routes to lessen dependence on the routes through Senegal and the port in Dakar. The commission suggested the rehabilitation of the port in Buba, Guinea Bissau, for this purpose. Meanwhile, President Kumba Yala continued to press for the resumption of the court process in respect of charges against those implicated in the sale of arms to the Casamancaise with a view to punishing them.[60]

The problem of General Ansumane Mane however was wider than the immediate question of the Casamance and Senegal, because it had pan-regional implications owing to the irredentism of the Mandingo and their espoused determination to create the Republic of Gabou out of the present Gambia, Guinea Bissau and Casamance. This constituted a threat to President Lansana Conte because Guinea Conakry is integral to any initiative to recast the existing configuration of states in the sub-region. For Conakry, three factors seemed to underline problems with Guinea Bissau. These factors include the fear of pan-regional Mandingo irredentism, institutionalization of personal relations as the basis of inter-state relations and the hurt to the national pride of Guinea Conakry arising from the losses it sustained in its failed intervention in Guinea Bissau. The interplay of these elements seem to provide some explanations on the nature of the alliances implied in the interventions in the Bissau Guinean domestic crisis.

It is uncertain that there was widespread consciousness of the need for the Mandingo and peoples of close cultural affinity to them, such as the Papel in Guinea Bissau, the Diolla, and the Kalinge to form one state. But it is certain that the radical faction within the Casamance based rebels, the MFDC, had espoused their ultimate political objective as the merger of the Casamance, Gambia and Guinea Bissau into a Republic of Gabou. The Mandingo spread into Guinea Conakry and as far as Mali. Sekou Toure, the first president of Guinea Conakry, was a Mandingue. Since then, despite the overwhelming numerical superiority of the Madingue throughout West Africa, they constitute a minority in most states and therefore lack the levers to influence the direction of policy in the sub-region. They also do not control any state. The pan-regional irredentism of the Madingue therefore poses a significant threat to the integrity of Guinea Conakry as a state. As such, the secession of the Casamance province from Senegal conjures the spectre of agitation in Guinea Conakry. It is to be highlighted that Gabou, the acclaimed spiritual home of the anticipated Gabou Republic, is today the capital of the region that goes by its name in East Central Guinea Bissau. Most Casamancaise trace their roots back to Gabou and recall that the flight of the population to the Casamance was to escape the religious wars of very recent memories. The Mandingue are concentrated around the area of Mansoa, Bissora and flow across the northern borders with Senegal into Diolla country. If the population of the Gambian basin, including the Casamance, along with the two Guineas, were put together, the whole of the region would qualify to be called Mandingo country. Thus sub-regional Mandingue irredentism would create instability throughout the sub-region and in all the states having Mandingue populations. For President Kumba Yala, his much touted Balanta majority in Guinea Bissau would become a small minority in an expanded political space that would be dominated by the Mandigue.

For Guinea Conakry, the fear of a pan-regional Mandingo political consciousness was real, and a possible threat to the integrity of emergent postcolonial African stateswas equally plausible. Under Sekou Toure, who was a Mandingo, it was possible to invoke the Mandingo affinity toward positive consolidation of pan-regional efforts, especially given the circumstances of Guinea Conakry's severance from France in 1958 when it rejected French proposals to formalize its neo-colonial arrangement. The Mandingo factor was a centripetal force then. The pervasive presence of the Mandingo which was a vital glue holding the sub-region together through a labyrinth of informal networks across countries and their capitals had become a liability under the evolved circumstances. President Lansana Conte's Guinea could not be said to enjoy the same privileges of a good historical conjuncture of forces as Sekou Toure. President Conte was an outsider in the strong Mandingo political circuit.

213

Given these threat factors around pan-regional Mandingo irredentism, Senegal, Guinea Conakry under Conte have a common long-term interest to undermine the spread of Mandingo political consciousness. These considerations appear to be relevant in the common perspectives that emerged in Dakar and Guinea over events in Guinea Bissau, particularly the prominent role of the MFDC on the side of General Ansumane Mane. Under a Balanta leadership that was soon in search of long-term hegemony in Guinea Bissau, pan-regional aspirations of the Mandingue put them at loggerheads with the Balanta, who held power in Bissau.

The problems of the status of the anti-democratic residues of the Junta in the democratic order were expressed in what became frequent personal confrontations between President Kumba Yala and the General Ansumane Mane. These affronts were serious enough to warrant the intervention of President Olusegun Obasanjo of Nigeria who on 24 October 2000 received President Kumba Yala and General Mane in Abuja. The clashes between the president and Mane however reached a head three weeks later during the celebration of the 36th anniversary of the Armed Forces of Guinea Bissau from which the General was conspicuously absent. Secondly, the internal schism within the military was manifest in the speech read on behalf of the military by Colonel Verissimo Seabra, who reaffirmed that the armed forces could not belong to any political party and was motivated by republican values. The statement underscored internal disagreements within the military over the continued high profile of General Mane in the affairs of the PAIGC, which was the main opposition party. At the celebration, President Yala announced the promotion of 28 senior officers to higher grades. General Ansumane Mane was promoted to the rank of a four star General. Colonels Seabra, Bothe Nabathcha, and Mamamdu Lamine Sahna were promoted the rank of major generals. The promotions in effect created three more generals in the military. Before then, the military had only one general in Ansumane Mane.

On 19 November 2000, General Mane ordered the top hierarchy of the military to his Base Aeirriene headquarters to denounce the promotions conferred on the top officers by the president. In the televised meeting, he also publicly ordered the officers to remove and dump their new stars in a trashcan at hand. Mane proclaimed himself as the Chief of Defence Staff, removing General Seabra from that position. He announced that from that moment on, he had assumed full responsibility for military affairs and appointed Bothce Nabatcha as his deputy Chief of Defence Staff. The political parties were divided in their pronouncements on the open defiance of the constitutional order. The Unioa para Mudanca (UM) of Amin Saad defended General Mane's actions as responses to injustices in the military. The PAIGC, as well as the seven-party Democratic Alliance called for dialogue between the two sides. The Minister of Defence reaffirmed the promotions of the officers and declared that the government would not capitulate before the General but suggested its readiness to negotiate differences with him. In between, General Mane placed under house arrests senior military officers, including members of the junta, perceived to be loyal to the democratic institutions. This included Col Verrismo Seabra. On 23 November, 2000 armed confrontations began between troops loyal to Ansumane Mane and those on the side of the democratic order. On 24 November, 2000, President Kumba Yala announced the neutralization of a rebellion led by the commander of the former junta, General Mane, to reverse the constitutional order. A few days later, the death of General Mane in battle in the outskirts of Bissau, where he had retreated with his depleted forces, was announced.

President Kumba Yala and the Ballantization of the Political Space

The events of November 2000 significantly changed the political environment in Guinea Bissau. The death of General Ansumane Mane removed the threat posed by the Military Junta to the full play of democracy in the country. This presented President Kumba Yala as well as the political class with the opportunity to begin to advance their political agenda without the shadow of the military looming over the process. The pro-democratic faction of the military, led by the new Chief of Defence Staff, General Verrismo Seabra, reaffirmed its loyalty to the constitutional order. This was demonstrated in the effective resistance of their former comrades from taking over power in November. However, two years after November 2000, the political process was again crisis-ridden with uncertainties on the direction of the new democracy. Political instability seemed to revolve around the determination of Kumba Yala to ensure Balanta domination of the political space. Also, internal schisms within the Balanta political elite were creating tensions within the government and the entire political process. These were compounded by the deteriorating socio-economic situation of the country, corruption in government, and, critically, by President Kumba Yala's personal agenda to subordinate other branches of the democratic order to the executive. He was motivated by three impulses in the post-junta years. The three dominant political goals set by the president included: consolidating the powers of the presidency vis-à-vis the legislative and judicial branches of the democratic order in order to dominate the political space; the creation of conditions that would guarantee his re-election as president; and firmly entrenching Ballanta ethnic control of the political and economic spaces. These constituted the elements of the emerging autocratic governance that destabilized the political system. The opposition's reaction to these was to organize into bigger units through a number of loose coalitions of small political parties with similar agendas.

The struggle of the political class against President Yala's political agenda, including his initiatives to acquire powers that the constitution had not bestowed on the presidency, as well as internal tangle of the ruling PRS characterized the political process up to his subsequent removal from office. By November 2002, President Yala had dissolved the National Assembly. The Supreme Court was in disarray following the interference of the presidency in the affairs of the judiciary that culminated in the arrest of the president of the apex court. The travails of the President of the Suoreme Court were intepreted by observers as principally designed by Kumba Yala to ensure that the the court was headed by a Balanta ethnic kinsman. His brazen drive for complete Balanta control of the judiciary, even when the speaker of the parliament was a Balanta, raised reservations even among key Balanta allies. The increasing protests against President Yala from his fellow Balanta resulted in the emergence of factions in the ruling Balanta-dominated PRS party. It boiled over from June 2002 when Alamara Ntchie N'hasse, the latest in the string of prime ministers appointed by the president, publicly criticised him for his handling of the affairs of state. Frequent cabinet reshuffles expressed internal wrangling in the PRS, as well as the changing balance of power in the party, particularly the unstable relations between the president and those he saw as rivals within the party who could make his renomination as the party's candidate for the next presidential elections difficult. Meanwhile, the RGB-MB party removed itself from government as a consequence of increased factional fighting along ethnic lines within the party. President Kumba Yala was perceived by the political class as responsible for political instability in the country. Many opined that the immediate future would be difficult in Guinea Bissau because of disillusionment in society, with deteriorating conditions of living and the seeming inability of the government to provide relief from the increasing suffering of the people. It was feared that the problems in the country would culminate in social upheavals sometime in October, 2002. If such social discontent was not properly handled, it could spur factions of the military to intervene And probably degenerate into a war.[61]

The political class also blamed the extant crisis on the ethnic politics of the PRS, which now equated the interests of the hegemonic ethnic group with the interests of the state. Within this ethnic group there appeared to be a struggle for control, leading to a constant flux in the balance of forces within the ruling PRS. The economic dimensions of the problems in the PRS revealed itself in the struggle within the party for the control of the fisheries, with the president angling to put his closer loyalists in charge of the sector. The international dimensions of the struggle in the sector came to the fore as Senegalese and Asian fishing entrepreneurs worked to cultivate their local allies in the ruling party. All these culminated in the split of the PRS party. One major faction attempted to create another Balanta party. The new party had a potential to divide the Balanta base of the PRS and leave President Kumba Yala with a very weak political base. It would also formally rubbish his claim of solely representing the Balanta interests.

In view of the high profile of the Balanta officers in the military and the close interaction between these and and their counterparts in the PRS hierarchy, tensions among the Balanta in politics was of concern to those in the military. This was reflected in the successful intervention of the military in the problems between President Kumba Yala and Prime Minister N'hasse. This was spectacular in the face of the failure of the National Assembly to resolve the problem. The success of military mediation raised issues about the continuing involvement of the military in political life, so soon after the tragic events of November 2000.

The resolution of the crisis between the President and the Prime Minister was achieved by the military through various meetings to find some accommodations on the differences that had threatened to snowball out of control. The immediate substantive contention, a minor cabinet reshuffle unilaterally announced by the president and rejected by the prime minister, that triggered the crisis, was not addressed.[62] The mediation brokered some understandings between the two top government officials, though not publicly acknowledged by both sides and the mediators. But it would appear that the agreement, among other things, stated that the vacancies created by the president's sacking of incumbent cabinet ministers, particularly the transport and justice ministers, would be filled through consultations between the president and the prime minister. The Office of Secretary of State for National Territory, also unilaterally abolished by President Yala, would remain abolished. It was indicated that the military mediators reiterated their support for constitutional rule and, on that basis, pledged loyalty to Kumba Yala as the elected official. They, however, also encouraged him to show greater respect for the provisions of the constitution in his actions as president of the country.

The crisis brought to the open deep divisions within the ruling party, exposed the difficult undercurrents of the political process, reflected the dangers inherent in the ethnic hegemonic project of the Balanta and, above all, demonstrated the fragility of the young democracy. Notwithstanding the commitments made to the military mediators that he would accord some respect to the Office of the Prime Minister, in September 2002, President Kumba Yala removed Alamara N'hasse from office. In mid-November 2002, President Yala announced the dissolution of the National Assembly. This created a vacuum that effectively limited mass participation in the nascent democracy. This further exacerbated fears of Balanta domination of the political process. On 2 December, the finance minister in the new government, who had been retained from the old government, was replaced. These developments all consolidated powers in the hands of the president. Following the dissolution of the National Assembly, President Kumba Yala expressed his intention to schedule early elections.

In the aftermath of the crisis, reactions among the political class to the confrontation between Prime Minister Alamara and the president were varied. Some commended the prime minister for his courage in drawing attention to the dangers posed to the stability of the country and good functioning of the democratic dispensation by the incessant breach of the constitution by President Kumba Yala.[63] Alternative views included outright condemnation of the prime minster for not availing himself of all channels of communication to reach the President before his statement on the radio that exacerbated the situation. The prime minister's public statement denouncing unilateral cabinet changes by the president was seen as an affront to the Presidency. Some opposition forces called for a thorough investigation of all the accusations that were bandied by the two sides in the heat of crisis. Such accusations included violations of the constitution by the president and allegations of corruption against Prime Minister Nhasse and the ex-minister of fisheries, Arthur Sanha. Indeed, one party, the Union para Mudanca (UM), with only 3 seats in parliament, indicated that it would work for the overthrow of Prime Minister Alamara Nhasse, following corruption charges made against him and virtually substantiated by the president in the course of the crisis.

Most actors in the political process were critical of the prominent role played by the military in achieving accommodation by the protagonists in the conflict. This included the PAIGC president, Carlos Gomes. The first concern appeared to be that mediation by the military was only possible because the two protagonists had constantly assessed their support in the military and had made veiled allusions to balance of forces within the military in their favor. Indeed, speculation about who stood where among the military was rife throughout the crisis. Thus, the political class had resorted to the manipulation of the military to attain their political goals. In resisting the overtures for partisan support, the military hierarchy chose the mediation option. Some however perceived the major actors in the military mediation as fellow ethnic Balanta protecting their emerging hegemony in the political process. Thus, the problem became part of the ethnic calculus between the Southern Balanta represented by Prime Minister N'hasse and the Northern Balanta led by President Kumba Yala.

In all these, institutional mechanisms, such as the National Assembly and Supreme Court, did not play any role. The President of the National Assembly, Jorge Malu, also a Balanta, argued that convening the Permanent Committee of the National Assembly to deliberate on the institutional crisis could only have complicated the mediation process. Against the background of seeming helplessness of democratic institutions to mediate the crisis, active intervention by the military in the political process was disturbing to the political class and civil society. In the long term, they argued, such mediation would endanger the viability of the democratic process.

The removal of prime ministers as well as incessant cabinet reshuffles unilaterally initiated by the president exacerbated problems within the ruling PRS. Also, the presidency's continued stoking of Balanta elements in the opposition RGB-MB, to ensure the take-over of the party by a Balanta, Salvador Tschongo, was weakening internal cohesion in that party. President Yala's interventions ensured that the party eventually split into two factions. Balanta elements in the RGB-MB were grouped in the Tschongo wing of the enfeebled opposition party. This destroyed one of the two potent opposition parties and left the PAIGC as the only credible alternative force in the political system against the PRS. It was against this background that President Yala ordered the arrest of the President of the Supreme Court, Justice Emiliano Nosonini. The arrest and sack and the problems contrived first to delay the re-election of a new supreme court president, and later the manipulation of the law to ensure that a fellow Balanta emerge as the new head of the judiciary proved to be part of the general plan for Balanta domination. Against this background, the destabilized judiciary was barely able to function not only because of the infrastructural constraints, but also because of the deliberate attempt by the president to paralyse other branches of democratic governance. The Executive under his firm control was dominant.

Finally, President Kumba Yala promoted Balanta domination and control of the military and consolidated the state security apparatus in Balanta hands. In December, 2002, three high-ranking intelligence officials were detained in connection with an alleged coup d'etat. The detained were Celcio de Calvalho, Ernesto Carvalho and Colonel Malama Camara. On 27 January, 2003, the Minister of Internal Administration, Antonio Sedja Mann, issued nine despatches to reorganize state security. The reorganization entailed the creation of a new Department of Analysis of Information to be constituted by three top-ranking Balanta police officers, namely: Major General Inhare Yala Nhante, Director of State Security as president of the new outfit, Brigadier General Bitchofula Na Fafe, Commissioner General of the Police as member and Brigadier General M'bana Na Sanha, Commandant General as member. Lieutenant Colonel M'bali M'bum was named Head of intelligence related Civil Office in the presidency while Colonel Jose Sanha was appointed Advisor to the Minister of Internal Administration. These appointments at the highest level of state intelligence, including the minister of internal administration, were all Balanta. The appointments, in effect, replaced non-Balanta senior officers with Balanta. By this, the firm domination of the state security by the Balanta was effected. The president explained that the new deployments in state security were to redress years of persecuting the Balanta. The new state security would later hound political opponents, stifle the freedom of the media with incessant arrests and shut down newspapers through denial of access to newsprint. The move to consolidate state security was, however, also directed equally at prominent figures in the PRS such as Alamara N'hasse and Arthur Sanha. The two had managed to build autonomous centers of power in the PRS party that were perceived as posing a threat to the renomination of President Kumba Yala as the party's flag bearer for the next presidential elections. They were subjected to increased attention from security operatives. Most top- ranking Balanta military officers owed their loyalty to Alamara N'hasse. A split among the Balanta now threatened a potential destabilization of the young and fragile Bissau Guinean democracy.

Avenging Past Balanta Grievance

Following the consolidation of state security in Balanta hands, President Kumba Yala proceeded to investigate the perceived injustices to Balanta in the past, including the 1985 executions of Balanta officers. This implied a direct confrontation with the entire leadership of the state for the period. In March 2003, state security, under direct instructions of the President, arrested all surviving members of the Council of State that had denied clemency to the executed officers. The PAIGC leadership, led by its Vice President, Carlos Gomes Domingos Jnr. and high-ranking member, Aristides Gomes, explained that the arrest of six members of the party who had served on the Council of State during the one-party era was unjustified. Interventions made by their attorney with the authorities to be formally informed of the charges against the six had not yielded any fruits. The leaders of the PAIGC observed that from pronouncements made by the government, the six members of the old Council of State had been arrested in connection with the Council's refusal to grant clemency to a group of Balanta officers who had been condemned by a military court for an attempted coup d'etat in 1985. They highlighted that the arrests were a dangerous development with serious implications for social and political stability because of the glaring ethnic dimensions implicit in the executive order for their arrests. The arrests therefore constituted political persecution.

The PAIGC leaders explained that many unfortunate things happened during the one-party era. This included summary executions at various times of those who were said to have collaborated with the colonial forces and some others for an attempted coup d'etat. Some of the victims of these executions belonged to other ethnic groups, such as Peuls and Biafada. The arrests of the members of the Council of State by State Security was related to the case of Paul Correia and five others who were executed following condemnation by a military court. The PAIGC stressed that President Kumba Yala was resuscitating their case simply because they were Balanta. Such ethnically selective review of the past constituted a dangerous political development for the country, the PAIGC leaders affirmed.

On the legal implications of the arrests, they asserted that the executive lacked the power to summarily raise such issues and give orders of arrest. Such powers, they contended, belonged to the National Assembly. Besides, it was strange that members of the Council of State would be legally held for decisions taken in their capacity as Council members, especially in a matter that had gone through a judicial process. To arrive at such arrests, at a minimum a new court process had to be initiated to review the decision of the last court. It was noted that the Minister of Internal Administration was out of step with the law in executing the arrest orders on former members of Council of State. These steps would also endanger harmonious relations among tribes, especially as President Yala had been tribalising the political process. Finally, they urged the international community to step into the matter as part of its preventive diplomacy to assure peace in the country.

On the immediate consequences of the arrests, the PAIGC leaders said that it had led to the formation of a technical committee of opposition parties to elaborate a common response to the slide in governance in the country. The Conference of Political leaders revealed that its response would aim to paralyze the country to stop the activities of President Kumba Yala. The Conference clarified that up to that point they had been reluctant to mobilize people into the streets because society and the political process were still fragile following the experience of the last civil war. Society was still traumatized and many were scared. Yet, concerns were mounting that the situation in the country would degenerate. This left them with no choice other than to mobilize the people into the streets.

A DEBILITATING DEMOCRACY

The PAIGC party, however, continued to prepare for the legislative elections scheduled for April 20, 2003 by processing its list of candidates. As required by law, it planned to submit the list to the Supreme Court on the last date set for it to receive nominations. The party was under no illusions that the elections could not hold as scheduled on April 20 because of technical delays that the National Electoral Commission could not possibly resolve by that date. Secondly, political party leaders expressed serious concerns about the internal political dynamics and wondered if elections could actually be held under the prevailing political climate. A formal announcement by the party to boycott the anticipated elections would give President Kumba Yala the chance to postpone the election indefinitely. PAIGC would, therefore, refrain from doing so. The matter of elections would, however, remain under constant review by the party.[64]

Meanwhile, the economy continued to pose serious constraints and concern. It had degenerated as the government remained unable to pay civil servants and could not mobilize international aid as a result of the politics of President Kumba Yala. This led to a series of strikes by various unions. This included the teachers union, SINAPROF, which insisted that reopening of primary schools would depend on the payment of 90% of arrears owed to teachers by the government.[65] The views of the political class on the evolution of the post-conflict democratic system were provided by Victor Madinga, who emerged as the leader of the democratic opposition.[66] The forum brought the Democratic Convergence Party (PCD), the Democratic Front (DF), the Social Democratic Front (DSF), the Front for the Total Liberation and Independence of Guinea (FLING), the first liberation movement to challenge Portuguese colonial regime in Guinea Bissau, under one umbrella. The economic situation was rather difficult, he emphasized. With government monthly expenditure out-stripping revenue by 5 to 6 million, it was a question of time for workers to rise in protest. He noted that the government owed workers four months of salary arrears. Yet, there seemed to be no imaginative way out for the government. He said that there was nothing to salvage in the Alamara government, except the fact that President Kumba Yala would sacrifice Prime Minister Alamara Nhase in time to appease workers demand for payment of back wages. The recent agreement on wage increases had not helped matters. Yet, the solution would not lie in changing governments, but in instituting immediate reforms of the public service. Such a reform should involve rationalization of staff to reduce the heavy wage burden of the government.

On the state of the military, Victor Mandinga observed that two major blocs existed within it. The Democratic Opposition expressed doubts about the loyalty of the chief of staff to the president. It observed that General Verissimo Seabra had been playing the two blocs against each other for his own political survival. In the time being, the Democratic Opposition did not think that the politics of the military did pose any immediate danger. The gravest danger to stability was the rising social discontent and the increasing loss of hope and faith in the political process. The discontent might encourage an obscure officer to intervene in the political process, and probably leave no option for the suffering population. In that case, one could not be sure of the eventual outcome of such a move. He expressed serious reservations about the manner of intervention of the military in resolving the last crisis.

Mr. Madinga noted that a joint open declaration of the Bishops of Bissau and Bafata that was very critical of the state of affairs reflected the true pulse of the country. He justified the intervention of the cleric in the political process. These bishops had listened to the sufferings of the people and had been forced to increase their humanitarian initiatives to provide relief to society. The Catholic Church was thus overwhelmed and had become necessary for the bishops to draw attention to the worsening plight of the people. Traditionally, the Catholic Church, he added, had very strong influence in the country. He did not think that President Kumba Yala's overtures to the predominantly Muslim Foula community to counter-balance the influence of the Catholic Church would detract in any way from the influence of the Church or even translate into political support for the president. He noted that the emergent situation had elicited serious apprehensions about the future from all segments of civil society, led by Bishop Caminate of the Catholic Church and including prominent businessmen Carlos Domingos Gomes and Rosa Enrique Rosas(later prime minister and interim president respectively), Carmen Pereira, former minster of justice in the early PAIGC regime, and respected leaders at grassroots level, Madam Barai, as well as youthful leader Nelvina Barreto. It was the national consensus that the evolution of the country had become debilitating.

In the discourse of representatives of civil society,[67] the general consensus emerged that the overall situation in the country was untenable, with the real danger of implosion. This applied equally to the social, the political and the economic life of the country. Society was described as fragile, materially and psychologically. Civil society was said to have no moral force in the face of the assault on democratic values by President Kumba Yala. The dire social situation that was characterized by increasingly depreciating conditions of living, including pervasive hunger, had led to a sense of hopelessness in the general population. In this connection, society had been weakened and was now fragile. Many Bissau Guinean families survived only because of remittances from family members abroad. These funds from abroad were what indeed sustained the largely informal economy in which the preponderant number of Bissau Guineans participated. Otherwise, the formal economy was perceived to be on the verge of collapse. Crime was on the increase and homicide was increasingly becoming an issue. Some saw the rise of homicide as part of the hidden psychological impact of the difficult situation in the country. The collapse of the education sector was cited as frustrating and that it could aggravate the alienation of the population further. Demonstrations by pupils were said to be imminent and the political fallout of student street rallies was generally dreaded. It was noted that there was no universal understanding of a common vision for the country. In the absence of such a vision, many were not surprised that though Bissau Guineans had clamored for change, *mudanca,* they had forgotten to ask for concrete programs of action from candidates during the electoral campaign. It was concluded that the malaise that was manifesting in all facets of national life resulted from this situation.

Civil society was unanimous in its perception that President KumbaYala was principally to blame for political instability in the country. It was observed that the ethnicisation of the political process, especially the concentration of political power in Balanta hands, was a worrying development. The ethnic factor had never played a role so blatantly and prominent in Bissau Guinean politics, they asserted. Indeed, many explained the crisis in the country in terms of the closure of the political system, where only the Balanta and a few others were privy to the conduct of the affairs of state. In that scenario, personality clashes and individual differences played a significant role in the instability of the whole political system. Intra-ethnic cleavages also aggravated political tensions. On the character of the political class, it was felt that, indeed, most of the political actors had been compromised. In this connection, spokespersons of civil society commended the Pastoral Letter of the Bishops of Bissau and Bafata for its forthrightness and for giving vent to the major problems that the average Bissau Guinean had been grappling with for some time. It was acknowledged that the pastoral letter, which forcefully brought home to the president the dire straits in which the people were, constituted a serious call on him to get his acts together. The call for radical change in that letter was appreciated by civil society. It was gratifying, they noted, that Bishop Caminate had condemned ethnic politics even though he was a Balanta himself.

A myriad of reasons was adduced for the poor quality of governance in post-conflict Guinea Bissau. Civil society actors noted that the leadership was made of largely inexperienced people, who had not been prepared in any way for the challenges of political leadership and development. It was also observed that the post-conflict democratization process had brought in its wake many innovations. One of such changes with far-reaching consequences was the introduction of systematic and rule-based administration following the introduction of true multi-party democracy in the country. These new administrative procedures and processes, involving formalized channels of communication and respect for bureaucratic ethics ad values, were novel in the administration of the country. This lack of a formalized culture of governing could also, in part, explain the attitude of those in high positions in government.

The political and economic situation in the country continued to deteriorate as President Kumba Yala consolidated personal power with scant regard for the constitution. The situation is captured in the report of the European Union Election Observation Mission that noted that

> ...President Kumba Yala was democratically elected with 72% of votes, but quickly he opted for an erratic governance system characterized by frequent changes of government and human rights abuses. The harassment of judges and censoring the press, the refusal to promulgate the new constitution approved by Parliament, dissolution of the Parliament and frequent adjournment of legislative elections contributed to a constitutional crisis. The situation dis-

couraged donors and placed the country in a deep financial crisis and rendered the government incapable of paying salaries of military and civil servants, including these key sectors as education and health. Between 2000 and 2002, the country faced social instability with street manifestations, repeated strikes due to unpaid salaries and a deep social discontent.[68]

By September 14, 2003, the Unity Platform announced that a military coup to overthrow the government was inevitable. The same day, the Chief of Defence Staff, General Verissimo Seabra publicly charged President Kumba Yala with violating and disrespecting the constitution and announced the formation of a new government. Kumba Yala refused to acknowledge his overthrow but was forced to step aside after being put under house arrest as General Verissimo Seabra took over as head of state. The new government however reassured that it had no intention of staying in power. On 17 September, Kumba Yala publicly renounced his mandate. Following prolonged negotiation led by ECOWAS to dissuade Kumba Yala from carrying out threats to resume his mandate that was truncated by the intervention of a section of the military, prominent attorney and businessman Rosa Enrique Rosas assumed the presidency on an interim capacity, pending the holding of new democratic elections.

The military named Henrique Rosa as president and Arthur Sahna, a former critic of President Kumba Yala, was named prim minister during the transition to a new democracy. Commentaries on Guinea Bissau at this time observed that

> ...the armed conflict that ravaged Guinea Bissau in 1998-1999 caused important damage to the infrastructure, disrupted the economic growth and impoverished the country. The incoherent economic and fiscal policies and the absence of a trustworthy government in the post conflict phase created the conditions for the September 23 coup d'etat.

Nevertheless, Guinea Bissau is still facing a 'structural emergency' characterised by a significant disruption of State capacity to deliver services to its citizens, persistent political tensions, the fragility of the civilian authorities vis a vis a tradition of high politicised interventionist Armed Forces and growing manipulation of ethnicity for political purpose. [69]

The ousting of Kumba Yala, notwithstanding the tensions and instability that his policy was perceived to have had plunged the country into, was unpopular among the Balanta officer corps who were mostly loyal to the deposed presidency because of his ultra-Balanta hegemonic aspirations. Shortly after, on 6 October, a military mutiny led by a group of Balanta officers assassinated General Verrisimo Seabra and the military spokesperson, Colonel Domingos de

Barros, for their role in the toppling of President Kumba Yala, who had clearly identified himself as a champion of Balanta control of Guinea Bissau. The mutineers insisted on the appointment of Major General Tagme Na Waie, a Balanta, as the Chief of Defence Staff. Thus the authority of the new government was compromised early as it succumbed to the demands of the Balanta military officers. The European Union observers highlight that

> This, and other appointments of the new military high commands were widely perceived as caving in on the part of the civilian authority of the constitutional Government and institutions. The mutiny also increased the danger of the polarization of Guinea Bissau society along ethnic lines, especially given widespread perception that the revolt was inspired by Balanta elements in the armed forces intent on assuming control of the military establishment.[70]

The appointment of civilians to head the new government did not pacify the political class that was determined to resist the outcome of the military inspired changes to the executive. The PAIGC promised to prosecute its resistance until "final victory", among other political forces. Negotiation between the interim President Rosa Enrique Rosas and Prime Minister Arthur Sahna with the political forces led to the signing of a National Transition Charter by political forces on 28 September, 2003. The charter provided for the transfer of power to civilian authority, the nomination of a Transition President, and the holding of legislative elections within six months of its signing and the conduct of presidential elections within one year of the swearing-in of the elected legislators.[71] The presidential elections were scheduled for 19 June, 2004. As the legislative and presidential elections approached in the first quarter of 2004, President Henrique Rosa affirmed the neutrality of the military in the electoral process.

Fifteen political parties contested the legislative elections that were held on 28 March, 2004. Three political parties between them won 99 of the 102 seats in the Peoples' National Assembly. The PAIGC got 33.8% of the vote. This secured the party 45 seats in the Assembly. With 26.50% of the vote, the PRS had 35 seats; the United Social Democratic Party (PUSD) received 17.60% of the vote that gave it 17 seats in the Assembly. Two other parties received 2 seats and 1 seat respectively.

28 MARCH 2004 NATIONAL PEOPLE'S ASSEMBLY ELECTION

Registered Voters	603,639
Total Voters (Voter Turnout)	460,254 (76.2%)
Invalid/Blank Votes	31,317
Total Valid Votes	428,937

PARTY/(COALITION)	NUMBER OF VOTES	% OF VOTES	NUMBER OF SEATS (100)
African Party for the Independence of Guinea and Cape Verde (PAIGC)	145,316	33.88%	45
Social Renewal Party (PRS)	113,656	26.50%	35
United Social Democratic Party (PUSD)	75,485	17.60%	17
United Platform [PLATAFORMA]	20,700	4.83%	-
Electoral Union [UE]	18,354	4.28%	02
Democratic Socialist Party (PDS)	8,789	2.05%	-
Union for Change (UM)	8,621	2.01%	-
Resistance of Guinea-Bissau-Bafatá Movement (RGB-MB)	7,918	1.85%	-
Party of National Unity (PUN)	6,260	1.46%	-
United Popular Alliance [APU]	5,817	1.36%	01
National Union for Democracy and Progress (UNDP)	5,042	1.18%	-
Guinean Civic Forum-Social Democracy (FCG-SD)	4,209	0.98%	-
Guinean Democratic Movement (MDG)	4,202	0.98%	-
Manifest Party of the People (PMP)	3,402	0.79%	-
Socialist Party of Guinea-Bissau (PS-GB)	1,166	0.27%	-

The first round of presidential elections was held on 19 June, 2005. It was contested by 13 candidates, as flag bearers of 13 of the political parties that had presented candidates for the legislative elections. The return of former President General Bernardino Vieira from exile and his rejection by the PAIGC reflected the divisions within the party, in particular within the military faction of the PAIGC, since the civil war that had pitted him against the dominant Ansumane Mane faction of the party. The party had also not forgotten his invitation to Senegal and Guinea Conakry to rescue his government. Many had interpreted the invitation as an invasion of the country by foreign forces. The PAIGC was particularly resentful of the Senegalese because it recalled the refusal of Senegal to permit the use of its territory to launch the revolutionary war that eventually liberated the country from Portuguese colonialism. With the turning tides in the political evolution of the country, the PAIGC, under Ansumane Mane, had found itself in alliance with a sympathetic Portuguese establishment against the Senegalese, who were also seen as proxies of France.

Against this background, the PAIGC was determined to ensure victory at the polls, if only to validate its sentiments that General Bernandino Vieira remained unacceptable to the people of Guinea Bissau. Also, the revelations of the atrocities against the Balanta under his presidency remained fresh in the minds of the population. The Balanta, it was felt, would challenge the legitimacy of the elections if Bernardino Vieira won the presidential elections. Yet, this was precisely how the elections turned out to be.

JUNE/JULY 2005 PRESIDENTIAL ELECTION

First Round (19 June 2005)

Registered Voters	538,471
Total Votes (Voter Turnout)	471,843 (87.6%)
Invalid/Blank Votes	25,350
Total Valid Votes	446,493

CANDIDATE (PARTY)	FIRST ROUND	
	NUMBER OF VOTES	% OF VOTES
João Bernardo "Nino" Vieira	128,918	28.87%
Malam Bacai Sanhá (PAIGC)	158,267	35.45%
Kumba Yalá (PRS)	111,606	25.00%
Francisco Fadul (PUSD)	12,733	2.85%
Aregado Mantenque Të (PT)	9,000	2.02%
Mamadú Iaia Djaló	7,112	1.59%
Mário Lopes da Rosa	4,863	1.09%
Idrissa Djaló (PUN)	3,604	0.81%
Adelino Mano Queta	2,816	0.63%
Faustino Fudut Imbali (PMP)	2,330	0.52%
Paulino Empossa Ié	2,215	0.50%
Antonieta Rosa Gomes (FCG-SD)	1,642	0.37%
João Tátis Sá (PPG)	1,378	0.31%

With three Balanta candidates in the race, Malam Bacai Sanha, former interim president put forward as the candidate of the PAIGC, former President Kumba Yala returning from exile in Morocco to contest as the candidate of the Party for Social Renewal (PRS) and Faustino Imbali, a former prime minister, the votes of those Balanta who might have voted on ethnic lines were divided among the three. Significantly though, with Malam Bacai's 35.45% and Kumba Yala's 25.00% of the total votes cast in the first round, the 2 Balanta candidates between them received over 60% of the votes. Yet, with 28.80% of the votes received by Bernardino Vieira, who stood as an independent candidate, he received enough votes to edge out former President Kumba Yala, as the second candidate for the run-off presidential elections. Despite reports that there had been an influx of arms in the weeks leading up to the election and reports of some "disturbances during campaigning" — including attacks on government offices by unidentified gunmen — foreign election monitors labeled the election as "calm and organized".[72]

The edging out of Kumba Yala threatened to derail the process as he refused to recognize the result. Many of his loyalists challenged the results of the elections as designed to eliminate him, whom they perceived as the authentic arrowhead for the continued pursuit of Balanta domination of the political space. In the second round of presidential elections that were held on 24 July, 2005, Bernardino Vieira received 52.35% of the votes and thereby was elected to the presidency. The announcement of the final results of the elections was delayed owing to complaints by Malam Bacai Sanha's and the PAIGC of fraud and demanded recounts in the capital Bissau and districts in the eastern and western parts of the country. Malam Bacai remained unconvinced, but eventually accepted the results.

Second Round (24 July 2005)

Registered Voters	538,472
Total Votes (Voter Turnout)	422,978 (78.6%)
Invalid/Blank votes	10,052
Total Valid Votes	412,926

CANDIDATE (PARTY)	SECOND ROUND	
	NUMBER OF VOTES	% OF VOTES
João Bernardo "Nino" Vieira	216,167	52.35%
Malam Bacai Sanhá (PAIGC)	196,759	47.65%

The second presidency of Bernardino Vieira, notwithstanding his pledge for peace and not to persecute anyone, was troubled. Prime Minister Carlos Gomes refused to accept Bernardino Vieira's victory. The hierarchy of the military establishment that was dominated by the Balanta and headed by General Tagme Na Waie was hostile to his victory, in particular with the protests of former President Kumba Yala that he had been schemed out of the race. The chief of defense staff had been appointed under duress following the assassination of his predecessor General Verissimo Seabra for his role in the ousting of President Kumba Yala and the insistence of the military to have Tagme Na Waie occupy the highest post in the military. Relationship between the president and the chief of staff was based on mutual suspicion. President Vieira was sworn into office on October 1. On October 10, he dismissed the government of Carlos Gomes. He appointed Aristides Gomes as prime minister on October 15. President Bernandino Vieira's control over the Peoples' National Assembly was tenuous. Lounging from one problem to another, on March 27, the major political forces in the Peoples' National Assembly; the PAIGC, PRS and PUSD, called for a 'government of consensus. Following the refusal of the president to accept the demand, the Peoples' National Assembly passed a vote of no confidence on the government of Aristides Gomes, who resigned on 29 March. A new Prime Minister, Martinho Ndafa, took the reins of governing after much resistance by President Bernandino Vieira. The PAIGC withdrew its support for Prime Minister Martinho Ndafa Kabi in February 2008. In July, the party also pulled out of the government of consensus. The prime minister was replaced by Carlos Correia. Meanwhile, the Supreme Court ruled the postponement of the legislative elections that was due in March, 2008, and the prolongation of the life of the People's National Assembly as unconstitutional.

Also, given the instability and the very weak capacity of the state to maintain law and order on the mainland and the virtual abandonment of the Viragos islands, international drug mafia had infiltrated the country as a transit station to the market in Europe and America. In these circumstances, many of the political elite and the military hierarchy had been implicated in the drug trade. The political complexities of Guinea Bissau had been rendered more complicated by the transformation of the country into a narco-state. The drug mafia from South America had vested interests in the political evolution or continuing chaos in the country.

On March 1, 2009, General Tagme Na Waie was killed by explosives planted at the military headquarters. The day after, March 2, his Balanta loyalist officers stormed the residence of President Bernandino Vieira early in the morning and hacked him to death with machetes. This was followed by gunshots to his body to ensure that he did not survive. The attackers, as in the previous assassination of General Seabra, announced that they did not seek to take over political power. They had acted to avenge the killing of the Chief of Staff that was presumed to have been orchestrated by President Vieira.

The assassinations of the Chief of Staff, General Tagme Waie and President Bernardino Viera may be attributed to the inability of Bissau Guinean society since independence to wean the state from the debilitating control of the military wing of its liberation movement, the Pan African Party for the Independence of Guinea and Cape Verde (PAIGC). The execution of President Bernna-dino Viera, ostensibly a revenge for the killing of Chief of Staff General Tagme Waie on Sunday, 1 March, brought the sanguine trajectory of Guinea Bissau's political evolution full cycle. With the executions of Generals Ansumane Mane, former Chief of Staff of the Bissau Guinean military, in November 2000, General Verrisimo Seabra, former Chief of Staff, three years later, assassinations of Tagme Waie and President Bernandino Viera, all the old generation of 'militicians' that had imposed their will on the political process in Guinea Bissau had finally left the scene. The development thus marked the end of the domination of the political space by the vanguard of the PAIGC, a party that did not shed its military character and that inflexibly imposed its will on the socio-political domain of Guinea Bissau. The decay, the loss of internal coherence and rivalries and schisms in the PAIGC, interacting with the ethnic struggle for state control reverberated in perpetual turmoil that easily degenerated into political violence. The death of Bernandino Viera seemed to have presented the opportunity for the country to turn a page. Yet, the violence persisted.

The death of President Bernandino Vieira had removed the constitutional head of state but left intact the government headed by Prime Minister Carlos Domingos. To preserve the constitutional government and since the military explained that their action was not intended to stage a coup, Raimundo Pereira, the President of the National Assembly, consistent with the Constitution, was appointed as the interim head of state, pending the holding of presidential elections that was fixed for 28 June, 2009. With the many political assassinations that had followed in quick succession, the political atmosphere remained tense during the transition. The situation deteriorated again on June 3, when with Prime Minister, Carlos Domingos away in Portugal, one of the candidates for the June 28 presidential elections, Baciro Dabo, was assassinated. Baciro Dabo was a former intelligence officer who had testified against the aides of President Bernandino Vieira during the General Ansumane Mane instigated trials of those alleged to have aided and abetted the invasion of the country by Senegalese and Guinean Conakry forces.

The same day, the General Management of State Information Services, the State Intelligence, announced that it had foiled a coup d'etat against the interim government perpetrated by a self-described "High Commandership of Republican Forces for the Restoration of Constitutional and Democratic Order". The announcement claimed that the group was led by Helder Proenca, a former leader of the PAIGC, and included the assassinated Baciro Dabo. State Intelligence informed it was compelled to deploy the Military Police to quell the planned 'act of subversion of the constitutional order'. Despite the heightened tensions all over the country, the presidential elections were held on June 28.

REPUBLIC OF GUINEA–BISSAU
PRESIDENTIAL ELECTIONS HELD ON 28TH JUNE 2009
Total Number of Votes Obtained

CANDIDATES	TOTAL # OF VOTES
Baciro Dabo	0
Francisca Vaz Turpin	1,219
Serifo Baldé	1,794
Pedro Infanda	0
Aregado Mantenque Té	1,736
Malam Bacai Sanhá	133,786
Henrique Pereira Rosa	81,751
Luis Nancassa	1,195
Kumba Yalá	99,428
João Cardoso	4,115
Mamadu Iaia Djaló	10,495
Paulo Mendonça	949
Ibraima Djaló	1,489

In the first round of presidential elections, Malam Bacai Sanha, the candidate of the PAIGC, and Kumba Yala, flag bearer of the PRS, both Balanta, received the two highest votes of the 13 candidates to qualify for the second round of the Presidential elections that was conducted on 26 July 2009. In the second round of the elections Malam Bacai Sanha received 63% of the votes to Kumba Yala's 36%. Kumba Yala expressed satisfaction with the outcome of the elections. Another Balanta was to take over the Presidency of Guinea Bissau with effect from 8 September, 2009 when Malam Bacai Sanha was scheduled to be formally inaugurated into office.

Notes

1. Amilcar Cabral, *Return to the Source: Selected Speeches of Amilcar Cabral*, ed. Africa Information Service, Monthly Review Press, New York, 1973, p. 9.
2. Patrick Chabal, *Amilcar Cabral: Revolutionary Leadership and People's War*, Africa World Press, Trenton, 2003, p. 65.
3. Amilcar Cabral, op. cit., p. 9.
4. Patrick Chabal, *Amilcar Cabral: Revolutionary Leadership and People's War*, op. cit., p. 9.

5. Patrick Chabal, *Amilcar Cabral: Revolutionary Leadership and People's War*, ibid., p. 2.

6. Background Note: Guinea Bissau, Bureau of African Affairs,. US State Department. Internet Source: http://www.state.gov./r/pa/ei/bgn/5454.htm

7. Patrick Chabal, ibid., p. 16.

8. Background Note: Guinea Bissau, Bureau of African Affairs,. US State Department. Internet Source: http://www.state.gov./r/pa/ei/bgn/5454.htm

9. Background Note: Guinea Bissau, Bureau of African Affairs,. US State Department. Internet Source: http://www.state.gov./r/pa/ei/bgn/5454.htm

10. Background Note: Guinea Bissau, Bureau of African Affairs,. US State Department. Internet Source: http://www.state.gov./r/pa/ei/bgn/5454.htm

11. Background Note: Guinea Bissau, Bureau of African Affairs,. US State Department. Internet Source: http://www.state.gov./r/pa/ei/bgn/5454.htm

12. Patrick Chabal, *Amilcar Cabral: Revolutionary Leadership and People's War*, ibid., p. 10

13. Amilcar Cabral, op. cit. p. 9.

14. Amilcar Cabral, ibid., p. 9.

15. Patrick Chabal, *Amilcar Cabral, Revolutionary Leadership and People's War*, (Africa World Press, Trenton, 2003) p. 10

16. Patrick Chabal, *Amilcar Cabral: Revolutionary Leadership and People's War*, op. cit., p. 135.

17. Patrick Chabal, *Amilcar Cabral: Revolutionary Leadership and People's War*, ibid., p. 10

18. Patrick Chabal, *Amilcar Cabral: Revolutionary Leadership and People's War*, ibid., p. 65

19. Patrick Chabal, *Amilcar Cabral: Revolutionary Leadership and People's War*, ibid., p. 134

20. Reuter report of 9 October, 1999. Also cited on Portuguese television on Saturday

21. Interviews with Spokesman for the PRS.

22. Roy van de Dwight, "Democracy, legitimate warfare in Guinea Bissau," paper presented at conference "Webs of War," Africa Studies Center, Leiden, Holland, March, 1999.

23. "Instant War," *The Economist* 347, no. 8073, June 20, 1998, p. 50.

24. "Unhappy Soldiers," *The Economist* 348, no. 8085, September 12, 1998, p. 53.

25. Roy van de Dwight, op. cit.

26. Lars Rudbeck, "Guinea Bissau: Military Fighting Breaks Out," *Review of African Political Economy*, September 1998.

27. Lars Rudbeck, ibid.

28. Roy van de Dwight, op. cit.

29. Lars Rudbeck, op. cit.

30. "Senegal's separatists resume offensive," *AFP/Newsedge*, June 5, 1999.

31. See AFP/Newsedge report, Senegal's separatists resume offensive, 5 June, 1999. See also Newsedge report, Senegalese rebels meet to prepare talks with government, 12 December, 1999.

32. Adekeye Adebajo, *Building Peace in West Africa: Liberia, Sierra Leone, and Guinea-Bissau*, Lynne Rienner Publishers, Boulder, CO, 2002.

33. Roy van de Dwight, op. cit.

34. Lars Rudbeck, op. cit.

35. Adekeye Adebajo, op. cit.

36. "Unhappy Soldiers," op. cit.

37. "Unhappy Soldiers," ibid.

38. Roy van de Dwight, op. cit.

39. Adekeye Adebajo, op. cit.

40. Lars Rudbeck, op. cit.

41. Roy van de Dwight, op. cit.

42. Adekeye Adebajo, op. cit.

43. Roy van de Dwight, op. cit.

44. Adekeye Adebajo, op. cit.

45. Statement by the Presidency of the European Union concerning recent developments in Guinea Bissau, issued on 18 May, 1999.

46. Dr. Rui Mendes, interview by author, July, 1999. Dr. Mendes said that he voted for the amendment because his constituency in the North was overwhelmingly for the amendment, even though he is part Senegalese and was equally affected by the law. He said a contrary vote would have put his political career on the line. He predicted that the interim President would not jeopardize his political career by vetoing the amendment.

47. OCHA (Office for the Coordination of Humanitarian Affairs), "Humanitarian Situation Report," Guinea Bissau, July 16-31, 1999. On 23 July, 1999, Portuguese radio reported troop movement in the southern regions bordering the Republic of Guinea. A government source in Bissau explained the deployment of Guinean Bissau forces to the southern border was part of routine troop rotation. On 28 July, it reported alleged presence of former President Nino Vieira in Conakry. On July 19, expressly forbade Nino Vieira from making political statements.

48. At the meeting of the European Union in Brussels to discuss the case of Guinea Bissau, the three countries voted against the applicability of article 366 (bis) to Guinea Bissau. Austria abstained.

49. OCHA, "Humanitarian Situation Report," Guinea Bissau, 1-15 July, 1999.

50. OCHA, "Humanitarian Situation Report," Guinea Bissau, 16-31 July, 1999.

51. Amin Saad spoke to the Representative of the Secretary General, Samuel Nana Sinkam, on the need to prolong the transition. General Mane also warned the RSG against holding the elections on 28 November, 1999.

52. OCHA, "Humanitarian Situation Report," Guinea Bissau, 1-15 July, 1999.

53. An example was the marches in Bafata of senior officers held there by guards loyal to General Ansumane Mane.

54. During the transition, General Mane voided an invitation issued by President Malam Bacai Sanha and Prime Minister Fadul to President Lansana Conte to visit Bissau on grounds that the Guinea President was "playing tricks with Guinea Bissau".

55. Visit of General Ansumane Mane to Burutuma, October 1999.

56. Notes on rallies of the PRS leader by author.

57. In his pronouncement on national Television (RTGB) on 12 February, 2000 Attorney General Amin Saad publicly identified the Portuguese Ambassador as one of those standing in the way of this trial. He later apologized to the Ambassador.

58. Prime Minister Caetano's address to the diplomatic corps in Bissau on 3 May, 2000.

59. To find solutions to the recurrent problems among communities living across international borders, the governors of the provinces of Oio, Bafata and Farim in Guinea Bissau and their counterparts in Kolda and Ziguichor established a forum to meet to lessen tensions. One of such meetings held in Farim on 20 September 2000 broke up in acrimony as the two sides insisted on demands for their interlocutors to produce goods allegedly stolen by elements that crossed over from the borders. The highly politicized forum generated more concern than the confidence building it was designed to achieve.

60. President Kumba Yala's statement on the National Day against Corruption and Impunity on 15 September, 2000. The President reiterated this call in his message to the nation on the 27th anniversary of the independence of Guinea Bissau on 24 September 2000. He emphasized that the court had a responsibility to shed full light on the sale of arms to the Casamance.

61. Separate discussions with leaders of the opposition including Helder Vaz, former minister of State for Economy, and Victor Mandinga, leader of the Platform National Unidade, a coalition of four opposition parties in August 2002.

62. President Kumba Yala had also in September 2000 through decree 23/2000 unilaterally removed the 5 ministers of the coalition partners RGM-MB from the Government without consultations with Prime Minster Caetano N'tchama. It took the intervention of his party leadership to rescind the decision in a counter decree 24/2000 days later.

63. Most members of the National Assembly expressed support for the Prime Minister.

64. Notes on meetings with PAIGC leaders in March 2003.

65. Statement by Vensen Mendes, President of National Syndicate for Teachers (SINAPROF) on Radio Pindjiquiti, 21 November, 2000.

66. Many other groups of opposition emerged. They included:

The Democratic Opposition,

The PAIGC,

Platform National Unidade:

Parti Convergence Democratic... Victor Madinga

The Front Democratic................Jorge Mandinga

The Front Democratic Social...Rafael Barbosa

Front Liberation Independence National Guinea....Catengul Mendy

Alliance Popular Unidade

PUSD.............Josez Fadul

Union para Mudanca.....Amine Saad

Alliance Socialist and Parti Popular Guinea

Union Electoral

PSD	Joaquin Balde
LIPE	Mustapha Blade
PRP	Bubakar Sanni
PDSSG	Serifo Balde

67. Interviews held in the last weeks of April, 2003 and pastoral letters issued by the Catholic Bishops of Bissau and Bafata, Caminate.

68. Report of European Union Election Observation Mission Guinea Bissau-2005. Internet source: http://www.eueomgbissau.org/2005/Info.htm

69. Report of European Union Election Observation Mission Guinea Bissau-2005. Internet source: http://www.eueomgbissau.org/2005/Info.htm

70. Report of European Union Election Observation Mission Guinea Bissau-2005. Internet source: http://www.eueomgbissau.org/2005/Info.htm

71 Report of European Union Election Observation Mission Guinea Bissau-2005. Internet source: http://www.eueomgbissau.org/2005/Info.htm

72. Guinea Bissau: Wikipedia.

Chapter 6

LIBERIA: CONFLICTS FOR STATE APPROPRIATION

The underlying source of conflicts in Liberia is traceable to the philosophy that underpinned the founding of the republic in 1847. The exclusivist character of governance and the hierarchical structure of relations between the settler groups and the various indigenous peoples before and after the founding of the republic entrenched a culture of hegemonic control of the state as a political norm. Absolute and exclusive control of the state therefore became the goal to which all the major constituent groups of the Liberian state aspired. Since April 1980, consistent with the norms established during the exclusivist Americo-Liberian rule, the monopoly of partisan hegemonic control of the state has been the main thrust and motivation of the political process. This has instigated the turbulence that has defined political interaction among protagonists in the Liberian state. In the struggle to assert control of the political space or the legitimacy of their identity in the republic, all Liberian indigenous groups have depended on the support and active collaboration of their affiliates across the country's borders, in Guinea, Sierra Leone and Cote d'Ivoire. The conflicts in Sierra Leone and Liberia have involved elements from both countries crossing the border to fight alongside their kith and kin on either side. The consequence was the implosion of the these neighboring states in that intermestic environment as well as instability across the whole of the sub-region. The struggle for hegemonic control of the republic by all major constituent groups of Liberia remains a strong undercurrent of the evolution of the political process in the post-conflict democratic system that emerged on 16 January, 2006.

The American Colonization Society (ACS), the motivators of the removal of freed black slaves from the United States for resettlement in Africa to resolve "the dilemma of 'negroes, mulattos and other persons of color residing in the United States who had been liberated from slaver vessels on high seas under the act of 1808"[1] under a humanitarian guise, did not establish a democratic country in West Africa for freedom and for receptive Africans living in the United States. On the contrary, it designed and established a highly autocratic and racially exclusive pateraltarian order. By this arrangement, the indigenous peoples were treated as subjects rather than citizens of the settlement.[2] By 1841 when the settler community took effective control of the colony, the policies of the ACS and its agents had poisoned relations between the black settlers and the indigenous communities. This impacted future relations, especially as the settler community continued with the hierarchical social order that drove the exclusivist political system that had emerged from the policies of the ACS.

Against this background, the political evolution of Liberia since its founding to the early years of the twenty first century can be divided into broad two phases. These are the years of Americo-Liberian hegemony dating from the founding of the Republic in 1847 to April 1980; and the period thereafter. Violent struggles among Liberia's major constituent groups to dominate the social and political space have characterized this latter period. The contending groups include descendants of a settler community generally known as Americo-Liberians and the Congos, various communities of peoples indigenous to the territory predating the arrival of the settlers, as well as the Mandingo community, whose Liberian*ness* has been challenged by the other indigenous groups. April 1980 marked the beginning of two and a half decades of turbulent struggles among indigenous groups for total control of the political space opened up by the violent end to the rule of the hegemonic True Whig party. The conflict, or the long and violent interregnum from Americo-Liberia rule, which began in 1980 and ended with the post-conflict transition guided by the Comprehensive Peace Agreement of August 2003, was a struggle for the appropriation of the post-hegemonic Liberian state. Contending domestic forces acted in concert with their extra-territorial allies in the ensuing confrontations.

The involvement of extra-territorial communities and ethnic groups from neighboring states across international frontiers in the internal affairs of Liberia locates developments in the state in an intermestic environment. This intermestic character of the environment drives Liberian communities and their extra-territorial extensions to act as corporate units and as legitimate stakeholders in the affairs of the state. Through their interventions they influence the outcome of the domestic processes of the states in which their members are found. These transnational corporate groups play an active part in the political bargaining and have been fully involved in the conflicts that have ensued to configure power among the constituent groups of the post-hegemonic Liberian state. The struggle to retain some of the significant features of the True Whig era and the struggles between disparate indigenous forces for control of the post-hegemonic state have defined the country's violent political conflict since 1980. These struggles also form the critical undercurrents of the evolution of the political process in the emerging democratic order in post-transition Liberia. Twice, the struggles have led to the implosion of the state. On both occasions, international interventions by the United Nations, in collaboration with the sub- regional organization, the Economic Community of West African States (ECOWAS), were put in place to reconstruct the state.

Along the line, the scramble for estates in Africa in the nineteenth century by traditional colonialists, France and the Britain, compounded the course of Liberian history. It forced a temporary accommodation between the state and its hitherto unpacified hinterland. This was necessary to ward off the territorial ambitions of the colonialists in the country's hinterland. French and British activitiesalong the coast and the hinterland forced the settler community to come to terms with the reality that it could not pacify its hinterland without some form of collaboration with the indigenous peoples. This became imperative in the face of serious efforts by the British and French to expand their territories to the west and east of Monrovia respectively. Jeremy Levitt opines that the motive for the reevaluation by the settler community of its approach to the natives was to ward off challenges from the British and French.

The same considerations gave rise to the decision of the settlers to break away from ACS' administration and declare statehood. The British government reminded the nascent state that the Royal Navy had in the past protected the local groups with which it had traded, making it clear that it planned to continue to safeguard legitimate its commercial interests and to ensure the freedom of trade in those areas claimed by Liberia. In effect, the British did not recognize the claims of sovereignty over the territories and peoples of the areas that the new state claimed to be protecting. Numerous incidents that followed the British refusal to recognize Liberian sovereignty convinced Governor Roberts that the settlers' only course of action was to break their ties with the ACS and change the territory's status in international law from that of a private venture to that of an independent state.[3] In this connection, Levitt notes that

> In 1886, Monrovia was forced to reevaluate its native policy due to increased British and French aggression. As, mentioned, it could not wage war against natives and simultaneously ward off foreign land encroachments. Great Britain and France actively sought to annex Liberian territory to expand the jurisdictionof Sierra Leone and the Ivory Coast, respectively. French aggression and occupation of Liberia's southeastern border was of particular concern to the government. Hence it had good reason to be sensitive about Grebo and Kru calls for the establishment of a French protectorate in Maryland County.[4]

Liberia thus began as a forced enterprise if the settler group was to survive the challenges posed by its British and French adversaries or competitors for its hinterland. The state was created on a foundation of distrust and despera-tion imposed by the political and commercial exigencies of mid-nineteenth century. At one level, the disaffection emanating from this foundation has been expressed in the deeply entrenched antagonistic relations between the descen-dants of the settler community and the indigenous peoples. At another level, the continued attempt by the majority indigenous people to delegitimize and alienate some communities as stakeholders in the Liberian state and resistance to these efforts by the minority Mandingos, with the effective collaboration of other Mandingos in the sub region, in particular Sierra Leone and Guinea, have been a dominant undercurrent in the turbulent contest to appropriate and dominate the total political space by the contending forces, namely: the Gios, Manos, Bassa, Kru/Krahn, Lomas, etc. It is equally clear that even at present many Liberians continue to regard Mandingos as not authentic claimants to citizenship. They are perceived as people who do not belong in Liberia, not-withstanding that they have lived there for generations.[5] This has been a major factor in the ethnic divisions, alliances and alignments that have characterized inter-communal political violence to take control of the state since 1980.

These inter-communal struggles for state appropriation, articulated by the various armed factions that represented their ethnic groups, underpinned the construction of the National Transitional Government of Liberia (NTGL) and the National Transitional Legislative Assembly (NTLA) that were cobbled together in October 2003 in Accra as the pivotal institutions of the transition from war to a post-conflict dispensation to be guided by the Accra Compre-hensive Peace Accord (CPA). These factors also played themselves out in the democratic elections of October and November 2005 that brought to an end the post-conflict transitional arrangement guided by the CPA in August 2003. The structure of the post-transition political party system, the alignments between them as well as the major forces that emerged during the transition reflected the interaction of a triad of opposing social, political and economic forces and interests closely constructed along the partisan lines between the major contending communities of power in Liberia.

The thirty odd parties registered by the National Elections Commission (NEC) for the presidential and legislative elections of October and November 2005 may be grouped under three major broad political tendencies as well as a distinct Mandingo political force. The interaction between these four major political forces constitutes the dynamic of Liberia's post-hegemonic democratic dispensation. At the polar ends of the spectrum are status quo forces that act as guardians of the legacy of the Whig hegemony. They are opposed by nativist forces with an agenda to dominate the state in the post-conflict era and consolidate their gains made possible by the Samuel Doe regime. The third major political tendency, whose vision of Liberia clashes with those of the first two, is the progressive nationalist force bringing together moderates in the system. The nationalism of this new force is in reaction to the absolute outlook of the hegemonic era when Liberia was treated as a rent colony by the Americo-Liberians, to be exploited and the spoils invested in the United States of America. This third major force is also populated by elements that originally belonged to the two polar forces. Many of the leading lights in the progressive nationalist camp had transformed their previous identities to distance themselves as well as repudiate the tenets of the two antagonistic forces.

Compounding the dynamics generated by the struggle of the three major forces is the radical intervention of a Mandingo political force determined to sustain its new-found prominence in national affairs in the post-conflict era. The rapid rise of Mandingos political leverage in Liberia resulted mainly from the decisive leadership of Mandingos in creating the United Liberia Movement (ULIMO) in Sierra Leone and Guinea, later the Liberia United for Reconciliation and Development (LURD) founded in Guinea and funded and supplied mainly by Guinea. Improved Mandingo political leverage was thus achieved through effective collaboration with Mandingo kith and kin in Sierra Leone and Guinea. The national unity professed by both Mandingo-led ULIMO and LURD broke down under the tension of inter-communal maneuvers to protect their partisan interests. Finally, the ULIMO splintered into a Mandingo faction led by Alhaji Kromah and a Krahn faction under Roosevelt Johnson. The LURD, which started off as a coalition of Mandingos and Krahns, was formed in 1999 by Sekou Conneh with the religious, political, military and logistical support of Guinea, complete with a base.

Observers note that LURD had a significant Muslim element and reportedly received arms from sources such as the United Arab Emirates.[6] And 70% of the fighting forces of LURD were of the Mandingo ethnic group.[7] The Movement for Democracy in Liberia (MODEL), dominated by the Kru and Krahn, at one time collaborating with the LURD and also in bitter opposition, and largely associated with the nativist cause, was backed by the Ivorian state. MODEL was also implicated in the civil war in Cote d'Ivoire, mostly on the side of the state. The central theme in the conflict in Liberia was the struggle for the appropriation of the state by contending groups aligned first along the broad divide of Americo-Liberians and Congos, and on a second plane, on divisions among indigenous groups who questioned the legitimacy of Muslims and Mandingoes as stakeholders in the affairs of a state founded as a Christian nation. This struggle remained the dominant motive of the democratic elections of October and November 2005.

Conflict in Liberia was also a struggle by contending forces and constituent groups in the state to build the state in the image of the dominant force. These developments unfolded against the background of strong transnational ethnic affinities that encouraged domestic protagonists in the conflict to openly seek intervention from ethnic allies outside the country. Indeed, key contending forces in the conflict were mobilized from outside Liberia, and they enjoyed open support from extensions of their communities across the frontiers. The deleterious consequence of the interactive dynamic of conflict partly accounted for the implosion of Sierra Leone to the west and the exacerbation of the conflict in Cote d'Ivoire to the east of Liberia, the country soon became the epicenter of conflict in the whole sub-region.

THE CONSTRUCTION OF A HEGEMONIC STATE

The Commonwealth Constitution was brought to Liberia by a new governor, Thomas Buchanan. This constitution, which preceded the creation of Liberia as a sovereign state, divided the country into two counties for administrative purposes. These were Montserrado, comprising the original ACS colony of Liberia, and Grand Balsa (Balsa Cove). The new arrangement claimed sovereignty over all the settlements between Cape Mount and the Cestos River. A survey conducted in 1838 counted 2,247 colonists, 20 churches, 10 schools, and four printing presses; the ACS reported the following year that the right bank of the Saint Paul River presented an almost continuous line of cultivated farms up to the fall line. In 1841 a settler, Joseph Jerkins Roberts, was appointed to succeed Buchanan as governor of Liberia. Within a few years of his administration he extended the jurisdiction of Liberia as far as the Grand Cess River, which was the western limit of the Maryland colony. Liberia also claimed sovereignty in the other direction up to the Sewa River bordering Sierra Leone, but exercised no authority beyond Cape Mount. An important aspect of this consolidation was Roberts' effort to put an end to the slave trade. By asserting Liberian sovereignty over an even larger stretch of the coast he expected to counter similar claims that might be made by Britain and France. In 1842 the Mississippi colony was formally admitted as Sinoe County, leaving only the Maryland colony outside the commonwealth.

As an extension of a settler community forced to declare statehood, incorporating adjoining lands and peoples, by circumstances well beyond its control, conflict inhered in the principles on which the Liberian state was founded. The inherent sources of instability included the declared character of Liberia as a Christian state, the circumstances that led to the emergence of the Liberian dominion, and the evolution of a hierarchical society as well as an exclusivist political community. As a result, between 1820 and 1847 six deadly conflicts occurred between the settlers and the indigenous peoples.[8] The situation was exacerbated by the process through which the implanted Liberian state, which was dominated by the newly arrived settler community, continued to consolidate a hierarchical national society. Throughout the nineteenth and early twentieth centuries, indigenous Liberians, most notably the Gola, Bassa, and Kru, generally believed that the settlers should integrate with them, rather than erect a hostile competitive nation. However, the integration did not occur.[9] The social hierarchy that emerged from the policies of the ACS and which was later continued by the settlers, underpinned the development of a segregated national political community that fossilized divisions among the constituent groups of the Liberian state. Despite constituting only 5 per cent of the population, the coastal settler elite established an oligarchy that excluded and oppressed the indigenous inhabitants. Commentators note that the Americo-Liberians set their community apart:

> The Americo-Liberians presided over the development of a social system in which they assumed superiority over the tribal peoples. The term kwi first used in the nineteenth century by indigenous Africans to identify the settlers and other foreigners (including Europeans), was adopted by the Americo-Liberian community as a synonym for civilized. The state of being kwi was defined by family background, education, church membership (preferably in a mainline Protestant denomination), and certain other social relationships. Kwi status thus became a prerequisite for a favored position within the Americo-Liberian social setting.
>
> In general, Americo-Liberians constituted a circumscribed set of people, and the social boundaries were permeable only on the initiative of members of the set. If tribal Africans entered the privileged preserve, they normally did so when individual Americo-Liberians acted as their sponsors by means of formal or informal adoption. The tribal people accepted through adoption or intermarriage became kwi by taking American or European names, by acquiring a Western education, and by adopting Americo-Liberian customs and patterns of behavior.
>
> The social, political, and economic distinctions between these two segments of the population were associated with major differences in values and ways of life. The settlers from the New World and their descendants possessed a completely different culture one rooted in American customs and values from those of the tribal African peoples.[10]

The 133 year rule of the Americo-Liberian oligarchy created deep-seated resentment and divisions within Liberian society and left historical scars[11] that have plagued contemporary developments in the country. Up to the 1930s[12] the various ethnic groups living along the littoral areas and the hinterland within modern-day Liberian territorial expanse resisted their subjugation by the state, which was synonymous with Americo-Liberian control. Amos Sawyer notes that Liberia's declaration of independence in 1847 was rejected by some indigenous communities with whom the state was in conflict over trade. These indigenous communities were recognized by several European countries, including Britain and France, and by the governments of Hanseatic German Confederation.[13] Amos Sawyer, a prominent Liberia scholar, concludes that

> ... the proposal to form a unitary state, put forward by leaders from Monrovia and supported by the American Colonization Society (ACS) was hotly contested by representatives from the coastal settlements, especially the Bassa. Those opposing the establishment of a highly centralized system argued mainly for a constitutional arrangement that would cede some degree of autonomy to the counties and for curtailment of the control the ACS exercised over certain portions of land.[14]

In spite of these protestations, the settler community consolidated its hegemonic rule in Liberia. It was not until 1951, that Americo-Liberians granted the indigenous peoples marginal participatory rights in the affairs of the state, and under stringent conditions. Sawyer affirms that

> Most settler-leaders struggled to establish relationship of tutelage with surrounding indigenous communities with a view to gradually incorporate (sic) individuals from those communities into the Liberian body politic, as such individuals would have been seen to have acquired the qualities to be considered 'civilized'. These qualities included acceptance of the Christian religion and the cultural traits and social practices of the settler society.[15]

PROBLEMATIC FOUNDING PRINCIPLES

The founding of the modern state of Liberia was inspired by a number of prominent white Americans concerned with slavery, the slave trade, and the untenable position of the 'free persons of color in the United States following the formation of the Federal Republic in 1787.[16] The state was established by returning slaves from America and those rescued on the high seas, who, imbued with a sense of superiority over their native hosts, replicated the hierarchical and discriminatory social organization to which they had been exposed during their enslavement, and configured the new state in like manner.

In many cases, official contact between the state and the indigenous groups has been very recent. In the more remote hinterland of Liberia, Americo-Liberian official contact has been limited largely to the last century.[17]

The state was also founded on Christian principles that were at variance with the dominant indigenous faiths in the immediate societies and environment in which the state was planted. The motivators of the founding of Liberia saw the colony of American Black as a beachhead in West Africa for Protestant Christianity and Western Civilization, not only spreading the gospel to the 'dark continent' but also implementing some of the fuzzy nineteenth century ideas regarding pacifism, alcoholic prohibition, and other novel experiments in morality and social relationships.[18] Liberia's founding fathers, or the eleven men who signed the country's Declaration of Independence on 26 July 1847 were all Christians.[19] In the social habitat in which it was planted, Liberia was thus created an elitist state that alienated the people and the environment in which it had now become an oasis of some kind. The oasis, in terms of the social distances between the settler group and indigenous peoples forged by the subsisting socio-political organization, ran for a century and a half on dualist principles of complete appropriation of economic and political control by the minority settler group and absolute subjugation of the majority natives. The state belonged to the returnee Americo-Liberians and the Congos, while the vast native majority rested along the margins. As Gus Liebenow notes

> The expansion of the Americo-Liberian community beyond the pockets of settlements at the coast created a highly complex political, social, and economic situation. It was not a simple case of one society dominating another. Rather it was a relationship that ultimately subordinated sixteen or more tribal societies to Western oriented community of Americo-Liberians. The dominated groups differed radically in culture, degree of political cohesion and organization, ability and resolution (sic) to resist Americo-Liberian domination, and responsiveness to modernization.[20]

The decay of the hegemony of the Americo-Liberia rent state in the late 1970s, which coincided with the emergence of an international community with evolving notions of morality, minority and human rights as well as participatory democracy, ushered in an era of internal struggle among the elites within the ruling Americo-Liberians. This struggle also implicated a generation of the leaders of an emerging nativist force that also formed the nucleus of a pro-democracy constituency that challenged the status quo and demanded the opening up of the political space through democratization. These new demands created schisms within the True Whig hegemony as well as among the democratic forces. The divisions provided the planks for another struggle among contending nativist groups to dominate the re-appropriated social, economic and political space earlier occupied by those who protected the legacy of the diffused and now depleted returnee slave community. Samuel Doe's April 1980 coup d'etat exploited the massive social discontent manifest in the 1979 rice riots to bring to an end the total control of the political space by what was left of the descendants of the original settler community.

The brutal and unending conflict that saw Liberia through two bloody regimes between 1980 and 2003 was brought to a final end by international intervention that culminated in the October and November 2005 democratic elections that brought to power the presidency of Madam Ellen Johnson Sirleaf. Elsewhere on the continent, the primary concerns with dislodging European minorities from their positions of privilege in areas south of the Sahara has tended to focus attention during the past two decades upon only one kind of imperialism.[21] In the aftermath of the liquidation of apartheid in South Africa, this attention has shifted to overthrowing the various hues of political hegemonies established in African states by military and civilian despots alike, as well as indigenous black minorities. For the most part, these imperial expansions found Africans subordinating other Africans for the purposes of political, economic, and religious exploitation.[22] Liberia was no exception to this tendency.

THE DECAY AND FALL OF AMERICO–LIBERIAN HEGEMONY

Liberia presents a classic case of the decay of a long-lasting hegemony established by a settler minority that appropriated the total political, economic and social space for a century and a half and failed to exploit the opportunities to negotiate democratic transition in a structured setting during the outset of the third wave of democratization. In 1980, from the marginalized indigenous peoples, new forces emerged to forcefully reassert historic native challenges to the construction of the Liberian state and the status quo set up by the settler community since 1847. The outcome was the overthrow of the True Whig oligarchy that brought in its wake an unending brutal struggle for total control of the political space by various indigenous forces. The struggle ended first through the bifurcation of the Liberian space and finally in the implosion of the state. The first factor that led to the ultimate implosion was the internal decay of the Americo-Liberian hegemony.

Fuelled by increasing internal contradictions and lack of policy convergence among major groups of the Americo-Liberian hegemony, the decay spawned pro-democracy movements within the oligarchy. The democratic forces were led by new-entrant natives into the privileged realm, drawing support from the widespread opposition among indigenous communities to the status quo on the margins of the Liberian hegemonic state and society. These developments delegitimized the prevailing construction of the state around the exclusive control of the True Whig Party, the hegemonic party since the founding of Liberia. The rise of pro-democracy movement in Liberia in the late seventies presaged the late eighties and fed into a larger movement in Africa expressed in the third wave of democratization through sovereign national conferences initiated in the Republic of Benin that brought down the one-party state of Kerekou. This constituted a second factor in the timing of the era of conflicts in Liberia. The April 1980 coup d'etat came in time to merge into the process of evolving sensitivities and emergence of a powerful global pro-democracy constituency channeling support of the international community for participatory democracy in developing countries. This conferred legitimacy on various struggles by hitherto oppressed communities for participation in the affairs of their states. The overthrow of the Liberian oligarchy was indeed welcome.

The coup that brought down Liberia's first republic was the manifestation of 158 years of pent-up settler–native and civil society-government hostilities, spawned by a socio-political order that never evolved fully to accommodate the nation's diverse and dynamic population.[23] President Tubman's Unification and Open Door policies were at base a calculated strategy of economic development designed not only to enhance the foundations of privilege for the Americo-Liberian elite, but also to give them the revenues for maintaining a more modern and efficient system of control over the tribal majority. In effect, the policy was designed to further entrench the hegemony of Americo-Liberians over the social, economic and political space.[24] Yet, the improving economy that partly forced the government into instituting limited economic openings to the emerging indigenous elite contained the seeds of agitation for greater participation by the indigenous population..

The limited openings begun by the Tubman administration and subsequent initiatives created stresses and strains that were exploited by democratic activists who began to manifest themselves in an emerging students' radicalism. First, the limited openings began the process of alienating the old guards of the oligarchy from the Tubman administration, especially as Tubman squeezed them from the economy through the instrumentality of his purported reforms. His Open Door Policy disenfranchised those settlers and natives who were not integral to his loyal patronage network. Moreover, he neutralized all potential competitors by stifling the capacity of settlers, especially those in opposition to the True Whig party, to accumulate wealth through denial of licenses, and official coercion by government auditors, and by extending to indigenous Liberians various civil and political rights.[25] Yet, attempts by the Grebo intelligentsia to register a political party in 1951 and to contest elections were suppressed.[26] More recent challenges to the settler oligarchy may be dated to the massive demonstration of students at the Executive Mansion in April 1970 led by Calvin Cole, the President of the University Student Government, the 1973 formation of the Progrssive Alliance of Liberia by Gabriel Bacchus Matthews, a native son earlier closely associated with the Americo Liberians, and the registration of the Progressive Peoples Party in 1975 as the instrument of the first direct democratic challenge to the Whig hegemony[27]. These developments primed society and prepared the ground for changes brought by Samuel Doe's April 1980 coup d'etat. With the failure of the half-hearted initiatives of the Tubman and Tolbert administrations to integrate indigenous peoples into the mainstream of national life, developments within the hegemonic elites and increasing rumblings in constituencies along the margins of national life posed a threat to the longevity of the status quo. Secondly, notwithstanding the overarching concerns about the maintenance of despots if they professed the right ideological cant, international sensitivities in the late 70s and early 80s were beginning to weigh against dictatorships.

Pressure was building up by the continued alienation of increasing numbers of educated indigenous people locked out of the system and by increasing consciousness among this indigenous class to assert its autonomy and repudiate the system that rested on the assumed superiority and privileges of the Americo-Liberians. Notwithstanding the fact that many indigenous Liberians had acquired education to compete effectively with their compatriots of Americo-Liberia heritage, the social distances widened between educated indigenes and Americo-Liberians. For the national society in general, the cultural integration of the settler and tribal communities was far from complete, even though education abroad had started to create common bonds among a growing cadre of Americo-Liberian and tribal youths who were raising serious questions about the continued course of the political, economic and social development of their country. [28] The liberalization of the space undertaken by the hegemonic forces in the seventies were indeed designed to preserve the status quo, yet accommodating enough changes to pacify the subordinate strata of the hierarchical social system in place.

The demands of a changing economy and social pressures emanating from the contradictions of the status quo under President Tolbert elicited rebellion from its own ranks as urban educated democratic forces from within the settler elite community found common cause with natives. Many educated natives, partially accommodated in the decaying system, were beginning to repudiate the status quo and call for radical overhaul of the social order. A synopsis on one of the key leaders of the democratic movement of the 1970s is illustrative:

> Togba–Nah Tipoteh was born Rudolf Roberts because his father, a
> Kru by ethnic origin, adopted a settler name – a common tactic in
> the past, representing an effective passport for access to certain jobs
> and other opportunities. However, after he ccompleted his doctoral

studies in economics in the United States and returned home, he changed his name to what it should have really been. This move was seen as an affront to the settler establishment, who then ostracized him politically. Tipoteh's outspokenness about government mal-practice further alienated important political figures. Consequently, he was sacked first as Director of the Bureau of Budget and second as Chair of the Dept. of Economics, University of Liberia. By 1973, he, along with other university lecturers and students formed the Movement for Justice in Africa (MOJA); an organization promi-nent in the struggle for social transformation in Liberia.[29]

The final failure of the limited integration projects was pronounced by the rice riot of 1979. The riot was equally the expression of the frustration of the marginalized victims of the hegemony of the Americo –Liberians in their demand for full participation in the national processes. In 1979, Tolbert's min-ister of agriculture Florence Chenoweth increased the price of rice from the subsidized $22 for a 100-pound bag to $26. This was designed to keep indig-enous farmers from moving into the cities, as rationalized by the minister who explained further that the increase would induce rice farmers to stay on the land and produce food for themselves and for sale instead of leaving to work for wages in the cities or on the rubber plantations. Yet, the democratic forces opposed to the oligarchy condemned the increase, noting that Chenoweth and the Tolbert family were large-scale rice farmers who stood to profit handsomely from the price increase. It was also felt that the real aim of the price increase was to write off government debt, as there was an "annual import and subsidy bill amounting to $8 million". Indeed, most Liberians considered the increase as an attempt to generate resources to pay the subsidy bill and, more importantly, to line some pockets.[30] This resulted in a massive protest called by the Progressive Alliance of Liberians (PAL) on April 14.

About 2,000 activists who assembled to march on the Executive Mansion to protest the proposed price hike were joined en route by more than 10,000 "back street boys" who quickly transformed the orderly procession into an orgy of destruction. Policemen and troops were deployed, and they brutally suppress the march and protests. In 12 hours of violence in the city's streets, at least 40 demonstrators and rioters were killed by the troops and policemen. More than 500 were injured. Hundreds more were arrested, and police were ordered to storm the PAL headquarters.[31] PAL leaders who were responsible for the riots were rounded up along with many other political dissidents. The old guard in the True Whig party blamed Tolbert for his earlier leniency toward the political opponents of the regime, charging that he could have acted sooner to check unrest by cracking down on their subversive activities. Under pressure from hardliners in the True Whig Party, Tolbert closed the university and suspended due process. Tolbert, however, subsequently reduced the price of rice to $20.[32] The rice riot demonstrated the vulnerability of the decaying hegemony, particularly as it revealed the deep divisions between hardliners and reformers in the establishment.

The prospects for conflict, deriving from the manner of the founding, the construction, the hierarchical structure of society, as well as the character of the evolution of the Liberian state, remained latent for over a century and a half. Long-suppressed antagonisms began to manifest strongly from 1979 and continued in the past two and a half decades when a number of factors, both internal to Liberia and related to developments in the global inter-state system, converged to trigger conflict. Beginning with the institution of sovereign national conferences to remove one-man-one-party states and patriarchal regimes in Benin, Congo Brazzaville, Mali, these "imperial" regimes were removed. In most other cases where these regimes either defied regime change through the instrument of negotiated transitions, armed revolts and hostilities would appear to have recommended themselves, as in the dinosaur state of Mobutu's Zaire and Cote d'Ivoire in the post-Houphouet Boigny era exemplify. In Liberia, the hegemony of the True Whig party, the sole political forum where Americo-Liberians decided the fortunes of the state to the exclusion of the indigenous peoples, elicited a bloody response from the foot soldiers of the Armed Forces of Liberia (AFL), largely constituted by the indigenous peoples.

Samuel Huntington dates the third wave of democratization to the April 25, 1974 coup against the Marcello Caetano dictatorship in Portugal[33]. As Huntington further notes, the processes of the third wave of democratization, which is one way of understanding original motives behind the events of 1979 that preceded the coup of April 1980, were overwhelmingly indigenous. The processes of regime change can be located along a continuum in terms of the relative importance of governing and opposition groups as the sources of democratization.[34] The role of the government in advancing the transformations that were sought by the marginalized, through its continued maneuvers to control the political space, was to unwittingly create an enabling environment for the system collapse that later occurred. In terms of conceptualizing the process of the overthrow of the Whig hegemony in Liberia, the events of 1980 neatly fit into what Linz describes as 'rupture,' Huntington calls 'replacement,' and Donald Share and Scott Mainwaring term system "collapse or breakdown," where the opposition, the indigenous forces in the case of Liberia, took the lead or mobilized exclusively in bringing about the collapse and overthrow of the hegemony. Samuel Huntington asserts that the nature of regime replacements:

> ... involves a very different process from transformations. Reformers
> within the regime are weak or non existent. The dominant elements

in government are standpatters staunchly opposed to regime change. Democratization consequently results from the opposition gaining strength and the government losing strength until the government collapses or is overthrown.[35]

Consistent with this mode of regime change[36], the leaders of the hegemonic regime in Liberia suffered unhappy fates.[37] Following the regime change, the institutions, procedures, ideas, and individuals associated with the Whig domination were considered illegitimate. The future of Liberia was to make a clean break with the past. Those who took over the reins of power in post-hegemonic Liberia based their acceptance on "forward legitimacy,"[38] implying the hope that their visions of a new society and the implementation of their programs would advance the interests of the nation. This hope did not materialize. The 1980 Liberian coup presaged later massive revolt against perpetual oligarchies, one-man, one-party patriarchal states, which began to tumble from the early 1990s in West and Central Africa and eventually brought down the apartheid regime in South Africa.

The pro-democracy sentiments, which began with the third wave of democratization, came to its fullest blossom barely two decades later, as reflected in the support for democratic forces during the third wave of democratic transitions in Black Africa through the avenues of sovereign national conferences initiated by the Republic of Benin as earlier noted. At the beginning of the 1990s, national conferences were organized in sub-Saharan Africa with the aim of finding the ways and means to transition from authoritarian or dictatorial one-party regimes to pluralist and democratic political regimes. Eight countries organized such conferences.[39]

These conferences were sometimes "sovereign," and often "non-sovereign," depending on whether the Acts which they adopted were binding and had a strong impact on the political and social evolution of the countries concerned. Sometimes, the political transition midwifed by such assemblies resulted in democratic regime changes, but sometimes, as in the case of Liberia under the Samuel Doe and Taylor, such hopes were dashed. In other cases, African countries launched the democratization of their political regimes without holding a national conference[40]. Yet, often, the death of dictatorship did not ensure the birth of democracy. In Liberia also, the end of the True Whig hegemony in 1980 unleashed a huge array of popular, social, and political forces that had been effectively suppressed during the hegemony.[41] The struggle among these forces for control was even more intense than the bloody act of removing the hegemony.

The confluence of internal and external factors has influenced the character of Liberia's recent tumultuous political evolution whose undercurrents are the continuing struggle for the appropriation of the state and the domination of the political space by all the major contending stakeholders. The seeds of a system of domination and control were planted at the founding of Liberia.[42]

SAMUEL DOE AND THE RISE OF LIBERIA'S MARGINS

The April 1980 coup by a Master Sergeant Samuel Doe reflected the failures of reforms undertaken by both the Tubman and Tolbert administrations to pacify the restive indigenous population. It also reflected the internal decay of the Whig hegemony and weaknesses deriving from the contradictions of the status quo. Initiatives to mitigate the impact of these contradictions, such as Tubman's 'Open Door', and 'Integration' and Unification Programs, failed to achieve a cultural integration of the peoples of the country. While these policies appeased native Liberians by giving them a larger political stake in the country, they were designed not to extend to the natives enough economic and political clout to unseat the oligarchy.[43] Rather, the tribal youths who had received education from abroad were raising serious questions about the continued course of political, economic, and social development in the country.[44] Prince Yormie Johnson is the leader of the Independent National Patriotic Party of Liberia (INPFL), a breakaway faction of Charles Taylor's National Patriotic Front of Liberia (NPFL), and a key actor in the national political process since the return of relative peace. He notes that

> Before 1944, when the late Tubman 'ascended to the throne of the Liberian Presidency' and ushered in his Unification Policy, the indigenous population of Liberia, which constitutes those in the majority, were taxed without reference or consultations, and compelled to work for government officials who claimed to be the so-called 'Pioneers' and their descendants for whom all rights and privileges were reserved.

Soon the indigenes became aware of their unfulfilled and oppressive life, and although some began to lift their voices in protest against such inhumane treatment, they were soon silenced and made to succumb to the forces of oppression.[45]

Rapid economic growth tends to create a strong base for democracy. It however, also raises expectations, exacerbates inequalities, and creates stresses and strains in the social fabric that stimulate political mobilization and demands for political participation.[46] Although, in relative terms, the material lot of tribal people was substantially improved by the rapid economic exploitation of Liberia's resources, in absolute terms, their gains were small when contrasted with those of the Americo-Liberian elite.[47] Such was the division in the country that even after the 1980 coup, many tribal people still tended to regard themselves as Bassa, Kpelle, or Loma, reserving the title 'Liberian' for the Americo-Liberi-ans.[48] The divisions have been expressed in the factionalization of the conflicts since the 1980 coup and also in the structure of the political party system that emerged following the end of the transition guided by the Comprehensive Peace Agreement signed by Liberia's ethnic warring factions in Accra in August 2003. These factors ensured almost universal support for the Samuel Doe coup among the indigenous people. Yet, the coup, as it ultimately revealed itself as an instrument of partisan Krahn and Kru domination of the state, set in motion the struggle by other constituent units to take over.

Master Sergeant Samuel Doe's April 1980 coup was originally embraced by the population as the insurrection of indigenous forces. It was with great joy and relief that they welcomed into power a 'native son' through a military coup.[49] But, as the coup soon became an instrument of Krahn domination of the state, Mandingo elements were readily co-opted into the project, the Mandingoes having been alienated by both the Americo-Liberians and other indigenous groups who questioned the legitimacy of their claims to Liberian citizenship. Samuel Doe's regime took state brutality to a higher level in his designs to create a Krahn-dominated state

> The brutality of Master-Sergeant Samuel Doe's regime was heralded by his assassination of Tolbert and thirteen of the Americo-Liberian president's senior officials within a week of taking power. Over the next four years, Doe eliminated potential rivals through assassina-tion or enforced exile.[50]

In so doing, Samuel Doe purged the military of other rival ethnic groups. He perpetuated existing divisions and animosities in society by filling the most important military positions with fellow Krahns and removing the Gios and Manos.[51] Adekeye Adebajo further notes that

> He (Doe) effectively turned a national institution into a Krahn dominated instrument of oppression ...The brutality of Doe's rule and his parochial, ethnic power base deepened ethnic divisions within Liberian society. Krahns, making up only about 5 per cent of the population were disproportionately represented in the cabinet...

Given the structure of Liberian society and a general perception of the illegitimacy of Mandingo claims to be stakeholders, Samuel Doe exploited this historic antipathy by incorporating a few Mandingo elements into the political system. The net effect of Krahn occupation of the total political space was deepening resentment among other indigenous forces, especially as Doe began to effectively repress all dissent, banning all opposition media as well as issuing threats "to use military force against those few Congo people against his government"[52]. To achieve this goal, he created the Special Anti-Terrorist Unit (SATU) that owed loyalty to his person and was the spearhead of his force to crush any dissent. On 12 November 1985, General Thomas Quiwokpa, a Gio from Nimba County and former commander of Doe's army, led a failed military coup. Doe executed the general and his fellow putchists and seized the opportunity to purge the army of Gios. The Krahn-dominated military went on the rampage in Nimba County where they burned villages and indiscriminately reportedly killed a 3000 Gios and Manos.[53] This exacerbated ethnic tension and heightened the security dilemma which all constituent elements of the state, with the exception of the Krahn/Kru, confronted in the emergent dispensation. Although Samuel Doe advocated multiparty democratic government, Prince Yormie Johnson, one of Liberia's many warlords, observes that

> ... in practice he ruthlessly suppressed any and all opposition. The lives of members of the various opposition parties were character-ized by constant harassment, intimidation, unexplained disappear-ances, and secret executions.[54]

The absolute control of the political space by the Krahn gave rise to armed opposition which struck on 29 December 1989 from Nimba County. Soon the armed opposition to Samuel Doe's regime gave birth to a competing center of power in a proto state established by the National Patriotic Front of Liberia (NPFL) in the north of the Liberian territory around Gbarnga. It ultimately led to the implosion of the Liberian state, as rival ethnic groups that had also suf-fered in the hands of the Samuel Doe regime, as well those who were perceived as allies of the Doe regime, were targeted by the National Patriotic Front of Liberia

PARTISAN CONSOLIDATION OF STATE SECURITY AND PERVASIVE SECURITY DILEMMA

Essentially, a security dilemma occurs when two or more states or groups feel insecure vis-à-vis other states. None of the states involved want relations to deteriorate, let alone bring war, but as each state acts militarily or diplomatically to make itself more secure, the other states interpret its actions as threatening. An ironic cycle of unintended provocations emerges, resulting in an escalation of the conflict which may eventually lead to open warfare.[55] The conditions for generating a security dilemma in Liberia were first created by the consolidation and deployment of the coercive apparatus of state by the Krahn-dominated Samuel Doe regime to overwhelm other constituent groups and stakeholders in the affairs of the state. The resultant power asymmetry among indigenous forces was reinforced by the exacerbation of tensions along ethnic lines, as well as the long-held denial of the legitimacy of Mandingos as stakeholders in Liberia. The association of the Mandingo with the Samuel Doe regime further marked them out for revenge when the opportunity presented itself. The system's skewed hierarchical arrangement, which had seemingly justified the April 1980 coup, further worsened with the rise of Krahn hegemony to replace the historic oligarchy that had been the focus of the animosity of the indigenous peoples. This transformation implied that the Krahns began to see themselves as masters of the post-hegemonic Liberian state thereby inheriting the legacy of the Americo-Liberian oligarchy. This situation wiped out whatever tenuous social trust and credibility had held the constituent groups together, the indigenous groups in particular. This encouraged the formation of ethnic militias by each group to protect its members. In this situation, each group was suspicious of the intent of the others and took positive action to defend its interests, including physical protection of the community. In this, they enjoyed the support of the ethnic affiliates across the border that watched and supported their kith and kin engaged in the struggle to appropriate the political space.

The security dilemma engendered by the firm control of the Liberian state, first, by the Americo–Liberians and then by the Krahn and Kru, formed the permanent undercurrent of the conflict in Liberia. This impacted on the fractiousness of the political and military alliances among various political forces that emerged to oppose the Doe and, later, the Charles Taylor regimes. The various attempts to forge a pan–Liberia opposition always failed, as the forces eventually all broke up along ethnic lines. The factions emerging from the breakup depended heavily on support from extensions of their community in neighboring states, rather than trusting their compatriots in the deadly enterprise of insurgency. The brutality and absolute control of the state under the Doe regime ensured its own demise. The bankruptcy of Doe's regime, its ethnic agenda, as well as its brutality against perceived enemies, set the stage for external forces in collaboration with domestic forces to facilitate the immediate trigger of his fall. One seed of the downfall was sown at the non-aligned summit meeting in Harare in 1985. At this summit, President Doe, at a hastily called international press conference, publicly upbraided the African heads of state present at the summit for their critical stance against the invasion of Grenada by the Reagan administration in America. He openly condemned the policy of Libyan President Muammar Gaddafi and challenged him to a public duel that the Liberian president suggested he was going to win. Doe unceremoniously departed Harare shortly after his public tirade against his peers. Following this, Liberia was one of only four countries that supported the United States and voted against a United Nations General Assembly resolution condemning the invasion of Grenada. This diplomatic gaffe assured that not a few African heads of state, particularly those of his immediate sub-region, were prepared to rid the continent of Samuel Doe.[56]

In Liberia, as noted in our earlier chapters in respect of post-colonial African states, the search for participation often implied the search for total control of the political space by the formerly excluded communities. This zero-sum mindset, exhibited by the Krahn-controlled Doe regime, which had raised brutality a notch higher, reenacted similar ambitions for the control of the state across the spectrum of constituent groups of Liberia. While political forces sought all along to build unified fronts, these attempts always faltered on the altar of the partisan agendas of the constituent groups of those coalitions. This led to a brutal conflict between all the contending forces struggling for control of the Liberian political space. The cruelty of the Samuel Doe regime, which was consolidated through rigged elections in 1985, left no room for peaceful dissent. Samuel Doe contested the elections on the platform of the National Democratic Party of Liberia (NDPL) that he had created to advance his candidacy. In spite of a sprinkling of political actors coerced or blackmailed to recant their sins of earlier opposition to Samuel Doe, the prominence of the Krahn and other ethnic groups from Grand Gedeh County, (his home area), was evident not only in the leadership of the party, but in terms of its electoral support later.[57] This resulted in many opponents taking up arms in various attempts to oust his regime. Against the background of the total domination of the political space by the Krahn and their allies the Mandingos, the 1980 bloody restatement of the historic grouse of the indigenous population against the Americo-Liberian oligarchy and the unfolding implications of the Krahn control of the state, set into motion a new dynamic that emphasized political violence. This political culture of violence was sustained for two and a half decades.

This prepared the grounds for the emergence of a national anti-Doe coalition, with considerable resentment against the Mandingo, attempting to stave off the calculus of ethnic animosities between other indigenous populations and the Krahn and to remove the source of the increasing ethnic polarization. The anti-Doe coalition claimed responsibility for the failed coup by General Quinwokpa, which had led to brutal reprisals against his Gio ethnic group in Nimba County. This coalition, the National Patriotic Front of Liberia (NPFL) probed different avenues for support, training facilities and launching pads for their military operation. Envoys were dispatched to Sierra Leone, Burkina Faso, Senegal, Cote d'Ivoire and Nigeria. Under the leadership of Mrs. Ellen Johnson-Sirleaf, these envoys combed the sub-region for support. Thomas Woewiyu was assigned to Cote d'Ivoire, Duopo went to Nigeria, Harry Yuan to Senegal, and Charles Taylor to Burkina Faso. It was Taylor who first found the possible avenue to accomplish the mission of an armed invasion of Liberia.[58]

On the eve of Christmas 1989, the NPFL under Charles Taylor invaded Liberia from Nimba County. Almost immediately, Charles Taylor's NPFL did not rise to the occasion as he began to rival the Doe regime in the application of violence against those perceived to be political enemies who had come under the control of his forces. These enemies turned out to be mostly, but not exclusively, Krahns and Mandingos. The persecution and massacres of ethnic groups defined as anti-Taylor began almost immediately with the inception of NPFL's insurgency on Liberian territory. Internal schisms within the NPFL and the massacres of perceived Krahns, Mandingos and other presumed enemies by the Taylor insurgency further entrenched a security dilemma, such that all contesting groups resolved through the establishment of their own armed forces to protect their communities and defend their interests in the violent political bargaining that was taking place. Stephen highlights the impact of the early failures of Charles Taylor's insurgency on the proliferation of ethnic forces that characterized the Liberian conflict from 1989. In this connection, he observes that:

> In Lofa County, for example, the first incursion by the NPLF culminated in a major massacre of Mandingo at the town of Makedu ... The memory of Makedu massacres was one of the chief motives for Mandingo exiles to join ULIMO-K in Sierra Leone and Guinea in 1991. When ULIMO-K invaded upper Lofa County from its Sierra Leone bases in 1992-3, the Mandingo fighters took cruel revenge, occupying towns where they had previously had no permanent rights of residence. To the outrage of Loma and Kpelle inhabitants, they systematically pillaged sacred groves of the Poro society...It was in retaliation for these attacks that some Loma and Kpelle refugees with military and organizational experience set up the Lofa Defence Force in 1993, established in refugee camps in Guinea with the primary aim of hitting back at the hated ULIMO-K. The faction was undoubtedly organized with the support of zoes of the Poro religious society from their places of exile in Guinea. Hence in many places, the LDF fighters had the full support of the communities on whose behalf they were fighting, turning the war in upper Lofa area into an ethnic contest between the Mandingo on one side, and Loma and Kpelle on the other. This feud had a long history, since the area had been the limit of the conquests of nineteenth century of Malinke warlord, Samory, whose memory is still alive in the area.[59]

This conflict pitted all contending political forces in Liberia against one another. Each of the eight armed factions involved was broadly associated with one or two ethnic groups. As such the forces deployed fought for partisan control of the political space, which was now open for the taking to all constituent groups with the requisite military force. In the least, by fielding armed elements in the fray, these groups enhanced their political leverage, and by implication, the clout of their ethnic groups in the peace negotiations and often in the transitional arrangements. This state of affairs also led to convenient, shifting and short-lived military alliances among the various forces. This however did not alter the ultimate individual group agenda of seeking to dominate the political space or gain respectable political leverage in the final settlement of the conflict whenever it came. The break-up of the ULIMO into the 'K' faction (K for Alhaji Kromah) and the 'J' faction (J for Roosevelt Johnson) was a major setback for the Krahn/Mandingo alliance.

The break-up of ULIMO along ethnic lines, a movement founded on 6 April, 1996, was instructive of the future factionalization of the Liberian conflict. ULIMO-K, founded to defend the Mandingo from massacres by the NPFL, later teamed up with the NPFL to arrest Roosevelt Johnson. The Mandingo alliance with Charles Taylor's NPFL elicited the alliance of all Krahn armed groups including the ULIMO-J faction, the Krahn dominated Armed Forces of Liberia/Government of Liberia (GoL) led by Hezekiah Bowen, Krahn,, George Boley, Krahn, led Liberia Peace Council. The attack on Johnson galvanized the creation of a pan-Krahn resistance and defense of him. Along with these was the Gio/Loma-dominated Independent National Patriotic Front of Liberia (INPFL), an early splinter faction of the NPFL led by Prince Yormie Johnson.

INPFL was determined to reverse Krahn control of the state and avenge the death of General Quinwokpa who was killed in the abortive coup attempt in 1985. In September 1994, NPFL further splintered when Samuel Dokie, Laveli Suluwood and Tom Woewiyu (all of them close allies of Charles Taylor) created the Central Revolutionary Council (CRC-NPFL) out of the front. In these engagements and the alignment of forces, all the contending forces mobilized their kith and kin across Liberia's international frontiers to defend their transnational communal interests in the struggle to possess the prized national estate. This made the Liberian conflict a war among various transnational communities in the immediate sub-regioncomprising Sierra Leone, Cote, d'Ivoire and Guinea, using their cousins in Liberia as the main protagonists. These included the Gios, Guerre, Yacouba, Krahns, Mandigo, Mano who straddle the territories of these countires. In the intense struggle for appropriation by contending forces within and without, the Liberian state twice, from 1990-1997 and in 2003, collapsed in the absence of a central authority perceived as legitimate by all protagonists in the conflict.

The unending peace initiatives under the auspices of a badly divided ECOWAS yielded fruits when a peace agreement was signed in Abuja in April 1996 by the main warring factions, with a supplement to the Abuja II Accord signed in August. The Abuja Accord was the twelfth peace agreement by the warring groups since the inception of peace negotiations at the Inter-

Faith Mediation Committee meeting in Freetown, Sierra Leone, in June 1990. The peace process went through various meetings and agreements, such as the Bamako ceasefire in November 1990 that agreed to the creation of an Interim Government of National Unity (IGNU); the Banjul agreement in December 1990; the Lome Agreement in January 1991; the thwarted All Liberian Conference in March 1991; a reconciliation gathering, sponsored by Ivorian President Houphouet Boigny in collaboration with President Jimmy Carter's International Negotiation Network in Yamoussoukro; and a subsequent Yamoussoukro peace plan in October. In July, at the invitation of the United Nations and the Organization of African Unity (OAU), the peace talks among the warring factions in Geneva led to the signing of the Geneva ceasefire by NPFL, ULIMO and IGNU. The promising Akosombo Peace Agreement of September 1994, another pact by all warring faction in December, which anticipated the holding of general elections in November 1995, failed to achieve peace. It was not until 1996 that the sustained initiatives of ECOWAS paid off in the signing of Abuja Accords I and II that guided the conduct of presidential and legislative elections on 19 July 1997. Charles Taylor won a landslide victory, while the NPFL also won the majority of seats in the National Assembly. Almost immediately, Charles Taylor repudiated essential provisions of the Abuja Peace Accords aimed to create legitimate national institutions and inspire confidence in them for post-conflict Liberia.

CHARLES TAYLOR AND THE INTENSIFICATION OF THE PARTISAN STRUGGLE FOR STATE APPROPRIATION

Charles Taylor's victory at the polls has been explained by the phenomenon of perceived war weariness on the part of Liberians who wanted peace at all costs. Given the brutality and tenacity of his campaign for the Executive Mansion in Monrovia, Liberians were convinced that long-term peace could not be assured if Charles Taylor did not win the elections. However, Liberians' expectations in conceding victory to him in the 1997 elections did not materialize. Almost immediately he assumed power, Charles Taylor began a vicious campaign against political opponents, including some of the leaders of the warring factions that had contested against him. He murdered many of his old lieutenants, clamped down on the media and rendered the judiciary prostrate.[60] By April 1998, the political climate had deteriorated, and there was unease over a string of extra-judicial killings and over Taylor's 'tightening of his grip on the security forces in defiance of the Abuja Accord,' which ended the civil war.[61] He confronted the ECOWAS, and relations between him and the ECOMOG Force Commander soured over the modalities for the restructuring of the military as agreed in the Abuja Accords.

The reign of terror imposed by Charles Taylor gave birth to another civil war. In the ensuing conflict, neighboring states to the west, east and north of the country availed Liberian groups with which they were affiliated the use of their respective territories to strengthen the capacity of these groups to launch war against President Charles Taylor and against rival contending ethnic forces in Liberia. Sierra Leonean Mandingos had supported the launching of the militia group ULIMO in the insurrection against Samuel Doe. In the war against Charles Taylor, LURD, another Mandingo-centric reincarnation of ULIMO, was financed from Sierra Leone and Guinea. Another major insurgency led by the Krahn-dominated MODEL was supported and financed by the government of Cote d'Ivoire. All the warring groups had effective support from their ethnic cousins across the borders, and all the communities that shared borders with the country were thus fully implicated in the instability in Liberia from 1980 onwards. They contributed significantly to the fighting cadres of their ethnic affiliates in the Liberian conflict.

In 1999, LURD announced itself and declared its intention to oust Charles Taylor from power through military means. It was formed by Liberian refugees in Sierra Leone and Guinea and was led by Sekou Conneh. Aisha, Sekou Coneh's wife, was reputed to be closely associated with President Lansana Conteh of Guinea. It was believed that the group was strongly supported or controlled by the government of neighbouring Guinea[62] and assisted by Sierra Leone. The group is also believed to have received the tacit support of Britain and the United States. Initially, LURD used Guinea as a base, with religious, political and military support from the Muslim–dominated government of that country. Observers note that LURD had a significant Muslim element and reportedly received arms from sources such as the United Arab Emirates.[63] In a statement issued on 25 April 1999 in the United States, the Liberia Coalition for Reconciliation and Democracy (LCRD), referring to itself simply as RESISTENCE, said it had decided to carry out tactics of "positive resistance" to degrade and disable Taylor's ability to reign in Liberia. The group confirmed that it was made up of former fighters of Taylor's NPFL, the disbanded Liberia Peace Council of George Boley, the break-away ULIMOs of Roosevelt Johnson and Alhaji Kromah, the Armed Forces of Liberia and the Lofa Defense force of Taylor's incumbent Youth and Sports Minister, Francois Massaquoi. The provincial city of Voinjama in Lofa County is a one-time stronghold of the former ULIMO-K leader, Alhaji G.V. Kromah.[64] In a further statement in September 2004, LURD explained that its primary focus was the unification and integration of all Liberians, with an unending desire to promote ethnic harmony and religious tolerance. In this regard, it affirmed that the healing of national wounds could only be attained through a genuine reconciliation process.

LURD however soon suffered the fate of its precursor ULIMO and broke into factions along ethno-religious lines. It became associated with Mandingo and Muslim political interests in the war to oust Charles Taylor from power, splitting into Krahn, Mandingo and Gio factions. The earlier split between the Krahns and the Mandingos in 1994 that gave birth to ULIMO-K and -J had to do with the ethnic hatred that developed between Ziah and Sheriff at the Council of State elections. The leader of LURD was a Mandingo, and it is understood that 90% of its forces was of the Mandingo ethnic group. Meanwhile, continuing violence in Lofa County exacerbated ethnic tensions between the Mandingos, on the one hand, and the Lormas and Kissis, on the other hand. Against this backdrop of mutual security apprehensions among the various ethnic groups, MODEL emerged. It was believed that the movement was backed by the government of Cote d'Ivoire.[65] Besides the ethnic affiliations of the Krahns and Kru with the ethnic groups of west Cote d'Ivoire, in particular the Guerre, close to the home of President Gbagbo, the radical changes implied by the election of Gbagbo in Abidjan denied Charles Taylor the support he had enjoyed from Houphouet Boigny. President Gbagbo had opposed Houphouet Boigny throughout his political career and had domestic reasons to encourage ethnic Krahns in Liberia who were already under arms to gravitate around the west of Cote d'Ivoire in defense of their common cause to reclaim their homeland under what was perceived as a threat from immigrants.

The radical transformations in the domestic politics of Cote d'Ivoire had turned the table against President Taylor. Further, MODEL forces that were mainly recruited from ethnic groups sympathetic to President Gbagbo could also be deployed to fight against the Force Nouvelles insurgency in Cote d d'Ivoire. Grand Gedeh, on the border with Cote d'Ivoire, is dominated by ethnic Krahns who share affinity with the Guerre, who are the dominant group in western Cote d'Ivoire. Both ethnic groups speak the same Kru language and have maintained a support network that has been effective during instability and conflict with other groups. Conveniently, they mutually traverse the international frontiers to find refuge on either side. Following the onset of civil war in Liberia to oust Doe, a Krahn from Grand Gedeh, Krahn refugees fled into Liberia. The Krahn created MODEL in Liberia and formed the sister LIMA force, a pro-Gbagbo militia, in Cote d'Ivoire. In 2003, ethnic Krahns were to support their ethnic affiliates in the fight against the Ivorian rebels from rival tribes as well as immigrant communities, mostly Burkinabes, that had acquired demographic superiority over the Guerre in their traditional homelands in the west of Cote d'Ivoire. The LIMA force in Cote d'Ivoire, based in Toulepleu, was reputed to have sub-units of Liberian Krahns. Other militias in this connection include the Union Patriotic de Resistance du Grand Ouest (UPRIGO). It was a Guerre movement, based north of Guiglo. Among others, there were also the Alliance Peuple We (WE) and Mouvement Ivoirien Liberation Ouest Cote d'Ivoire (MILOCI). The creation of the Movement for Democracy in Liberia (MODEL) was announced in early 2003 as an integrated force of a dissident movements operating in the south-eastern region of Liberia. MODEL, composed mainly of Krahn and Kru elements, quickly gained ground in the south-eastern counties, namely, Grand Gedeh, Sinoe and Grand Kru. Its main target seemed to be the port of Buchanan in Grand Bassa County, from where the GOL was exporting the country's major produce, timber. On 27 April 2003, fighters belonging to MODEL engaged in a major battle to take the town of Greenville, the main port of south-eastern Liberia, where several logging companies based their operations. The rebels also attacked government troops on the road between Tappita and Gborlor-Diallah towns close to the Ivorian border.[66] Through these initial exploits, MODEL became recognized as a fighting force with considerable leverage in the conflict.

By 2003, the activities of the two insurgencies, LURD and MODEL, had reached Monrovia, the capital, which was under the control of four different warring groups threatening to take the Executive Mansion. President Taylor was weakened, but retained enough armed power to cause havoc with potential calamitous consequences for the civilian population trapped in the city. He was forced to negotiate himself out of power into exile. The central motive driving the conflict since 1980 was to edge the Americo-Liberians from the control of the Liberian state and, importantly, with each constituent group aided by its ethnic affiliate across the borders.

The April 1980 coup, executed by marginalized indigenes led by Master Sergeant Samuel Doe, a Krahn, ushered in a long period of war and instability that pitted all the major ethnic groups in the country against one another. In the ensuing conflict, ethnic groups across Liberia's international frontiers mobilized material and financial support for their ethnic cousins to prosecute the war. The attempt by a coalition of national political actors to create a national patriotic front to counter the Doe regime went awry in the hands of Charles Taylor, who hijacked the front to pursue an alternative agenda. In the process, the prospects of a latent security dilemma in the anarchic environment became real. The National Transitional Government of Liberia and the National Transitional Legislative Assembly, the pivotal institutions of the transitional arrangement that emerged from the Accra Comprehensive Peace Agreement, represented the interests of warring factions associated with the various ethnic constituencies. Each member of the government defended its partisans, and often personal interests, at the expense of the interests of the country. As a result, the implementation of the CPA bred corruption[67] and ethnic jingoism as major undercurrents of the democratization process as well as the presidential and legislative elections of November and October 2005 and their outcome. The CPA process was marked by turbulence as the various political forces sought to gain advantage over one another.

The CPA-guided transition unfolded within a clearly defined social and political context. The intervention of the international community in the distress implies, as expressed in the deployment of the UN peace mission in Liberia, at least de facto, the suspension of the prevailing rules governing the political process and the norms of social interaction. This was a cardinal provision of the CPA. In general such interventions are aimed at freezing or, often, replacing the old rules for social and political engagements, as well as economic relations between all stakeholders in politics, society and business. This is with a view to creating a new foundation for a more harmonious political process and moving the system away from the sources of its conflicts. To succeed in giving birth to a new society, the projected changes must necessarily alter the character of society and the nature of social interaction. This goal has far-reaching implications for the socioeconomic and political power structure in the post-intervention phase. This creates a pool of potential antagonists of the process who are drawn from the most powerful segment of the political, administrative and business elite determined to retain the basic structure of the state and the norms underpinning society in that state.

Yet, against this background, the very forces whose political struggles were responsible for the implosion of the political system do not simply stop as a result of the intervention, especially in a negotiated end to the conflict, which often consolidates the political leverage acquired by those forces through the instrument of violence. These forces are entrenched in the peace process which is able to begin only because they have agreed to a compromise in order to break the destructive stalemate in the armed encounters. In the transition to long-term peace, their struggle continues but constrained within the framework of new rules that have been established by the external intervening forces which now regulate how the game in the transition is going to be played. In Liberia, the principal intervening forces included the ECOWAS and the United Nations. Paradoxically, while the contending forces struggled against one another to exploit the interregnum provided by international intervention to lay foundations to gain political ascendance in the new republic, a second struggle pits all of them, as national elites with entrenched interests in the maintenance of that ruinous status quo, against the intervening forces whose mandate is essentially to change the status quo, reconstruct the political landscape to entrench democratic principles and reorient societal attitudes in support of the new democracy and mass participation in national life.

COALITIONS FOR THE STATUS QUO
AND THE BENEVOLENT COALITION FOR CHANGE

Initiatives by the international community to intervene in a failed state create a dynamic of interactions among domestic forces within the context of the internationally mediated process, and also between domestic and international forces in the country. This dynamic of the reconstruction process leads to the evolution of major coalitions based on political, social and economic interests in society. This reflects a major divide in attitudes to international efforts to resuscitate the failed state. The first coalition may be described as the coalition for the status quo or a coalition of the unwilling. This coalition is constituted by all groups that are apprehensive of changes to the status quo and, therefore, actively or passively work to undermine the success of the transformation that international intervention is mandated to achieve in the political process as well as in society at large.

In Liberia, the coalition for the status quo spread across the spectrum of the leadership of the political class, administration and business. This coalition brought under its umbrella all the leaders of the Americo-Liberian hegemony as well as the top echelons of the three major armed gangs that had had the country in a stranglehold in the quarter of a century before the third coming of the United Nations. Their goal was to prevent the implementation of radical changes that would destroy their individual careers or reveal the extent of personal and group implication in the destruction of the country. In their collective confrontation with the international community, the principal goal of the coalition for the status quo or the coalition of the unwilling was thus to preserve the basis of their continued domination of Liberian national life as a group.

The coalition manifested itself in several ways. The first group within the coalition stood against the conduct of elections in October 2005. This was to prolong the short-term interest of remaining in office with the transitional structures put in place to manage the peace process. The paradox was that the Comprehensive Peace Agreement signed in August 2003 by all the armed elements could be also interpreted as providing legitimacy to the gang leaders and their methods. For many of these elements, what they had failed to gain through violence had been offered through the peace talks and they sought to prolong the dividends of the armed struggle. They saw themselves as liberators. A second group within the coalition sought the delay of the elections as a strategic move to undercut those well placed within the transitional dispensation to gain political advantage. For these elements, this was an extension of the internal struggle of the political and business elites to retain the status quo in post-transition Liberia.

One major expression of the coalition for the status quo came in an open rejection of an investigative team despatched by the ECOWAS mediator to establish the facts of some high-profile cases of corruption involving both the transitional executive and legislature. The decision to send ECOWAS investigators arose from complaints from civil society and development partners in Liberia against what was described "as rampant corruption, lack of accountability, and transparency in financial and economic matters on the part of high government officials".[68] Following allegations of corruption levelled against the executive by highly placed interlocutors of General Abdulsalam Abubakar during the ECOWAS mediator's visit to Monrovia from 28 February to 6 March 2003, the general, in consultation with Chairman Gyude Bryant, set up a six-man team to investigate allegations of corruption brought to his attention. The team comprised 2 members each from Nigeria, Ghana and Sierra Leone. Also, on 10 March, deliberations on the report of a Special Investigative Committee (SIC) set up by the National Transitional Legislative Assembly (NTLA) to examine allegations of financial and administrative mismanagement in the legislature led to a fracas in the assembly. This followed a motion to suspend the leadership of the assembly on the basis of the report of the SIC. Consequently, the assembly leadership was suspended, and on 17 March, the assembly elected an interim Speaker and a new deputy speaker. The suspended leadership of the NTLA challenged the legality of the action of the assembly on the ground that due process had not been followed.

As a result of the tension at the NTLA over corruption, the investigation of the allegations was added to the brief of the ECOWAS investigators. At the invitation of Chairman Bryant, the investigators arrived in Monrovia on 18 March, with a mandate to investigate corrupt practices as well as provide evidence for the prosecution of those behind any financial malpractices. The investigators, who were scheduled to stay in Monrovia for two weeks, were to submit their report to the mediator on 15 April. By 31 March, the investigators had collected a number of documents on cases of corruption. The team had, however, observed the fact that many of the principal officers of the government whose activities were relevant to the investigations had generally been reluctant to honour their invitation. They had also not been enthusiastic about providing documents pertinent to the investigations. The investigators sensed that there was a conspiracy "orchestrated" across the spectrum of the political and administrative hierarchy in the country to undermine the effectiveness of their work. Mr. Adinkra Donkoh, the team chairman, felt that the little progress made by his team had "sown fear" in government officials as well as the top echelons of the executive and the political class.[69] The investigations were severely constrained by the unavailability of key ministers, government functionaries, and private-sector individuals, who were not available in the country when needed.[70]

On 4 April, an application for a writ of prohibition was filed by attorneys representing the Liberia Institute of Certified Public Accountants (LICPA).

Having failed to frustrate the team through stalling and other obstructive devises for a week, the whole spectrum of national leadership in politics, business and administration ganged up to derail the investigations. The principal officers of the relevant ministries refused to honour the invitations of the investigators. On 6 April, Associate Justice Ishmael P. Campbell of the Supreme Court, presiding in Chambers, in a directive dated 5 April, "ordered to stay all further proceedings" with respect to the application for a writ of prohibition submitted on 4 LICPA. The application by LICPA seeks to restrain "the Minister of Finance, the Governor of the Central Bank of Liberia, the Director of the Bureau of Budget and all other persons working under their authorities or in the aforementioned agencies, or otherwise involved in the fiscal affairs of the Government of the Republic of Liberia" from cooperating with the ECOWAS team investigating corruption in Liberia. The investigators only found out about the Stay Order through a letter dated 6 April from the Comptroller General to the team to explain his inability to continue to provide additional information and related documents to it.

In a related development, the NTLA at its regular sitting of 7 April criticized the visiting ECOWAS team, and described the intervention of Community as a subterfuge to save the suspended leadership of the assembly. Parliamentarians, who had earlier claimed to have suspended the speaker of the assembly on charges of corruption, now argued that the ECOWAS investigations into corruption in the country infringed national sovereignty. They proposed that the investigations could proceed only if confined to financial matters and undertaken in conjunction with the Liberian auditors.

Yet, against the powerful coalition for the continuation of the status quo was an aggregation of concerned citizens organized under various associations which desired change and supported the effort of the international community to begin the process of entrenching accountability and transparency in national life. The coalition brought together human rights activists, pro-democracy movements outside the mainstream of the political process, the church, and specific national NGOs to force the interim legislature to accede to the examination of the financial records of the interim government and its institutions. These associations provided the leadership for, and give voice to, the vast majority of the citizens of the failed state, who are virtual hostages to the political ambitions of the armed, rich and powerful members of the coalition for the status quo. This benevolent coalition for change constituted the domestic allies of the intervention forces, who provided the domestic anchor in society that helped international efforts to navigate the treacherous waters of state reconstruction. Good intentions are not enough. In the subsisting climate, the leaders of the coalition risked personal safety by defending the cause of international intervention as they took on the whole leadership of the country and faced the danger of possible reprisals, especially after the international forces may have withdrawn, from the scene from the coalition of the unwilling.

The coalition for change revolved around the Center for Democratic Empowerment (CEDE). In the gang-up of the Liberian political and business elite against ECOWAS investigations into corruption, the coalition voiced the determination of responsible and principled civil society organizations against the attempt of the status quo forces to represent the presence of the ECOWAS team of investigators in Liberia as an effort to undermine the sovereignty of the Liberian state. It observed that any pretension of hiding behind sovereignty to derail the efforts of the international community during the transitional period was not only a disservice to the nation and its people, but also a disdainful denial and a dangerous misreading of the prevailing circumstances of the nation.[71]

As earlier observed, the internal workings of the transitional government were turbulent and characterized by tensions along factional lines throughout, as the representatives of MODEL, LURD and Charles Taylor schemed and maneuvered to get the best out of the transition in preparation for the October elections that were to formally terminate the CPA process. Meanwhile, allegations of corruption continued, with the government being accused of manipulating the supply and prices of staple commodities to derive profits to fight elections. In March 2005, the shortage of rice in the market became an issue, especially as the Government of China had just donated 100,000 bags to ameliorate the suffering of the people. Allegations were rife that much of the rice had ended up with an aspiring presidential candidate who was a political associate of the Chairman. Moreover, the government importation of rice was handled mainly by two expatriate enterprises with close relationships with the highest political authorities in Liberia.

The issue of rice, a politically sensitive subject in Liberia, became the podium to even out political scores. The government set up the Rice Commission headed by Ellen Johnson-Sirleaf Johnson, who was also the chair of the Good Governance Reform Commission, to investigate the rice problem. Her findings were critical of the government and led to a heightened campaign by all sides to gain the moral high ground with the populace. Ellen Sirleaf Johnson resigned her chairmanship of the Good Governance Reform Commission, but the government claimed to have relieved her of the office to enable her concentrate on the pursuit of her presidential ambition. On the same matter of rice, the Minister of Commerce, Samuel Wlue, was invited several times by the transitional legislature to testify before the plenary session. The jostling for vantage position had begun in anticipation of the October elections to terminate the transition to a new order.

This contest among the elite was also discernible in the manner in which political forces negotiated alliances and political cooperation with one another

. Discussions of a possible merger of the UPP, UP, LPP, etc. to make Ellen Johnson-Sirleaf (UP) the presidential candidate of this alliance demonstrated the imperatives of the contest among political elites. The push for the coalition came mainly from Ellen Johnson-Sirleaf's main supporters in the LPP, Conmany Wesseh and chairman Dusty Wolokie, who had been plotting for some time to remove Dr. Togba-Nah Tipoteh, key founder of the LPP and long-standing standard bearer of the party, considered by his supporters to be the most principled politician. He was, however, heavily despised by the average Americo-Liberian for his prominence as the principal instigator of the movement to end 133 years of the rule of the True Whig Party. He was also reputed to have encouraged the coup by Samuel Doe on 12 April 1980 and blamed by Americo-Liberians for the execution of their prominent leaders by the putschists. He was considered by most of the anti-True Whig/anti-Americo-Liberian rule to be the godfather of the progressive movement which led to the creation of the Movement for Justice in Africa (MOJA) chapter in Liberia and the Progressive Alliance in Liberia (PAL) along with Bacchus Matthews and Amos Sawyer

INTERNAL STRUGGLES WITHIN THE COALITION FOR THE STATUS QUO

The partisan struggle among political forces for the upper hand in the post-transition era also took place in the interim legislature. The leadership crisis of the assembly epitomized the pervasive struggle among all political forces against all. Investigations by the SIC into allegations of corruption had led to the suspension of the legislature's leadership by 50 of the 75 legislators present at a special session to deliberate on the report on 14 March. Those suspended were the Speaker, Deputy Speaker and the Chairman of the NTLA Committee on Ways, Means and Finance as well as the Chairman of the Rules and Order committee. Though the legislature explained the decision as more related to the violent disruption of legislative session by the speaker on 10 March than to the main issue of corruption which was the original charge against the leadership of George Dweh, it went ahead on 17 march to elect an interim speaker, George Koukou, and a new deputy speaker, David Gbala.

This at the NTLA raised many political as well as legal and constitutional issues. It also offered an opportunity to look at the state of some of the conflicting interests driving the Liberian political process. Principal among these factors are ethnic rivalry among the Americo-Liberians, the Mandingos, and Krahn and Kru; party loyalties involving the pro-Taylor National Patriotic Party (NPP); factional fighting among LURD; as well as personal affiliations, interests and ambitions of major political actors such as Charles Taylor, Chairman Gyude Bryant, Sekou and Aisha Conneh and Ellen Johnson-Sirleaf.

Changes in the Distribution of Power among Political Forces

The immediate consequence of the overthrow of George Dweh as the as speaker of the transitional legislature was a profound change in relative power held by various interests and political forces in the assembly. This change was interpreted as a dimunition of the the political power of some ethnic groups, such as the Krahns and associated ethnic groups from the south-east of the country. It was also read as the enhancement of the power in the hands of pro-Taylor political forces in the transitional legislature. Against the gains of pro-Charles Taylor forces, mostly a sub-set of the Americo–Liberian constituency, both the LURD, implying Mandingos and Muslims, and MODEL, a reference to Krahn and Kru, lost political influence as a result of the crisis.

In the ensuing struggle for the leadership of the legislature, ethnicity and political party affiliation were strongly at play. The deposed speaker, George Dweh, being one of a minority of Krahns affiliated to the predominantly Mandingo LURD, was, in the context of the struggle between the two ethnic groups (Krahns and Mandingos), a compromise of sorts. Despite his political affiliation to the LURD, Dweh was seen by the Krahns and the people from the south-east, who were mostly affiliated to MODEL, as an assuring strategic presence in the legislature. MODEL, it may be recalled, was created to stop the Mandingo drive to power in the post-Taylor era. With Jackson Doe, the Minister for Presidential Affairs in the executive branch and George Dweh as speaker of the legislature, the Krahns felt adequately represented in the system and compensated for their armed struggle. This was more so as the prospect of the emergence of a Mandingo as Chairman of the National Transitional Government of Liberia, troubling to other ethnic groups, was avoided in the distribution of portfolios after the CPA had been agreed to. For LURD and MODEL it was a major political victory that the position of deputy speaker, allotted to Eddington Varmah, represented the defunct Taylor government, was the highest office in the legislature available to elements affiliated to the deposed Taylor regime in post-CPA Liberia.

The election of George Koukou, a Charles Taylor loyalist, to the office of Speaker of the NTLA, as a result of the crisis in the assembly, reversed the post-CPA gains of LURD and MODEL. It led to many speculations regarding the true motives behind the George Koukou's initiatives in leading the anti-corruption crusade that ousted George Dweh. From that perspective, the anti-corruption campaign was seen as a ploy to achieve two main goals, namely: to remove a Krahn from the leadership of the NTLA; And to reinstate the control of the legislature in the hands of pro-Taylor forces. The suspension of the former NTLA speaker, therefore, did not go down well with the Krahns as well as some prominent Grand Gedeans and kinsmen. At a well-attended re-union program for Grand Gedeh citizens on Sunday, 27 March, 2005 at the Monrovia City Hall, Mr. Chie Gaye, Gbarzon Statutory District and Mr. J D Slanger, Commissioner of the Bureau of Maritime Affairs, denounced the suspension of George Dweh, describing it as an attempt to sideline Krahns from the government. Participants at the meeting cited the dismissal of Mr. Charles Bennie, former Commissioner of Customs, for criticizing the NTGL publicly and the attempted dismissal of Mr. Sam Wlue, the Commerce Minister, as part of the continuing manipulation of the process to sideline Krahns and their affiliate groups. They also denounced Mr. David Gbala, the new acting deputy speaker and a fellow Grand Gedean, for teaming up with legislators from other tribes to deprive his fellow tribesman of power.

Former Speaker George Dweh also received open support from elements of some formerly armed factions. The most prominent has been a group of four "generals" who wrote to express their frustration over the possible suspension of Dweh, warning that no group had a monopoly of violence in the country. Furthermore, George Dweh was associated with most of the ex-combatants at the center of the crisis at the Guthrie plantations. They were perceived to constitute a reservoir of willing loyalists that could be used in the event of a relapse into armed hostilities.

Meanwhile, as the elections to terminate the CPA drew nearer, indigenous forces began massive mobilization and alliance talks under the auspices of the Grassroots Opinion Leaders Forum (GOLF) to forestall the emergence of an Americo-Liberian as the next president. The mobilization took place under the Only Indigenous Liberians (OIL) movement.

Only Indigenous Liberians Movement

The movement OIL brought together students and their union, elements in civil society and prominent political actors, with the sole agenda of ensuring that only an indigenous Liberian became president in the coming elections. As the name suggested, membership in the organization was made up of indigenous Liberians who were determined to ensure that no Americo-Liberia emerged as the President of Liberia from the October elections. The group included key personalities in society and politics such as Thomas Nimley, Sekou Conneh, Moses Blah, J D Slanger - all linked to former armed factions. Others include Romeo Quiah (FDA/MODEL), Edward Farley (GSA/LURD), Paul Thomas (Dep MD at FDA/LURD), George Koukou (Acting Speaker/ex-GOL) and George Dweh (LURD). Members with no war pedigree included Bacchus Matthews (UPP), Cllr Fredrick Cheru, described as a staunch member of the LAP; Milton Teejay, a potential candidate against Marcus Dahn as presidential candidate for UPP; as well as Marcus Dahn, considered a founding member of the Progressive Alliance of Liberia, former deputy minister for administration at the Ministry of Education and who was elected chairman of UPP in January 2005. Roosevelt Quiah facilitated the meetings of the group. The Student Unification Party (SUP) at the University of Liberia was associated with the group, whose main strategy was to come up with a single indigenous candidate to contest the presidential elections. Apart from Moses Blah indicated by Quiah as a serious contender for the post, other potential candidates included Milton Teejay and George Weah.

Although seen as an umbrella for indigenous forces, the activities of OIL, paradoxically, not only fostered anti-Americo Liberian sentiments, but also anti-Mandingo as well as anti-Krahn feelings. This brought to the fore again difficult ethnic relations. In the short term, it created a situation which threatened the integrity of the electoral process, should an indigene not emerge as the winner of the presidential elections. Following the signing of the Alliance for Peace and Democracy (APD) by the LPP and UPP out of the four registered parties (LPP, UPP, UP, NDPL) that had been consulting on the possibility of forming an alliance for more than ten months, Conmany Wesseh explained why UP and the NDPL had stayed away from the signing ceremony on 27 April. He noted that the UPP and LPP were born out of the struggle against the old oligarchy of the True Whig Party and Americo Liberians and **were** thus blamed for the consciousness of the military which eventually led to the coup of 1980. Ironically, Samuel Doe, fearing the militancy of the UPP and LPP, banned them from taking part in politics, accusing them of being radicals.

On the other hand, the Unity Party, which was formed by Dr Kesssely in 1984, provided a platform for Johnson-Sirleaf after she pulled out of LAP. UP was acceptable to the military regime. Thus, the NDPL, which was Doe's political party, and the UP became the direct beneficiaries of the military regime. LAP, on the other hand, came from a reformed True Whig Party, it did not look kindly on the LPP and UPP, as it blamed them for their loss of power. The idea of an alliance of the UPP and LPP with the UP and the NDPL was an attempt to realign the political forces to overcome historical lines of cleavages in the country. The alliance was meant to transcend political partisanship; it was an alliance of clashing political traditions and forces of two dominant, if contending, forces. Again, an attempt to create a unified political platform embracing all stakeholders in Liberia failed on the altar of ethnicity and the political ambitions of the major actors.

It was against this background that the October and November 2005 elections were held. The pull and push of the transition gave rise to four major political tendencies, which were still, however, rooted in the continuing struggle for appropriation of the state by partisan groups, even in the Liberian post-conflict political process. These forces included a coalition of forces determined to sustain the legacy of the Americo-Liberian oligarchy; a nativists group of forces determined to push for the emergence of a president with an indigenous background; a couple of actors with an agenda to protect the legitimate Mandingo interests as well as consolidate the gains made by them and Muslims in the Liberian political system during the war. A fourth tendency was the coming together of many political actors in the old pro- democratic movement on a new platform of moving Liberia from its politics of antagonism to realign the national focus internally.

DEMOGRAPHIC CONTEXT OF THE OCTOBER AND NOVEMBER 2005 PRESIDENTIAL AND LEGISLATIVE ELECTIONS

With an estimated population of 3.4 million, 1,352,730 voters registered for the October elections. Out of the registered voters, 676,390 were women and 676,340 men. The Liberian electorate was largely youthful, with 40% of the registered voters in the 18-27 year age group. Most of the registered voters were concentrated in three counties. In general, each of the fifteen counties of Liberia is associated with a particular ethnic group, often the vast majority along with one or two other related ethnic groups. In terms of voter distribution and the implications for the continuing struggle of the nativist forces to wrest power from Americo-Liberians , Montserrado County (Monrovia), which had the largest number of registered voters (473,229) and the most enlightened part of the electorate, was the most critical county for the presidential elections. However, Nimba County (190,270 registered voters), Bomi County (146,338 registered voters) and Grand Bassa County ((100,601) were also crucial in the final configuration of power that was expected to emerge from the elections. In the south-east, Grand Gedeh County is predominantly Krahn (former President Doe's tribe), while Sinoe, Grand Kru, River Cess, River Gee and Maryland counties (all with under 90,000 registered voters) are mainly populated by the Kru Sapo and Grebo ethnic groups. Grand Bassa County, which is also counted as part of the southeast, is mainly populated by the Bassa tribe, although commercial activities have drawn a significant number of people from other ethnic groups to Buchanan, the county capital. In Nimba County, the Gio and Manos dominate, while in Lofa County, the Loma, Kissi and the Mandingo are pre-eminent. In Bomi County, the Gola are prominent, while Bong, Gbarpolu and parts of Margibi County are mainly populated by the Kpelle. The outcome of the elections, in particular the presidential, starkly reflected the stout allegiance of the electorate to those perceived as representing their respective ethnic agenda, a prominent factor in the calculus of the electorate and candidates alike.

However, other variables that mitigated the ethnic factor in the election included education, gender, charisma, the age of the electorate, and the record of individual candidates in previous governments, as well as their role in the various conflicts which had endeared some to the local constituencies and at the same time made them controversial elements on the national scene. Another important element was religious affiliation, which, in the case of Liberia tends to converge with ethnicity, such that it can be predicted that Americo-Liberians and ethnic groups that have imbibed Western education and culture are most likely to be Christian, nominal and otherwise. As one moves north, Christian religiosity gradually fades into animism. Clusters of Mandingo communities found mostly to the north of Liberia are Moslems. There is, therefore, a high correlation between being Americo- Liberian and southerner and being Christian. In the same manner, being Mandingo is as good as being Moslem, but the Vai, Gbandi, Lorma and Kissi in Grand Cape Mount and other counties in the northwest are also largely Moslem.

In all, it is estimated that 55% of Liberians are Christian, 25% adhere to indigenous belief system, and 20% are Moslems. It is worth reiterating that there are strong anti-Mandingo and significant anti-Americo-Liberian sentiments among other Liberian ethnic groups. The Americo-Liberians along with other ethnic groups generally consider the Mandingos as foreigners and have traditionally questioned the legitimacy of the ambition of any Mandingo to rule Liberia. On the other hand, the Mandingos and other ethnic groups have also long ago declared that they would never allow an Americo-Liberian to rule Liberia again. A final critical variable was the funds at the disposal of the candidates and political parties to fight the elections. The more sophisticated the environment was, the greater the number of factors that influenced voter behaviour in that constituency. For example, the interplay of many of these factors were manifest in Monrovia, but much less so in the hinterland such as Lofa, Grand Gedeh and the southeastern counties. The more heterogeneous the setting, the more several variables were salient in determining the outcome of the elections.

In compliance with Article IX para 2 of the Accra CPA of 18 August 2003 which called for the conduct of national elections not later than October 2005, the National Elections Commission (NEC), reconstituted in conformity with Article XVIII para 2a of the CPA, decided to hold the presidential and legislative elections on 11 October, 2005 consistent with constitutional provision in Article 83 para a, which stipulated the holding of national elections on the second Tuesday of October of each election year. An electoral calendar was established with timelines to achieve these goals within the timeframe of the CPA and consistent with the provisions of the constitution. The electoral time table set 6 August as the final day for the nomination of candidates and for the submission of applications to register as an independent candidate. On 12 August, the NEC completed its review of the 779 applications received from the prospective candidates for the October elections. It approved the applications of 762 candidates, including 22 presidential, 22 vice-presidential, 206 senatorial, and 512 House of Representatives candidates. The Commission rejected the applications of 17 candidates, including 5 presidential, 3 vice-presidential and 9 House of Representatives candidates. On 13 August, Cornelius Hunter, acting on his own behalf and other rejected candidates, wrote to NEC requesting opportunity to rectify discrepancies in their documentation, but their requests were denied. The reasons given by NEC for rejecting the applications ranged from the failure by some of the aspiring presidential candidates to submit applications for their running mates, to deficiencies in the petition lists of some of the candidates. Independent candidates whose applications were rejected included Marcus Jones and running mate Mohamed Sangbeh Kromah, Cornelius Hunter and aspiring vice presidential candidate Cecilia Siaway Teah as well as Isaac Johnson running for a seat in the House of Representatives as an independent.

THREATS TO THE ELECTIONS

On 10 August 2005, the Coalition for Transformation of Liberia (COTOL) petitioned the Civil Law Court for Montserrado for a declaratory judgment, arguing that each voter was entitled to cast two votes in the senatorial elections, being one vote for each senatorial seat in the county. The judge of the Civil Law Court ruled in favor of COTOL, whereupon NEC appealed the ruling to the Supreme Court. On 22 September, 2005, in a split decision, the majority of the Supreme Court bench ruled in favor of COTOL that each voter was entitled to cast two votes in the senatorial elections. However, the Chief Justice delivered a dissenting ruling. The majority of the bench accepted the arguments that had been put forward by COTOL, and they accepted that the two senatorial posts were separate and distinct offices and that a voter had a right to vote for each public elective office. The Court therefore ruled that the final ruling of the Civil Law Court be affirmed and confirmed, and mandated the lower court to order that the ballots be printed in a manner to allow each voter the right to vote once for each of the senatorial posts in a county, and to order NEC to publicise and disseminate information to the public to educate them that they were entitled to vote separately for two senatorial candidates.

Arguments in the case centred on the interpretation of Section 1.3 of the Electoral Reform Law which provided that in relation to elections for the office of senator "each voter shall have one vote". It was argued by NEC that the provision in question was clear and unambiguous and that each voter was, therefore, only entitled to one vote in the senatorial election. It contended that the Civil Law Court had no jurisdiction to hear the application for declaratory judgment. It averred that the legal remedy of declaratory judgment could not apply in the circumstances of the case, and that the provision in question had been promulgated following extensive discussions and deliberations with the political parties including members of COTOL who had agreed that each voter should have just one vote. In response, counsel for COTOL argued that declaratory judgment was the appropriate remedy because NEC itself had refused to give a ruling as to the interpretation of the sentence in question – COTOL had specifically requested NEC to provide its interpretation of the particular provision in question, in response to which NEC stated that it was unable to interpret the law as it was only the court that was empowered to interpret laws. COTOL further argued that the positions of senior and junior senator were two separate offices, each post carrying a different term of office and that in the circumstances each voter was entitled to vote for the two persons that they wanted to represent them in the Senate. COTOL therefore argued that the Electoral Reform Law should be interpreted to mean that each voter should have one vote for each senatorial post.

On 27 September, the court handed down its ruling on the Marcus Jones et al v. NEC case, which had been filed on 22 August 2005 by Marcus Jones et al requesting an opportunity to cure errors in their nomination papers. The court ruled against the NEC and granted presidential candidate Marcus R. Jones and Mohamed Sangbeh Kromah, his running mate; presidential candidate Cornelius Hunter and his running mate, Cecilia Siaway Teah; and D. Garkpe Gedepoh the opportunity to cure errors in their nomination papers, which if cured, would enable them to be put on the ballot for the 11 October 2005 elections. Similarly, the court granted Mr. Isaac M. Johnson, an independent candidate for House of Representatives in District No.1 in Gbarpolu County an opportunity to cure errors. The court upheld the NEC's decision to refuse to certify presidential candidate Gedepoh whose running mate failed to file any papers. The court reasoned that the NEC gave an advantage to political parties by allowing political parties to register six months before the elections, along with the distinction between the requirements for political parties to submit petitions of *"eligible voters"* instead of *"registered voters"* as required for independent candidates were among the substantive findings. Additional facts cited against the NEC were that fewer meetings were held with independent candidates than with political parties, that independent candidates did not have a mailbox in the lobby of the NEC, as did political parties. The court held that the NEC was unfair to independent candidates because it denied them the same access as political parties.

The ruling of the Court was that the NEC was required to give the independent candidates seven days from the date of the ruling to cure the defects in their Petition Lists, and to place them on the relevant ballots if the papers were satisfactory. The ruling of the Supreme Court of 22 September implied that the NEC had to issue new instructions to voters to vote for two candidates in the senatorial elections. The Supreme Court's ruling of 27 September on the Marcus Jones case was issued barely 13 days to the conduct of the elections when preparations were far advanced, including the printing of ballots. To comply with the ruling, the NEC suggested that the conduct of the elections would have to be postponed to some time after October. It noted that this would contravene the relevant provisions of the CPA. It argued that since the elections were governed by the CPA, it had no powers to postpone the elections. Meanwhile, Marcus Jones resubmitted his nomination papers as required by the court's ruling.

REACTION OF THE POLITICAL CLASS TO THE RULING

The political class reacted strongly to the ruling of the Supreme Court. Ms. Johnson-Sirleaf , presidential candidate of the Unity Party, called it "political mischief," while Mr. Sherman, the flag bearer of COTOL, thought that the uncertainties around the elections arose from the blunder of NEC lawyers who were not a match to the more experienced trial lawyer Marcus Jones, the principal litigant in the matter. However, even though Marcus Jones et al won the court case, it was important for all to recognize that not all court judgments are enforceable. This was an instance where the ruling of the court violated the CPA by prescribing steps that could not be accommodated within the established timelines of the CPA. The rulings could, therefore, not be enforced. He criticized the court for the undue delay in making their ruling.

INITIATIVES TO RESOLVE THE STALEMATE

The weeks following the ruling of the Supreme Court up to October 6, were dominated by initiatives from all sides, involving the NTGL, the presidential candidates, the Implementation Monitoring Committee (IMC), as well as the International Contact Group on Liberia (ICGL), to overcome the difficulties besetting the conduct of the October elections. On 28 September, the IMC met to discuss the way forward. On 29 September, the group ICGL met with Chairman Bryant in the continuing search to resolve the impasse. NEC, encouraged by the international partners of Liberia, continued to seek avenues to ensure that the 11 October elections were conducted as scheduled. IMC and the ICGL called on the ECOWAS Mediator to initiate decisive actions to resolve these issues and any similar issues in the future in a manner consistent with the CPA to ensure that the elections were held as planned. On 30 September, an Abuja extraordinary summit of regional leaders issued a communiqué which, in paragraph 11, took note of the holding of the next elections in Liberia on 11 October and called on all institutions of state, all political actors and civil society to respect the letter and spirit of the CPA. In the follow-up to the summit, the ECOWAS Secretariat in Abuja wrote to Chairman Gyude Bryant to underline that the CPA was paramount vis-a-vis the constitution, laws and statutes of Liberia relating to the elections and to declare a firm stand on the holding of the elections on 11 October.

On 1 October, an independent presidential candidate, Mr. Marcus Jones, along with his running mate, another independent presidential candidate, Mr. Cornelius Hunter, and a House of Representatives aspirant, Isaac Johnson, left Monrovia for Abuja at the invitation of the ECOWAS Mediator for consultations on how to resolve issues arising from the 27 September Supreme Court rulings. The weekly meeting of the ICGL held on 5 October focused principally on the 11 October elections. Chairman Gyude Byrant informed participants of the decision of the transitional government to proceed with the conduct of the elections on 11 October. The chairman noted that consultations initiated between the NEC and the Supreme Court on the court's ruling which preceded the decision of the transitional government to hold elections on 11 October had been testy. NEC had undertaken to execute the ruling of the Supreme Court in respect of dual voting by voters in the senatorial election and was working with its partners to educate voters on the changes entailed. He added that the government's engagement with Counsellor Marcus Jones, the main litigant in the ruling in respect of independent candidates, was also going well.

Following consultations with stakeholders in the elections after his arrival in Monrovia on 5 October, the ECOWAS Mediator announced that the independent candidates had withdrawn their candidacies. He also confirmed that the elections would take place on 11 October. The independent presidential candidates, who were present at the meeting, acknowledged their decisions, on 6 October, Marcus Jones and Cornleius Hunter spoke on Radio Veritas to publicize the withdrawal of their candidacies. President Olusegun Obasanjo of Nigeria arrived on a one-day visit to Liberia on 7 October. His visit brought certainty that the elections of 11 October were indeed going to take place and that the CPA transition was going to terminate on schedule. In spite of the uncertainties, political forces had long commenced the process of consolidating themselves, while the process of reconfigurating some of the old forces into newer political visions progressed.

THE MAJOR POLITICAL FORCES IN THE POST-CONFLICT ERA

The pull and push of the transition gave rise to four major political tendencies, which reflected the continuity of the entrenched polarities of political forces in the evolution of the Liberian state. At the same time, the coming together of prominent political actors from the progressive camp with a new vision to break from the past led to the emergence of a coalition of progressive nationalist forces that transcended existing divisions. Three of the broad political tendencies reflected the old divisions in society, and appeared to be rooted in the continuing struggle for the appropriation of the state by partisan groups in the post-conflict political process in Liberia. These forces included COTOL, which was determined to sustain the legacy of the Americo-Liberian oligarchy; another aggregation of nativist forces revolving around George Weah's Congress of Democratic Change (CDC); and the Togba Na Tipoteh-led Alliance for Peace and Democracy (APD). The nativists were motivated by their agenda to ensure the emergence of a president with an indigenous background in the coming elections. A sub-set of the nativists included a couple of actors, such as Sekou Conneh's PRODEM and Alhaji Kromah's ALCOP , with an agenda to protect Mandingo interests and legitimacy, as well as consolidate the gains made by them and Muslims in the Liberian political system during the war. They were, however, on the margins, given the perpetuation of historical prejudices against the Mandingo in the mainstream nativist caucus. A fourth tendency was the coming together of many political actors in the old pro-democratic movement on a new platform of moving Liberia from its politics of antagonism to realign the national focus internally. This revamped progressive nationalist force came together under a reconstituted UP.

THE PROGRESSIVE NATIONALIST FORCE UNDER THE UNITY PARTY

The flagship of the reconstituted progressive camp was the Unity Party. The party had been established twenty years earlier by its founder, Dr Edward B. Kesselly, in order to provide a democratic alternative in the Liberian political process. It affirmed its vision of a united and stable Liberia, in which all citizens are guaranteed equal rights and opportunities. The party asserted that one of the greatest tragedies of Liberia was the 1980 coup d'etat and the failed attempt at democracy,, that followed and ushered in years of brutal conflict.[72] In effect, the party repudiated the agenda which was central to the Samuel Doe regime, around which the prominent indigenous actors were mobilized. In a more direct challenge to the notion of Christianity as the founding religion of the state, the UP manifesto urged each Liberian to invoke guidance from God or Allah in moving the country forward. Consistent with this philosophy, membership of the party was more broad-based than any other party, as it shunned ethnicity and actively sought to build a more national character. The manifesto stressed that its agenda was to lay a solid foundation for creating a strong and productive new Liberia that belonged to all. On restoring the nation's pride and dignity, the party proclaimed:

> A Unity Party led government will promote unification and integration of all our peoples. Through civics and citizenship education, we will encourage each Liberian to think and consider himself/herself to be first ad foremost Liberian-not a member of a group or a particular tribe...

> We believe a full, balanced and unbiased research of our country's history will reveal accounts that are inclusive of all our people...

> Our firm belief is that Liberia is for all Liberians, and knowing who we are, as a people, will promote a social and political environment that unites all Liberians as ' One People with One Destiny.[73]

The party thus advocated a policy that was inclusive and nationalistic, putting Liberia first and recognizing the importance of fundamental principles at the heart of a democratic process.

One of its central planks is the importance of the citizens in the development of the economy in collaboration with its international partners. UP boldly deviated from past political tendencies by forging a national front that was motivated to take power and transcend the traditional gulfs in Liberia's national life. No major ethnic group was left out in the party. Yet, as if to acknowledge the strong national mood against the return of Americo Liberian rule, Mrs Johnson-Sirleaf, the party's presidential candidate, was pragmatic in accentuating her indigenous antecedents and distanced herself from the image and perception of being an Americo-Liberian to which she had been associated throughout her political career. Mrs. Sirleaf, who was married to a Mandingo, made it known that she was Gola and a granddaughter of a German. This implied a repudiation of the long-held popular perception of her antecedents as an Americo Liberian, who, as a descendant of the settler community, was linked to the era of True Whig hegemony. Influential Mandingo organizations and political figures, led by Mrs. Aisha Conneh, the estranged wife of former LURD leader Sekou Conneh and spiritual advisor of President Lansana Conte of Guinea, and who, arguably, had become the de facto leader of the Mandingos, joined Mrs. Sirleaf's camp. Her marriage to a Mandingo served to bridge her past association with Americo-Liberia with the new popular requirement to have an indigene rule the country. She was singularly placed to integrate the

Mandingos into the mainstream of the national process and help to consolidate the gains made by her tribe during the war years.

The association of Aisha Conneh was significant in this project. Through this association, the virtually token presidential candidacies of the other Mandingos, Alhaji Kromah and Sekou Conneh, further suffered serious setbacks. President Conte of Guinea, who has been implicated in supporting Mandingo political aspirations in Liberia, provided significant financial support to the Mandingo political leadership via Aisha Conneh. Aisha Coneh was instrumental to the contact between Guinean President Conte and Johnson-Sirleaf. President Conte donated a significant amount of money and some vehicles to the Aisha Conneh Foundation, which went to support Mrs. Sirleaf's campaign. Mrs. Conneh coordinated Mrs. Sirleaf's national campaign. Against the background of the entrenched crisis of the legitimacy of Mandingo political aspiration fuelled by those who perceived themselves as representing nativist interests, Aisha Conneh's support for Johnson-Sirleaf appeared to be a most realistic option left to consolidate the massive political gains the Mandingo acquired through the ULIMO-K and later the LURD insurgencies.

With only about 5% of the population and labouring under widespread prejudices that tended to question the legitimacy of their stakes in national life and process, the Mandingo could not go it alone politically. The political problem of the Mandingo was compounded by their association with the infamous Charles Taylor regime. The Mandingo were neither very welcome in the COTOL, which represented the interests of the old Americo-Liberian oligarchy nor at home with the conservative nativist parties. The nativists did not extend to the Mandingo the status of a true indigenous Liberian. Meanwhile, Mrs Johnson-Sirleaf's running mate, Mr. Joseph Boakai, is a Vai from Lofa County with a strong ethnic affiliation with Grand Cape Mount County. The Bassa were represented in the UP by prominent political figures including Dr. Togba McIntosh. The southeast, the heartland of the nativist forces, was represented by a prominent civil society figure, Conmany Wesseh, and former Chief Justice Gloria Musu Scott.

The Americo- Liberian constituency was represented by Dr. Amos Sawyer. Mrs. Johnson Sirleaf's political party's broad national spread was also strengthened by the support of the majority of women of voting age, a gender factor which proved to be significant, too. Among Liberian women, there was some disenchantment with the leadership of men who were perceived to have failed the country. However, some faulted Mrs. Sirleaf for failing to actively champion the cause of women over the years. UP was favoured among the more enlightened and sophisticated electorate of Monrovia who also very well respected Mrs. Sirleaf. The progressive nationalist force was centered in the UP, which also reached out to the marginalized constituency of women.

THE NATIVISTS

The second major political force that emerged in the post-conflict era was an attempt at coming together of all political forces dedicated to the political ascendancy of indigenous peoples. Rooted in the struggle for indigenous participation in national politics in the early 1950s when a Grebo nationalist stood for the presidency under the Liberian Reformation Party and was later hounded into exile, the nativists hoped that under the envisaged one umbrella it would consolidate its votes to effect a desired change from the hegemony of Americo-Liberian rule to indigenous rule through the ballot. The name of George Weah's CDC was indicative of this main political objective. CDC was joined in this by Nah Togba Tipoteh's two-party coalition, the Alliance for Peace and Democracy (APD). These parties were complemented by well known anti status quo political actors like Bacchus Mathews. The nativists planned to achieve the political goals of change through non-violent means. It was in this sense that George Weah carried the legacy of the indigenous struggle for liberation. Indeed, the organization, Only Indigenous Liberians (OIL), formed by the caucus of the nascent nativists to advance this goal, had contemplated drafting George Weah as its flag bearer. Mr. Weah, who is of the Kru ethnic group of the south-east, was projected to dominate all the counties in that region comprising Grand Kru, Sinoe, Rivercess, Grand Gedeh and Maryland, where Samuel Doe was seen as a hero. Without a coherent and formal political platform other than a perceived general sentiment that the people wanted the Americo-Liberians off their backs and desired to assert the vision of the majority indigenes in the affairs of Liberia, Mr. Weah's greatest asset was his celebrity status as a former world best footballer, which drew support for him among bulk of the youth in Montserrado and other counties. His personal fortune, accumulated during his years as an international soccer star also greatly assisted his political campaign.

Mr. Weah's humble background and modest education earned him the support of the uneducated, dispossessed, disenchanted and disoriented urban mass, which saw itself in him. This urban mass was composed of the many young Liberians who grew up in the last twenty-five years without a notion of how organized societies function. They were the product of pervasive anomalies that had characterized Liberia since the advent of the turbulent era that began in April 1980 with the rise to power of Master Sgt. Samuel Doe. Apart from sharing much in common, Master Sgt. Doe and Mr. George Weah were reported to be personal friends. The nativist agenda was strong and orbited around the Kru and Krahn who deserted their own traditional political party, the NDPL, which was founded by Doe, to join Weah's CDC. By virtue of the emergence of an Americo-Liberian as its flagbearer in the elections, the Kru/ Krahn considered the NDPL high jacked by status quo forces. One Krahn faction had orchestrated the selection of Mr. Winston Tubman (an Americo-Liberian) as its presidential candidate. The CDC thus became the best hope for the indigenous plan to acquire power. Indeed, MODEL and its leadership had formally declined to form a new party, hoping to strengthen Samuel Doe's NDPL to achieve continuity in the visions around which the late founder of the party was mobilized.

A number of prominent political figures, from among the early progressives and pro-democracy camp, abandoned their parties to join Weah's CDC. These included Bacchus Matthew, Milton Teahjay, Rudolph Johnson who became Mr. Weah's running mate, and Mr. Eugene Nagbe, former NPP partisan and Minister for Posts and Telecommunications. Yet, there were, implicitly, contradictions within the nativists' camp. Samuel Doe's legacy had left a war between the Kru/Krahn and the Mandingo, on the one hand, and the Gios, Manos, Lormas and others, on the other hand. As such, while all parties formed against the resuscitation of the Americo-Liberian hegemony in the post-conflict era had a tinge of the nativist agenda, the indigenous forces were by no means united. In attempting to build a broad-based alliance, while a few Mandingos had ventured to join the OIL movement, it was clear that the movement, at heart, also questioned the legitimacy of the claims of Mandingos to be stakeholders in the affairs of the Liberian state. This led some prominent Mandingo to go it alone by creating their own parties.

THE MANDINGO FRONT

The prominence of Mandingo armed forces throughout the civil war was facilitated by the unstinting financial and materiel support for them from Sierra Leone and Guinea. This support ensured that the Mandingos in Liberia, estimated to be just less than 5% of the population, were prominent in negotiations that finally led to the creation of transitional administrations and also held important positions in those transitional governments. The prominence acquired in the political process by the Mandingo through the use of arms was not sustainable in a democracy because with less than 5% of the population, the voting leverage of the group was quite limited. Mandingo leaders floated parties to advance the community's partisan interests, especially as their aspiration was not recognized by the nativists. Alhaji Kromah, erstwhile leader of ULIMO-K, created the All Liberia Congress of the People (ALCOP), while Sekou Conneh, leader of the LURD, formed the Progressive Democratic Movement (PRODEM). Internal schisms within the Mandingo caucus resulting from strained marital relations between Sekou Conneh and his wife Aishat, the vital link between the Liberian Mandingo political elite with President Lansanna Conteh of Guinea, had a debilitating impact on the cohesion of the Mandingo in the last days of the post-conflict transition. Aisha Conneh's support for the UP candidate helped to bring the Mandingo into the mainstream of post-conflict political process and assured that the group was not consigned to the margins as had been the case both during the True Whig hegemonic rule and the Samuel Doe era when they were partially integrated to strengthen the agenda of the Krahn to dominate the political space.

CONSERVATIVE STATUS QUO FORCES

Mr. Varney Sherman was the presidential candidate of COTOL which brought under one coalition political forces struggling to keep the Americo-Liberian status quo alive as well as protect their big-business interests. Given the large presence of the old political and business elites, and the sympathy of the Chairman of the NTGL that was largely perceived as corrupt, the coalition was generally perceived as a bastion of corruption. The political fortune of COTOL was strictly perceived to be dependent on the ability of its candidates to influence the process through the use of money. Widely perceived as the best financed among all the partis contesting in the elections, the coalition made some impact in Montserrado County, the economic nerve center of Liberia. Chairman Bryant, who was a member of Mr. Sherman's Liberia Action Party (LAP), made efforts to assist the coalition's political fortunes by appointing its members as superintendents in most of the counties. The superintendents were expected to play a key role in mobilizing local support for their political parties.

Notwithstanding this tripod of dominant forces, the influence of the charisma of personalities at the county level was critical in the outcome of the elections. From county to county, the vision and leverage of the local leader made a decisive difference. Mr. Charles Brumskine's relatively strong showing in Montserrado County was accounted for by the ethnic factor. In Montserrado, 12% of the population was of Brumskine's Bassa ethnic group. He also enjoyed the support of the majority of the electorate in Grand Bassa, which was one of the critical counties with over 100,000 registered voters. However, elsewhere he was perceived as a former associate of Charles Taylor, although they fell out in the early stages of the regime.

PERSPECTIVES ON THE OUTCOME OF THE OCTOBER/NOVEMBER 2005 ELECTONS

Mr. George Weah of the CDC led in the first-round presidential election, wining 28.3% of the 1,012,673 votes cast. He was followed by Mrs. Ellen Johnson-Sirleaf of the UP who won 19.8%. Mr. Charles Brumskine, the flag bearer of the Liberty Party (LP) had 13.9% of the votes, while Mr. Winston Tubman of the National Democratic Party of Liberia (NDPL) came in fourth place with 9.2%. In the parliamentary elections, COTOL won 7 of the 30 seats in the upper house. The National Patriotic Party (NPP), UP, CDC, APD, LP won 3 seats each. NDPL got 2 seats, and the All Liberian Coalition Party (ALCP), and the National Reformation Party (NRP) had a seat each, while three independent candidates also got elected into the chamber.

In the lower house, the CDC won 15 of the 64 seats, followed by the LP with 9 seats. UP and the COTOL obtained 8 seats each. APD got 5 seats and the NDP had 4 seats. The New Deal Movement (NDM) got 3 seats, ALCP had 2 seats and NDPL , NRP, and United Democratic Alliance (UDA) won one seat each, with 7 independents making up the balance.

The sources of the votes for the four leading candidates, county by county, illuminate the factors and forces that determined the outcome of the elections. Ethnicity, age (youths) gender, and the strength of campaign funds, in that order, would appear to have influenced the results.

Each of the four leading candidates, as well as the other candidates that got significant votes in the race, received the bulk of the votes from their ethnic bases. In the south-east Krahn/Kru/Sapo land of Grand Gedeh, Grand Kru, River Gee, and Sinoe Counties, Goerge Weah, a Kru, attained 88.0 %, 51.0%, 50.0 % and 45.5% of the votes respectively. This is replicated, although in a less accentuated manner, by Ellen Johnson-Sirleaf in her home state of Bomi with 43.0 % and 26.0 % in neighbouring Lofa where she beat off a spirited challenge from Alhaji Kromah, a Mandingo and leader of the ALCOP. The structure of Charles Brumskine's 13.9% of the vote highlights the potency of the ethnic factor in the race. Of the total 135,093 votes secured by him in the presidential election, 98,609 of the votes, representing 76.1% of his total votes, were received from the Bassa belt that groups Grand Bassa, Montserrado, Margibi as well as River Cess Counties. Indeed, his score of 12.2% of the votes in cosmopolitan Montserrado tallied with the estimated 12% Bassa portion of the county's population. Ethnic influence was further illustrated by Varney Sherman, the candidate of the status quo COTOL whose 63.0 % score in his Vai home county of Grand Cape Mount was a far cry from his national average score of 7.8%. He received less than 10% of the votes in two-thirds of the fifteen counties. Ethnic affiliations and the impact of the respective numerical strengths of ethnic groups in the presidential race confirmed the old axiom of politics as a game of numbers.

The east and west wings of the country, largely removed from the day-to-day interaction of the national processes because of their relative geographical isolation, exemplify the impact of relative insularity on voting. In Sinoe County, in the remote south-east, the presidential race was between two native sons,

Nah Togba Tipoteh, who scored 38.1%, and George Weah with 49.9%. No other candidate scored up to 8% in that county. As noted earlier, George Weah won a resounding 88.3% of the votes in Grand Gedeh. Similarly in the west, Varney Sherman garnered 62.8% of the votes in Grand Cape Mount. In Montserrado, while ethnicity may explain the 12% received by Charles Brumskine, only the massive support of youths provided an informed explanation of 37.5% scored by George Weah. The strong support of women may also account for Ellen Johnson-Sirleaf's 29.8% of the expressed mandate in the county. Three major factors may thus explain the voting behavior in Montserrado County: ethnicity, youth and gender. In adjoining Marghibi County, four contenders scored at least 15%, with the highest being Ellen Johnson-Sirleaf, reflecting the impact of the cosmopolitan character of the county. In other counties, with the exception of Montsserado and Nimba, only two candidates made significant impact on voters.

In the second round of presidential elections, Ms. Ellen Johnson-Sirleaf, the UP presidential candidate, obtained 478,526 (59.4 %) votes out of 805,572 valid votes from all the 3,070 polling places. CPC's flag bearer, Mr. George Weah, received 327,046 (40.6 %) votes. On a national average, the voter turnout was 61 %. CDC's reaction to its electoral defeat was that of incredulity. Vice-presidential candidate Rudolph Johnson, CDC political advisor Bacchus Matthews and leaders of parties that had aligned with it mainly in the cause of the nativist agenda, notably Dr. Togba-Nah T Tipoteh, standard bearer of the APD explained that the party believed fundamentally that it won the 11 October elections, and was surprised that a run-off was required. Mr. Johnson explained that, based on the commitments made by leaders of several political parties such as COTOL, NDPL, Union of Liberian Democratic (ULD), as well as APD and ALCOPS in the run-off election, the party believed that it had secured vast support from the populace to win a landslide victory. In this connection, he stressed that the support for George Wear went across all warring factions, including Sekou Conneh and former interim president Moses Blah. He concluded that these endorsements boosted the assumptions of victory in the CDC and had made it difficult for the party to accept the outcome of the 8 November run-off elections.

CDC noted that it had been demonized in the eye of the public for protesting alleged fraud in the elections. The party had been forced to adopt a defensive posture because of a general public perception of the party as a collection of lawless people. Mr. Matthews and Dr. Tipoteh associated themselves with the allegations of the CDC. They called on President-elect Johnson-Sirleaf to come to the table with the CDC standard bearer to negotiate a solution to the political problem posed by the elections. Mr. Matthews stressed the need for some form of accommodation of all political parties in the new democratic dispensation as critical for long-term stability in the country. UP did not react publicly to those demands. On 21 December 2005, against the backdrop of internal strife between the hardliners and moderates within the CDC over how to proceed with its complaints on the presidential elections and defections from the party, George Weah, the flag bearer of the CDC in the elections, announced the decision of the party not to exercise its option of pursuing their allegations of massive fraud in the run-off election to the Supreme Court. By this declaration, he closed the challenge mounted by the party to the outcome of the 8 November presidential run-off election and to the declaration of Ellen Johnson-Sirleaf as president-elect.

CDC explained its decision in terms of the party's commitment to peace in the interest of Liberians as well as "by the NEC admission of fraud" in the elections, which it interpreted as the ultimate remedy to the wrong that was committed against the party. George Weah defined the paramount interest of his party as how Liberians could take advantage of the new opportunities presented by the emerging democratic dispensation and in concert with international security to improve the lives of Liberians in a very secure atmosphere. George Weah added that the decision was taken after an exhaustive meeting of the party with leaders of ALCOP, APD, and ULD.

Meanwhile, anti-Americo-Liberian propaganda leaflets began appearing in Monrovia and its environs, drawing attention to the fact that the status quo forces, now under the control of the Masonic Order, was about to take control of the country again. Following the outcome of the November presidential run-off election, one of such leaflets was photocopies of an e-mail message dated 21 October, 2005 purported to have been sent by Mrs Ellen Johnson-Sirleaf for the attention of Dr. Amos Sawyer under the "brotherhood of Liberia" of "the Order of the Great Masonic Craft and the Auxiliary of the order of the Eastern Star". The e-mail informed readers that at an exceptional meeting of the UP , the party had decided on 23 names of Americo-Liberians and their associates to be appointed ministers if the party won elections. The message added that the "Pioneer Brothers" from Philadephia and Virgina (in the United States) would soon submit their nominees for appointments. Finally, it highlighted that it was important to use scare tactics to "keep our inferior native rivals" out from winning the elections.

The results of the October and November 2005 elections showed that the post-conflict political system remained fractious. The process rested on a delicate balance between status quo forces, represented by COTOL, which had managed to entrench itself in the legislature; and conservative nativist forces, partially represented by George Weah's CDC, as well as progressive nationalist forces, which the UP represented. The results of the presidential run-off significantly altered the political landscape, with the triumph of progressive nationalist forces, abundantly expressed in the Ellen Johnson-Sirleaf-led UP rendering the situation more complex. In the posy-conflict democratic system that emerged, the newly cobbled progressive nationalists under the banner of the UP won control of the executive. Meanwhile, status quo forces and the nativist forces dominate the legislature. The former hegemonic forces held sway in the Senate and the nativists constituted the largest single block in the House of Representatives. This development helped to lessen the intensity of the political face-off between nativists and entrenched status quo actors in COTOL who were at the different ends of a spectrum of visions on the way forward in the country.

In the senatorial elections, at least 9 political parties won a seat. COTOL won a relative majority with seven seats in the 30 seat upper house, representing 23.3% of the vote in the senate. NPP came second with four seats. Four parties, namely, the UP, the CDC, the APD, and the LP won three seats each, 10% for each in the Senate. NDPL got two seats, while the ALCOP as well as the NRP received a seat each, three independent candidates were voted into the Senate. Of the total membership, there were five females (16.7%), including Jewel Taylor, wife of ex-President Charles Taylor. The result of the senate race indicates that there was no correlation between voter behavior in the presidential race and that of the Senate.

In broad terms, the result of the House of Representatives election replicated the pattern of the results of the presidential elections. While the dynamic that produced the results at that level might be closer to that of the senatorial race, representation in the House reflected more closely the outcome of the presidential elections, although in much lower percentages. With 15 seats in the 64-seat assembly, the CDC controlled 23.4%. It was followed by the LP with nine seats or 14.1% and then the UP and COTOL with eight seats or 12.5% each. In the House, 13 parties won seats, and there were six independents.

Two reasons may be adduced for the different voting patterns between the presidential and senatorial races. Most of the political parties focused their strategies on the presidential race. This was with the notable exceptions of COTOL, which was the petitioner in the case for dual voting in the senatorial election, and also the NPP that deliberated seriously on its approach to the legislative elections. This lack of serious attention by most of the parties left the legislative elections largely to local influence and the resources available to each candidate. The results of the senatorial race also revealed the limits of the influence of senatorial candidates on the performance of the respective party flag bearers in their constituencies. It pointed rather to the strong play of personalities at the local levels to thwart the influence of powerful political actors from Monrovia. The impressive number of COTOL seats in the Senatorial election, in contrast its poor showing in the presidential race, demonstrated that most of the winners were relatively strong personalities, and sometimes backed up by a formidable resource base to fight elections. The consequence of the relatively inferior attention given to legislative elections in general also showed in the success of a number of controversial personalities like Prince Yomi Johnson of the Independent National Patriotic Front of Liberia, Howard Jewel Taylor and Aldophus Dolo into the Senate.

The political configuration that emerged was the product of a number of interacting interests and forces driving the process. These included historical, political, social and economic forces. The outcome of the elections reflected the strong influence of ethnic affinities, highlighted the paradoxes of historic resentment against Americo-Liberian hegemony and all those who were generally associated by the masses of people party with the status quo, and demonstrateed the power of local influence and the vast political leverage held by the disenchanted, dispossessed and disoriented youth who constituted a potent majority of Liberia's population.

With Ellen Johnson-Sirleaf's victory in the presidential election, a new force with nationalist credentials emerged at the center of Liberian politics. It joined the conservative and exclusivist Americo-Liberian hegemonic forces that had ruled the country from its founding until April 1980 and the "nativists" who rose from the margins of society and the political process to take over the control of the Liberian state in the 1980s. In spite of the multitude and diversity of parties in the legislature, representation in both chambers reflected the institution of a tripod of political forces drawn across the broad spectrum of society. The diversity in representation denied any one party or political orientation, including the party of the president-elect, a monopoly, or even preponderant influence, in the legislature. This had implications for the dynamics of the process that would emerge and impact the character of the legislature as well as how the legislature would respond to the challenges and priorities set by the executive.

It was projected that, to garner enough clout to influence the legislature, the executive and UP legislators would need to collaborate with the seven legislators of the NPP, the majority of 11 on the ticket of the LP and representatives of an assortment of smaller parties such as the NRP and the NDM as well as the independents. This was critical if undue wrangling in the legislature was not to be a stumbling block to the implementation of the executive's policies. The "nativists", led by the CDC and supported by the APD, and possibly the NDPL that represented the Krahn and Kru counties of the south-east, might pose serious challenges should they seek to undermine the policies of Ellen Johnson-Sirleaf. It was postulated that COTOL had economic interests to protect and would, therefore, cooperate with the executive. The LP's three senators and nine representatives as well as the NPP's three senators and four representatives would seem to be potential balancers who, in the final analysis, might opt to collaborate with Sirleaf's UP.

THREE MAIN TENDENCIES IN THE LEGISLATURE

From the outcome of the elections, the three main political tendencies emerged in the legislature. The "nativists" comprised a crisis-ridden CDC, what remained of the coalition of political forces under Togba Nah Tipoteh's APD, the NDPL and arguably ALCOP. Grounded in narrow ethnic constituencies and focused on the interests of many indigenous groups, these forces combined had 22 seats in the House of Representative and seven in the Senate. They constituted a relatively strong group that would be able, if it retained some internal cohesion, to influence deliberations in the legislature. In the post-election period, the mainstream (George Weah) CDC and a faction of APD decided to consolidate their collaboration and formed the nucleus of the indigenous platform in the legislature.

The conservative and status quo forces were represented by the four political parties operating under the umbrella of COTOL. This coalition was the strongest single political force in the Senate, with some influence in the House of Representatives. As direct offshoots of that flagship of Americo-Liberian hegemony, the old True Whig Party, it aimed to protect its legacies, in particular the social and economic prerogatives acquired over the period up to 1980. It was the exclusivist character of this group and its preeminence in all facets of national life that led to the original rise of "nativism" in Liberia. The struggle between the two forces at the two polar ends of the political divide has been the dominant theme of Liberia's political evolution since 1980. A small minority of UP representatives embodying the progressive nationalist force completed the three major forces in the legislature.

The jostling for the position of the Speaker of the House of Representatives reflected the high value attached to the leadership of the legislature and the direction that the legislature would go in relation to the reform agenda of the executive. Three main candidates were in the contest, including Edwin Snowe, ex-son-in-law of Charles Taylor and former Managing Director of the Liberia Petroleum Refining Corporation, was supported by a faction of the CDC; and Dusty Wolokolie, a recent crossover to the UP from the LPP where he was chairman, economist and former country director of the International Foundation for Electoral Systems (IFES) and Commissioner for the Contract and Monopolies Commission. The third candidate was Edward Forth of the CDC.

A Transformed Political Landscape

The newly elected legislature was unique in Liberian history. It had representation from 11 political parties. The Senate was dominated by the conservative status quo force under the umbrella of the COTOL. The "nativist" forces, led by the CDC, had the largest bloc of seats in the House of Representatives. Along with the progressive nationalists occupying the very powerful presidency, the three forces constituted the pivotal elements around which the political process in the post-conflict legislature revolves. The emergence of the progressive nationalists to prominence from the core of Liberia's radical protest movements and mainstream opposition was novel in the context of Liberian politics, and their presence represented a significant change in the political landscape.

By transforming and diluting the dichotomous struggle between the Americo-Liberian hegemony and the "nativists" that had dominated the Liberian political process since the late seventies, the agenda of the UP in the presidency shifted the theme from the struggle for the appropriation of the state by the two old forces to a new substantive plane of building a nation, development and remaking Liberia as a constructive actor in a difficult neighborhood. The legislature was expected to be the main theater of the continuing contest between the three forces to dominate the new dispensation. The outcome of the struggle for control, if not domination, of the legislature was critical to the future direction of the overall social, political and economic climate of the country. It might also determine whether the post-conflict democratic system would be consolidated as well as enhanced. It would also ultimately impact on the prospects of long-term stability in post-conflict Liberian political process.

Notes

1. Jeremy L. Levitt, *The Evolution of Deadly Conflict in Liberia: From 'Paternaltarianism' to State Collapse*, Carolina Academic Press, Durham, NC, 2005, p. 35.

2. Jeremy L. Levitt, ibid., p. 85.

3. GeoSecurity

4. Jeremy L. Levitt, op. cit., p. 125.

5. Stephen Ellis, *The Mask of Anarchy: The Destruction of Liberia and the Religious Dimension of an African Civil War*, Hurst and Company, London, 1999, p. 39.

6. Internet

7. Internet

8. Jeremy L. Levitt, op. cit., p. 31.

9. Jeremy L. Levitt, ibid., p. 3.

10. GeoSecurity

11. Adekeye Adebajo, Building Peace in West Africa: Liberia, Sierra Leone, and Guinea-Bissau, Lynne Rienner Publishers, Boulder, CO, p. 45.

12. J. Gus Liebenow, "Chapter III: The Origins of the Modern Liberian State," in *Liberia: The Quest for Democracy*, Indiana University Press, Bloomington and Indianapolis, 1987, p. 36. Liebenow cites that, for example, the Kru resisted the Liberian state until the 1930s.

13. Amos Sawyer, *Beyond Plunder: Toward Democratic Governance in Liberia*, Lynne Rienner Publishers, Boulder, CO and London, 2005, p. 13.

14. Amos Sawyer, ibid., p. 13.

15. Amos Sawyer, ibid., p. 15.

16. J. Gus Liebenow, op. cit., p. 12.

17. J. Gus Liebenow, ibid., p. 37.

18. J. Gus Liebenow, ibid., p. 13.

19. Jonathan Paye-Lahley, "Cleansed," *BBC Focus on Africa Magazine*, October-December 2006, p. 16.

20. Gus Liebenow, *Liberia: The Evolution of Privilege*, Cornell University Press, Ithaca and London, 1969,

21. J. Gus Liebenow, *Liberia: The Evolution of Privilege*, Cornell University Press, Ithaca and London, 1969, p. xv.

22. J. Gus Liebenow, *Liberia: The Evolution of Privilege*, ibid.

23. Jeremy L. Levitt, op. cit., p. 194.

24. J. Gus Liebenow, "Chapter IX: Class and Caste Stratification in the First Republic," in *Liberia: The Quest for Democracy*, Indiana University Press, p. 59.

25. Jeremy L.Levitt, op. cit., p. 189.

26. Jeremy L. Levitt, ibid., p. 189.

27. Jonathan Taylor dates the earliest beginnings of the democratic struggles to the student demonstrations of 1971.

28. J. Gus Liebenow, "Chapter X: The Gathering Storm," in *Liberia: The Quest for Democracy*, Indiana University Press, p. 54.

29. Background Briefing: Liberia Critical Perspective on the Elections and Beyond, Unknown Author , p.7.

30. Jeremy L. Levitt, op. cit., p. 195.

31. GlobalSecurity.org

32. GlobalSecurity

33. Samuel P. Huntington, *The Third Wave: Democratization in the Late Twentieth Century*, University of Oklahoma Press, Norman and London, 1991, p. 3.

34. Samuel P. Huntington, ibid., p. 114.

35. Samuel P. Huntington, ibid., p. 142

36. Samuel P. Huntington, ibid., p. 147.

37. Thirteen of the cabinet ministers of the

38. Samuel Huntington, ibid., p. 147.

39. Dominique Bangoura, "National Conferences: The Only Means to Overcome Crisis," 2002, *Africa Geopolitics*: http://www.african-geopolitics.org/show.aspx?ArticleId=3844.

40. Dominique Bangoura, ibid.

41. This was consistent with Huntington proposition that the end of a dictatorship, while unleashing these forces, may not necessarily lead to a democratic outcome.

42. Amos Sawyer, op. cit., p. 12.

43. Jeremy L. Levitt, op. cit., p.185

44. J. Gus Liebenow, Liberia, op. cit., p.154.

45. Prince Yeduo Johnson, *The Gun That Liberates Should Not Rule: The Philosophy of the I.N.P.F.L.*, Pax Cornwell Publishers Ltd., Lagos, Nigeria, 1991, p. 16.

46. Samuel Huntington, op. cit., p. 68.

47. Samuel Huntington, ibid., p. 155.

48. Samuel Huntington, ibid., p. 154

49. Prince Yeduo Johnson, op. cit., p.16.

50. Adekeye Adebajo, op. cit.

51. Adekeye Adebajo, ibid.

52. J. Gus Liebenow, Liberia, op. cit., p. 258.

53. Adekeye Adebajo, op. cit., p. 46.

54. Prince Yeduo Johnson, op. cit., p. 17.

55. From Wikipedia, the free encyclopedia on internet.

56. Jonathan Taylor, interview with author in Monrovia between 2005 and 2010.

Prof. Taylor was Minister of State in the Presidency under President Samuel Doe.

57. J. Gus Liebenow, Liberia, op. cit., p. 274.

58. Thomas Woewiyu, Open Letter to Madam Ellen Johnson Sirleaf, Augst 30, 2005, The Informer, Tuesday February 21, 2006

59. Stephen Ellis, op. cit., p. 128-129.

60. The atrocities of Charles Taylor are well documented by Levitt, Adebajo and other writers who provide a more historical account of that era.

61. Jeremy L. Levitt, op. cit., p. 212.

62. Internet source: http//:en.wikipedia,org/wiki/Liberians_United _for_Reconciliation_and _Democracy.

63. GlobalSecurity.org accessed through http://www.globalsecurity.org/military/world/para/lurd.htm.

64. GlobalSecurity, ibid.

65. Jeremy L. Levitt, op. cit., p. 223.

66. GlobalSecurity.org accessed through http://www.globalsecurity.org/military/world/para/model.htm.

67. Many investigative reports, in particular the Report of the ECOWAS on , indicted all the major actors, from the Chairman of the NTGL, Vice Chair to the Cabinet ministers, of the NTGL for various forms of corruption. This is also reaffirmed in the investigations conducted by the IMF and the European Union on the awards of contracts and concessions by the NTGL.

68. Final Report of ECOWAS Team of Investigators into Economic Crime in Liberia, Background, p. 1.

69. Mr Donkor, interview by author in Monrovia.

70. Final Report of ECOWAS, p. 3.

71. Ezekiel Pajebo, interviewed by author, Monrovia.
Pajebo is Director, Center for Democratic Empowerment (CEDE).

72. Unity Party Platform, Move UP for a better life, page 1, para 1.1

73. Unity Party Platform, Move UP for a better life, page 6-7, para 2.3.1

Chapter 7

CONCLUSION

This book explored conflicts across two linguistic zones in West Africa: Anglophone and Lusophone. This was to generate theoretical insights into the sources and dynamic of conflicts in the post-colonial African state; and also explain the fragility of its interconnected state system. Although it was inevitable to discuss in some detail the evolution of the processes entailed in the conflicts and peace processes, the aim was not to present literal blow-by-blow narratives of those conflicts. The literature of conflict in the post-colonial African state is replete with this genre of analysis. What the book has sought to do is to distill the facts to allow for the general characteristics of interactions among domestic, intermestic, sub-regional and systemic forces to emerge and to highlight how they instigate and impact conflict in the post-colonial African state as well how their interactions fracture its fragile state system. The book has thus endeavored to undertake analytical explorations in order to derive explanations on two interrelated fundamental puzzles: the pervasive proneness of the African post-colonial state to conflict; and the ease with which the conflicts metamorphose and spread to neighboring countries across international borders. In focusing on this main *problematique* of the post-colonial African state, the inescapable reality of the deleterious impact of the activities of systemic and hegemonic powers (imperial and colonial) on the internal affairs of the post-colonial African state imposes itself as an important conflict element to be understood. The interaction of these external forces within the peculiar structure of the post-colonial African state and its immediate intermestic environment, constituted by nonstate actors and state actors alike, was explored. A final vital element that promotes the implosion of the post-colonial African state is the fear factor and the security dilemma associated with the zero-sum struggle for control and total appropriation of the political space by constituent protagonists. All the protagonists envision themselves as the next hegemon of the state. The security dilemma arises from the predatory goals of all the constituent groups who are competing with one another to dominate the political space in the state.

Richard Ned Lebow, writing from an alternative theoretical plane, captures the summation of the security dilemma that emerged in this study

> When not held in check by reason, competition for either standing or wealth can transgress the accepted constraints and lead to a rapid unraveling of order...This fear becomes paramount when one actor or faction (or state or alliance) appears on the verge of capturing the mechanism of state (or abusing its power to establish unwanted authority over others) in pursuit of its parochial goals. In these circumstances, violence or warfare may break out, precipitated by a bid for power by one side or pre-emption by the other ...[1]

In examining the conflicts and the peace processes in the two cases, the studies reveal that underlying the perplexing twists and turns of the political process in these post-colonial African states is a struggle that has common motivations. The conflicts are driven by identical forces that are motivated by a similar struggle for the domination of the political space, and they assume similar dynamics and characteristics. It is evident that the internal construction of the post-colonial African state and its intermestic environment generate the unending struggle for the appropriation of the levers of power by the competing constituent groups. Inherent in the struggle for the appropriation of the post-colonial state, which is the main contention of conflict, is a paradox. The post-colonial African state is an orphan state, to the extent that none of the protagonists struggling to possess it want it for its intrinsic worth. Yet, at the same time, it is the object of violent contests among its constituent members, acting in concert with their transnational affiliates who perceive a legitimate stake in the struggle for its possession. It emerges that the violence in the post-colonial African state is not just about its mere instrumentality for the hegemonic agenda of the competing domestic protagonists and their affiliates in the intermestic neighborhood. For, at another larger systemic level, the articulation of the parochial agenda of the competing groups is often linked to the interests of powerful systemic forces. These forces align themselves with whichever of the contending forces is amenable to be used to consolidate their interests in the state. This is even more so in the post-Cold War world. The clashing agenda of the domestic forces and the interests of external forces that are also competing to dominate the state reflect the double instrumentality of the post-colonial African state.

The ghastly double instrumental character of the post-colonial African state is imposed on the state by a number of important factors. We found these to be the incongruous internal structure that creates a complex intermestic external environment. Its complexity impacts significantly on the volatile nature of the internal workings of the state. Other important factors in this regard include the fragility of the immediate environment in which the state is located, the historical antecedents of the state as the mechanical creation of powerful elite forces, as well as the inherent weakness of the post-colonial African state in the global inter-state system. The subordinate role of the post-colonial African state as a handmaiden of imperial elite states in the global world system is imposed by the systemic structure. Accordingly, in coming to the appreciation of the sources of conflict and the forces that interact to create a dynamic of conflict, the major focus has thus been on structural factors: the construction at the domestic, intermestic, sub-regional and systemic levels. It is significant that at the last two levels, the rules of interaction are formalized, while ay the first two, interactions are governed largely by informal codes. If intermestic affinities appear to be so potent as to serve as a counter-weight to formal state structures, we are reminded that

> In developing his concept of organic solidarity, Durkheim observes, and subsequent research tends to confirm, that legal and social norms are more in accord, and informal mechanisms are more effective, in smaller and less developed societies ... Order is more difficult to achieve and sustain at higher levels of social aggregation.[2]

In the contest between the post-colonial African state and competing entrenched nationalities that act as corporate protagonists across state boundaries, the state is at a disadvantage. While these nationalities are often small and governed by informal codes and motivated by an almost mythic sense of loyalty to the group and its agenda, irrespective of which side of the state boundaries they are physically located, the formal state is unable to elicit the same loyalty or generate the same intense solidarity that naturally characterizes interaction among those who define themselves as one. The human tendency to generate social cohesion by creating distinctions between 'us' and 'others' work in favor of intermestic corporate groups. Richard Ned Lebow notes that the research of Tajfel and others on 'entativity' suggests that this binary may be endemic to all human societies.[3] Besides, the dependence on weak formal institutions by the post-colonial African state puts it on a losing run against transnational forces. The state tends to implode because all the constituent groups seek to protect their partisan interests rather than those of the 'orphan' state. The state is protected by the hegemonic force that at a particular historical juncture dominates the political space and determines the character of the state.

The protection of the state is to facilitate its unhindered exploitation by the dominant force at given historical points. This is a tenuous base for the legitimacy of the ruling hegemonic group which seeks to protect its hegemony by achieving total control of the political space. We see this at play in Guinea Bissau under President Kumba Yala's persistent pursuit of Ballanta hegemony in the immediate post-conflict era. The Ballanta problem thus remains the enduring complexity of the political conundrum of Guinea Bissau. It may also be recalled that Guinea Bissau's slide to conflict began with the repudiation of the philosophy of the organic solidarity of all Guinean identity that undergirded Amicar Cabral's revolutionary war to liberate the country. This rejection was given expression by General Bernandino Viera's coup d'etat of 1980 against the mulato leadership of the country. The same phenomenon lies at the heart of the Ivorian conflict in the post-Houphouet Boigny pro-Baoule hegemonic era. The intractable problem in the instance of Liberia between the hegemonic Americo-Liberian settler group and the indigenous peoples of the county is bedevilled by the same issue.

It is in this context that we delineated another structural layer that is crucial for a complete appreciation of the dynamic of conflict in the post-colonial African state and the crisis of its state system: the intermestic environment. The intermestic environment has attributes, character and role that are quite distinct from the sub-regional. While the operation of intermestic factors in the post-colonial African state environment are basically driven by informal codes, sub-regional forces may act on the basis of power calculus or on the basis of institutional collaboration. The impact of forces from these different levels of operations is qualitatively different. Yet, depending on the structure of the sub-region, intermestic factors may be the dominant influence in the formulation of state policy in relation to conflict in that environment. This is clearly the case in the implication of Burkina Faso in the conflict in Cote d'Ivoire. Also, the perennial intrusion of the Tutsi- dominated Rwandese regime in the crisis in the Democratic Republic of Congo may be attributed to this factor.

This intermestic environment, an intermediate layer between the domestic and subregional, proved to be crucial in enhancing our explanatory capacity of the transnational complexities of conflicts in the post-colonial African state since the end of the Cold War. The critical implications of the intermestic structure of the immediate neighborhood in which the post-colonial state is located highlight the weaknesses which constrain the state in the pursuit of a single-minded security policy or adoption of a formal monist stand that is acceptable to all its constituent groups. The policy of the state may not necessarily merge with the interests of crucial groups and transnational actors in relation to a conflict in which its ethnic affiliates are engaged. Intermestic groups, acting in concert across international frontiers of their states, have a will and pursue policies that may openly be at variance with the official policy of the state. Depending on the peculiarities of its internal construction of the state, the intermestic character of the environment imposes certain constraining imperatives on conceptions of the national goals and interests that must be pursued. In this setting, conflicts are hardly internal to any one state trapped in an intermestic environment.

As such, Burkina Faso and Mali were deeply implicated in the conflict in Cote d'Ivoire. Accordingly, the resolution of the conflict must seek to pacify the interests of Burkina Faso which derive from the intermesticity of the immediate environment shared by the three states. The pro-Forces Nouvelles sympathies of Senegal were predicated on religious affinities as well as broad ethnic closeness with the Mande-speaking peoples of the Sahelian region. As noted by partisans close to the radical nationalist camp, the Ivorian civil war would be the first civil war waged in the interests of foreigners. The interpretation is that Ivorians with ethnic links to Burkina Faso and Mali had resolved to enhance their chances of taking over the Ivorian state by fighting to legitimize the emergent demographic structure that was in its favor. In this they had the support of the Burkinabe government. The interests of the block of pro-Forces Nouvelles actors converged broadly with those of France that sought to overthrow the radical nationalists led by President Laurent Gbagbo from power, with a view to protecting its hegemonic interests in the sub-region. For Cote d'Ivoire remained the pivot of French power in West Africa, and the reputation of France as the foremost power in Africa would be greatly diminished if it lost Cote d'Ivoire.

The conflict in Guinea Bissau revolved around the management of inter-mestic complexities linking that country to the Casamance. This became inevitable in the face of political considerations that forced President Nino Viera to radically alter the policy of intense collaboration of the state with the irredentist movement MFDC in the Casamance. The war in the country began over the acrimonious claims and counter-claims of President Nino Vieira and his Chief of Defence Staff, General Ansumane Mane, over the arming of the MFDC. The evolution of the internal politics of Guinea Bissau, and its relations with Senegal and Guinea Conakry are better understood in terms of the management of the consequences of the intermesticity of their immediate environment. The Ballanta hegemony that emerged in the immediate transition from the post-conflict era was less sympathetic to the historical legacy between the Bissau Guinean military and state, and the Casamancaise, who had fought along with their Mandigue ethnic affiliates in the war of liberation. This granted the Casamancaise virtual citizenship rights in independent Guinea Bissau, and virtually blurred the line between MFDC rebels and the Bissau Guinean military as well as sustained the irredentism in the Casamance for over two decades. The unending political killings in Guinea Bissau were closely linked to the management of the tensions over widespread discontent with state policy on the struggle in the Casamance.

The radical policy change forced on President Nino Vieira, a veteran of the war of liberation who had subscribed to the prevailing sentiments, until he was confronted with the challenge of winning a democratic re-election, was against the general mood of the country. Senegal's intervention in the ensuing conflict on the side of the embattled presidency was a strategic response to the challenge posed by potential continued support for the MFDC should President Bernandino Vieira be deposed, as it eventually happened. President Kumba Yala's determination to establish a Ballanta hegemonic rule in the post-transition clashed with the rise of Mandigue power under the Ansumane Mane-led military junta. For Kumba Yala demographic superiority conferred on the Ballanta the right to lead Guinea Bissau. Ansumane Mane's vision of a liberated Casamance would create the necessary conditions for the emergence of a Republic of Gabou, incorporating Guinea Bissau, the Casamance and the Gambia. Such a development would have transformed the structure of the immediate sub-region profoundly. It would have rendered the Ballanta a minority in Guinea Bissau and threatened the territorial integrity of Guinea Conakry.

Senegal's interests were consistent with the French drive to incorporate Guinea Bissau into its orbit of influence through the retention of the country in the sub-regional francophone CFA zone. Accordingly, Portugal, the colonial metropole of Guinea Bissau, was clearly sympathetic to the anti-Senegal and anti-France stance of the General Ansumane Mane- led military junta that drove President Nino Viera out of power. The deployment of intermestic zone and intermesticity as analytical concepts and frameworks helped to define the potential catchment areas for protagonists caught in conflict within the post-colonial African state and helped to explain the problematic ease with which conflicts spread across transnational borders. Our narratives in earlier chapters vindicate the crucial importance of anchoring conflict analysis in an understanding of the determinant social constructions. As the degree of order and its character determine the character of politics, any explanations of international relations must be rooted in a broader theory of society.[4] Richard Ned Lebow further illuminates the problem of political order:

> As politics and society are inseparable, the first requirement of a
> good theory of international relations is that it provides a theory of
> society, or at least those aspects of it most relevant to the character
> of the evolution of politics at the state, regional and international
> level (sic).[5]

By this, we enter into the theoretical fray about the role of agency as the motor driving conflict in the post-colonial African state. This discourse has acquired salience at a time when many horrendous rulers have been hauled before various international tribunals to account for violent and flagrant violations of the human rights of innocent victims of war believed to have been spearheaded by them. Indeed, these monstrous leaders have more than deserved their fate. Yet, there is a need to begin to closely examine how entrenched traditional affiliations, structures and institutions that are transnational and more potent than the new-fangled states have militated against the development of democratic values and ethics, whose absence have so critically been responsible for the catastrophe that has become the hall- mark of the operation of the post-colonial African state.

It is in this context that the exploration of the structural forces at work in conflict situations leads to a rejection of the romantic notions of innocent people who are perceived to be manipulated by the monstrous leaders. Much of the literature on conflict in the sub-region has mainly provided descriptive accounts of the conflicts with particular emphasis on the role of leaders. Much of the attempt to explain conflict in the post-colonial African state has placed undue emphasis on agency and contingency. This analysis, which puts emphasis on individual actors and the confluence of haphazard and fortuitous developments, often obscures the structural context that invariably and inevitably produces the role play that the characters at the center of the conflict assume and also drives the trajectory of the conflict that is generated. In a sense, agency and contingency analysis often seems to develop narratives that can be better appreciated when located as expressions of larger structural forces at play. While such approaches place the responsibility for certain acts of war squarely on specific individuals, it has a tendency to put into obscurity the responsibility of collectivities and aggregates that constitute the structure and whose interaction is the dynamic that produces, or indeed manufactures, the monsters. The understanding that emerges from the conflicts discussed here suggests that in accounting for the roles that are ascribed to leaders and the horns they often develop, which is not the aim in this book, conflict analysis must be firmly rooted in the structural contexts that throw up these leaders. Such multi-level diagnosis of conflict is necessary if we are to begin to design realistic strategies to combat the incidence of conflict and system implosions in the post-colonial African state. The post-colonial African state is thus a problematic reality that must be confronted in fashioning long-term solution to the problem of conflict that afflicts it.

The structure of the African state, from the very inception of the process that led to its emergence as a new entrant into the state system, elicits a struggle for its partisan appropriation. This parochial struggle implicates the colonial creators of the state who sought to establish strong allies in order to protect their long-term interests in the emerging independent post-colonial African state. The contest for appropriation of the new state engenders Lucien Pye's multiple crises of identity, integration, distribution, participation, that under-pin the major crisis of legitimacy that besets the African post-colonial state, and indeed, the state system that it constitutes. The process of the legitimation of the state is undertaken through violence unleashed by the state when it is temporar-ily under the control of one domestic hegemonic force that is acting in concert with its affiliates in the intermestic environment. Against this background, in spite of the death of Fonday Sankoh in Sierra Leone, the indictment an 50 year imprisonment of Charles Taylor in Liberia, the ultimate fate of Jonas Savimbi in Angola, the killing of Ansumane Mane in Guinea Bissau, the uneasy lives of deposed Mengitsu Mariam in Ethiopia and Hissen Habre of Tchad, the post-colonial African state still produces the likes of Kones of Uganda and Laurent Nkundas of the Democratic Republic of Congo.

Compounding the nature of the post colonial African state is its deviations from the established character and norms governing the modern Westphalian state and the evolving post-modern state. Fixated in an archaic era of the abso-lute rights of the sovereign state, the African state and its state system seem impervious to emerging norms and values of the twenty-first century that are radically transforming the internal character of the classic Westphalian state, its society and the international society that has emerged to break the traditional yoke of sovereignty over the will of international society. Paradoxically, the more the post-colonial African state seeks to apply coercion to force its legitimacy on society, the greater the challenge it confronts from competing internal aspirants for control of the state. The challenge of national security remains at multiple levels for the post-colonial African state. Ultimately, these internal challenges lead to the emergence of a proto state, which lives side by side along with the state system and participates in formal interactions in the sub-regional political space. The internal construction of the post-colonial African state emerges as its principal burden.

Notes

1. Richard Ned Lebow, *Fear, interest and honour*, p. 447.
2. Ibid., p. 439.
3. Ibid., p. 443.
4. Ibid., p. 439.
5. Ibid.

Bibliography

Adebajo, Adekeye. *Building Peace in West Africa: Liberia, Sierra Leone, and Guinea-Bissau.* Boulder: Lynne Rienner Publishers, 2002.

Adow, Mohammed. "At the Frontier." *BBC Focus on Africa Magazine*, October-December 2006.

AFP/Newsedge report, Senegal's separatists resume offensive, 5 June, 1999. See also Newsedge report, Senegalese rebels meet to prepare talks with government, 12 December, 1999.

Africa Confidential 48, no. 1, 12 January, 2007. "Central Africa: On the Brink."

Africa Confidential 47, no. 15 (July 21), 2006. "Uganda/Sudan: Opening Broadside."

African Center for Development and Strategic Studies. Editorial. *Africa Conflict, Peace and Governance Monitor*, 2006.

Africa Newsfile, August 29, 2000, *Time*: http://www.time.com.daily/newsfile/africa/central.html.

Agence France Press: "Chad Declares Victory over Rebel Column." *http://reliefweb.int/report/chad/chad-declares-victory-over-rebels*

Akinyemi, Bolaji. *"Nigeria, a Mere Geographical Expression."* Public lecture in commemoration of June 12 and the creation of the Ondo State, Akure, June 21, 2001. http://cometnews.com.ng/20062001/p171901.htm.

Ake, Claude. Development and Democracy in Africa. Washington: Brookings Institution, 1996.

Apter David E. and Rosberg, Carl G. "Changing African Perspectives." in *Political Development and the New Realism in Sub-Saharan Africa.* Charlottesville: University Press of Virginia, 1994.

Araoye, Ademola. *"Conflict and Cooperation in Central Africa: Explaining Behavioral Transformations of States in the Post Cold War,"* Ph.D. diss. Claremont: Claremont Graduate University, 1999.

Arbetman, Marina and Kugler, Jacek. *Political Capacity and Economic Behavior.* Boulder, Westview Press, 1997.

Ash, Lucy. "France-Superpower or Sugar Daddy." in *France's New Mission special issue.* BBC News:http://news.bbc.co.uk/1/hi/special report/1998/12/French_in_ Africa/235589.stm, December23, 1998.

Ayissi, Anatole and Poulton, Robin, Edward. *Bound to Cooperate: Conflict, Peace and People in Sierra Leone.* Geneva: United Nations Institute for Disarmament Research, 2000.

Ayittey, George B. N. *Africa in Chaos.* New York: St Martin's Press, 1998.

Background Briefing: *Liberia Critical Perspective on the Elections and Beyond.* Unknown Author.

Background Note: *Guinea Bissau, Bureau of African Affairs.* US State Department. Internet Source: http://www.state.gov./r/pa/ei/bgn/5454.htm

Bangoura, Dominique. "National Conferences: The Only Means to Overcome Crisis," 2002, *Africa Geopolitics*:http://www.african-geopolitics.org/show.aspx?ArticleId=3844

BBC News, "Chad and Sudan Unite over Rebels." http://news.bbc.co.uk/2/hi/ africa/5218064.stm accessed on July 29, 2006.

Boeck, Filip De. "Postcolonialism, Power and Identity: Local and Global Perspectives from Zaire." in *Postcolonial Identities in Africa*, edited by Richard Werbner and Terence Ranger, New Jersey: Zed Books, 1996.

Bonner, Raymond. "France Linked to Defense of Mobutu." *The New York Times International*, May 2, 1997.

Bourg, Albert. "Un Yalta Africain,"in "En Verite." *Jeune Afrique*, no. 1896, May 7- 13, 1997, p. 6-7.

Braeckman, Collete. "Rebel Official Rejects Secession, Wants Mobutu to leave." March 3, 1997, *Foreign Broadcast Information Service*: http://wnc.fedgov.com.

Brzezinski, Zbigniew. *The Choice: Global Domination or Global Leadership.* New York: Basic Books, 2004.

Bur, Ason. "Nigeria's National Conference on Political Reform: Will it Constitute the Laying of the Foundation for a New Democratic Order in the Country? *Africa Conflict, Peace and Governance Monitor.* Ibadan: Dokon Publishing House, 2005.

Burns, John F. Panel asks how Britain Got Involved in Iraqi War. The *New York Times* (Europe), November 4, 2009.

Cabral, Amilcar. *Return to the Source: Selected Speeches of Amilcar Cabral, A*frica Information Service ant the African Party for the Independence of Guinea and the Cape Verde Islands, 1973.

Catholic Bishops of Bissau and Bafata, Caminate. Pastoral letters issued Interviews held in the last weeks of April, 2003.

Central Intelligence Agency, "Sudan." *The World Factbook 2006.* Potomac Books, Washington, D.C, 2005.

Chabal, Patrick and Daloz, Jean-Pascal. *Africa Works: Disorder as Political Instrument.* Bloomington: Indiana University Press, 1999.

Chazan, Naomi. Introduction. *Asian and African Studies, Vol 26*, 1993.

Chomsky, Noam. Hegemony or Survival: *America's Quest for Global Dominance*. New York: Metropolitan Books 2003.

Clapham, Christopher. *Africa and the International System: The Politics of State Survival*. Cambridge: Cambridge University Press, 1996.

Coq, Guy. "Why France Values its Religious Neutrality." *International Herald Tribune*. February 2, 2004.

Crawford, James. *The Creation of States in International Law*. Oxford: Clarendon Press, 1979.

Deng, Francis M. and Medani, Khalid M. "Civil War and Identity in Sudan's Foreign Policy." in *Africa in the New International Order. Rethinking State Sovereignty and Regional Security*. edited by Edmond J. Keller, Donald Rothchild, Boulder: Lynne Rienner Publishers, CO. 1996.

Doyle, Mark. "Sudan's Interlocking Wars." *BBC News*: http://news.bbc.co.uk/1/hi/world/africa/4759325.stm, accessed on December 12, 2006.

Drift, Roy van de. Democracy, legitimate warfare in Guinea Bissau," paper presented at conference "Webs of War," *Africa Studies Center*. Leiden, Holland, March, 1999.

Eckhardt, Andy .*Old Europe Unrepentant*. MSNBC: http://www.mnsbc.msn.com. id/4379560, accessed on March 14, 2004.

Ellis, Stephen. *The Mask of Anarchy: The Destruction of Liberia and the Religious Dimension of an African Civil War*. London: Hurst and Company, 1999.

Enahoro, Anthony. "*The National Question: Toward a New Constitutional Order*." lecture delivered at the Yoruba Tennis Club, Onikan, Lagos, July 2, 2002.

Europa. "European Union institutions and other bodies." http://158.169.50.70/institutions/index_en.htm, accessed on March 12, 2004.

Europa. "The EU at a glance" http://158.169.50.70/institutions/index_en.htm

Field, Catherine. "Wrangle over EU Constitution Masks a Seismic Shift." *International Herald Tribune*. October 31, 2003.

Final Report of ECOWAS's Team of Investigators into Economic Crime in Liberia.

French, Howard W. "In Congo, Province's Dreams of a Better Life Fade." *The New York Times International*, December 10, 1997.

Galtung, Johan .C. G. Jacobsen, and Kai Frithjof Brand-Jacobsen, Searching For Peace: *The Road to Transcend*. Sterling: Pluto Press, 2002.

Gambari, Ibrahim A. "The Role of Foreign Intervention in African Reconstruction." in *Collapsed States: The Disintegration and Restoration of Legitimate Authority*. I. William Zartman, Boulder: Lynne Rienner Publishers, 1995.

Gellar, Sheldon. "France in Black Africa, 1958-1990,"*Asian and African Studies* 26, 1992, p. 101-117.

Gomes, Solomon. Africa in the New International Order: *Rethinking State Sovereignty and Regional Security*. edited by Edmund Keller and Donald Rothchild, Boulder: Lynne Rienner Publishers, 1996.

Greenway, H.D.S. "The Diagnosis: Narcissism." *International Herald Tribune*, February 3, 2004.

Harsh, Ernest. "Setting foreign fighters on the road home.". *Africa Renewal*. United Nations Department of Public Information, Vol. 23, No 2, July 2009.

Horowitz, Donald L. *Ethnic Groups in Conflict*. Berkeley, Los Angeles: University of California Press, 1985, p. 188.

Howard, Michael E. *The Invention of Peace: Reflections on War and International Order*. New Haven: Yale University Press, 2000.

Huntington, Samuel P. *The Third Wave: Democratization in the Late Twentieth Century*. Norman and London: University of Oklahoma Press, 1991.

Ibrahim, Garba. "Repositioning of Focus in the NYSC Scheme." address at 2002 NYSC Annual Management Conference, Maiduguiri, June, 2002.

Ihenacho, David Asonye. "Sharia's Late Nullification a Timely Fight," *Nigeria world*: http://nigeriaworld.com/columnist/ihenacho/032302.html, accessed on March 25, 2002.

Inglehart, Ronald. *Culture Shift in Advanced Industrial Society*. Princeton: Princeton University Press, 1990.

IISS (International Institute for Strategic Studies) "Nigeria's Political Prospects." *Strategic Comments* 12, no. 5 (June), 2006.

International Herald Tribune, "Greens Meet to start up a Europe Wide Party." February 21-22, 2004.

Irele, Dipo. "The Nation State in Africa: A Fresh Look." *Africa Quarterly* 38, no. 2, 1998.

Isaac, Dan. "Nigeria's Turbulent Prospects," *BBC News*:http://news.bbc.co.uk/hi/English/world/Africa/newsid_1753000/1753559.stm, accessed on January 11 2002.

Jacques, Martin. "Divided We Stand." *The Guardian*: http://books.guardian.co.uk/print/0.3858.4871153-99793.00.html, accessed on March 3, 2004.

Karaganov, Sergei. "The Perils of Pressuring Russia: Brussels vs. Moscow." in *International Herald Tribune*. February 25, 2004.

Kayode, Fayemi. "Entrenched Militarism and the Future of Democracy in Nigeria," in *Political Armies: The Military and Nation Building in the Age of Democracy*. Edited by Kees Koonings and Dirk Kruijt, London and New York: Zed Books, 2002.

Keller, Edmund and Rothchild, Donald. *Africa In the New International Order*. Boulder: Lynne Rienner Publishers, 1996.

Kissinger, Henry A. *A World Restored: Metternich, Castlereagh and the Problems of Peace, 1812-1822*, Boston: Houghton Miflin Company, , 1973.

Kouassi, Edmond Kwam and John White, "The Impact of Reduced European Security Roles on African Relations." in *Europe and Africa: The New Phase*, edited by William Zartman, Boulder: Lynne Rienner Publishers, , 1993.

Krasner, Stephen. "Compromising Westphalia." *International Security* 20, no. 3 (Winter), 1995-96, p. 115. [152] Stephen D. Krasner, Sovereignty: Organized Hypocrisy, Princeton: Princeton University Press, 1999.

Laitin, David D. *Hegemony and Culture, Politics and Religious Change among the Yoruba*. Chicago: University of Chicago Press, 1986.

Lake, David A. and Rothchild, Donald. "Containing Fear: The Origins and Management of Ethnic Conflict." *International Security* .21, no. 2 (Fall), 1996.

Levi, Margaret. *Of Rule and Revenue*. Berkeley: University of California Press, 1988.

Levitt, Jeremy L. *The Evolution of Deadly Conflict in Liberia: From 'Paternaltarianism' to State Collapse*. Durham: Carolina Academic Press, 2005.

Liebenow, J. Gus. *Liberia: The Evolution of Privilege*. Ithaca and London: Cornell University Press, , 1969.

Liebenow, J. Gus. "The Origins of the Modern Liberian State." in *Liberia: The Quest for Democracy*. Bloomington and Indianapolis: Indiana University Press, 1987.

Linklater, Andrew. "The Transformation of Political Community: Carr, E.H. Critical Theory and International Relations," *Review of International Studies* 23, 1997.

Lyall, Sarah. "For Young Europeans, Identity Questions." *International Herald Tribune*, March 5, 2004, p. 10.

Mane, Joao Seco. "Presidential Closing Address," address to 1st Congress of the Social Democratic Party of Guinea Bissau, Farim, March 17, 2002.

Mazrui, Ali Al'Amin and Tidy, Michael. *Nationalism and New States in Africa: From About 1935 to the Present*. Nairobi: Heineman, 1984.

Mcgreal, Chris. "French calls for Zaire Force is Spurned." *Mail and Guardian*. March 14, 1997.

Mendes, Rui. interview by author, July, 1999.

Milnor, Andrew J. *Comparative Political Parties*. New York: Thomas Y. Crowell, 1969.

Narawane, Vaiju. "The Stakes in Africa," *Hindu Newspaper*, November 10, 1996

Ned, Lebow Richard. Fear, Interest and Honour: Outlines of a Theory of International Relations." *International Affairs*, 82, no. 3, 2006.

Newbury, C.W. *British Policy Towards West Africa*: Select Documents, 1786-1874, Oxford: Clarendon Press, 1965.

Ngang Kevin. and 11 others vs. the Federal Government of Nigeria before Justice Roseline Ukeje of Federal High Court in Abuja, Federal Republic of Nigeria. February –March 2002.

Nigerian Tribune. Saturday, 1 July, 2006. Secession: Bakassi indigenes write OBJ, Biya, UN - New Republic to take off after Nigeria's withdrawal.

O'Brien, Donal B. Cruise. "*The Show of State in a Neo-Colonial Twilight: Francophone Africa*." in Rethinking Third World Politics. London: Longman, 1991.

Oji, George and Olugbode,Michael. "Shoot-out in Maiduguri as Soldiers battle fanatics." *Thisday Newspaper*, 29 July, 2009

Organski, A.F.K. and Kugler, Jacek. *The War Ledger*. Chicago: University of Chicago Press, 1980.

Osterud, Oyvind. "The Narrow Gate: Entry to the Club of Sovereign States." *Review of International Studies* 23, 1997, p. 167-184.

Palmer, John. "Let Europeans Help Choose EU Leaders," *International Herald Tribune*, March 6-7, 2004.

Pajebo, Ezekiel. interview by author, Monrovia.

Paye-Lahley, Jonathan . "Cleansed." *BBC Focus on Africa Magazine*, October-December 2006, p. 16.

Pfaff, William. "Expansion Jeopardizes EU'S Founding Vision- Redefining Europe." *International Herald Tribune*, February 21-22, 2004.

Power, Jonathan . "United Nations: Much maligned, but much needed." *International Herald Tribune*, February 26, 2004.

Preece, Jennifer Jackson. "Minority rights in Europe: from Westphalia to Helsinki." *Review of International Studies* 23, 1997.

Rothkopf, David. Cited in Karen de Young, *Soldier. The Life of Colin Powell*. New York: Alfred A. Knopf, 2006.

Rouvez, Alain, Coco, Michael and Paddack, Jean-Paul. *Disconsolate Empires: French, British and Belgian Military Involvement in Post-Colonial Sub-Saharan Africa*. Lanham : University of America Press, , MD, 1994.

Rudbeck, Lars. "Guinea Bissau: Military Fighting Breaks Out." *Review of African Political Economy*, September 1998.

Sami, Cyrus. .*Peace Operations in Africa: Capacity, Operations, and Implications*. Report of the 34th Annual Vienna Peacemaking and Peacekeeping Seminar.

Sands, Philippe. Lawless world: *America and the making and breaking of global rules from FDR's Atlantic Charter to George W. Bush's illegal war*. New York: Viking, 2005.

Sawyer, Amos. *Beyond Plunder: Toward Democratic Governance in Liberia*. Boulder: Lynne Rienner Publishers, and London, 2005.

Schwab, Peter. Africa: *A Continent Self-Destructs*. Basingstoke: Palgrave MacMillan, 2002.

Sciolino, Elaine. "Same-Sex Marriage Ties the French in Knots." *International Herald Tribune*. May 21, 2004.

Seton-Watson Hugh. *Nations and States: An Enquiry into the Origins of Nations and the Politics of Nationalism*. Boulder: Westview Press, 1977, p. 339.

Smock, David. Report from conference "Crises of War and Governance." United States Institute of Peace, January 16, 1997, http://www.usip.org.

Smock, David R. *Making War and Waging Peace: Foreign Intervention in Africa*. Washington, D.C: United States Institute of Peace Press, 1993.

Somerville, Keith. "Burkinabes in Ivory Coast Firing Line." *BBC News: news.bbc. co.uk/2/hi/africa/2306087.stm*⊠

Sorensen Georg. "An Analysis of Contemporary Statehood: Consequences for Conflict and Cooperation." Review *of International Studies*. 1997.

Soudan, Francois. "Humiliation Francophone." *Jeune Afrique*, no. 1896, May 7- 13, 1997.

Taylor, Jonathan. Interview with author in Monrovia between 2005 and 2010.

The Economist. May 22 –28, 2004 "Another thirty Years War in the making?" http://www.highbeam.com/doc/1G1-117017242.html.

The Economist. June 20, 1998. "Instant War." http://www.highbeam.com/doc/1G1-20827318.html

The Economist, September 12, 1998. "Unhappy Soldiers." http://www.economist.com/node/164525

This Day News Online , "Ivorian Government Accuses Burkina Faso of Backing Dissident Soldiers." September 22, 2002, allafrica.com/stories/200209230150.html

Unity Party Platform (Liberia), Move UP for a better life, page 6-7.

Vensen Mendes, President of National Syndicate for Teachers (SINAPROF) Statement on Radio Pindjiquiti, 21 November, 2000

Waltz, Kenneth N. "Chapter 3." in *Theory of International Politics*. New York: McGraw-Hill, 1979.

Welsh, Paul. "Ivory Coast: Who are the rebels?" *BBC News*: http://news.bbc.co.uk/2/hi/Africa/2662655.stm, accessed on January 15, 2003.

Woewiyu, Thomas . Open Letter to Madam Ellen Johnson Sirleaf, August 30, 2005. *The Informer (Liberia)*. Tuesday, February 21, 2006.

Woodward, Peter. *Sudan, 1898-1989: The Unstable State*. Boulder: Lynne Rienner Publishers, 1990.

Young, Crawford. *Politics in the Congo*. Princeton: Princeton University Press, 1965.

Zartman, William. "Regional Security and Changing Patterns of Relations." paper presented at conference, "James Coleman African Studies Center Conference on the End of the Cold War and the New African Political Order," University of California, February 17-19, 1994.

Index

Madrid 85

Magna Carta 182, 188-190, 192, 193, 209

Mahamids 13

Mali 15, 40, 131, 169, 180, 183, 213, 250, 299

Mali Empire 169

Malu, Jorge 200, 201, 218

Mandela, Nelson 149

Mandinga, Victor 199, 222

Mandingo 40, 69, 170, 212-214, 238, 240, 241, 253, 255-258, 260, 261, 269, 272, 273, 278-280, 282-284

Mandinka 170

Mane, Ansumane General 57, 68, 69, 135, 152, 166, 175-178, 180-184, 187-197, 202-212, 214, 215, 227, 228, 231, 299, 300, 302

Mano River Union 15

Mark Leonard 90

Marshal plan 37

Martin Wight and Rosalyn Higgins 42

Maryland County 239

Massaquoi, Francois 260

Matthew, Gabriel Bacchus 248, 268, 270, 285

Mazrui and Tudy 38

Mearsheimer, John 122

Mende and Temne 54

Metternich 108

Mina, Manuel 207

Mississippi / Sinoe County 242, 284

Modern states 27, 31-37, 47, 80, 81, 83-85, 87, 89, 90, 92, 93, 95, 96, 98, 100-104, 106, 107, 117, 124

Monetary Union of West African States (UEMOA) 175-177, 183

Monetary zones 101

Monnet, Jean 100

Monopoly 43, 70, 72, 79, 84, 124, 142, 143, 270, 288

Monrovia 2, 71, 239, 244, 259, 262, 265, 270, 272, 273, 277, 280, 286, 287

Montevideo Convention 28, 104

Montserrado 242, 272, 274, 281, 283-285

Morocco 8, 60, 125, 228

Mosque 36

Mouvement Ivoirien Liberation Ouest Cote dÍvoire (MILOCI) 262

Movement for Democracy in Liberia (MODEL) 17, 30, 31, 33, 34, 43, 44, 46, 241, 260-262, 267, 269, 270, 282

Movement for Justice and Peace (MJP) 148

Movement for Justice in Africa (MOJA) 249, 268

Movement for the Actualization of the Sovereign State of Biafra (MASSOB) 11

Movement for the Emancipation of the Niger Delta (MEND) 2, 10

Movimento Popular de Libertacao de Angola/Popular Movement for the Liberiation of Angola (MPLA) 58, 71, 122, 148, 229, 243, 265, 281, 286

Mozambique 42, 49

Mullato 163, 164

Musa, Yahya Kane 207

Museveni 149

173-188, 191, 192, 194-197, 201,
204-206, 227-231, 299, 300
Viorst, Milton 31, 32

Wade, Abdoulaye 209
Waltz, Kenneth 118, 122
Washington 86, 93, 149, 181
Watson, Seton 38, 39
Weberian 42, 43
Wesseh, Commany 268, 271, 280
Western Europe 87, 91
Westphalian state 4, 9, 20, 31, 33-37,
42, 44-47, 72, 73, 81, 83, 87, 89,
91, 102-104, 106-108, 136-138,
140, 141, 143, 144, 146, 302
Whitney, Craig 148, 153
Wight, Martin 42, 182
Wilsonian Idealism 91
Wlue, Samuel 267, 270
Woewiyu, Tom 256, 258

Yala, Kumba 51, 57, 69, 152, 155,
166, 174, 175, 186, 198, 201-209,
211-226, 228-230, 232, 298, 300
Yoruba 11, 40, 51, 52, 55, 56, 153
Yoruba Council of Elders 52
Young, Crawford 7
Yusuf, Addulahhi 4

Zagawa 2
Zaire 7, 8, 14, 19, 60, 62, 67, 69, 71,
116, 121-123, 125-127, 149-151,
250
Zairoise 7, 8, 125, 126, 148, 149
Zambia 8, 14, 22, 42, 59

Zapatero, Rodriquez Luise 93
Zartman, William 129
Zenawi, Meles 149
Zimbabwe 8, 9, 22, 42, 47
Zuguinchor 154, 179